Criminology and Public Policy
An Introduction

James F. Gilsinan
St. Louis University

PRENTICE HALL, Englewood Cliffs, New Jersey 07632

Library of Congress Cataloging-in-Publication Data

Gilsinan, James F.
   Criminology and public policy : an introduction / James F.
Gilsinan, Jr.
     p.   cm.
   Includes bibliographical references.
   ISBN 0-13-193665-4
   1. Criminology. 2. Criminal justice, Administration of--United
States. I. Title.
HV6025.G515 1990
364.973--dc20
                                        89-23216
                                             CIP

Editorial/production supervision and
   interior design: Marianne Peters
Cover design: Diane Conner
Manufacturing buyer: Ed O'Dougherty

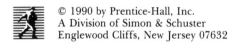 © 1990 by Prentice-Hall, Inc.
A Division of Simon & Schuster
Englewood Cliffs, New Jersey 07632

Printed in the United States of America
10 9 8 7 6 5 4 3 2 1

ISBN   0-13-193665-4

Prentice-Hall International (UK) Limited, *London*
Prentice-Hall of Australia Pty. Limited, *Sydney*
Prentice-Hall Canada Inc., *Toronto*
Prentice-Hall Hispanoamericana, S.A., *Mexico*
Prentice-Hall of India Private Limited, *New Delhi*
Prentice-Hall of Japan, Inc., *Tokyo*
Simon & Schuster Asia Pte. Ltd., *Singapore*
Editora Prentice-Hall do Brasil, Ltda., *Rio de Janeiro*

To Erma Gilsinan,
Christine Gilsinan, and Kathleen Gilsinan

Women of different generations
who have shared the same spirit

Contents

Preface

While definitions vary somewhat, most major criminological texts assert that criminology is concerned with both why people violate the law and how society responds to such violations. At first glance, then, traditional criminological concerns would seem to dovetail nicely with the concerns of those who formulate and implement public policies regarding crime. In fact, however, they do not. Most major texts in criminology fail even to list the subject "public policy" in their indexes. On the other hand, the attitude of many policymakers toward scientific criminology is at best suspicious and at worst distinctly hostile.

This book attempts to bridge the gap between criminology and public policy. It deals with the etiology of crime and with what governments—local, state, and federal—in the United States can do, choose to do, and choose not to do about it.

The boundaries of a policy area are sometimes quite vague. Furthermore, the social-political landscape is populated by a large number of policy areas, each of which can be broken down into subareas of concerns and policy options. Policy areas impinge on one another, so that decisions in one area affect policies and problems in another. To understand and sort out this complex landscape, it is helpful to think of a policy area occupying a particular space. Part I of this book, Chapters 1, 2, 3, and 4 deal with the question of boundaries in criminal justice policy and criminology. The different roles of the policy maker and scientist are described, as are the distinctions among the legal, scientific, and common sense definitions of crime. The major locations of criminal justice policy and decision making are also reviewed, together with the primary sources of information about crime in our society. The kinds of resources currently being used by the criminal justice system, both monetary and personnel, are discussed. Finally, the term program evaluation is introduced, and its application to crime control policy is analyzed.

Once boundaries have been described and analyzed, it is possible to describe in detail the elements of the enclosed area. Part II of this book provides descriptions of the kinds of things that fill the policy area of criminal justice, including ideologies (Chapter 5), criminological and organizational theories (Chapters 6, 7, and 8), people and organizations (Chapters 9—victims, 10—criminals, 11—the police, 12—the courts, 13—the correctional system, and 14—state legislators).

Part III of this book deals with the changing shape of the boundaries that encompass the criminal justice policy area. Changes in these boundaries are the result of other policy areas bumping into and sometimes invading the criminal justice policy domain.

Chapters 15, 16, and 17 deal with a major trend that is reshaping criminal justice policy area boundaries and the collection of ideas, actors, and programs that fill up the space—*privatization*. These three chapters deal with this phenomenon by examining the role of the private sector and volunteers in security work, dispute resolution, and the running of correctional facilities. The privatization of social control and justice responsibilities may prove to be the most significant policy change since government initially assumed the major share of such responsibilities less than 150 years ago.

The final chapter of the book discusses confusion. The policy area of criminal justice is filled with competing ideas, people, organizations, standards of judgment, and problem solutions. Increasing confusion in a policy area may be a sign of either breakdown or breakthrough. The final outcome depends upon the ability of policymakers, policy implementers, and policy analysts to confront confusion with imagination. Thus, Chapter 18 concludes the book with a discussion of how to keep the imagination stimulated.

ACKNOWLEDGMENTS

My own imagination has been continually stimulated by the creativity and insights of my colleagues at Saint Louis University in both the Center for Urban Programs and Graduate Programs in Public Policy Analysis and Administration. I wish to thank especially George D. Wendel, Donald P. Sprengel, E. Allan Tomey, Frank Avesing, Steven Puro, Kenneth Warren, Thomas Kramer, Brian Nedwek, and Patrick Welch.

While colleagues stimulate the imagination, graduate students often end up doing the more tedious work of checking references and finding obscure source material so that imagination is given form and substance. Graduate students in the Public Policy Analysis and Administration Program were particularly helpful as both research assistants and friendly critics. I wish to thank especially Mary Domahidy, Patrick Kelly, Elizabeth Fitzwater-Williams, Will Miller, Kathleen Flannery, Julie Sutter, Pierrette Bentivegna, and Ann McDonald.

Manuscripts begin in many forms: audio-tapes, handwritten sheets, word processed drafts, and so on. All of these forms have to eventually be made into a consistent, readable whole. The ability to do this is no small feat, and without the able assistance of my secretary, Kathleen Straatmann, the manuscript would not have been completed. It would have instead remained disparate bits and pieces. For her craftsmanship, insistance on clarity, and long hours, I thank her.

I would also like to thank the following reviewers for their comments and suggestions: Thomas J. Bernard, Penn State University; Raymond A. Eve, University of Texas at Arlington; Gary Jensen, University of Arizona; and George F. Stine, Millersville University.

Finally, for her support and her own insights and imagination, I thank my wife, Christine Gilsinan. She is able to continually bring order out of chaos.

I

Public Policy and the Study of Crime

At the end of this chapter, the student will be able to:

A. Define public policy.
B. Distinguish scientific problems and procedures from public policy problems and procedures.
C. Define the terms policy area, policy statements, policy issue, and policy argument.
D. Define policy analysis.

ISSUE BACKGROUND

Public Policy and Criminology

Public policy has been defined as "whatever governments choose to do or not to do."[1] A popular textbook in the field defines criminology as "the objective, systematic study of how criminal laws are enacted, why some people break these laws, how we and our representatives react to the breaking of law, and our methods of dealing with convicted offenders."[2] While definitions vary somewhat, most major criminological texts assert that criminology is concerned with both why people violate the law and how society responds to such violations. At first glance, then, traditional criminological concerns would seem to dovetail nicely with the concerns of those who formulate and implement public policies regarding crime. In fact, however, they do not. Most major texts in criminology fail even to list the subject "public policy" in their indexes. On the other hand, the attitude of many policy makers toward scientific criminology is captured in the comments of a Senate aide who, when asked about the need of having a research component in The Safe Streets Act of 1968, said:

> The Congress doesn't cotton to the research and studies approach. The thing, for example, in the area of "research" that would impress many of the senators most is a new type of bullet (for use by the police) that would have better and more effective results, i.e., killing someone faster and more totally, that is what you have to deal with when you talk about research with Congress. . . .[3]

The Goal of This Book

This book attempts to bridge the gap between criminology and public policy. It deals with the etiology of crime and with what governments, local, state, and federal, in the United States can do, choose to do, and choose not to do about it.

CRIMINOLOGICAL/CRIMINAL JUSTICE CONSIDERATIONS

The Sociological Connections

Criminology has been largely the concern of those trained in the social sciences, particularly sociology. Sociologists who study crime divide the subject into three component areas. Criminological theory attempts to explain why people break the law. The sociology of corrections (penology) describes how societies deal with those defined as criminals and the consequences for both the individual and society of particular forms of punishment. Finally, the sociology of law deals with the causes of law, that is, how laws come into being, how their enactment and application are influenced by various groups, and how laws relate to the values and organizing principles of a society. All three of these subfields manifest a concern for applying the knowledge gained to helping resolve the problem of crime. Why they have been less than successful in doing so can be understood when the scientific approach to problem solving is compared with problem solving in the world of social policy.

Scientific Problem Solving

All problem solving requires simplification. The multiple facets of a problem need to be sorted out and specified. Such sorting and specification yields a restricted problem definition. This problem definition highlights certain elements of a general problem while ignoring or understating other elements.

The social scientist generally takes as a model the problem-solving strategies of the natural sciences. While the activity of scientific problem solving is quite complex and there are many different models of scientific reasoning, the following represent broad principles that seem common across the dominant models operating in the natural sciences.[4]

First, a scientist begins with his or her discipline in formulating the precise nature of the problem to be studied.[5] This theoretical anchoring is how a scientist simplifies or restricts the problem to be addressed. For example, a sociologist asked to account for the increased rate of delinquency beginning in the 1960s and continuing through the mid-1970s might utilize the theoretical concept of socialization to narrow the boundaries of the problem. Socialization is the process by which one internalizes the norms of one's group while simultaneously developing a unique personality. The social scientist's use of this concept narrows the general problem of increased delinquency to the more specific and therefore more manageable problem of the nature of the relationship between socialization and delinquency. The scientist might suspect that the socialization process within the family underwent a change sometime during the early 1950s. Demonstrating the nature of this change, its likely causes, and its link to delinquency then forms the framework for investigating the problem of increased rates of youthful law violation. The theoretical concept of socialization helps the scientist organize the search for an explanation of why the delinquency rate increased.

This connecting of the concrete (a rise in the rate of delinquency) with the abstract (the process of socialization) forms a basic element of scientific problem solving. Social science is in part an attempt to move beyond specific questions and answers to arrive at general statements about the nature of social life.

The concern with formulating general statements leads to a second distinguishing characteristic of scientific problem solving. The scientist is only secondarily concerned with the usefulness of the information discovered. The primary concern is to add to the knowledge base of one's science. In the above example, the major goal is to learn about the nature of the socialization process and its relationship to youthful law breaking. Whether the information is also immediately useful is a less important consideration. Suppose the scientist discovered that during the period in question the proportion of second- and third-born children in the teenage population increased significantly. This is, in fact, exactly what happened.[6] Since the concept guiding the research is socialization, the scientist might then ask whether birth order affects the way children are raised within a family. Available data already suggest a relationship between birth order and intelligence. Firstborns generally do better on standardized intelligence tests than their siblings, particularly when there is a short interval between births.[7] A firstborn appears to be influenced almost exclusively by the parents, while those born later are mostly influenced by older brothers and sisters.[8] A large increase in the proportion of second- and third-born children in a population might account for an increase in delinquency if such children are less socialized to adult values. This guess about how the concrete phenomenon of increased rates of delinquency is linked to the abstract notion of socialization is called a hypothesis. The scientist, once the hypothesis is formulated, then attempts to find if the linkage proposed is true. This requires careful testing. If evidence could be obtained that supported the hypothetical relationship, the finding would be an interesting one. It would add to our understanding of family socialization and to the significance of both birth order and age spacing for family dynamics. But would the finding that increased rates of delinquency are related to a changed pattern of family socialization, which in turn is influenced by birth order and age spacing also be useful? It is difficult to see how a government in a democratic society could utilize such information to lessen the problem of delinquency.

The abstract statements that form the body or theory of a particular discipline must be empirically testable.[9] Therefore, scientific problem solving has a third characteristic. It involves a painstaking process of carefully controlling and eliminating other possible explanations for a phenomenon. In the example, to solidly establish the relationship among the variables of birth order, socialization, and delinquency, other explanations for the rise in delinquency during the decade would have to be eliminated. Television violence, increased divorce rates, increased labor force participation by women, the assassinations of the Kennedys and Martin Luther King, the Vietnam War, and the sheer size of the youth population are all alternative explanations for increased youth violence during the period. The elimination of these alternatives would be an extremely large undertaking involving enormous amounts of time and money. But a scientist, to maintain credibility within the scientific community, must follow the accepted procedures of science. Time and money are of less concern than accuracy and showing one's colleagues that the rules were followed. A scientist writes for other scientists who are as interested in the procedures of problem solving as in what was discovered.

Finally, the scientific process is circular. The scientist starts with a problem statement informed by his or her discipline and ends with a conclusion that can add to the disciplinary knowledge base. This circular process is important, because the goal of science is prediction and control. It is thus a search for basic causal relationships among phenomena.

To summarize, scientific problem solving has the following characteristics:

1. Problems are theoretically formulated, based on the particular disciplinary perspective of the scientist.
2. Knowledge rather than utility is emphasized.
3. The elimination of competing explanations through the rigorous application of standard methods is required.
4. It is a circular process, beginning and ending with a disciplinary perspective to uncover basic causal relationships among phenomena.

POLICY CONSIDERATIONS:
THEORIES/ARGUMENTS/APPLICATIONS

Problem Solving in Public Policy

Like scientists, policy makers must begin their problem solving with a process that simplifies the complex issues they encounter. In the realm of policy, however, problems are simplified by connecting them to available solutions instead of to an abstract, logically integrated system of causal statements.

To understand this process, it is necessary to picture a world where problems and solutions exist simultaneously with one another. Solutions seldom emerge from carefully constructed analytical procedures. Rather, they develop from cultural, historical, political, and economic answers to the question, "What's possible?"

Restricting problems within a framework of available solutions means policy makers stress the value of utility. Knowledge for its own sake is not a goal. Policy makers are expected to solve problems. If they do not, or perhaps more accurately, appear that they do not, then they risk not being reelected or reappointed.

Policy makers, therefore, want to define problems in a way that allows for their solution or at least the appearance of a solution. Indeed, in the world of policy, the appearance of a solution may at times be more important than the fact of one.

At any rate, the search for basic causes, the kind traditionally of interest to the social scientist and the criminologist, is not very useful to the policy maker. First, there is little the government can do to change basic social dynamics. Thus, while an increase in delinquency may be due to a change in the proportion of firstborns in the juvenile population, it is unclear what role government can play in affecting this. Second, since terms of office are for a limited period, solutions need to have fairly immediate effects, either real or perceived. Long-term studies to determine ultimate cause do not fit this restricted time frame. Yet, since we really are not sure of the causes of crime, it is precisely these kinds of studies that scientists would like. Third, policy makers operate in a world of finite resources. They do not have unlimited amounts of time, staff, or money. Therefore, problems that are defined in a way that permits the efficient use of resources are most likely to get the policy makers' attention. Finally, the search for ultimate causes suggests the possibility of ultimate solutions. Ultimate solutions do not have a good history in the realm of public policy.

Believing that problems of public policy can be solved once and for all ignores the fact that decision makers and their constituents are involved in a fundamentally political process. In a political environment, truth is relative.

There is no single explanation for a phenomenon, nor is there a single strategy that will obviously solve a problem. Thus, when a policy maker connects a particular solution with a particular problem, alternative solutions and problem explanations do not thereby disappear. These alternatives remain and continue to compete for recognition and limited resources. This is a world in which the ability to persuade is more highly prized than the ability to uncover the indisputable fact, since there is considerable skepticism about the existence of an indisputable fact. Further, since policy makers operate in a political context, retention in office is often a dominant consideration. The public articulation of a problem and solution therefore may actually be in response to the need to be reelected rather than in response to a condition about which something should or could be done. Of course, in this regard, the policy maker and the scientist may share a common orientation, namely ensuring job security. Publications by the latter may at times be more influenced by the quest for tenure than for truth or usefulness.

To summarize, problem solving in public policy has the following characteristics:

1. Problems are formulated within a framework of available solutions.
2. Utility rather than knowledge is the primary goal of the problem-solving process.
3. Basic causes of problems are usually beyond the ability of a policy maker to change, and thus there is less interest in uncovering them.
4. Since competing explanations of problems cannot be eliminated, persuasion rather than analysis often determines which problems get connected with which solutions.

Definitions for Policy Studies

Before attempting to further penetrate the complex and sometimes sloppy world of public policy, a few signposts in the form of definitions are appropriate. These will hopefully provide a point of reference and direction in exploring the complexity of crime and society's response to it.

There are specific, long-lasting social concerns in our society. These form the focal point around which regularized governmental coping strategies develop. Such regularized responses result in the formation of one or more institutions that routinely assume responsibility for formulating policies and enacting programs related to the area of concern. Such institutions and their focal concerns constitute the center of what will be referred to in this book as a *policy area*. Education, health care, national defense, and crime are focal concerns around which core institutions have developed. These can therefore be considered policy areas. A policy area also contains groups that try to influence the activity of those at the center. These interest groups can either be stable residents of the policy area or they can represent temporary alliances put together to influence a particular policy. Further, a policy area contains categories of people affected by the decisions and actions of those at the center. The categories of "victims," "patients," and "students" represent the populations affected by crime and criminal justice, health care, and education, respectively. The categories remain stable, while membership in them continuously changes. While the focal concerns, core institutions, interest groups, and client categories of a policy area are fairly clear, the boundaries are not. There is no neat, clearly agreed upon division of labor and responsibility for each set of social concerns. In a complex society, action or inaction in one policy area can and does affect a number of other policy areas. Thus, boundaries are often quite vague. The fact that Johnny can't read is an educational problem. But it can also be a problem for the system of commerce if Johnny cannot get a job. His inability to get a job not only adds to the unemployment rate, but potentially to the crime rate as well. Finally, if Johnny can't read, he may not be able to follow the instructions of a physician on how often to take a certain medication or on how to properly care for a newborn infant. Education, commerce, criminal justice, and health care are all potentially affected by Johnny's reading ability. Thus, at the boundaries, policy areas collide with one another over problem definitions, the allocation of resources, and the impacts of one area on another.

Turmoil, however, is not only located at the boundary of a policy area. Those institutions regularly associated with a policy area generate *policy statements*. These statements contain a goal and a program for obtaining the goal. They can be general in describing both the goal and the program for obtaining it, or they can be quite specific as to one or the other or both.

Policy statements are found lurking in a variety of places. A candidate for office who says that government must do more to stop crime by increasing respect for law and order has made a policy statement, albeit a very general one. He or she has enunciated a goal (stopping crime) and a program for securing it (increasing respect for law and order). Were this politician to be elected to office, a more specific statement of goals and/or programs might then be formulated.

A police chief faced with carrying out the wishes of our newly elected official might further specify the original policy statement by directing his officers to concentrate on reducing burglaries (a goal) through increasing the arrests of suspicious persons (a program). The chief might argue that such a program will ultimately increase respect for law and order.

Thus, policy statements are found not only in political speeches, but also in agency directives that organize the work of particular governmental units. Policy statements are also found in laws, in state and federal constitutions, and in the detailed operating manuals of specific programs or agencies. As policy statements become more specific, however, particularly in regard to programs for obtaining goals, they are likely to lead to the development of *policy issues*.

Coplin and O'Leary define a public policy issue as a disagreement between two or more elements of a society over the way that the society's government deals with a given condition.[10] We have seen that such disagreements can erupt at the boundaries of a policy area, but they can also develop among the core institutions of a policy area, for example, between police officials and prosecutors as to what constitutes adequate cause for arrest. People assigned to client categories and/or the general public can become concerned about the policy initiatives of the core institutions and form either temporary or permanent groups to lobby for their point of view. Currently, victim's rights organizations appear to be forming a stable interest group within the policy area of crime and criminal justice to ensure that crime control policies are congruent with the interests of victims. Those who work in the criminal justice system also form interest groups that lobby for changes in policy if current or suggested strategies are viewed as detrimental to their occupational interests. Increasingly, police officer associations are demanding more stringent gun control legislation. Of course, one group's idea or solution becomes another group's cause for concern. Turmoil therefore can exist in all parts of a policy area, as policy statements generate policy issues.

Since policy specification is likely to generate at least some policy issues, most such statements are accompanied by *policy arguments*. Such arguments contain statements of value (what is good and what is bad) and assertions of fact (*x* will result in *y*). It is this mixture of value and fact that makes the analysis of a policy argument difficult, and further complicates the role of the criminologist in trying to understand and contribute to the resolution of policy issues.

The Sloppy World of Criminal Justice and Public Policy

The perils of attempting to resolve the public policy problems and issues within the realm of criminal justice are illustrated by Karl Weick when he describes some of the facets of the crime problem and its attempted solution:

> To solve the problem of soaring crime rates, cities expand the enforcement establishment, which draws funds away from other services such as schools, welfare, and job training, which leads to more poverty, addiction, prostitution, and more crime.[11]

Notice the elements of both the problem and the solution represented in this quotation. First, a single policy issue such as what to do about crime is not an isolated phenomenon. As we have seen, it touches a whole host of other issues including education, employment, and welfare. Second, given the complex interrelationships among policy areas, a solution aimed at solving a single problem affects a whole host of other problem areas in sometimes unanticipated ways. Third, because of the inability to anticipate all the actions and reactions caused by a single problem-solving strategy, problems are often made worse rather than better. Finally, add to this bubbling morass the factor of ideology, of personal, subjective beliefs about the world, and you have a complexity that is truly staggering. Given this last factor of ideology, people may not even agree that there is a problem, much less agree on its nature. For example, considerable disagreement exists about whether the crime wave of the 1960s and 1970s was really a crime wave. Some argue that it was more of a reporting wave.[12] A dramatic increase in reported crime does not mean that there was a dramatic increase in the actual amount of crime.

The world of policy is a sloppy one. It is so sloppy, in fact, that decision making within it has been compared to a garbage can.[13] Problems and solutions float around in a random manner. Occasionally, a problem links up with an appropriate solution, but more often a solution bumps into and sticks to a problem for which it has little relevance. Criminal justice policy is ripe with examples of inappropriate solutions sticking to problems.

Violent crime is of concern to most citizens. A solution that continually bumps into this concern is the elimination or modification of the exclusionary rule. This rule says that evidence obtained by police officers in violation of the search and seizure protection afforded by the Fourth Amendment to the Constitution cannot be used in criminal proceedings. Some fear that such a rule lets dangerous criminals free on a mere technicality. Further, some view the police as "handcuffed" in their attempts to remove violent wrongdoers from our midst. Some believe that by eliminating or modifying the rule, violent crime will be better controlled. At least that is the solution that continually bumps into the real concern about violence in our society. However, research shows that the exclusionary rule has nothing to do with violent crime.[14] Less than 1% of felony cases are dismissed because of the rule. Moreover, as Samuel Walker has argued, attempts to modify the rule appear to have benefitted defense lawyers more than prosecutors.[15]

In 1982, California passed Proposition 8, which had as one of its components a "Right to Truth in Evidence" clause. All relevant evidence was to be admitted during criminal proceedings except hearsay evidence and information pertaining to a rape victim's past sexual conduct.

Defense attorneys have used this modification very effectively. Background checks on police officers and other prosecution witnesses bring to light such things as bad credit histories, lost jobs, and so on which can be used to impeach the credibility of these witnesses. Some victims are now choosing not to proceed with prosecution because of the scrutiny they might have to endure.[16] An inappropriate solution sticking to a problem has not solved the original problem and has created a whole new set of problems.

This example illustrates two more facets of the sloppy world of policy problems. First, solutions sometimes come before problems. In other words people have their pet solutions and look for problems to apply them to. If elimination of the exclusionary rule is one of your pet solutions, it can be applied to solving the problem of violent crime in our society, or the problem of how victims are treated in our justice system, or the tendency of judges to be "soft" on crime. Unfortunately, the solution is applied without much thought being given to the nature of either the problems identified or one's favorite nostrum. Second, the example clearly illustrates the tendency of policy to create other problems. In brief, policy problems are created by previous attempts to solve other problems. The current problem of prison overcrowding also illustrates this point. This problem arises in large part because of a previous policy decision to get tough on crime.

"Getting tough" was translated into legislation that provided for both mandatory and longer sentences. More people went in, fewer came out. Laws passed in the early 1980s had an immediate effect. By 1984, the prison population had increased 40%.[17] By 1987, about 40 state prison systems and many city and county jail systems were operating under court orders because of overcrowding, poor conditions, or both.[18] State legislators expressed surprise and consternation, both because of conditions and because of court interference in the operation of *their* prisons. They were forced to act. Several state legislatures responded by repealing their mandatory sentencing laws and instituting early release programs. Ironically, this "solution" had been seen as the "problem" a few years previously!

In this kind of world, problems are not often solved. They are supplanted by other problems. The original problems are still around, but policy makers move on to other ones, as public concerns shift and eddy in the jetsam and flotsam of numerous policy arenas.

Clearly, the world of the policy maker and the world of the scientist are different. Effective answers to the question, "What can we do about crime?" require, however, a blending of these two worlds.

The social scientist can offer the policy maker tools for thinking systematically about the kinds of problems and the kinds of solutions that might be available in a particular policy area. The policy maker, on the other hand, can challenge the social scientist to think in terms of real-world limitations, both political and monetary. To operate in this world, the scientist must reexamine the nature of the problems he or she typically addresses and the methods utilized to solve them. Working together, both the scientist and the policy maker can stick appropriate solutions to appropriate problems and perhaps unstick the inappropriate solutions. But the task is a messy one. The person doing it cannot rely solely on the favorite problem-solving strategies of either the scientist or the policy maker. A mixture of strategies is required. The emerging hybrid is called policy analysis.

The Art of Policy Analysis

Policy analysis is a union of opposites.[19] It uses the rational, objective approaches of science, but it also uses the art of politics and persuasion. Its problems come from the immediate, everyday concerns of those expected to manage the society, but it relies on disciplinary theory to generate different ways of looking at the practical problems of policy makers. Thus, it is just as concerned with formulating good problems as with discovering solutions. Since social policy is fundamentally a political phenomenon, influenced by the values of decision makers, policy analysis, unlike science, does not seek to eliminate alternative explanations for problems. Rather these explanations are sought after for their ability to contribute to informed public debate.[20] To summarize, policy analysis has the following characteristics:

1. It seeks knowledge about the cause and effects of government policy.[21]
2. It seeks to formulate problems about which something both should and can be done.[22]
3. It seeks to give advice to those in authority.
4. It is both objectively diagnostic and subjectively judgmental.

Policy analysis uses the following tools:

1. Rational, quantitative, social scientific procedures including cost/benefit analysis.
2. Qualitative social science procedures including oral history, ethnography, and case studies.
3. Political skills including persuasion and the ability to know whom to persuade of what.
4. Theoretical insights from a wide variety of social science disciplines.

Organization of This Book

We have already seen that the boundaries of a policy area are sometimes quite vague. Further, the social-political landscape is populated by a large number of policy areas, each of which can be broken down into subareas of concerns and policy options. Policy areas impinge on one another, so that decisions in one area affect policies and problems in another. For example, the deinstitutionalization of the mentally ill may have resulted in the reinstitutionalization of this population in another policy area, namely criminal justice. Jail overcrowding may in part be related to the lowering of populations in mental hospitals. To understand and sort out this complex landscape, it is helpful to think of a policy area occupying a particular space. The first problem then faced by the policy analyst is to determine the boundaries of that space. What distinguishes one policy area from another? What are the unique characteristics of a particular space? Chapters 2, 3, and 4 deal with the question of boundaries in criminal justice policy and criminology. Chapter 2 distinguishes among the legal, scientific, and common-sense definitions of the crime and describes the major locations of criminal justice policy and decision making. Chapter 3 discusses the primary sources of information about crime in our society. Questions concerning the amount of crime and how we count it are the focus of this chapter. Chapter 4 presents the different categories of criminal behavior as defined both formally and informally by the system. The kinds of resources currently being used by the criminal justice system, both monetary and personnel, are discussed. Finally, the term program evaluation is introduced and its application to crime control policy is analyzed.

Once boundaries have been described and analyzed, it is possible to describe in detail the elements of the enclosed area. Part II of this book provides descriptions of the kinds of things that fill the policy area of criminal justice. A main component of any policy area is the fund of ideas available to shape the problems and the solutions within it. Again, these ideas are a mixture of values and facts and they become the basis for the policy statements, issues, and arguments of a policy area. At particular times, certain ideas will become dominant. These ruling ideas then shape most of the problem definitions and solutions of a policy area until they are subsequently replaced by new conceptualizations. Chapter 5 provides an historical overview of the ideas and policies that have influenced the activities of those seeking to control crime. The relatively of crime and what one does about it is underscored. Chapter 5 also discusses the ideologies influencing today's view of crime and compares some of the commonly accepted notions of crime with recent data on its type and occurrence within our society.

A major source of our ideas on crime is the wealth of criminological theory that has been developed within the last 100 years or so. Chapters 6 and 7 present the major schools of criminological thought. Chapter 6 covers the biological, psychological, and psychiatric approaches to the study of crime. Chapter 7 deals with the various sociological explanations of the phenomenon, including the conflict and Marxist perspectives. Each chapter concludes with a discussion of the contribution standard theories of crime causation have made to actual crime control policy.

A policy area is filled not only with ideas, but also with people who act upon them, change them, and create new ones. Mostly, people within a policy area act as part of an organized group. They want to protect not only their own personal interests but also the interests of the group to which they belong. Chapter 8 is devoted to recent developments in organizational theory. Understanding how people organize themselves and their environment lays the groundwork for understanding why the criminal justice system operates as it does.

The degree of organization will vary among different groups within a policy space. Groups that form the core institutions of a policy area will be highly organized and thus their interests will be among the best represented within the area of concern. Other groups, such as those representing a temporary coalition of views, may not be as well organized. Consequently, their interests will not be as well represented. Chapters 9 and 10 deal with the least well-organized groups within criminal justice. Chapter 9 discusses the various types of victims, while Chapter 10 describes the various types of criminals. As will be seen, neither of these groups has much to say about criminal justice policy or how it gets implemented.

Chapters 11 through 14 describe how the core institutions within the criminal justice policy area, those that usually assume the policy-making and -implementing functions, operate. Their effects on each other and the overall doing of justice in this society are also discussed. Chapter 11 details the police function in society and the typical operations of a police department. Chapter 12 discusses the workings of the courthouse and the roles played by prosecuting attorneys, defense attorneys, and judges. Chapter 13 deals with the correctional system including both institutional corrections and community corrections. Chapter 14 looks at one of the primary sources of criminal justice policy, the state legislatures, and discusses the various influences on their members as they formulate the laws.

Part III of this book deals with the changing shape of the boundaries that encompass the criminal justice policy area. Changes in these boundaries are the result of other policy areas bumping into and sometimes invading the criminal justice policy domain.

Chapters 15, 16, and 17 deal with a major trend that is reshaping criminal justice policy area boundaries and the collection of ideas, actors, and programs that fill up the space. Chapter 1 began with a definition of policy as that which government chooses to do or not to do. Increasingly, government is choosing to look to the private sector and to interested volunteers for help in solving the problem of crime. These three chapters deal with this phenomenon by examining the role of the private sector and volunteers in security work, dispute resolution, and the running of correctional facilities. These correspond to the functions traditionally filled by the police, courts, and corrections. The privatization of social control and justice responsibilities may prove to be the most significant policy change since government initially assumed the major share of such responsibilities less than 150 years ago.

The final chapter of the book discusses confusion. The policy area of criminal justice is filled with competing ideas, people, organizations, standards of judgement, and problem solutions. Increasing confusion in a policy area may be a sign of either breakdown or breakthrough. The final outcome depends upon the ability of policy makers, policy implementers, and policy analysts to confront confusion with imagination. Chapter 18 concludes the book with a discussion of how to keep the imagination stimulated. It notes the changes occurring in both scientific understanding and in political assumptions. From the resulting confusion, imaginative programs are beginning to emerge that can harness what we know about crime and justice in a way that provides useful as well as interesting knowledge.

Chicken Little thought the sky was falling. Had he taken the broader view, he would have spotted those problems about which something should have and could have been done. Willingness to change old understandings is important if workable solutions to vexing problems are to be found.

SUMMARY

What Was Said

- Despite assumptions to the contrary, criminological concerns do not dovetail nicely with the concerns of those who formulate and implement public policies regarding crime.
- All problem solving requires simplification, but policy makers and criminal justice researchers use different methods to arrive at specific problem definitions and solutions.
- Social scientists generally take as a model the problem-solving strategies of the natural sciences, which involve:
  - a. Theoretically formulated problems
  - b. The search for knowledge
  - c. The elimination of competing explanations
  - d. A circular process beginning and ending with a disciplinary perspective
- Public policy problem solving has the following characteristics:
  - a. Problems are formulated within a framework of available solutions.
  - b. Utility rather than knowledge is the primary goal.
  - c. There is less interest in uncovering basic problem causes.
  - d. Persuasion rather than analysis often determines which problems get connected with what solutions.
- Policy areas overlap with one another and thus an initiative to solve one problem can have either positive or negative effects in a host of other problem areas.
- Policy statements (programs and goals) often raise policy issues (disagreements about how government deals with a given condition), which create policy arguments (statements containing a mixture of value fact propositions about a policy initiative).
- The wrong solution often gets attached to the wrong problem.
- Policy analysis is a union of opposites drawing on both the techniques of science and the art of politics and persuasion.
- Willingness to change old understandings is important if workable solutions to vexing problems are to be found.

What Was Not Said

- Liberals have the answer to crime control.
- Conservatives have the answer to crime control.
- Politicians have the answer to crime control.
- Criminologists and social scientists have the answer to crime control.
- One group is morally and intellectually superior to the others.

- The desire for job security only affects the problem-solving strategies of public servants.

NOTES

1. Thomas R. Dye, *Understanding Public Policy*, 3rd ed. (Englewood Cliffs, NJ: Prentice-Hall, Inc. 1978), p. 3.

2. Charles W. Thomas and John R. Hepburn, *Crime, Criminal Law, and Criminology* (Dubuque, IA: Wm. C. Brown, Co., 1983), p. 5.

3. Thomas E. Cronin, Tania Z. Cronin, and Michael E. Milakovich, *U.S. v. Crime in the Streets* (Bloomington, IN: Indiana University Press, 1981), p. 54.

4. See R. Harre, *The Philosophies of Science, An Introductory Survey* (Suffolk: The Oxford University Press, 1972).

5. Robert A. Scott and Arnold R. Shore, *Why Sociology Does Not Apply: A Study of the Use of Sociology in Public Policy* (New York: Elesevier, 1979), pp. 1–2.

6. Landon Y. Jones, *Great Expectations* (New York: Ballantine Books, 1980), p. 161.

7. Ibid.

8. Ibid.

9. Robert Rosenthal and Ralph L. Rosnow, *Essentials of Behavioral Research* (New York: McGraw-Hill, 1984), p. 20.

10. William D. Coplin and Michael K. O'Leary, *Analyzing Public Policy Issues* (Croton-on-Hudson, NY: Policy Studies Associates, 1978), p. 1.

11. Karl Weick, "Small Wins. Redefining the Scale of Social Problems," *American Psychologist* (January, 1984), 40.

12. Eugene Doleschal, "Crime—Some Popular Beliefs," *Crime and Delinquency* (January, 1979), 1–8.

13. Michael D. Cohen, James G. March, and Johan P. Olsen, "A Garbage Can Model of Organizational Choice," *Administrative Science Quarterly*, 17 (1972), 1–25.

14. U.S. Department of Justice, *The Effects of the Exclusionary Rule: A Study in California* (Washington, DC: U.S. Government Printing Office, 1982). James J. Fyfe, "The N.I.J. Study of the Exclusionary Rule," *Criminal Law Bulletin*, 19 (May–June 1983), 253–60. Also quoted in Samuel Walker, *Sense and Nonsense About Crime* (Pacific Grove, CA: Brooks/Cole Publishing Co., 1985), p. 94.

15. Walker, *Sense and Nonsense*, p. 142.

16. Ibid.

17. *The CJSA Forum*, Vol. 3., No. 3 (July 1985).

18. Peter Applebome, "States Spend Billions But Lag Behind Rate of Imprisonment, *New York Times*, March 2, 1987, p. 5E.

19. Aaron Wildavsky, *Speaking Truth to Power: The Art and Craft of Policy Analysis* (Boston: Little, Brown and Co., 1979), p. 15.

20. Lee J. Cronback and Associates, *Toward Reform of Program Evaluation* (San Francisco: Jossey-Bass, 1980). See also, James F. Gilsinan and L. Carl Volpe, "Do Not Cry Wolf Until You Are Sure: The Manufactured Crisis in Evaluation Research," *Policy Sciences*, 17 (1984), 179–91.

21. Dye, *Understanding Public Policy*, p. 5.

22. Wildavsky, *Speaking Truth*, p. 36.

II

What Exactly Is Crime?

At the end of this chapter, the student will be able to:

A. Describe the elements necessary for an act to meet the legal criteria of a crime.
B. Discuss the difficulties in defining the term crime, and the elements necessary for a sound scientific definition of the phenomenon.
C. List the major sources of criminal justice policy and the extralegal influences operating on policymakers and citizens in classifying something as a crime.

ISSUE BACKGROUND

Is There a Problem?

In the past two decades, the United States has experienced a rapid and alarming increase in crime.[1]

Contrary to the impression of increasing crime conveyed by much public discussion, most data sources suggest that crime rates have recently remained fairly stable in the United States.[2]

The contradiction in these two statements is all the more startling since the statements are made, albeit by different authors, in the same book 11 pages apart! The statements underscore, however, the ease with which the concept of crime becomes an issue of public debate rather than a problem with readily agreed-upon components. In fact, the concept of crime seems stubbornly resistant to bounding as a scientific problem. Why this is so will become evident by the end of this chapter. Two questions are posed. First, what is meant by the term "crime"? Second, what influences our perceptions of the problem? Policy makers, scientists, and interested citizens must analyze the various responses to these preliminary questions before strategies of crime control can be reasonably discussed and assessed.

The first part of this chapter presents the various definitions of crime. Of course, how the problem is defined influences the policies that are adopted to cope with it. But the relationship is circular. Policies, in turn, affect problem definition. It is necessary, therefore, to distinguish the different groups of criminal justice decision makers and their relationship to the policy process. This constitutes the second part of the chapter.

Definitions of Crime

Sense making is the ability to classify. It is the ability to put things into categories of like occurrences. Such categorization skills allow us to efficiently organize into meaningful patterns the hundreds of thousands of stimuli we encounter daily. Without these skills, we would not be able to act. Our interpretive ability would be overwhelmed if each item in our environment had to continually be assessed to determine what it was, what it meant, and how to act toward it. To illustrate, as you read this book, you are not stopping at each letter to ask what it is, what it means, and what you should do about it. You are continually categorizing letters into words, words into sentences, sentences into paragraphs, paragraphs into pages, and so on, into sections, chapters, and finally into a large category of things called "books." Of course, the process is helped by the use of space, but even the blank areas need categorization. Differences in spacing separates letters, words, sentences, and so on, but your categorization ability, your ability to judge that so much space means a distinction between two letters or two words, allows you to pattern the text so that it is sensical.

Categorizing and pattern making are so highly developed in human beings that we are often not conscious of either doing it or of how much skill it takes. A term like "crime," however, forces us to recognize the strengths and weaknesses of our categorization ability.

As Gwynn Nettler cogently remarks, "Crime is a word, not a deed."[3] To fully appreciate the import of this remark, it is necessary to recognize that the term crime is also part of a scheme of classification. It constitutes a category of events that contains within itself numerous subcategories. At the same time, the category of crime is itself a subcategory of a larger set of events. Figure 2-1 illustrates the classification scheme of which crime is a part.

The illustration underscores the fact that terming an event a crime

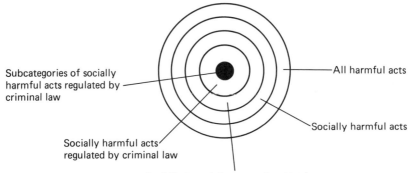

Subcategories of socially harmful acts regulated by criminal law

All harmful acts

Socially harmful acts regulated by criminal law

Socially harmful acts

Socially harmful acts regulated by law

Figure 2-1

involves a series of judgments or evaluations. The term "crime" is therefore not a term of empirical description. It does not specify the inherent qualities of an act that would automatically designate it as criminal. Rather, a series of judgments are called for to place an act in the category of crime. The first judgment is to decide if the act is harmful. This general class of event, however, contains many acts that are not considered criminal. Thus, cigarette smoking or getting drunk in your own home are not classified as crimes. When something is judged to be a crime, the harm is thought to extend beyond the individuals involved and to in some way affect the whole of society.

Like the more inclusive category of "harmful," the category of "socially harmful" contains actions other than those thought to be criminal. Air pollution, while judged socially harmful, is not necessarily classified as a crime. Nevertheless, the element of social harm is a key component of the definition of crime and separates these acts from acts that are thought to affect only the individual.

The definition of what constitutes a crime is narrowed further by judging whether the act is or ought to be regulated by law. Air pollution has only recently been reclassified from something judged harmful to something judged to be in the category of needing legal regulation. Thus, calling something a crime also puts an act into a category of occurrences that should be treated in a particular way. The system of legal classification itself contains subcategories, one of these being acts governed by the criminal law.

The designation of something as within the purview of criminal law means that the state, using its coercive power, will process the event. In our society, the criminal justice system—police, courts, and corrections—deals with such matters. Criminal law is therefore distinguished from civil law by the degree of involvement the state exercises in regard to an incident. In civil law, the state merely regulates the adjudication procedure between two parties. If I think you have harmed me by not living up to the terms of an agreement, I can bring suit against you and pursue my claim in accord with the legal regulations governing the keeping of contracts. But the responsibility for initial action rests with me, not with the state. The state's interest is in regulating how such issues will be decided. On the other hand, a robbery victim does not pursue the individual responsible with a piece of paper that says he will sue him to recover lost revenue. Instead, the state takes over and pursues the individual on its own, regardless of what the victim thinks. The state's interest in the matter is underscored by noting that in a criminal procedure the case is described as *The State of Illinois* v. *Escobedo*, not *John Jones* v. *Escobedo* as it would appear in a civil matter.[4]

Crime is further subcategorized by the seriousness of the events placed within it. Each subcategory of seriousness is designated by the increased punishment it contains.

The term "crime" obviously involves a number of classification judgments about an occurrence. As the examples illustrate, these judgments can change over time. Something classified as harmful at one point can move into or out of a series of increasingly more serious judgments about its nature. Cigarette smoking has, for example, moved from the category neutral or even beneficial to the classification scheme of harmful. In the 1940's tobacco companies used physicians to endorse their products or made claims of beneficial effects. Now cigarette smoking is regularly decried by the medical profession. Within the classificatory framework, it appears to be moving even further. It is now considered socially harmful due to the effects of secondary smoke, smoke exhaled but then ingested by a nonsmoker, and is increasingly subject to regulation by law. Clearly, such categorizing decisions are influenced by the values and moral beliefs of those making them. As Chapter 4 discusses, such beliefs change over time in response to a variety of circumstances. At this point it is sufficient to note that the term "crime" is a term of classification. To understand what this means, it is necessary to explore those rules by which events are placed in this category. Since the dominant set of rules for classifying events as crimes are contained within the framework of the criminal law, we explore this categorizing process first.

CRIMINOLOGICAL/CRIMINAL JUSTICE CONSIDERATIONS

Elements of the Legal Definition of Crime

Consider the following incident:

Charles Jones was found at 2:00 A.M. in an attached garage by Officer Malone. The police report states that Mr. Jones appeared to be under the influence of alcohol when apprehended. He had taken three tires out of the garage and placed them in the driveway. He had urinated in the corner of the building. Finally, he rattled the handle of the door connecting the garage with the house. This noise woke the home owner, who called the police. The garage door had been left open.

Is this incident a crime? There are five decision criteria used to determine if an incident involves a violation of the criminal law. An exploration of these criteria will demonstrate the problems inherent in the legal scheme of crime classification.

To be considered a crime, an act must:

1. Be observable.
2. Be a violation of either statute or case law.
3. Have a prescribed punishment called for in law.

Concerning the actor:

4. He or she must intend to commit a crime.
5. He or she must be acting without defense or justification.[5]

While these criteria may seem straightforward, they become somewhat less so in their application. For example, in the case above, only one of the criteria applies unambiguously. The act was an observable phenomenon. In our society we cannot be prosecuted for what we think. We can only be subject to criminal law for engaging in specific, observable activities or for failure to do something the law requires. In the latter instance, failure to act presumably has visible consequences. Thus, child neglect, where a parent fails to do that which the law requires for the care and protection of one's children, is criminal by an act of omission. But the omission has visible consequences such as a malnourished, sickly child. Conspiracy laws also underscore the necessity of observability if an act is to be classified as criminal. For a conspiracy to be shown (conspiracy to commit murder, for example), some concrete action needs to have been taken. Thus, if I only think about murdering my next-door neighbor, I have committed no crime. If I attempt to hire someone to do it, I can be guilty of conspiracy even though the act of murder itself was not carried out. I took a concrete action towards that end.

In the case above, it is clear that Charles Jones did something. He did not simply *think* about doing something. After this rather obvious conclusion, the waters become considerably more muddied. For example, the application of the second criterion requires knowing where the incident took place.

The Sources of Law and Punishment: Statute and Case Law

In the United States, there are two primary sources of law. Statutory law is that law which is enacted by legislative bodies. The statutes defining criminal conduct vary from state to state and between states and the federal government. The second major source of law is case law. Case law is based upon various court decisions and provides judges with a guide for deciding a

Table 2-1 The Different Definitions of Burglary

State A	State B
• breaking and entering (excludes through open door or window)	• entering
• the occupied or unoccupied	• house, room, shop, tenement, apartment, warehouse, store, mill, barn, stable, outhouse, other building, tent, vessel, railroad car, trailer coach, house car, camper used as a dwelling, or mine
• dwelling house or sleeping apartment of another	
• in the night-time	
• with intent to commit a felony or larceny	• with intent to commit a felony or larceny

Source: *Dictionary of Criminal Justice Data Terminology*, 2nd ed. (Washington, DC: U.S. Department of Justice, Bureau of Justice Statistics, 1981), p. 33.

particular case by telling them how cases of a similar type were decided in the past. Case law in turn is heavily influenced by English Common Law, a collection of past customs, traditions, and judicial decisions that developed in England after the Norman Conquest in 1066.[6] Case law, like common law, is applied on the principle of *stare decisis*, or let the precedent decide. But, again, case law varies from state to state and between state and federal judiciaries.

Common law may also influence statutory law by providing a guide to law makers for structuring specific criminal statutes. Most states have incorporated at least some common law elements into their statutory definition of crime. The exact elements incorporated, though, will vary. The common law definition of burglary is "unlawfully entering an occupied dwelling at night with the intent to commit a felony or larceny."[7] Compare the differences between States A and B in their interpretation and integration of this common law definition shown in Table 2-1.

Mr. Jones did not commit a burglary if he happened to be in State A. If Mr. Jones was in State B, he is much more likely to have his act classified this way.

The statute covering first-degree burglary in State B carries a penalty of 5 to 15 years in the state penitentiary. The degree of punishment divides the various subcategories of burglary. Thus, burglary in the first degree involves a dwelling unit as opposed to a factory, which would be burglary in the second degree. The latter carries a lesser penalty than the former (one to seven years). Mr. Jones's act meets the statutory definition of first-degree burglary (at least in State B), burglary of a dwelling place, and therefore he faces a more severe punishment. The third criterion of our definition is met. As noted, then, punishment not only distinguishes the general category of a criminal act but, in its various degrees, it also specifies the subcategories of such acts. One set of subcategories includes the distinction between felonies and misdemeanors.

Felonies and Misdemeanors

Criminal statutes distinguish between felonies and misdemeanors. Such distinctions reflect both the seriousness of the event and the place and degree of punishment. More serious crimes are generally placed in the felony category, less serious crimes in the misdemeanor designation. Felony punishment can be anything from death to confinement in a state or federal institution. Misdemeanor offenses are generally punished by fines or incarceration for a period not exceeding a year in a local jail. Given the seriousness of the punishment attached to the crime of first degree burglary, we need to ask if the actor, Mr. Jones, was legally culpable of committing the act. This question leads to consideration of the two remaining decision criteria.

Intent

Intent forms a major element of the legal definition of crime. Intent or *mens rea* means that the perpetrator of the act consciously sought to cause harm. Again, the straightforward explanation of intent belies a thicket of complex issues. The law distinguishes, for example, between general intent and specific intent. Only the former is required to establish criminal culpability. Thus, if I am playing with a revolver in a dangerous manner and accidentally shoot and kill a passerby, did I have the requisite intent to be charged with a crime? The answer is yes. Even though I did not specifically intend to kill the passerby, I should have been aware that playing with a weapon in a reckless way might have resulted in harm to others. Therefore, the law assumes that I generally intended such harm. Statutory rape laws also illustrate the idea of general intent. Although the violator may not have specifically intended to have intercourse with an underaged female, general intent is assumed. The law requires that sufficient regard be given to the possibility that the female cannot give her legal consent.

Criminal intent is a more subtle legal doctrine than it appears on the surface. Further, there are clear exceptions to the intent requirement. The major exception is the felony murder doctrine. This doctrine stipulates that an individual is responsible for any death resulting from the commission of a felony. A burglar is spotted by a police officer getting into a car. The officer gives chase. Both vehicles reach speeds far exceeding those allowed on residential streets. During the course of the chase, the officer hits and kills a pedestrian crossing the street in an appropriate location. Who is responsible for the pedestrian's death? The felony murder doctrine would hold that the burglar is responsible for the death, since it occurred during the course of his felony action. The burglar could now be tried for murder.

Did the hapless Mr. Jones have the necessary intent to lead us to classify his garage caper as a crime? What if he stumbled into the garage, thinking it was a public restroom? What facts can be adduced to show criminal intent? The most obvious fact is the taking of the tires and putting them in the driveway. Of course, if there is no vehicle for transporting the tires, this may suggest that there was neither a prior nor a concurrent intent to steal them. Obviously, establishing intent is a difficult enterprise.

Lack of Justification or Defense

Finally, the last element for determining the criminal nature of an act is lack of justification or defense. A homicide, for example, can be justifiable if the killing was in self-defense. The law also recognizes that there are degrees of responsibility for harm caused. The notion of defense refers to the degree of responsibility we possess for committing an act. Use of the insanity defense is a claim that requisite responsibility was absent for the designation of an act as a crime. Intoxication is also a defense against certain criminal charges. This defense is of course the most relevant for the case we are considering. If Jones was intoxicated at the time of the incident, this may be a sufficient defense against the charge of burglary. He did not know what he was doing and therefore cannot be held criminally liable for what occurred.

Of course, this defense by solving one problem may raise a number of others. While Jones may not have had the necessary control over his actions to be guilty of burglary, he was drunk and trespassing. Is he guilty of a crime, albeit a less serious one, by allowing himself to get into such a condition? We could start the process all over, and apply each of the criteria again, to see if his act fits into a less serious crime category (as it would have in State A), perhaps peace disturbance or drunk and disorderly conduct. The issue is of more than academic interest, at least to Jones, who could face anything from a night in jail to 15 years in the state penitentiary, depending on how his act is classified.

Deciding whether Jones committed a crime, and, if he did, what kind of crime it was, illustrates the judgmental nature of the term "crime." Calling something a crime or someone a criminal is an exercise in evaluation rather than description. This means that use of these terms often tells more about the values of the people applying the terms than about the inherent characteristics of situations or people to which they are applied. Jones can be classified as a burglar, a drunk, a person committing a trespass, or a poor unfortunate who just needs a hot meal and a biblical admonition. The term you pick to describe him is more indicative of your values than of some essential characteristic of Jones.

The above discussion again underscores the moral, value-laden nature of our criminal laws. Such laws ultimately involve value judgments about the nature of life, right and wrong, our place in the scheme of things. Exactly whose values and morals get enshrined into law, however, has been a matter of some debate.

POLICY CONSIDERATIONS:
THEORIES/ARGUMENTS/APPLICATIONS

Theories of Law and Levels of Policy

The value consensus theory of law argues that law represents the commonly agreed-upon mores of a community.[8] Only the most important values of the community, then, those that everyone assents to, are protected by law. This theory contrasts with the interest group model, which views law as representing the values and interests of the most powerful groups within a society. Finally, law can be viewed as a rational response to the problems of social order. What becomes law are those norms that contribute to the efficient functioning of the society.

There is no need to vote for a single theory of law. Egon Guba argues that social policy, of which law is a premier example, can be conceptually divided into three different levels. There is policy-in-intention. This consists of the goals and values that the policy maker intends to achieve in enunciating a particular policy. What is intended, however, is not necessarily what is implemented. The last chapter noted that those charged with specifying a method for achieving the goals of a policy statement have wide latitude in determining exactly what programs will be instituted. Policy-in-implementation, Guba's second level, can be considerably different, therefore, from policy-in-intention. Finally, there is policy-in-experience. Policy-in-experience is how a policy is viewed by those on the receiving end of it.[9]

Policy-in-intention often describes general goals and general means for achieving them based on the commonly accepted values of a society. Statements that condemn evil and support good can be readily agreed to by most citizens. Even more specific statements in the form of laws showing abhorrence of crime and a desire to protect society can garner a fair share of support in a society. Stealing should be illegal, and engaging in it should result in some form of punishment. The harshness of the penalty is, of course, an issue. Sentencing structures that provide a range of punishment can, however, encompass both liberal and conservative views. For example, a one- to seven-year sentence for stealing, with the possibility of probation or parole, can be seen as either harsh or lenient.

While not all laws represent value consensus within society, many do. It is in the implementation of the law that interest group values may become most predominant. What is to be considered stealing? What specific punishment will be given? What specific groups will be most likely focused upon as potential violators? Policy implementers responding to their own organizational values and to the interest group pressures exerted on them often determine the answers to such questions. Value conflicts often occur then between and among implementers and those subjected to the implementation. Why the police patrol the streets and not the corporate boardrooms may be a question posed by those subject to a specific kind of legal implementation. Finally, the rationality of the law is in the eye of the beholder. As will become clear, what appears rational from the standpoint of one set of organizational demands or values may be nonsensical from the standpoint of another group's goal and value orientation.

Legal codes attempt to systematically and rationally frame these underlying values, so that at least the values can be expressed consistently. Nevertheless, as is evident, there is plenty of room for individual interpretation. The law only attempts rationality, it does not consistently achieve it. Therefore law is ultimately based on the experience of the people who formulate it, interpret it, enforce it, and live by it.

Extralegal Considerations
in Criminal Justice Policy

This notion of lived experience introduces a second set of criteria for assessing whether something is a crime and someone is a criminal. Criteria based on experience form an extralegal basis for such decision making. To illustrate, if you are a police officer just about to get off duty, it may not seem sensical to charge our hapless Mr. Jones with burglary since paperwork alone could keep you tied up for hours. On the other hand, it always looks impressive to show the sergeant that you arrested a burglar. If you are an overburdened prosecutor, with dangerous murderers, rapists, and robbers to worry about, it may not seem sensical to waste resources on this kind of incident. On the other hand, if the home owner is an influential individual in the community, it might be worth the time and the expense. Suppose it turns out that Jones is the brother-in-law of the home owner. Will that make a difference as to how the incident is judged? What if Jones is the home owner's son, who left home when he was 17. What is the appropriate decision then?

The point is that law and its application simultaneously manifest contradictory elements. Many laws may be an expression of commonly held values, but in their application a number of extralegal circumstances determine whether a specific act will be termed a crime. The same act with two different sets of circumstances can result in entirely different judgments about its criminal nature. If I am severely injured by an assailant who beats me, the assailant's act may or may not be termed a serious crime depending on a number of contingencies. Is the person who did it a stranger, my spouse, my parent? Table 2-2 shows how a nationwide sample of people judged the seriousness of 204 illegal events. An examination of these data shows that the common-sense definition of crime takes into account extralegal factors such as the ability of the victim to protect him or herself, the relationship between victim and offender, and, for property crimes, the type of business that was victimized. Notice the difference in rankings, for example, between a beating involving a stranger (a score of 11.8) and one involving a father and son, where the father is the victim (a score of 7.9). Notice also the different weights given to stealing

Table 2-2 How Do People Rank the Severity of Crime?

Severity score and offense

72.1—Planting a bomb in a public building. The bomb explodes and 20 people are killed.

52.8—A man forcibly rapes a woman. As a result of physical injuries, she dies.

43.2—Robbing a victim at gunpoint. The victim struggles and is shot to death.

39.2—A man stabs his wife. As a result, she dies.

35.7—Stabbing a victim to death.

35.6—Intentionally injuring a victim. As a result, the victim dies.

33.8—Running a narcotics ring.

27.9—A woman stabs her husband. As a result, he dies.

26.3—An armed person skyjacks an airplane and demands to be flown to another country.

25.9—A man forcibly rapes a woman. No other physical injury occurs.

24.9—Intentionally setting fire to a building causing $100,000 worth of damage.

22.9—A parent beats his young child with his fists. The child requires hospitalization.

21.2—Kidnapping a victim.

20.7—Selling heroin to others for resale.

19.5—Smuggling heroin into the country.

19.5—Killing a victim by recklessly driving an automobile.

17.9—Robbing a victim of $10 at gunpoint. The victim is wounded and requires hospitalization.

16.9—A man drags a woman into an alley, tears her clothes but flees before she is physically harmed or sexually attacked.

16.4—Attempting to kill a victim with a gun. The gun misfires and the victim escapes unharmed.

15.9—A teenage boy beats his mother with his fists. The mother requires hospitalization.

15.5—Breaking into a bank at night and stealing $100,000.

14.1—A doctor cheats on claims he makes to a Federal health insurance plan for patient services.

13.9—A legislator takes a bribe from a company to vote for a law favoring the company.

13.0—A factory knowingly gets rid of its waste in a way that pollutes the water supply of a city.

12.2—Paying a witness to give false testimony in a criminal trial.

12.0—A police officer takes a bribe not to interfere with an illegal gambling operation.

12.0—Intentionally injuring a victim. The victim is treated by a doctor and hospitalized.

11.8—A man beats a stranger with his fists. He requires hospitalization.

11.4—Knowingly lying under oath during a trial.

11.2—A company pays a bribe to a legislator to vote for a law favoring the company.

10.9—Stealing property worth $10,000 from outside a building.

10.5—Smuggling marijuana into the country for resale.

10.4—Intentionally hitting a victim with a lead pipe. The victim requires hospitalization.

10.3—Illegally selling barbiturates, such as prescription sleeping pills, to others for resale.

10.3—Operating a store that knowingly sells stolen property.

10.0—A government official intentionally hinders the investigation of a criminal offense.

9.7—Breaking into a school and stealing equipment worth $1,000.

9.7—Walking into a public museum and stealing a painting worth $1,000.

9.6—Breaking into a home and stealing $1,000.

9.6—A police officer knowingly makes a false arrest.

9.5—A public official takes $1,000 of public money for his own use.

9.4—Robbing a victim of $10 at gunpoint. No physical harm occurs.

9.3—Threatening to seriously injure a victim.

9.2—Several large companies illegally fix the retail prices of their products.

8.6—Performing an illegal abortion.

8.5—Selling marijuana to others for resale.

8.5—Intentionally injuring a victim. The victim is treated by a doctor but is not hospitalized.

Table 2-2 (*continued*)

Severity score and offense

8.2—Knowing that a shipment of cooking oil is bad, a store owner decides to sell it anyway. Only one bottle is sold and the purchaser is treated by a doctor but not hospitalized.

7.9—A teenage boy beats his father with his fists. The father requires hospitalization.

7.7—Knowing that a shipment of cooking oil is bad, a store owner decides to sell it anyway.

7.5—A person, armed with a lead pipe, robs a victim of $10. No physical harm occurs.

7.4—Illegally getting monthly welfare checks.

7.3—Threatening a victim with a weapon unless the victim gives money. The victim gives $10 and is not harmed.

7.3—Breaking into a department store and stealing merchandise worth $1,000.

7.2—Signing someone else's name to a check and cashing it.

6.9—Stealing property worth $1,000 from outside a building

6.5—Using heroin.

6.5—An employer refuses to hire a qualified person because of that person's race.

6.4—Getting customers for a prostitute.

6.3—A person, free on bail for committing a serious crime purposefully fails to appear in court on the day of his trial.

6.2—An employee embezzles $1,000 from his employer.

5.4—Possessing some heroin for personal use.

5.4—A real estate agent refuses to sell a house to a person because of that person's race.

5.4—Threatening to harm a victim unless the victim gives money. The victim gives $10 and is not harmed.

5.3—Loaning money at an illegally high interest rate.

5.1—A man runs his hands over the body of a female victim, then runs away.

5.1—A person, using force, robs a victim of $10. No physical harm occurs.

4.9—Snatching a handbag containing $10 from a victim on the street.

4.8—A man exposes himself in public.

4.6—Carrying a gun illegally.

4.5—Cheating on Federal income tax return.

4.4—Picking a victim's pocket of $100.

4.2—Attempting to break into a home but running away when a police car approaches.

3.8—Turning in a false fire alarm.

3.7—A labor union official illegally threatens to organize a strike if an employer hires nonunion workers.

3.6—Knowingly passing a bad check.

3.6—Stealing property worth $100 from outside a building.

3.5—Running a place that permits gambling to occur illegally.

3.2—An employer illegally threatens to fire employees if they join a labor union.

2.4—Knowingly carrying an illegal knife.

2.2—Stealing $10 worth of merchandise from the counter of a department store.

2.1—A person is found firing a rifle for which he knows he has no permit.

2.1—A woman engages in prostitution.

1.9—Making an obscene phone call.

1.9—A store owner knowingly puts "large" eggs into containers marked "extra large."

1.8—A youngster under 16 years old is drunk in public.

1.8—Knowingly being a customer in a place where gambling occurs illegally.

1.7—Stealing property worth $10 from outside a building.

1.6—Being a customer in a house of prostitution.

1.6—A male, over 16 years of age has sexual relations with a willing female under 16.

1.5—Taking barbiturates, such as sleeping pills, without a legal prescription.

1.5—Intentionally shoving or pushing a victim. No medical treatment is required.

1.4—Smoking marijuana.

1.3—Two persons willingly engage in a homosexual act.

1.1—Disturbing the neighborhood with loud, noisy behavior.

1.1—Taking bets on the numbers.

1.1—A group continues to hang around a corner after being told to break up by a police officer.

0.9—A youngster under 16 years old runs away from home.

Table 2-2   (*continued*)

Severity score and offense		
0.8—Being drunk in public.	0.6—Trespassing in the backyard of a private home.	0.2—A youngster under 16 years old plays hooky from school.
0.7—A youngster under 16 years old breaks a curfew law by being out on the street after the hour permitted by law.	0.3—A person is a vagrant. That is, he has no home and no visible means of support.	

Source: Marianne W. Zawitz, ed., *Report to the Nation on Crime and Justice*, U.S. Department of Justice, Bureau of Justice Statistics, (Washington, DC: U.S. Government Printing Office, October, 1983.)

$1,000 from a home (9.6) and from a business (7.3). Thus, a second source of rules for categorizing events as criminal are the extralegal, commonsense criteria applied by different groups in society.

Individual values, interest group considerations, and organizational demands all affect the judgments made when attempting to place events into legal categories. Clearly, the law is not and cannot be applied in a mechanical fashion, and this is simultaneously its strength and a source of dissatisfaction. The law can be flexible and tailored to unique individual circumstances. At the same time, such flexibility generates a great deal of public debate as different groups are more or less successful in establishing their definition of an event as criminal or noncriminal. Thus, the concept of crime is more likely to be encountered in public discussions as an issue vulnerable to the persuasive powers of a given interest group and the dynamics of political compromise rather than as a problem with objectively evident elements.

From a policy perspective, the legal definition of crime is probably the most significant. And yet, as the discussion indicates, the application of such definitions cannot be understood without also knowing something about the values and interests of the group applying them. Finally, the danger of bias and subsequent erroneous conclusions about the nature of the crime problem is underscored by noting the problems of both legal and common-sense definitions of crime for scientific understanding. To unravel the interactions among all these different definitions of crime and the consequences of such interactions for policy responses to the problem, it is necessary to describe the various locations for criminal justice decision making and the forms such decisions take. We turn to these issues in the following section. Later in the text we shall examine the decision-making process of each location in detail.

Where Criminal Justice Policy Is Made

Criminal justice policy emerges in a wide variety of settings. The purpose of this section is to familiarize the student with the major sources of criminal justice policy. Each source will be briefly described together with its specific policy activity. In-depth treatment of the specific agency or group will be given in the appropriate chapters of Part II of this book.

Groups and agencies involved in criminal justice policy can be analytically classified according to one of three major policy roles: policy making, policy implementation, or policy advocacy. As we have seen, these distinctions are somewhat arbitrary, since policy is made through its application in specific instances and all policies develop their own cadre of advocates including those who make and implement specific policies. Nevertheless, such distinctions help begin the process of understanding the complex world of criminal justice policy.

Policy Makers

There are three major groups involved in criminal justice policy making: legislative bodies, appellate courts, and regulatory agencies. There are approximately 39,800 legislative bodies in the United States that can formulate criminal justice policies. These include the 50 state legislatures, the Congress of the United States, and the large number of city, county, and township local governing boards. These diverse legislative bodies make criminal justice policy in three ways. First, they determine what kinds of behavior will be subject to criminal law. Each state has its own distinct body of criminal law, defining the acts designated as criminal and the appropriate punishment for engaging in acts so specified. State legislatures are the most significant policy makers in this regard. While there is a body of federal criminal law, most crime is designated by state statutes. About 85% of criminal cases are heard in state courts, with only 15% heard in federal courts.[10] City or town ordinances also have a section on criminal violations, but these regulate public nuisance–type offenses, for example, smoking on public conveyances, and usually involve penalties no greater than a monetary fine.

Besides making policy by passing substantive laws, legislative bodies also make criminal justice policy through budgetary decisions. State legislatures control budgets for the major judicial and correctional functions within states. The major fiscal burden for the law enforcement function, however, generally rests with the local municipality. Thus, local government spends about 64% of its total criminal justice budget on police protection. State government spends less than 22% of its total criminal justice budget on police protection.[11] On the other hand, the major expenditure in state criminal justice budgets is for corrections, 55.1% of the total, compared with 16.8% of total for local governments.[12]

Finally, legislative bodies generate criminal justice policy by passing enabling legislation to set up various criminal justice agencies. Such agencies either aid criminal justice practitioners or enforce substantive laws. The Bureau of Justice Statistics is an example of an agency designed primarily to aid others in the criminal justice field. The Federal Bureau of Investigation, on the other hand, is primarily an investigation and enforcement agency, although it too has units primarily aimed at supporting the work of others in the law enforcement field. Once operable, governmental agencies in turn generate a body of law termed "administrative law."

Congress has empowered such agencies to make regulations for carrying out their mandate. These regulations represent a lawmaking function within the executive branch of government. Some of these administrative laws can and do carry a criminal penalty for their infraction. The Department of Treasury, the Commerce Department, the Department of Labor, and of course the Justice Department all have enforcement agencies that treat particular violations of administrative rules and procedures as violations of criminal law.

Passing substantive laws, governmental budgets, and agency-enabling legislation are the three ways legislative bodies make criminal justice policy. Agency-enabling legislation in turn allows agencies to make their own rules and regulations, some of which have the force of criminal law. Finally, judges also substantively affect criminal justice policy. Thus, the third major source of criminal justice policy making is the appellate courts.

The United States is known as having a dual court system. There is a state system of courts and a federal system of courts. Each system has two levels. Courts on the first, or lower, level hear or try the facts of a case. Most jurisdictions have inferior and superior trial courts. The inferior courts can try misdemeanor cases, review evidence and issue arrest warrants, set bail, and, in felony matters, decide whether there is sufficient cause to send a case to the superior court. The superior trial court hears felony cases.

Courts on the second, or higher, level hear appeals for reconsideration of the judgments rendered on the first level. The first level courts are courts of record. This means that appeals from the decisions of these courts are reviewed from the record. The appeals court will literally read the trial transcript of what occurred and will not rehear the entire case. Further, appeals are not reviews of the fact situation but of the trial judge's application of the law. In most states and in the federal system there is a trial court, at least one intermediate appellate court, and a final court of appeals, usually called the supreme court, except in New York where it is known as the superior court.

Contrary to popular belief, the state appeals courts are not subservient to the federal courts. The federal appeals courts are divided into 12 districts or circuits. Eleven hear appeals from the states within their jurisdiction, the twelfth hears appeals from the District of Columbia. Federal appellate courts can only review the decisions of state courts if it has been shown that a federal issue is involved. Otherwise, the supreme court of the state has the final word. Even if a federal appeals court overrules a particular decision of a state supreme court, only those states that are within the circuit of the federal court making such a judgment are bound by the ruling. Until such time as the United States Supreme Court rules on the matter, states in other federal circuits are bound by the judgments of their own appeals courts regardless of whether such judgments conflict with another federal circuit's ruling.

Table 2-3 Distribution of Criminal Justice
Employees by Level of Government
and Function

	Federal	State	Local
Police	61,342	107,606	568,793
Judicial	15,455	61,082	115,967
Prosecution	15,791	23,926	54,025
Public defender	356	6,003	5,733
Corrections	14,448	240,856	139,373

Source: *Criminal Justice Source Book—1986* Katherine M. Jamieson
and Timothy J. Flanagan, eds., *Sourcebook of Criminal Justice Statis-
tics-1986*, U.S. Department of Justice, Bureau of Justice Statistics
(Washington, DC: US Government Printing Office) 1987.

Appellate courts exercise a policy-making function by virtue of the
doctrine of *stare decisis*, alluded to previously in this book. The decision of an
appellate court is applicable to all similar cases within that jurisdiction.

Policy Implementers

Criminal justice policy is affected also by the agencies charged with
implementing either the substantive law as passed by legislative bodies or case
law as determined within the precedent-setting functions of appellate courts.
Enforcement agencies, trial courts, magistrate courts, juvenile courts, prosecuting attorney offices, and correctional agencies form the major groups of criminal
justice policy implementers. In 1985 there were over 1,340,000 individuals in
criminal justice policy-implementing positions.[13]
There are 14,707 law enforcement agencies in the United States.
Approximately 50 of these are under the jurisdiction of the federal government.
One thousand and sixteen are state agencies or special police bureaus such as
park rangers, harbor police, etc. The remaining 13,691 are dispersed throughout the United States and answer to the numerous local governments of the
cities, towns, and villages of our land.[14] Table 2-3 represents the distribution
of full-time employees by level of government and criminal justice function as
of October, 1985.
As can be seen from the table, law enforcement is largely a local matter.
The numbers represent a longstanding bias that favors local control of the
police. Police forces therefore vary greatly both in terms of size and in terms
of training given to new officers. Sizes range from one officer in some small
communities to over 23,000 officers in New York City.[15] Smaller departments
may require no training for officers other than that which they get "on the
job," while larger departments may require a three-month academy training
experience plus continuous in-service review. Most police departments have 10
officers or less.[16] In the United States there are a total of 470,678 sworn police

personnel, that is, personnel with the power to arrest.[17] If all of these officers lived in the same geographic area, they would constitute a city larger than Cincinnati, Ohio.

As previously noted, most serious crimes fall under the province of the state courts. The large number of judicial employees at the local level reflects resources committed to less serious legal infractions and to traffic ordinances. Such cases are heard in municipal or justice of the peace courts. These courts try petty cases, where the harshest penalty is the imposition of a fine. Such courts are not courts of record. That is, decisions appealed from this level result in a retrial of the whole case, as if no previous judicial action had occurred. Many of the judicial employees at this level are not attorneys. Depending on state statute, some of these courts may issue arrest and search warrants, inform an accused of his or her rights, and decide whether sufficient evidence exists to hold cases over for trial in state courts. These courts may also be responsible for setting bail. Thus, while these courts together with lower trial courts of record may have very restricted jurisdiction, they are often the first encounter an individual will have with the court system in a criminal matter. The tone set in these courts and the decisions made can therefore affect what will occur in the rest of the judicial system. Both in terms of numbers of employees and the sequence of decision making, these courts form an important element in the administration of criminal justice policy.

Another court of limited jurisdiction that is important, both in terms of the number of employees and its effects on implementation of justice policy, is the juvenile court system. The number of juvenile court judicial employees is reflected in both the state and local judicial totals. In some instances both state and local monies are used to pay the salaries of these court employees. The juvenile court system represents a blending of a legal and a social service philosophy. Historically, these courts have viewed their role as one of treatment rather than as one of fact determination. Unfortunately, this orientation led to the belief that the legal protections afforded adults in criminal matters were superfluous. In 1967, the Supreme Court of the United States in *In re Gault* held that juveniles were entitled to the protections afforded adults in criminal proceedings. Since as much as 50% of property crime and 20% of violent crime is attributed to juveniles, the operation of these courts form an important element in the implementation of criminal justice policy.

Prosecution of criminal cases is also largely a local function. Prosecutors are generally elected on a countywide basis within a state. The prosecutor's office is one of the most powerful offices in the criminal justice system. As will be seen, prosecutors have sole discretion in terms of the criminal cases they choose to pursue or not pursue. They are the key gatekeepers within our system of justice. As Table 2-3 makes clear, prosecution also garners a far greater share of resources in terms of numbers of people than does public defense. Public defender offices are notoriously understaffed. The difference

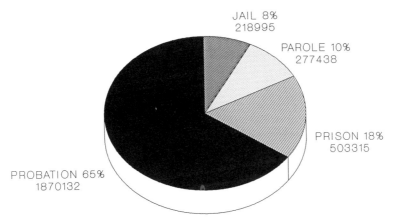

JAIL 8%
218995

PAROLE 10%
277438

PRISON 18%
503315

PROBATION 65%
1870132

Figure 2-2   Number of People Under Correctional Supervision.   *Source: Report to the Nation on Crime and Justice, 2nd ed.*, U.S. Department of Justice Bureau of Justice Statistics, (Washington DC: U.S. Government Printing Office, 1988). (Jail data are for June 30, 1983. All other data are for December 31, 1985.)

between prosecutors and defenders in the number of employees at all levels of government illustrates the point.

Finally, Table 2-3 illustrates the point that corrections is largely a function of state government. There are approximately 91,000 full-time employees working in state confinement facilities. Another 3,323 work in community-based facilities where inmates can leave for a certain portion of the day to utilize community resources such as schools, job assistance, and so on.[18] As of 1985, there was a total of 791 state prisons in the United States, housing 503,315 inmates.[19] There are approximately 69,000 state probation officers.[20] Probation is the typical correctional mode, and it is administered either on a statewide basis or on a local basis with the probation officer employed by the court. Thus, the number of local correctional employees includes both those who work in local confinement facilities (jails) and those who work for local probation departments. To get a clearer picture of the role of probation in corrections, consider the pie chart in Figure 2-2. As can be seen when comparing people under correctional supervision at both federal and state levels, the greatest percentage of people are on probation (65%). Nevertheless, both jails and prisons house a significant number of people. Each of these types of facilities face extensive problems of overcrowding, and each represents a significant drain on the resources of state and local governments. Chapter 4 will show the financial burden these institutions and indeed the whole criminal justice system impose on state and local governments.

If all of the individuals who have some role in the implementation of criminal justice policy were added together, including those not presented in Table 2-3, such as criminal justice planners and consultants, they would constitute our fourth largest city, replacing Philadelphia, Pennsylvania. While the criminal justice system is not famous for its uniformity of policy, given the vast number of people involved, it is a wonder that there is any semblance of uniformity at all. In part, the uniformity that is present can be explained by the tendency of organizations to routinize their responses to problems. Routinization provides a number of positive benefits for both organizations and the individuals within them.

Professional Interest Groups: Maintaining the Routine

To survive, an organization must demonstrate that it is worthy of the resources provided it. But since crime is encountered as an issue within the criminal justice policy arena and not as a clearly delineated problem, the actions of any group toward it will have ambiguous results. In situations where consequences of action are ambiguous, routines become substitutes for showing that the organization is doing what it is supposed to be doing. If a routine, therefore, is recognized as a standard one, it is therefore also assumed to be consequential. Thus, a police chief, who spends his or her appropriation on trying to figure out exactly what contributes to the crime problem and refuses to engage in any standard police preventative measures until he or she is sure that they work, will have a short tenure. Money spent on improving patrol capabilities with more squad cars, more personnel, and upgraded equipment will, however, likely be viewed as money well spent: this despite the fact that standard patrol has not been shown to have much effect on crime.

Routine also increases organizational efficiency while at the same time reducing job-related anxiety. Routines can increase the control a worker exercises over the environment, particularly ambiguous environments. If a public defender had to treat every single case he or she confronts as a brand new event, and therefore thoroughly analyze the circumstances surrounding it before recommending an action, the individual would be overwhelmed with detail and unable to function. The person would not be in control of the job, and the overall efficiency of the organization would suffer. Research by Sudnow shows that public defenders in fact routinize much of the decision making concerning case handling. He found that during the course of public defender work, the practitioner gains knowledge of the elements involved in "typical" occurrences of criminal behavior.[21] Crimes are carried out in a regular manner, so that most child molestation cases involve loitering around a school yard, assaults with a deadly weapon usually start with fights over a woman, petty thefts are generally unplanned and do not involve the use of a weapon, and so on. Routinizing cases in this way saves time, resources, and bureaucratic strain. The public defender knows what routine penalties routine cases receive, and can therefore advise the client on what to expect, and what to do "given the circumstances." Since such judgments are routine, the defense lawyer can be fairly certain what the prosecutor and the judge will do without even consulting these other workers.

Given the advantages of routine understandings, the core institutions of a policy area attempt to establish and maintain commonly accepted problem definitions, strategies of coping, and standard criteria for asserting that the job is being done. One vehicle for accomplishing these goals is the professional associations of criminal justice practitioners. Thus, their numbers and their ability to organize make criminal justice practitioners a potent force not only in the implementation of criminal justice policy but also in its development through their activity as members of interest groups.

Of course, these groups do not all have the same needs or interests. Thus, their ability to affect policy will in part depend upon their degree of organization, which in turn will depend upon how much agreement within each group there is concerning a particular issue. Moreover, there are other interest groups, besides criminal justice professionals, who lobby for their view of what criminal justice policy should look like. Thus, we have come full circle. We are now back at the legislature, only this time we examine how important interest groups are for the development of criminal justice policy. Three examples will illustrate the point.

In examining the development of sexual psychopathic laws, the criminologist Edwin Sutherland found that states usually passed such laws in response to a specific, heinous sex crime.[22] After the occurrence of such an event, citizens' groups would often lobby state legislatures to pass sexual psychopathic laws requiring mandatory commitment to a state mental facility. Interestingly enough, however, such citizens' committees were most often directly or indirectly influenced by psychiatrists. Thus, psychiatrists were the most important interest group behind such laws.

Not only is the formulation of substantive law subject to the influence of pressure groups, so too are the budgetary and administrative law decisions made by legislators. This was most clear in the development of the Law Enforcement Assistance Administration. Richard S. Allinson notes that LEAA, originally developed by the Johnson administration to fight what was perceived as an increasing crime problem, was subject to interest group pressure even prior to its passage in Congress. While it was still in its planning stages, LEAA was subject to input from a variety of interest groups including the National League of Cities and U.S. Conference of Mayors, the Council of State Governments, the International City Managers Association, the International Association of Chiefs of Police, and the American Correctional Association.[23] Thus, those who were to be the prime beneficiaries of the legislation were also the ones largely responsible for the shape it took. LEAA subsequently poured millions of dollars into the criminal justice system. In a span of just four years, LEAA's spending authorization went from $63 million in fiscal 1969 to $856 million in fiscal 1973.[24] The most noticeable beneficiaries of such increases were the criminal justice practitioners organized to take advantage of the program. Chief among these seemed to be police agencies. One study of LEAA thus concluded:

Table 2-4 List of Interest Groups Testifying before House and Senate Committees Considering Revision of the Criminal Code and Capital Punishment Legislation

Criminal Justice Group	Reform Groups	Govt. Agencies	Other
American Bar Association	National Council on Crime and Delinquency	U.S. Dept. of Justice	AFL-CIO
National Black Police Association	American Civil Liberties Union	State Judicial Conference	Business Round Table
International Association of Chiefs of Police	National Committee Against Repressive Legislation		The Association National Association of Manufacturers
National Legal Aid and Defender Association	National Coalition to Ban Handguns		Association of General Contractors
State Attorney Generals	National Coalition Against Death Penalty		

Source: Developed from an article by Barbara Ann Stolz: "Congress and Criminal Justice Policy Making: The Impact of Interest Groups and Symbolic Politics," *Journal of Criminal Justice* 13, No. 4 (1985), 307–19.

Instead of leader and initiator, the agency (LEAA) has consistently followed the whims and wishes of a limited constituency, the police.[25]

The results of such effective police lobbying are described in the quote below recorded by Cronin, Cronin, and Milakovich in their book, *U.S. v. Crime in the Streets.*

A small community, with five men on the police force, would want five cars, but after questioning could usually be talked down to two or three cars. Or a small force would order 20 gas masks, 20 bulletproof vests, 20 of everything— get it while the getting is good! Of course, they used the equipment—but not as much as they got.[26]

LEAA's impact on crime was negligible. Its main impact appeared to be a strengthening of groups within the criminal justice system.

Barbara Ann Stolz studied the number of interest groups involved in the effort to revise the federal criminal code and to consider creating a federal death penalty statute.[27] The list of these groups is instructive. Table 2-4 shows the strong presence of professional criminal justice groups. It also illustrates the importance attached to criminal justice legislation by a wide variety of organized interests, including agencies of the federal government itself.

How these interest groups specifically operate in the formation of criminal justice policy and legislators' response to them will be the focus of

Chapter 13. For now, it is sufficient to note that the criminal justice system is composed of many people, with diverse interests, who act in a variety of policy roles, including formation, implementation, and advocacy of various policies. It is also interesting to note the role of these groups in shaping our view of crime. As noted in the beginning of this chapter, "crime" is a word that has no inherent meaning. Therefore, not only our policies but our view of what constitutes crime is shaped by a variety of influences. Chief among these are the various interest groups that represent the criminal justice system and who have a vested interest in seeing to it that we conceive of crime in a particular way. Our view of crime is also shaped by the mass media, who report only particular kinds of criminal events, thereby giving a faulty impression of the type and amount of crime that is occurring. For example, a multiple homicide in the course of a robbery may make the front page. Such exposure may create the impression that violent crime is the most common type and that homicide is a relatively common occurrence. Yet, such crime represents the smallest proportion of crime that is committed and fortunately is rather rare. Nevertheless, our image of crime and the criminal is shaped by such reporting practices.

Since the crime problem involves such a large number of people-resources, it is important to know what sources exist for getting a clearer handle on the problem. While media is perhaps the major source of our perceptions about crime and justice, the pronouncements of various interest groups also shape our views. Neither, however, represents a particularly objective, unbiased description of the problem. We therefore need to know what other sources of information are available. We turn to this issue in the next chapter.

SUMMARY

What Was Said

- Terming an event a crime involves a series of judgements or evaluations, and thus, as Gwynn Nettler says, "Crime is a word, not a deed."
- Judgments about what is or is not a crime change over time.
- The dominant set of rules for classifying an event as a crime are contained within the framework of criminal law which contains five decision criteria:

An act must:
1. Be observable
2. Be a violation of either statute or case law
3. Have a prescribed punishment

The actor must:
4. Intend to commit a crime

5. Be acting without defense or justification
- Social policy, of which law is a premier example, can be conceptually divided into three different levels:
  Policy-in-intention
  Policy-in-implementation
  Policy-in-experience
- Depending on the level of policy or law, common values, interest group pressures, or considerations of rational planning will exert significant influence on a policy action.
- Extralegal factors thus influence the process of criminal law and crime classification.
- Groups or agencies involved in criminal justice policy can be analytically classified according to one of three major policy roles:
  Policy making
  Policy implementation
  Policy advocacy
- Criminal justice professionals form interest groups that attempt to shape our understanding of crime and policies for coping with it.
- Criminal justice organizations seek to maintain the legitimacy of their routine responses to problems and to gain resources to expand these.

What Was Not Said

- Crime is not a problem.
- Criminal justice decision makers set out to deceive the public.
- Interest groups are only concerned with their own welfare.
- Scientific judgments about crime should replace political judgments, cultural values, or administrative understandings.

NOTES

1. Glenn Dumke, preface to *Crime and Public Policy*, James Q. Wilson, ed. (San Francisco: ICS Press, 1983), p. xi.

2. Jan M. Charken and Marcia R. Chaiken, "Crime Rates and the Active Criminal," in Ibid., p. 11.

3. Gwynn Nettler, *Explaining Crime*, 3rd ed. (New York: McGraw-Hill, 1984), p. 16.

4. James F. Gilsinan, *Doing Justice* (Englewood Cliffs, NJ: Prentice-Hall, 1982), p. 11.

5. These elements are based on the legal definition of Paul Tappan, *Crime, Justice and Correction* (New York: McGraw-Hill, 1960), p. 10.

6. Sue Titus Reid, *Crime and Criminology* (Hinsdale, IL: The Dryden Press, 1976), p. 11.

7. George E. Rush, *The Dictionary of Criminal Justice*, 2nd ed. (Guilford, CT: The Dushkin Publishing Group, Inc., 1986), p. 27.

8. Gilsinan, *Doing Justice*, p. 11.

9. Egon G. Guba, "Perspectives on Public Policy," *Policy Studies Review*, Vol. 5, No. 1 (August 1985), 11.

10. Hazel B. Kerper, *Introduction to the Criminal Justice System* (St. Paul, MN: West Publishing Co., 1972), p. 210.

11. Katherine M. Jamieson and Timothy J. Flanagan, eds., *Sourcebook of Criminal Justice Statistics—1986*, U.S. Department of Justice, Bureau of Justice Statistics, (Washington, DC: U.S. Government Printing Office, 1987), p. 3.

12. Ibid.

13. Ibid., p. 6.

14. *Report to the Nation on Crime and Justice*, 2nd ed., U.S. Department of Justice, Bureau of Justice Statistics (Washington, DC: U.S. Government Printing Office, 1988), p. 63.

15. *Crime in the United States, 1983: Uniform Crime Reports*, U.S. Department of Justice, Federal Bureau of Investigation (Washington, DC: U.S. Government Printing Office, 1984), p. 291.

16. Harry W. More, Jr., ed., *The American Police: Text and Reading*, (St. Paul, MN: West Publishing Co., 1976), p. 29.

17. Jamieson and Flanagan, *Sourcebook of Criminal Justice Statistics—1986*, p. 14.

18. Edward J. Brown, Timothy J. Flanagan, and Maureen McLeod, eds., *Source Book of Criminal Justice Statistics—1983*, U.S. Department of Justice, Bureau of Justice Statistics (Washington, DC: U.S. Government Printing Office, 1984), p. 50.

19. Ibid.

20. Ibid.

21. David Sudnow, "Normal Crimes: Sociological Features of the Penal Code in a Public Defender's Office," *Social Problems*, 12 (Winter 1965), 255–76.

22. Edwin H. Sutherland, "The Diffusion of Sexual Psychopathic Laws," *American Journal of Sociology*, (Setptember 1950), 142–48.

23. Richard S. Allinson, "LEAA's Impact on Criminal Justice: A Review of the Literature," *Criminal Justice Abstracts*, (December, 1979), 608–48.

24. Ibid.

25. Luis P. Salas and Ralph G. Lewis, "The Law Enforcement Assistance Administration and Minority Communities," *Journal of Police Science and Administration*, Vol. 7, (December 1979), 379–99.

Also quoted in Thomas E. Cronin, Tania Z. Cronin, and Michael E. Milakovich, *U.S.* v. *Crime in the Streets*, (Bloomington, IN: Indiana University Press, 1981), p. 145.

26. Cronin, Cronin, and Milakovich, *U.S.* v. *Crime in the Streets*, p. 149.

27. Barbara Ann Stolz, "Congress and Criminal Justice Policy Making: The Impact of Interest Groups and Symbolic Politics," *Journal of Criminal Justice*, 13, No. 4 (1985), 307–19.

III

How Much Crime Is There and How Do We Count It?

At the end of this chapter, the student will be able to:

A. List the major data sources that describe the scope of crime in the United States.
B. Note the strengths and weaknesses of each data source.
C. Discuss the various schemes for improving criminal justice data.

ISSUE BACKGROUND

The contingent nature of law and crime can drive social scientists to distraction. If they attempt to explain crime scientifically, what do they use as a sample of incidents? If only those incidents that are officially designated crimes are to be explained, then do we explain crime or are we instead explaining the categorization practices of officials? The issue becomes even trickier when the term "criminal" is considered. If we attempt to explain criminal behavior, are we only counting those officially recognized as criminals or should we include people never caught but who have engaged in criminal acts? Once a person is recognized as a criminal, how long is the definition valid? During the time a criminal act was committed, a year later, 10 years later? All of these problems have led criminologists to be extremely careful about designating their field of study. Clearly, neither a legal definition of crime and/or criminals nor a definition based on extralegal, experiential criteria may be sufficient to meet the needs of the scientist who wants to study the causes of criminal behavior. Some researchers have even suggested that scientific rigor requires that legal criteria be abandoned altogether as a means of determining the appropriate area of study. According to these researchers, a more appropriate category of behavior to study is norm-violating activity.[1] Thus, for some scientists, the appropriate classification of acts to be studied may be all of those included in the category of "socially harmful."

Obviously, the problems of classification affect our ability to both accurately count crime and to say something meaningful about it. It should be clear that a student of crime must carefully analyze the populations upon which scientific and policy conclusions are based. Studies that purport to say something about illegal behavior but that rely solely on a sample of officially recognized persons constitutes a biased sample, and thus such findings are suspect.

To illustrate the difficulty, consider an explanation of crime from a study conducted in the early part of this century. Charles Goring, based on his study of English convicts, concluded that "weak-mindedness" caused crime.[2] English convicts turned out to be less intelligent than the nonincarcerated English population. Goring's idea was a novel one at the time and challenged existing theories. However, it was also based on a biased sample. Was Goring really explaining the link between intelligence and criminal behavior, or was he explaining the link between intelligence and getting caught? Presumably, smart criminals would be underrepresented in Goring's population. Social scientists need to be aware of the Goring fallacy when proffering explanations for crime based on a limited sample of incidents and/or people.

CRIMINOLOGICAL/CRIMINAL JUSTICE CONSIDERATIONS

Data Sources for Criminal Justice Information

The term "data source" has a certain objectivity about it. Indeed, data based on a large sample of phenomena tend to be less biased than information based on a select case. Therefore, it is reasonable to assume that the criminal justice data sources available in the United States will give a more objective picture of crime than will the nightly news. But it is a mistake to overestimate the objectivity and accuracy of official data sources, even when these are based on a large number of incidents. The following passage suggests why such caution is necessary.

> . . . the government are very keen on amassing statistics. They collect them, raise them to the nth power, take the cube root and prepare wonderful diagrams. But you must never forget that every one of these figures comes in the first instance form the village watchman, who just puts down what he damn pleases.[3] (Sir Josiah Stamp, English economist, 1880–1941)

As Sir Josiah noted, and as has been emphasized in this and the preceding chapter, the determination of what is or is not a crime is a judgment call. This element of subjectivity obviously affects the ability to accurately count crime. All such counts will reflect a certain bias. Therefore, in assessing various data sources, three questions must be posed. (1) "Why are certain categories of crime designated and not others?" (2) "What are the decision rules used to place a particular incident in a particular category?" (3) "To what use are the data and the interpretation being put?" With all of the various interest groups attempting to affect criminal justice policy, this last question is particularly important in assessing the objectivity of criminal justice data.

Each of these questions will be applied to the three data sources described below. These sources provide the major building blocks for an official description of crime in our society. It is therefore important not only to be familiar with what the sources are, but also with their major strengths and weaknesses.

1. UNIFORM CRIME REPORTS FOR THE UNITED STATES

This is probably the best known source of criminal justice statistics in the United States. It is published annually by the Federal Bureau of Investigation, and it is a compilation of crimes reported to the police.

The history of the Uniform Crime Report illustrates once again how a seemingly straightforward criminal justice problem becomes an issue. During the latter half of the 1920s, police administrators were increasingly concerned with the way the press reported crime.[4] Newspapers, by simply increasing the number of stories written about crime, could easily create the impression that a city was experiencing a crime wave. Obviously, this was detrimental to the image of a police department and its chief. The need for accurate crime data had been recognized in the United States as early as 1870, but it took a concerted effort by the International Association of Chiefs of Police (IACP) to finally get a uniform crime-reporting system operable. This effort itself was spurred in part by self-interest, and therefore the Uniform Crime Report was almost immediately embroiled in controversy. The question, "How much crime is there?" remained an issue of public debate, even after the establishment of a seemingly objective way of counting it.

The first point of disagreement concerned the type of data to use in determining the amount of crime. Prior to the 1920s, some experts argued that court data were the most reliable, since conviction of crime provided information on both the offense and the offender. Moreover, court procedures acted as an inherent check on the accuracy of police and/or citizen's descriptions of an event. By 1927, however, police administrators, as well as numerous academic researchers, had concluded that the more distant a counting category from an actual event, the less accurate the data. Thus, the number and kind of citizen complaints received by the police, presumably the closest category to actual crime occurrences, became the basis for the first Uniform Crime Report, issued in August of 1930. It would take almost 40 years before the problem of unreported crime would be addressed.

Although the issue of what to count had been largely settled by the late 1920s, considerable controversy still surrounded the issue of who should collect and analyze the data. Many individuals, including representatives of the American Prison Association and the national Conference of Criminal Law and Criminology, thought the Census Bureau should assume the burden of data collection and analysis. The police chiefs, however, wanted the Bureau of Investigation (soon to become the FBI) to collect the data. Those favoring the Census Bureau were concerned that a conflict of interest could too easily develop if data used to evaluate criminal justice agencies were collected by an agency itself involved in law enforcement. The IACP was better organized than the opposition, however, and, working closely with J. Edgar Hoover, was able to begin the process of collecting police data fairly rapidly. Congress then agreed to ratify what had already been started, and so the Bureau of Investigation was given in law the responsibility that they had already assumed in fact, collecting and analyzing crime data on a national basis.

Reporting crime data to the FBI was and is voluntary on the part of police agencies. But some agencies, at least, had an interest in reporting data in order to counteract negative publicity generated by newspaper stories about crime. The Bureau, therefore, was under some pressure to show results for their data collection and analysis efforts, and for the efforts of chiefs who voluntarily gathered and submitted local crime reports.[5] As a result, less than a year had elapsed between the first data collection effort (January, 1930) and the first published report on crime trends (November, 1930). How trend data could be established in so short a time with a relatively small sample of police agencies and a still-evolving data collection and analysis procedure was a puzzle. Immediately, the accuracy of such data became a source of debate. Although the F.B.I. *Uniform Crime Report* has improved over the years, debates about its accuracy still persist.

Today, the report covers 29 criminal acts, divided into two categories. The first category, "Part I crimes," are thought to be the more serious crimes, while "Part II crimes," are considered less serious. Part I and Part II offenses are shown in Table 3-1.

Part I crimes are also termed "index crimes." The rates of these crimes are calculated per 100,000 people (that is, indexed) and reported as shown in Table 3-2.

The *Uniform Crime Report* (UCR) also provides data on nationwide arrests. Data are given on total estimated arrests for the seven indexed crimes and for the nonindexed crimes as well. Arrest rates per 100,000 population are also calculated, and trends in arrests are provided for the previous 10 years. There are also various breakdowns by age, race, sex, and geographic locale

Table 3-1 Part I and Part II Crimes

Part I:	15. Weapons; carrying, possessing, etc.
1. Criminal homicide	16. Prostitution and commercialized vice
2. Forcible rape	17. Sex offenses (except forcible rape,
3. Robbery	prostitution, and commercialized vice)
4. Aggravated assault	18. Drug abuse violations
5. Burglary-breaking or entering	19. Gambling
6. Larceny-theft (except motor vehicle theft)	20. Offenses against the family and children
7. Motor vehicle theft	21. Driving under the influence
8. Arson	22. Liquor laws
	23. Drunkenness
Part II:	24. Disorderly conduct
9. Other assaults (simple)	25. Vagrancy
10. Forgery and counterfeiting	26. All other offenses
11. Fraud	27. Suspicion
12. Embezzlement	28. Curfew and loitering laws
13. Stolen property: buying, receiving,	29. Runaway
possessing	
14. Vandalism	

Source: Federal Bureau of Investigation (FBI), *Uniform Crime Reports*, (Washington, DC: Government Printing Office), app. II.

(city, suburban, rural) of arrests. Figure 3-1 shows the percent of crimes known to the police that are cleared by arrest.

There are two ways police agencies clear crimes. An offense cleared by an arrest means that the agency has arrested at least one person and charged him, her, or them with the offense and then turned the case over to the court for prosecution. Conviction is not an element in police reporting an offense cleared by arrest. Moreover, several crimes may be cleared by the arrest of a single person or one crime by the arrest of more than one individual. Police agencies also clear crimes by exceptional means. These are instances where

Table 3-2 Part I Crime Index Statistics: Rate per 100,000, and Percent Cleared by Arrest by Particular Crime 1985–1986

Part I offense	Number of crimes reported	Rate per 100,000	Percent cleared by arrest
Criminal homicide	20,613	8.6	70.2
Forcible rape	90,434	37.5	52.3
Robbery	542,775	225.1	24.7
Aggravated assault	834,322	346.1	59.4
Burglary	3,241,410	1,344.6	13.6
Larceny-theft	7,257,153	3,010.3	19.7
Motor vehicle theft	1,224,137	507.8	14.8

Source: Uniform Crime Reports 1986, pp. 44–45, 156.

CRIMES CLEARED BY ARREST
1986

CRIMES OF VIOLENCE

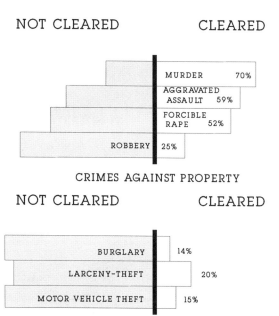

NOT CLEARED   CLEARED

MURDER   70%

AGGRAVATED ASSAULT   59%

FORCIBLE RAPE   52%

ROBBERY   25%

CRIMES AGAINST PROPERTY

NOT CLEARED   CLEARED

BURGLARY   14%

LARCENY-THEFT   20%

MOTOR VEHICLE THEFT   15%

Figure 3-1 *Source: Crime in the United States-1986: Uniform Crime Reports* U.S. Department of Justice, Federal Bureau of Investigation (Washington, D.C.: Government Printing Office), 1987.

circumstances are such that a formal charge is not possible. Such circumstances would include the death of the defendant, the victim's refusal to prosecute after the defendant has been identified, or the prosecution of the individual in another jurisdiction for another crime.

2. THE NATIONAL CRIME SURVEY

This annual report is published by the Bureau of Justice Statistics. Started in 1973 amid controversy about the usefulness of the UCR data for assessing the impact of the Law Enforcement Assistance Administration, it is based on a representative national sample of 49,000 households and 15,000 commercial establishments. The data are categorized according to (a) personal crimes (rape, robbery, assault, and theft, with subcategories); (b) household crimes (burglary, larceny, and motor vehicle theft, with subcategories); and (c)

Table 3-3 How Do UCR and NCS Compare?

	Uniform Crime Reports	National Crime Survey
Offenses measured:	Homicide Rape Robbery (personal and commercial) Assault (aggravated) Burglary (commercial and household) Larceny (commercial and household) Motor vehicle theft Arson	Rape Robbery (personal) Assault (aggravated and simple) Household burglary Larceny (personal and household) Motor vehicle theft
Scope:	Crimes reported to the police in most jurisdictions; considerable flexibility in developing small area data	Crimes both reported and not reported to police, all data are available for a few large geographic areas
Collection method:	Police department reports to FBI or to centralized State agencies that then report to FBI	Survey interviews, periodically measures the total number of crime committed by asking a national sample fo 49,000 households encompassing 101,000 persons age 12 and over about their experiences as victims of crime during a specified period
Kinds of information:	In addition to offense counts, provides information on crime clearances, persons arrested, persons charged, law enforcement officers killed and assaulted and characteristics of homicide victims	Provides details about victims (such as age, race, sex, education, income, and whether the victim and offender were related to each other) and about crimes (such as time and place of occurrence, whether or not reported to police, use of weapons, occurrence of injury, and economic consequences)
Sponsor	Department of Justice Federal Bureau of Investigation	Department of Justice Bureau of Justice Statistics

Source: *Report to the Nation on Crime and Justice, 2nd ed.,* U.S. Department of Justice, Bureau of Justice Statistics (Washington, DC: U.S. Government Printing Office, 1988).

commercial crimes (burglary and robbery). Table 3-3 compares the UCR and the NCS in terms of collection methods, categories, kinds of information, and sponsor.

The National Crime Survey represents a major addition to the source material available describing crime in the United States. Because it is a victimization survey, it includes unreported as well as reported crime. If it is true that the closer a counting category is to an actual event, the more accurate it is, then these data would represent a more accurate crime count than the UCR. The National Crime Survey does in fact give a considerably different picture of the volume of crime than does the UCR. Its major contributions have been the discovery that most crime goes unreported, that crime has not dramatically increased but appears to have been relatively stable during the period the UCR was showing such increases, and that regional and local differences in crime are not as pronounced as originally thought. On the other hand, when the UCR and the NCS are compared relative to the distribution of Part I offenses, they show a similar pattern with property crimes far outnumbering violent offenses in each measure.[6] While the victimization survey is an important addition to our ability to understand crime, it too has to be used with caution and some of its findings qualified.

3. SELF-REPORT SURVEYS

Since the majority of criminologists are interested in the theoretical components of crime, that is, in the dynamics of causality, they have generally found official statistics inadequate for their purposes. The sampling problem alluded to earlier (the Goring fallacy), the relative lack of information concerning offenders, and the possibility of bias in arrest statistics are serious obstacles to the use of such data for purposes of theory testing. Therefore, a number of criminologists have used self-report data to ascertain the correlates of criminal behavior.

Self-report surveys often consist of questionnaires with items that ask respondents about the frequency of illegal behavior in which they have been engaged. Such surveys are typically conducted among junior and senior high school students. In some studies, person-to-person interviews rather than anonymous questionnaires were utilized. The interviews had the obvious advantage of allowing either the respondent or the interviewer to clarify issues about which there might have been confusion.

At first, data from self-reports raised more questions than they answered. Early self-report research suggested that criminal behavior was equally distributed among the various racial and economic groups within the society. This finding was considerably different from what was showing up in the FBI data. The UCR arrest data showed, for example, that blacks were arrested in a far higher proportion to their numbers in the population than were whites. The reason for such overrepresentation was a point of debate. Some theorists argued that the justice system was discriminating against black people. They showed up more in official statistics simply because they were more likely than whites to be arrested by the police. Many of these theorists therefore supported interest group explanations regarding law and its application. Others, however, suggested that blacks actually committed more street crime than whites in response to the dynamics of racial and economic discrimination. Their over representation was due to greater criminal involvement. These theorists were more likely to accept a value consensus view of law and its application.

The question of whether blacks actually committed more street crime than whites was tackled directly in a seminal article by Michael Hindelang.

Since self-report data and official data on the issue were at odds, Hindelang argued the need for a third data source to answer the question. He turned to the National Crime Survey's data on offender characteristics as reported by crime victims. Based on his analysis, he concluded that while some of the variation between self-reports and UCR data could be accounted for by system discrimination, the majority of the difference appeared to be due to the greater involvement of blacks in street crime.[7]

If this was in fact so, the self-report studies were obviously flawed. In a 1980 study, Elliott and Ageton made a significant contribution to the understanding and correction of previous problems in self-report surveys.[8]

Elliott and Ageton noted that previous self-report studies had the following problems. First, items in self-report studies did not provide a good representation of criminal behavior. Thus, minor offenses such as cutting classes were overrepresented, while serious law violations such as sexual assault were often not included in the list of potential offenses. Second, some items overlapped. If I took something from a store, I would answer "yes" to a question that asked if I had shoplifted. I might also answer "yes" to a question that asked if I had stole something of value. Thus, one episode of criminal behavior would appear as two separate acts. Third, the type of responses demanded by the questions were often inadequate for determining the true frequency of the behavior. For example, if a respondent were required to choose among the responses "often," "sometimes," and "never" when asked how frequently he or she behaved in a particular way, a wide variation in the interpretation of the meaning of each category is possible. Such a response choice also precludes a precise count of actual incidents. Even when self-report surveys provided numbers to describe frequency, the highest choice possible would often be "three times or more." Thus a youth who shoplifted three times would be in the same category as one who did it 40 times.

In their research, Elliott and Ageton corrected these and other problems found in previous self-report studies. Their findings suggest that while virtually all youth report some involvement in delinquent behavior, race and class differences do emerge at the high end of the frequency range and in the more serious crime categories. These differences appear to support the correlates of delinquency found in official data concerning street crime.

Self-report studies can provide useful information regarding certain correlates of crime. However, they still confront problems of respondent truthfulness. Further, they are generally not useful for ascertaining the volume of crime in society given the uniqueness of the samples usually subject to self-report surveys or interviews.

There are a number of secondary sources available to students and researchers interested in crime and criminal justice. Chief among these is the *Source Book of Criminal Justice Statistics*. This should probably be the first reference source consulted by anyone needing statistical information about crime. If the information is not there, at least in summary form, it is probably not available.

A list of other source material is available through the Bureau of Justice Statistics. The Bureau regularly publishes technical bulletins on specific aspects of the justice system.

POLICY CONSIDERATIONS: THEORIES/ARGUMENTS/APPLICATIONS

Drawbacks of UCR

There are four major drawbacks to using the Uniform Crime Reports as the sole source of information about crime in the United States. First, the report is not a direct count of crime but is instead only the end product of a long series of decisions or judgments about whether to classify an incident as something that should be officially counted as a crime. Thus, the reports are based only on those crimes reported to the police. A great deal of crime goes unreported. Doleschal estimates that 82% of all larcenies, 60% of aggravated assaults, 56% of rapes, 54% of burglaries, 51% of robberies, and 32% of auto thefts go unreported.[9] Thus, it is difficult to tell whether an increase in reported crime actually means an increase in overall crime or simply an increase in people reporting. Clearly, the decision rules victims use to decide whether an incident should be reported to the police affect the accuracy of the UCR. The decision rule problem is compounded when you consider the fact that police participation in the FBI reporting system is voluntary.

While local cooperation has improved dramatically since the beginning of the reporting system in the 1930s, not all police agencies participate. Nevertheless, it is now estimated that the reports cover approximately 97% of the population.[10] But the ability of UCR data to accurately describe the amount of crime in the population is further affected by the decision rules participating departments adopt regarding what to include in the available categories.

The UCR is based upon crime incidents. The definition of an incident is different from the definition of a victim. To illustrate, if a series of 10 cars parked in front of one another are damaged in a singled escapade, the paint scratched, tires slashed, etc., the occurrence is counted as one incident of vandalism. If, on the other hand, 10 cars are damaged individually on 10 consecutive nights, that is counted as 10 individual incidents of vandalism. Notice also that degrees of crime are not specified in the categories. Thus, "forcible rape" includes attempts as well as completed incidents. What constitutes an attempted rape, however, may vary among police agencies. Thus, comparison between jurisdictions is hazardous without knowing the decisions rules departments use to place incidents in categories. Although the FBI does provide a manual that mandates appropriate decision criteria, a recent study by the Police Foundation found "widespread violation of the rules." Again, factors external to the crime incidents seem to affect how they are reported. Jurisdictions dependent on tourism, for example, are thought to underreport crime. While the Police Foundation report did not suggest intentional misrepresentation, it did report error rates of as high as 40%.[11]

A second major problem with the U.C.R. is its selection of crimes to report on. Not all serious crimes are included. Notice, for example, that skyjacking is not a category. Many varieties of corporate crime, such as the manufacture of unsafe cars, foods, or drugs, are not counted: this, despite the fact that such behavior is illegal and seriously threatening to our physical well-being. Thus, using the UCR as a description of crime in the United States is misleading, since it counts only certain kinds of illegal behavior, those likely to come to the attention of local police departments. The history of the Uniform Crime Reporting System demonstrates why there is this inherent bias in the system. But perhaps such behavior constitutes the most serious threat to the populace. Even using this criterion though, it appears that the Uniform Crime Report is misleading. To illustrate, data gathered by medical societies show that of the 320,000 practicing physicians, 16,000 (or 5%) are unfit to practice.[12] A 5% incompetency rate is perhaps no worse than in any other profession. Unfortunately, however, 7.5 million people are treated by this 5%. That is a lot of people risking victimization. Most are probably unaware of the threat to life and limb that they face and, if anything, are more worried by so-called street crime. The real danger they face, however, is not on the street. There are "nearly 2.4 million unnecessary operations each year in which 11,900 patients die as a result of complications."[13] The debilitating effects of drugs are also an area of concern, exemplified by recurrent governmental programs to eliminate pushers and suppliers. But, again, this danger is not only present on the street. Yearly, "at least 30,000 Americans accept the drugs their doctors prescribe for them and die as a direct result."[14] According to a recent report on the matter, "perhaps 10 times as many patients suffer life threatening and sometimes permanent side effects." Further, it has been estimated "that 22% of the antibiotics prescribed in hospitals are unnecessary."[15] Eliminating these would save 10,000 or more patients from untold pain, suffering, and, in some instances, premature death.

A third major problem also concerns categorization. A crime index is only computed for Part I offenses. It is clear that not all of these are of equal seriousness. For example, larceny-theft and homicide are not equal in seriousness, yet they are treated equally when computing the rate of indexed offenses per 100,000 people. This gives a misleading view of crime, since, as Figure 3-2 shows, most crime is not of the most serious type (about 10% of the index is violent crime and 90% is property crime).

Finally, the UCR since its beginning has been put to a variety of inappropriate uses. Thus, rises and falls in reported crime cannot be used to measure police effectiveness. Nor should the UCR be used to justify larger budgets for police agencies, a common practice during the 1970s. Regarding the first point, a rise in a particular crime category may in fact mean that the

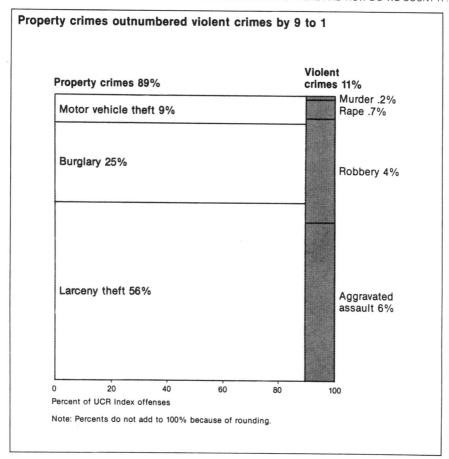

Figure 3-2 *Source: Report to the Nation on Crime and Justice, 2nd ed.,* U.S. Department of Justice, Bureau of Justice Statistics (Washington, DC: U.S. Government Printing, Office, 1988), p. 12.

police are doing their jobs, and the public has therefore increased their confidence in the police and reported more crime based on the belief that the crime will be solved. Even arrest data are not good indicators of police effectiveness, since an arrest may not in fact mean the guilty party was apprehended, a determination made at the judicial level of the system.

A recent study by the Department of Justice has suggested changes that would address some of the problems of the UCR.[16] First, it suggests sweeping changes in the way data are collected. Instead of merely submitting summary statistics on crime incidents, the study proposes that police agencies submit brief individual records for each incident and each arrest that occurred during the month. Thus, the categorizing of incidents would be centralized and made standard. Further, the report suggests that agencies distinguish between attempts and offenses actually carried out, since including both in a single category gives an inflated crime picture. Crimes against businesses should be distinguished from crimes against individuals, and additional information should be collected about homicides. The report recommends that more information should be collected about crime victims generally.

A second major area of concern in the study is the establishment of a new, more focused crime report that would be based on a sample of incidents from 300 cities or counties with populations over 100,000, plus a sample of at least 300 other agencies. Information in this "Level II" report would include significantly more detail on the nature of reported incidents and descriptions of the individuals involved. It would also include greater detail on the agencies reporting such incidents to assess changes in police practices over time. This recommendation addresses concerns raised as early as 1911 about the need for accurate data concerning offenders and the inherent unreliability of police statistics unless one knows the decision rules of police officers and their agencies.

Under the new system, agencies would also be audited much more closely. Close auditing would ensure greater accuracy in the data currently being reported.

Drawbacks of NCS

The problem of categories and decision rules again surfaces when considering the accuracy of the National Crime Survey. Victims untrained in legal categorization may tend to overstate or misclassify an incident in which they have been involved. Thus, if the UCR's data are suspect because of underreporting, the victimization surveys are suspect because of overreporting, at least in many of its categories.

However, personally degrading crimes, such as sexual assault or spouse abuse, may not be reported to an interviewer any more than they would be reported to the police. Further, the crime categories of the surveys are not directly comparable to those of the UCR. As noted, the UCR categorizes on the basis of incidents. The surveys count the number of persons victimized. In the example of auto vandalism cited above, the victimization surveys would count 10 victims in both kinds of occurrences, rather than one and 10 under UCR. Moreover, it is not clear how victims who are chronic victims report offenses. If a wife is consistently subject to abuse, does she report each occurrence as a separate incident? If so, this would inflate the rate of victimization. The victimization surveys only count people age 12 and over, while UCR includes every person. Finally, attempts are included as incidents in the UCR. In the victimization surveys they are counted in a separate category.

As is clear, if either the UCR or the NCS are used exclusively to paint a picture of crime in the United States, the image given will be faulty. Both used together, however, can give a somewhat less distorted picture of the problem.

Improving Our Crime Classification Schemes

The ability to classify allows human beings to make sense out of the hundreds of thousands of discrete items they encounter each day. From a scientific standpoint, an ideal crime classification scheme would possess the following characteristics:[17]

1. It would define boundaries of a total class of objects.
2. It would provide subclasses for every example of everything within the total class (the number of things categorized as "other" would be minimal).
3. It would establish levels of occurrences in such a way that subcategories could be easily incorporated into the higher category for purposes of aggregation and comparison.
4. Decision criteria for placing events within categories would be uniform and precise.
5. Categories would be mutually exclusive.

None of the classification schemes currently used to define the term crime possess all of these characteristics. It is unlikely that such a rigorous classification system could ever be devised for describing crime, since the judgment of what is or is not a crime is one based on values. The term "crime" is therefore not descriptive but evaluative. Thus, even the counting of crime becomes a policy issue and not simply a scientific problem.

There have been numerous reforms suggested to bring both legal and technical crime classification schemes closer to the ideal principles listed above. While there have been improvements in these schemes, there does not yet exist sufficient consensus among the various interest groups, who are the users and consumers of such data to resolve many of the issues raised. All crime data, therefore, must be approached with caution, and the decision rules of those collecting and interpreting them must be understood.

If all of these sources of information contain errors and omissions, how can they be useful to either policy makers or scientists? The answer to that question is twofold. First, even though individual sources may contain error, policy analysts can look for convergence among them to gain a more accurate picture than would have been possible with only one source. Second, we cannot expect the data to answer questions it was not meant to answer. Thus, the Uniform Crime Reports may be useful in uncovering reporting practices of both citizens and police but not useful in answering the question of actual changes in the amount of crime in the society and the police contribution to such changes.

Finally, a review of the data sources available shows that there are considerable gaps in the kinds of information we collect about crime and justice in our society. For example, we collect very little national data on the jail population. Jails, however, form a significant part of the criminal justice process in this country. It has been estimated that as many as six million Americans may pass through them in a given year—an incarceration rate of 2,900 per 100,000 population![18] Yet we know relatively little about the population, the effects of jail incarceration on the individuals subject to it, and the effects and uses of jail in terms of the overall criminal justice system.

Also lacking are uniform court data. We do not know, for example, the number of adult defendants who go through the court system in any given year. These data are of more than simply academic interest. Without adequate data, we have a difficult time evaluating either the effects of our intervention in crime or the economic sensibility of the decisions we make regarding it. As we will see in the next chapter, the cost of crime and justice in our society is enormous. Whether it is money well spent is open to debate, a debate that can in part be answered with better data and clearer definitions of problems and goals.

SUMMARY

What Was Said

- Even the counting of crime is encountered as an issue rather than as an undisputed fact.
- The *Uniform Crime Report* (UCR), published annually by the Federal Bureau of Investigation, is a compilation of crimes reported to the police.
- The Uniform Crime Report was originally instigated in part to protect police chiefs from unfavorable—and from their viewpoint unfair—reporting of crime by newspapers.
- The UCR divides crimes into Part I and Part II categories.
- Part I crimes are also reported as an index of crimes per 100,000 people.
- The UCR also provides arrest data.
- The *National Crime Survey* (NCS) is based upon a representative sample of 49,000 households and 15,000 commercial establishments and covers both reported and unreported crimes.
- The UCR and the NCS give considerably different pictures of the crime problem in the United States.
- Self report surveys have been used by social scientists interest in the dynamics of causality, but these too have suffered from various flaws.
- The four major drawbacks of the UCR are:
    - —Reports are based only on those crimes reported to the police.
    - —Not all serious crimes are included in the reports.
    - —A crime index based on Part I offenses gives a misleading view of the volume of serious crime.

—UCR has been put to a variety of uses that are inappropriate including as a measure of police effectiveness.

• NSC also suffers from certain flaws, most notably the assumptions that victims accurately report criminal occurrences.

• Using a variety of data sources together can help academics and policy makers overcome the inherent difficulties found when using a single source exclusively.

What Was Not Said

• All data sources are useless.
• Current sources cannot be further improved.
• It will eventually be possible to have value-free counts of the crime problem.

NOTES

1. Thorsten Sellin, "A Sociological Approach," in *The Sociology of Crime and Delinquency*, 2nd ed., Marvin E. Wolfgang et al., eds. (New York: John Wiley, 1970), p. 6.

2. Charles Goring, *The English Convict* (London: His Majesty's Stationery Office, 1913).

3. Gwynn Nettler, *Explaining Crime*, 2nd ed. (New York: McGraw-Hill, 1978), p. 57.

4. Michael D. Maltz, "Crime Statistics: A Historical Perspective," *Crime and Delinquency*, 23, No. 1 (January 1977), 32–40.

5. Ibid., p. 37.

6. Scott H. Decker, "Official Crime Rates and Victim Surveys: An Empirical Comparison," *Journal of Criminal Justice*, Vol. 5 (1977), 47–54.

7. Michael Hindelang, "Race and Involvement in Crimes," *American Sociological Review*, Vol. 43, No. 1 (February 1978), 93–109.

8. Delbert S. Elliott and Suzanne S. Ageton, "Reconciling Differences in Estimates of Delinquency," *American Sociological Review*, Vol. 45, No. 1 (February 1980), 95–110.

9. Eugene Doleschal, "Crime—Some Popular Beliefs," *Crime and Delinquency*, 25, No. 1 (January 1979), 1–8.

10. *Crime in the United States—1983: Uniform Crime Report*, U.S. Department of Justice, Federal Bureau of Investigation (Washington, DC: U.S. Government Printing Office), 1984, p. 3.

11. *Criminal Justice Newsletter*, Vol. 16, No. 14 (July 1985).

12. Boyce Rensberg, "Drugs," *New York Times*, January 26–28, 1976.

13. Ibid.

14. Ibid.

15. Ibid.

16. *Criminal Justice Newsletter*.

17. *Dictionary of Criminal Justice Data Terminology*, U.S. Department of Justice, Bureau of Justice Statistics, 2nd ed. (Washington, D.C.: U.S. Government Printing Office, 1981).

18. Eugene Doleschal, "Sources of Basic Criminal Justice Statistics," *Criminal Justice Abstracts*, Vol. 11, No. 1 (March 1979), 123.

IV

What Is It Worth?

At the end of this chapter, the student will be able to:

A. Discuss how the worth of a case is determined in the day-to-day doing of justice.
B. Discuss the factors that influence the informal definitions of crime and the effect of these factors on determining appropriate punishment.
C. Describe the monetary cost of crime and criminal justice.
D. Define evaluation research and note both its strengths and weaknesses.

ISSUE BACKGROUND

The Concept of Worth

The concept of "worth" pervades the categorization process of the criminal justice system. It is a concept, however, that has multiple meanings. In a market sense, worth refers to the price of an object. Such cost is in part determined by supply and demand. Generally, the more available an object, the less costly it will be. Things in short supply, on the other hand, will be dear. Worth also has a symbolic component. In this sense, worth is assessed in terms of the emotional or subjective attachment one has to an object or an outcome regardless of its absolute monetary value. The chemical components of the human body are only worth a few dollars. Most of us, though, would consider the body, at least our own, priceless, and with the advent of organ transplants, specific parts have become quite expensive. Finally, worth can be calculated based on the amount of work expended on an object or an outcome. This last definition contains both objective and subjective elements. What a worker is paid contributes to the price of an object. But an object also has worth for both the worker and those observing it based on the craftsmanship required to create the finished product. In this sense the product is symbolic of the worker's skill, an assessment that may or may not be reflected in its market price. Given the various definitions of worth, some of which may well conflict with one another, it is neither an easy nor a straightforward process to assess whether a particular criminal justice policy or decision is "worth it."

Consider the question of worth applied to an individual case within the criminal justice system. Police officers, prosecutors, defense attorneys, judges, and jurors, at different points in the system, have the responsibility of determining "what really happened." The answer to this question will determine the amount of punishment a person will receive for having committed a particular act. The amount of punishment considered appropriate is a determination of case worth from a largely symbolic standpoint. If a police officer expended a great deal of time on a case, he or she may feel it is worth more punishment given the amount of work necessary to bring the miscreant to the bar of justice. A prosecutor may, on the other hand, devalue the case if evidence and circumstances suggest that it will not have a great deal of "jury appeal." Therefore, the prosecutor may offer less punishment in exchange for a guilty plea. Thus, punishment becomes a medium of exchange, less or more being offered based upon largely subjective assessments of case worth.

Of course, formal legal statutes determine the amount of punishment available for exchange. However, as we have seen, punishments are attached to criminal activity largely on the basis of tradition or interest group pressure in response to particular crime occurrences. Punishments are seldom determined based on a careful calculation of their effects. Also, as noted in Chapter 2, a host of nonlegal factors help determine the seriousness of a criminal event, and therefore how much punishment an action deserves. Finally, these notions of worth have attached to them real monetary cost, a cost policy makers and/or implementers ignore only at their peril.

The price of justice is quite high, as a recent study of three "typical" New York City robbery cases demonstrates.[1] The first case cost the city of New York $851. The defendants pled guilty to a lesser charge the day after they were arrested. The majority of the costs were incurred for arresting and booking the individuals. Court costs were minimal. In the second case, the city expended $6,665. The defendant was incarcerated for 68 days after his arrest and prior to his plea of guilty. Thus, 70% of the cost was for pretrial detention. When the defendant pled guilty, he received a sentence of from 4 to 12 years. In the final case, the defendant opted to go to trial. The defendant was arrested soon after the commission of the act, so that costs for police activity were minimal. However, 250 days elapsed between the time of arrest and sentencing. Pretrial detention cost approximately $16,300. Police activity and the cost of a full trial added another $16,300 plus, so that the total cost of case processing amounted to $32,627. The individual was convicted of robbery and sentenced to 9 to 18 years. It costs approximately $23,000 a year to keep a person imprisoned in New York. Assuming our robber served his minimum nine-year sentence, he would cost the state an additional $207,000. Thus, this single case cost state and local authorities a minimum of $239,627. Was or is it worth it?

The answer to the question depends upon a number of contingencies. Is worth to be assessed symbolically, monetarily, or from a combination of these two perspectives? From whose standpoint is worth to be determined: the police, the prosecutor, the victim, or the public at large? Who benefits and exactly what is it that they gain?

CRIMINOLOGICAL/CRIMINAL JUSTICE CONSIDERATIONS

The Criminal Justice Wedding Cake

A number of authors have attempted to portray the complete interactions of formal and informal factors, symbolic and practical considerations and their influence on the process of crime categorization by proposing a wedding cake model of criminal justice.[2] Samuel Walker presented a pictorial representation of this concept (Figure 4-1).

Celebrated Cases

Celebrated cases, those in the top layer, are the relatively few cases that obtain a considerable amount of public attention because they involve famous people, landmark cases, or extremely brutal, infamous acts. While such cases receive considerable attention, they in fact represent the least typical cases dealt with by the system. Unfortunately, however, because they receive so much public attention, these become symbolic of the system at work. It does not matter that the system seldom works the way celebrated cases portray. If such cases are perceived as indicating a problem with the doing of justice, they become the reason for proposing new procedures. Because the public bases its perception of criminal justice on these cases, legislators often respond to constituent concerns by legislating solutions to problems that don't exist. At best such solutions remain symbols of concern, without practical effect. At worst, they create a problem where none existed before or put implementers in a position of using discretion often to the detriment of the least powerful in

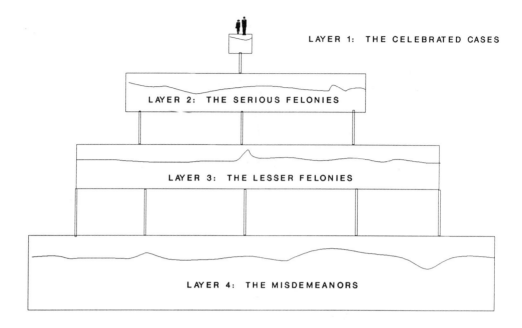

LAYER 1: THE CELEBRATED CASES

LAYER 2: THE SERIOUS FELONIES

LAYER 3: THE LESSER FELONIES

LAYER 4: THE MISDEMEANORS

THE CRIMINAL JUSTICE WEDDING CAKE

Figure 4-1 *Source*: Samuel Walker, *Sense and Nonsense about Crime: A Policy Guide* (Pacific Grove, CA.: Brooks Cole Publishing Company, 1985), p. 16.

our society. The recent debate about abolishing the insanity defense illustrates the first point. Prison overcrowding and the death penalty illustrate the last two points.

The Defense of Insanity

Steve Bruce Martin was killed during a domestic argument in Nashville, Tennessee. On the same day, Vernon Lassiter in Philadelphia, Antonio Jimenes in Chicago, and James Angus in New York were also killed.[3] These victims shared more, however, than just the day of death. All were killed by handguns. And the day they were killed, Monday, March 30, 1981, was the same day President Ronald Reagan was the victim of an assassination attempt by John W. Hinckley, Jr. Hinckley, too, used a handgun. What policy lesson might be drawn from these shootings and the 50 or so others that occurred on this day and that occur every day in the United States? Since, in terms of handgun shootings, March 30, 1981, was an average day, one might suspect that debate about the availability of handguns would hold the attention of policy makers as they grappled with the problem of violence in this society. In fact, just such a debate did occur. It was, however, soon overshadowed by a second debate. The issue of this second debate captured the attention of policy makers and resulted in a spate of legislation designed to correct what was perceived as an abuse in the criminal justice system. The issue was the insanity defense.

John Hinckley was found not guilty by reason of insanity of the 13 criminal charges that resulted from the shooting of the President and three others in his entourage. As discussed in Chapter 2, a person must have the necessary intent (*mens rea*) to be guilty of a criminal act. The insanity plea is a defense based on the argument that criminal intent was absent and therefore the person is not guilty of a crime. The jury in the Hinckley case believed that he was not guilty because the state of his mind prevented him both from appreciating the criminal nature of his act and from controlling his behavior. The Hinckley case and the events surrounding it illustrate three things about the nature of criminal justice and policy responses to the crime problem.

First, because of who the victims were, the case was a celebrated one that sparked policy debates and demands for reform of the insanity defense, even though the defense itself is not very important in the day-to-day doing of justice. Public attention focused not only on the President and his assailant, but on the family of the accused, the psychiatrist who treated him, the object of his delusions (actress Jodie Foster), and the witnesses and jurors in the case. Over a year passed between the incident and the trial, a year filled with pretrial motions and legal arguments about Hinckley's competence to stand trial and the nature of the evidence to be used if the case proceeded. When it was clear that defense attorneys were going to plead him innocent by reason of insanity, a storm of protest arose. Congress and at least two dozen state legislatures worked to close what was considered a loophole in the law that let dangerous criminals free. The profession of psychiatry was concerned with its image, as expert witnesses for the defense and the prosecution argued with each other over Hinckley's sanity. The contradictions that emerged in the psychiatric testimony challenged the objectivity and scientific élan of psychiatry. Finally, when a not guilty verdict was returned, people reacted with shock, outrage, and further demands for a changed policy regarding insanity pleas. During the trial and its aftermath, a number of states abolished the insanity defense and created a new verdict, "guilty but mentally ill."

What became lost in all the rhetoric was the fact that insanity defenses are used in relatively few criminal cases, something less than 1%. Further, it is seldom successful. Notorious figures such as Jack Ruby, Sirhan Sirhan, and John Wayne Gacy all attempted this plea and failed. Others, who certainly seemed to qualify for the label insane, did not even attempt to use it during their trials. Mark David Chapman, who killed John Lennon, "Son of Sam"

David Berkowitz, and Charles Manson never raised the issue at their trials.[4] John Hinckley's case was celebrated, and thus it became the focus for a policy debate and a desire to correct what was perceived to be a major problem. But because the debate and the problem formulation were based on an atypical occurrence, a problem was solved that really had little to do with the typical process of justice. Pleas of insanity are not only rare, they often are agreed to without trial and rarely involve incidents of violent crimes.[5] A problem was addressed that was not a problem with a policy solution that had little effect on the justice system.

The second thing the Hinckley case illustrates is the tendency for policy issues to be replaced rather than solved. The defense of innocent by reason of insanity has a long history in jurisprudence. Its modern application was first articulated in the 1840s in what became known as the McNaughten rule. Daniel McNaughten attempted to kill the British prime minister, Sir Robert Peel. He ended up, instead, killing the prime minister's private secretary, but was acquitted by a British jury who found him insane. The "McNaughten rule" holds that a defendant, to be adjudged insane, must not be able to distinguish right from wrong. Most courts in the United States adopted this test of insanity. Some courts, however, beginning with New Hampshire in 1871, added a second justification for the finding of insanity—irresistible impulse. Irresistible impulse, also known as "the policeman at the elbow test," says that if a defendant were to carry out an illegal act, even if a policeman were standing right next to him, he could be found innocent by reason of insanity. In 1954, the insanity defense was broadened by what is know as the "Durham rule." The U.S. Court of Appeals in Washington, DC ruled that if a defendant showed a crime to be a product of a mental disease or defect, he or she could be found innocent by reason of insanity. Under this ruling, the defendant could be found innocent even if he or she could distinguish right from wrong or did not have an irresistible impulse. The major effect of "Durham" was to increase the use of expert psychiatric witnesses in cases where the insanity plea was entered.[6] But "Durham" itself was overruled in 1972 by the same court of appeals that enunciated it in the first place. John Hinckley's verdict was decided based on a combination of a right/wrong test and irresistible impulse.

Throughout its history, the insanity defense has been a source of controversy. A nineteenth-century cartoon, for example, shows people lined up to receive certificates of insanity at reduced rates from "H. Looney, expert." The cartoon is titled, "The Slick Join the Sick."[7] But such controversy is short-lived. A celebrated case sparks debate and, at times, legislation, but interest in the issue fades as the celebrated case moves from the front page to the back page and then to the pages of history. The controversy and the issues surrounding it are replaced by new controversies and new issues. But since the problem is replaced rather than solved, a celebrated case can once again make a particular issue a source of policy debate and intervention. Usually, however, such interventions will little alter the daily doing of justice that goes on at the less visible levels of the criminal justice wedding cake.

Finally, the Hinckley case illustrates the difficulty in determining the worth of a case or a policy. Celebrated cases are like morality plays that display our concerns and values. But the specific lessons to be drawn from such events are often in the eye of the beholder. Did the Hinckley trial display a justice system that literally lets people get away with serious crimes? Did it display a system that is compassionate and that can take into account ancient principles of legal responsibility even when the president of the United States is a victim? Whatever lesson is drawn, such cases are expensive.

The Hinckley case took considerably longer than an "ordinary case." Further, the expert witnesses and the extensive pretrial maneuvering added greatly to the costs. Surveys of expert witnesses such as psychiatrists and psychologists have determined that the average fee for such services is between $500 and $1,000 a day.[8] Based on estimates of the cost of capital murder cases using the same type of experts and pretrial motions as used in the Hinckley case, it would not be surprising if this single case cost over $1 million. Worth it or not, the system cannot afford too many celebrated cases, and so the daily doing of justice is routinized to save everybody time and money.

The Rest of the Layers

The second layer of the criminal justice wedding cake consists of serious felonies. Serious felonies are ordinarily defined as stranger-to-stranger violent crime. This second layer constitutes about 10% of all felonies reported to the police. Besides seriousness and prior relationship, the past record of the defendant will often determine whether a case ends up in the second or third layer. In any event, a case ending up in this second layer is treated harshly by the system. Thus, routinization does not mean that cases are treated "cheaply" when it comes to punishments. Such cases are "worth more" than cases assigned to the lower tier.

The third layer contains those incidents considered less serious by criminal justice implementers. Thus, while certain acts may fit the technical, legal definition of serious crime, circumstances dictate that the case be treated as worth less than its formal definition would imply. The example of the man caught in the garage, discussed in Chapter 2, illustrates the point. Again, one of the circumstances that will dictate the placement of a case in the second or third tier is the prior relationship of the victim and the offender. A study of felony arrests in New York City by the Vera Institute illustrates the point. Comparing the disposition of prior relationship robbery arrests with stranger robbery arrests, the Institute found that less than half of the former (37%) resulted in a conviction. Convictions obtained in these cases were primarily for misdemeanor offenses (32%); only 5% of these cases resulted in a felony conviction. Twenty-one percent of those convicted were sentenced to jail or prison, but nobody was sentenced to felony time—over one year.[9]

The situation was quite different with the stranger cases. Eighty-eight percent of these resulted in convictions, the majority (68%) on felony charges. Most of those convicted were incarcerated, and half of these served a year or more.

The same pattern emerged in comparisons of prior relationship burglaries with stranger burglaries. In the former cases a little over half of those arrested (53%) were convicted on a charge, but all of these were put into the misdemeanor category, the third or perhaps even the fourth tier on our cake. Only 6% of the original cases were sentenced to jail or prison, but in no instance was it for more than a year. In the stranger cases, 89% resulted in a conviction. Interestingly, the majority of convictions (82%) were also on misdemeanor charges. Burglary cases overall are generally treated more cheaply than are robbery cases by the system. But in the case of stranger burglary, nearly 48% of those originally arrested were incarcerated, compared to 6% in nonstranger cases. Incarcerations were all for less than a year, however.[10]

Clearly, the courthouse weighs the worth of a case in terms of a number of circumstances. Further, placement on a tier of the cake dictates the amount of punishment considered appropriate. But since the variations in the amount of punishment are consistent—"cheap" cases receiving less punishment, serious cases more punishment—it is a mistake to view the criminal justice process as either too soft or too harsh. The system is simultaneously both soft and harsh.[11] This insight has major consequences for criminal justice policy. Those policies aimed at increasing sentence severity because the system is viewed as too lenient are solving a problem that does not exist. The end result may well be the creation of a problem. Reforms aimed at increasing the amount of punishment affect cases on the lower tiers of the cake, literally creating an inflationary spiral. Since serious cases are already treated seriously, increasing the amount of punishment affects less serious cases, not at all the kind with which reformers are very concerned.[12] Mandatory sentences and other efforts to restrict the discretion of courthouse personnel, who are mistakenly viewed as soft on crime, may well result in unnecessary overcrowding of our jail and prison facilities, as less serious offenders are added to the serious ones already there.

The largest category of crime, making up the bottom tier of the cake, consists of less serious misdemeanor offenses and what are sometimes known as public order offenses. These would include such things as public drunkenness, prostitution, and so on. The bulk of these cases are handled in lower courts. Because this is the most invisible layer of the system, these courts tend to be informal and are least affected by due process reforms. Lawyers, rules of evidence, and individual case processing are all hit or miss propositions within this layer of the justice system. Cases are handled assembly-line fashion with most people pleading guilty. If the time of the typical case in the higher courts can be measured in days, cases in these lower courts can be measured in minutes. According to one author, stepping into these courts is a step backward in time to the turn of the century, when our higher courts functioned without a great deal of concern about due process and other legal procedures that we now take for granted.[13] There is an irony in this. If lower courts take us back to the turn of the century in regard to implementation, those policy makers who want to limit the discretion of all criminal justice implementers take us even further back in time regarding policy-in-intention. Prison overcrowding of the 1870s and revulsion at the brutality and prison unrest that such overcrowding fueled moved policy makers towards giving more discretionary power to wardens, judges, attorneys, and parole boards.[14] And by 1920, plea bargaining together with indeterminate sentences had become an accepted part of the criminal justice system to cope with both overcrowded facilities and overcrowded court dockets.[15] Fixed, mandatory sentences at the turn of the eighteenth century were considered innovative. By the turn of the nineteenth century the lack of discretion that such sentences engendered was viewed as regressive and the cause of major problems within the system. Today, policy makers who suggest long fixed mandatory sentences are not innovative at all. Instead, they are taking us a step backward in policy time. The wedding cake model captures the interaction of the formal and informal aspects of law and demonstrates that the use of discretion within the system parallels to a great degree some common-sense notions of how much a case is worth.

The wedding cake of criminal justice appears most useful in understanding the policy dynamics of reform and implementation in terms of street crime and/or public order offenses. However, famous cases involving white-collar offenses and large corporate offenders seem to excite relatively little public indignation and/or demands for reform. The same is true for crimes against corporations such as employee theft and shoplifting. Yet, as will be discussed below, these types of crime together with organized crime, which excites public interest but little else, cost more in dollar terms than the typical crime for which the public demands a solution.

What Does Crime Cost?

Besides assessing worth on symbolic and/or practical criteria, it is possible to assess to some degree the dollar cost of crime and criminal justice. Figure 4-2 shows the growth in criminal justice expenditures from 1971 to 1985 on a per capita basis in constant 1985 dollars.

In 1971 the total expenditure for criminal justice was $11.2 billion. By 1985, the cost of justice services was over $45 billion.[16] Besides this cost of processing crime, there is the cost of crime in terms of loss to victims. The economic loss to victims of personal and household crimes in 1985 is shown in Table 4-1.

While personal and household crimes cost victims over $13 billion in 1985, this was only a small fraction of the total cost of crime. The loss to the

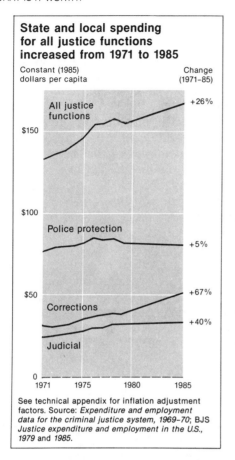

State and local spending for all justice functions increased from 1971 to 1985

Constant (1985) dollars per capita — Change (1971–85)

All justice functions — +26%

$150

$100

Police protection — +5%

$50 — +67%

Corrections — +40%

Judicial

0
1971   1975   1980   1985

See technical appendix for inflation adjustment factors. Source: *Expenditure and employment data for the criminal justice system, 1969–70*; BJS *Justice expenditure and employment in the U.S., 1979* and *1985*.

Figure 4-2 *Source: Report to the Nation on Crime and Justice, 2nd ed.*, U.S. Department of Justice, Bureau of Justice Statistics, (Washington, DC: U.S. Government Printing Office, 1988), p. 121.

American economy because of drug abuse has been estimated at $59.7 billion.[17] Moreover, the cost of white-collar crime is many times greater than that of street crime. The Subcommittee on Antitrust and Monopoly of the U.S. Senate Judiciary Committee estimated the cost of corporate crime, illegal acts that are carried out by corporate executives for the benefit of the corporation, at between $174 and $231 billion a year.[18] Other types of white-collar crimes such as fraud and embezzlement have been estimated to cost over $40 billion a year,[19] while federal income tax evasion is estimated to have cost the government $81 billion in 1981.[20] Yet, as noted, these types of crime excite relatively little public concern. In a symbolic sense, the detection and prosecution of white-collar crime isn't worth very much.

Concerning narcotics, symbolic and monetary assessments come closer

Table 4-1 Economic Cost of
Crime to Victims

*Total economic loss to victims of personal
and household crimes, 1985**

Types of crime	Gross loss (millions)
All crimes	$13,029
Personal crimes	3,363
—of violence	749
Rape	15
Robbery	492
Assault	242
—of theft	2,614
Personal larceny	
with contact	80
without contact	2,534
Household crimes	9,666
Burglary	3,499
Household larceny	1,607
Motor vehicle theft	4,560

* Includes losses from property theft or damage, cash losses, medical expenses and lost pay because of victimization (including time spent with the police in investigation and in court and time spent in replacing lost property) and other crime-related costs.

Source: BJS Data Report, 1987, U.S. Department of Justice, Bureau of Justice Statistics, (Washington, DC: U.S. Government Printing Office, April, 1988).

together. Policy makers and citizens generally consider drug violations as serious, and they do in fact represent a serious loss to the economy. The irony, however, is that policies aimed at controlling drugs are generally aimed at users rather than at suppliers. Thus, the laws seem ineffective at controlling the commodity and instead end up controlling the consumer. Many of these addicts are involved in relatively petty violations, and thus at the level of implementation such crimes are at times treated less seriously than the harsh laws would indicate. Even when laws are designed to incapacitate and deter dealers, their effect because of implementation problems seems minimal. Evaluation of the Rockefeller Drug Laws illustrate the point. These 1973 New York State laws provided a potential life sentence for those convicted of drug dealing and restricted the discretion of the prosecutor in plea bargaining such cases. New York was known as having the toughest drug laws in the nation. But since those indicted for such crimes now faced draconian sentences, the number of individuals demanding trials rose significantly. This required prosecutors to reduce the number of cases they accepted for prosecution in order to manage their work load. The net effect was to cancel out the deterrent and incapacitative effect of the law, since fewer people were being indicted and convicted.[21] The practical cost of implementation proved too great, so that prosecutors had to cheapen some cases they normally would have accepted for indictment.

The total dollar cost of crime in this country easily exceeds $140 billion a year. This cost is considerably more than the national defense budget in 1985.[22] Yet, symbolic and practical considerations make it difficult to assess whether expenditures to control crime are "worth it." Nevertheless, given the monetary resources involved in issues of crime, the stake society has in maintaining an orderly and relatively safe environment, and the toll crime occurrences extract from victims, offenders, and the community at large, it is important to develop procedures for assessing the worth and impact of particular crime control policies. It is to this issue that we now turn.

POLICY CONSIDERATION: THEORIES/ARGUMENTS/APPLICATIONS

The Legislator Considers Worth

State legislators are key architects of criminal justice policy. By passing substantive criminal laws that classify certain behaviors as illegal and prescribe a punishment for engaging in them, the legislators are usually the first group to determine a crime's worth. This activity, however, is only the beginning of a very long process that culminates in a specific punishment given to a specific individual enmeshed in a specific set of circumstances. As policy makers, then, legislators often operate at a level of policy-in-intention. Their activity and its outcome often express general values and goals, a desire to do the right thing. Thus, criminal laws are passed as much for their symbolic value as for their tangible effect. By passing laws, lawmakers show that they are doing what they were elected to do. Legislators, after all, are expected to legislate. Moreover, the passage of a law gives constituents the feeling that something is being done about a problem. Finally, a law acts to enshrine the beliefs and values of a group, whether a specific interest group or a broad-based constituency. Therefore, the penalties attached to violations of criminal law often reflect the symbolic needs of constituents and legislators alike. Punishments reflect both the degree of moral abhorrence of a particular act and the fact that legislators are listening to the concerns of voters. Policy-in-intention then often has more symbolic worth than tangible benefit. Such symbolic worth is not, however, without real costs. These points can be illustrated by examining the reenactment of capital punishment statutes in 37 of the 50 states.

The Worth of Capital Punishment

Most people in the United States now express support for capital punishment, particularly in cases of homicide. Attitudes toward capital punishment have, however, been remarkably unstable. A Gallup Poll found that 68% of the American public favored the death penalty in 1953. By 1966, those favoring the death penalty dropped to 42%. Now it appears that support has again increased so that close to 70% of the American public favors the death penalty.[23]

The fluctuation in public opinion regarding capital punishment has been matched by fluctuations in its imposition. As Figure 4-3 shows, by the late 1940s there was a significant decline in the number of executions in this country. The high watermark for executions was 1935, when 199 people were executed in a single year. By 1968 executions had stopped. This moratorium lasted through 1976.[24] Executions were resumed in 1977 with the death of Gary Gilmore before a Utah firing squad. As of July 1, 1988, 100 people have since been executed. Figure 4-4 shows that there are now over 1,500 people on death row in the United States.

During the moratorium on executions from 1968 to 1977, legal opinion itself shifted back and forth between condemnation and support of the penalty. In 1972, the Supreme Court, by a vote of five to four, declared in *Furman* v. *Georgia* that "the imposition and carrying out of the death penalty . . . constitutes cruel and unusual punishment in violation of the Eighth and Fourteenth Amendments."[25] Only two justices, however, were willing to declare that the death penalty was inherently unconstitutional. The other three justices in the majority objected to the way the penalty had been arbitrarily applied. Thus, states rushed to make the imposition of the penalty less arbitrary by trying to ensure greater procedural safeguards and/or by making the death penalty mandatory for certain specified crimes. In 1976, the Supreme Court in *Woodson* v. *North Carolina* declared that a mandatory death penalty was unconstitutional. At the same time, in *Gregg* v. *Georgia*, the Court ruled that "the punishment of death does not invariably violate the Constitution."[26] Thus, while condemning mandatory death sentences, the Court supported "guided discretion" statutes that imposed a regularized process of evidentiary review with objective standards to guide the imposition of the death penalty. Such a process involves the use of a bifurcated (two-stage) trial. The jury first decides guilt or innocence. If the person is found guilty, the second stage of the trial consists of the jury choosing between imprisonment and death in light of legislatively described aggravating or mitigating circumstances. In 1987, the Court in *McCleskey* v. *Kemp* held that despite statistical evidence of discriminatory application of the death penalty based on race of the victim, such evidence was not relevant to showing discrimination in the case of the particular individual.[27] Thus, by 1987 the Court seemed less concerned with systemic problems in the application of the death penalty.

Number of persons executed, by year, 1930–81

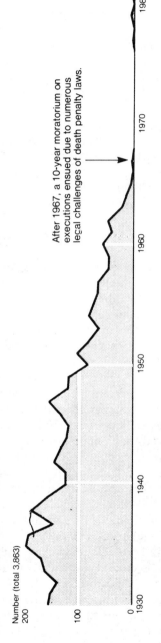

Figure 4-3 Executions—1930 to 1981 *Source:* United States Bureau of Justice Statistics, *Capital Punishment, 1981* (Washington, DC: U.S. Government Printing Office, 1982), p. 8.

**The number of persons on death row
reached an alltime high in 1985**

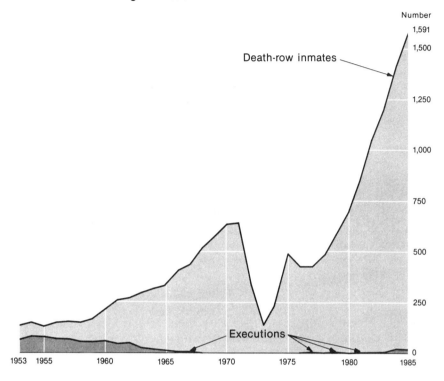

Figure 4-4   The number of persons on death row reached on all time high in
1985.   *Source: Report to the Nation on Crime and Justice, 2nd ed.,* U.S.
Department of Justice, Bureau of Justice Statistics, (Washington, DC: U.S.
Government Printing Office, 1988), p. 98.

While fluctuations in public opinion, imposition, and legal judgments
have marked the history of the death penalty in the United States, research
concerning its effectiveness has been generally consistent. The bulk of the
research fails to show any deterrent effect. In the few studies, among the
thousands that have been conducted, where a deterrent effect appears, the
studies have subsequently been shown to be methodologically flawed.[28] Not
only has research failed to demonstrate a deterrent effect for the death penalty,
some have actually uncovered what appears to be a stimulation effect. That is,
in the short run, homicides seem to increase after an execution. Bowers and
Pierce, for example, in examining data for a 57-year period in New York state
from 1907 to 1964, found that on average, one or more executions in a given
month added a net increase of two homicides to the total committed in the
next month.[29]

Finally, current research suggests that it may not be possible to avoid arbitrary and capricious application of the death penalty. The vast majority of homicides are not eligible for the death penalty, because they do not meet criteria such as premeditation, wantonness, or commission in the course of another felony. Some researchers estimate that only 10% of homicides are capital homicides. But even among those eligible for the death penalty, only one in 10 actually receives it.[30] Discretion is obviously still a significant factor in the application of the death penalty despite efforts to curb it. Prosecutorial discretion on what to charge and judicial or jury discretion on what to impose are two points of the process where inconsistency and arbitrariness can enter. Recent studies of prosecutorial discretion suggest that the race of the victim determines the likelihood of a prosecutor's seeking the death penalty. In those cases where the victim is white and the defendant is black, the perpetrator is more likely to be charged with a capital murder and the death penalty sought than in cases with any other racial combination.[31] As noted above, however, in *McCleskey* the Supreme Court rejected this argument as a basis for overturning the death penalty. Finally, the very process of selecting a jury in a capital murder case appears to result in jurors biased towards the prosecution and biased towards the imposition of death.[32]

Given the rather significant problems that surround the death penalty, it may appear surprising that most state legislatures quickly sought to reinstate the penalty after its temporary demise because of the *Furman* decision. But as the first chapter noted, scientists with their data are simply one more interest group that policy makers take into account when deciding an issue. In this case, they were not a particularly important group since most constituents appeared to support the death penalty. Thus, whether or not the penalty had some demonstrable effect, the reinstitution of the death penalty was a way to show constituents that legislators were concerned about crime and were willing to do something about it. This symbolic action is not, however, without real costs.

The Cost of the Death Penalty

If a typical case costs over $32,000 to process through the trial stage, a capital murder case easily surpasses this figure. Let us assume, using the cost figures presented previously, that the cost of a typical trial, including the extra police work necessary to provide both evidence and witnesses, is conservatively in the neighborhood of $16,000. A typical trial lasts two days, so that the cost per day is $8,000. Actually, a portion of this money is expended prior to the trial, as the attorneys prepare and as pretrial motions concerning evidence and other issues are decided upon. Again, however, given the work prior to trial, $8,000 per actual trial day is a conservative figure. While a typical trial lasts two days on average, a capital murder case can take a month or longer. Justice Thurgood Marshall stated in *Furman* the reasons for lengthy trials in capital cases:

At trial, the selection of jurors is likely to become a costly, time consuming problem in a capital case, and defense counsel will reasonably exhaust every possible means to save his client from execution, no matter how long the trial takes.[33]

Using a conservative estimate of 14 days for a capital murder trial, including pretrial jury selection, and multiplying this by $8,000 per day, means that a minimum of $112,000 is spent just at this first stage of the process. Appeals in capital murder cases are automatic to the Supreme Court of the state. The appeals process is at least the cost of the original trial, so that a minimum of $224,000 is expended prior to beginning federal court reviews. Some of these reviews can be in the courts for as long as eight years. Clearly the death sentence is a monetarily expensive penalty, more expensive than life imprisonment. Estimates of how much it would cost to pursue a capital case through the first three stages of litigation (trial, state appeal review, and U.S. Supreme Court review) have ranged as high as $1,828,100.[34] But even using conservative assumptions and estimates yields a cost factor that is quite high. Nor do these costs cease to escalate when legal avenues of appeal are exhausted.

The state of Georgia spent $250,000 in preparation for an execution that was aborted before being carried out.[35] The high cost is in part due to the number of personnel required to carry out an execution. Guidelines on execution procedures for the South Carolina Department of Corrections, for example, mandate the presence of 11 employees just in the execution chamber when the execution is carried out. These include one physician, one chaplain, two electricians, the warden, three executioners, two assistants to the warden, and one medical technician.[36] Preparations for the execution begin four days prior to the actual event with the installation and/or activation of special telephone equipment for handling last minute stays. Detailed responsibilities are assigned to numerous people during the days preceding the execution, all resulting in considerable expense to the state.

Is capital punishment worth it? Monetarily the answer seems to be no from both the standpoint of general deterrence and specific incapacitation. The penalty does not appear to deter others, and life imprisonment, which would serve the function of incapacitation, costs less. Estimates of the costs of imprisonment range from $9,000 a year to $23,000 a year per individual. Taking a middle-range figure of $15,000 a year means that a person incarcerated for 50 years would cost the state $750,000, significantly less than the cost of litigating, preparing for, and carrying out a death sentence. But as noted, worth can also be assessed symbolically. A death penalty statute shows that legislators are concerned about crime. Citizens can feel that something is being done to address their fear and concern. And an occasional execution can give the appearance of righting the scales and restoring the moral balance by taking a life for a life—even if it's only carried out in about 1% of the elegible homicide cases a year. And while the stimulation hypothesis discussed above suggests that taking a life for a life also causes others to solve their problems the same way the state does, that is, by killing an individual perceived to be the cause of a problem, these are fine points. A legislator faced with a constituency overwhelmingly in favor of the death penalty is under a great deal of pressure to legislate this punishment regardless of its practical effects.

Criminal Justice Implementers Consider Worth

Like legislative policy makers, criminal justice implementers, police, court, and correctional personnel also base their findings of worth on a combination of practical and symbolic considerations. Since, however, they operate with more clearly defined budgetary limits and with far less public scrutiny, practical considerations can often outweigh symbolic ones in their assessments of case worth.

The constraints of time, money, and resources force most policy implementers to routinize their processing of cases. Such routinization is exemplified by Sudnow's research on "normal crime" discussed in Chapter 2. Discovery of whether a crime was "normal" allows for its routine handling. If a crime has the typical elements, these elements can be used to fashion a plea bargaining arrangement whereby the defendant admits guilt to a lesser charge. The knowledge of what kinds of pleas will be accepted in what kinds of cases allows public defenders and prosecutors to process large case loads efficiently. The considerable time and money necessary for a full trial is saved. Further, such routine handling eliminates the uncertainty of trials, thus giving these criminal justice policy implementers more control over their work.

This informal, routine way of handling cases is of course influenced by the formal statutes of the criminal law. Again, these provide the currency, in the form of punishments available, that is exchanged in the determination of case worth. But the symbolic value that punishment provides legislators and constituents is significantly altered by the need to be practical when it comes to the implementer's job of applying the law. Thus, prosecutors do not routinely seek the death penalty, even in those instances where they could, because of the time and money it takes to pursue these cases.

Understanding the difference between assessing worth symbolically and practically clears up some of the inconsistency that appears in the data regarding average length of time served by inmates. In 1982, half of the murderers released from state prison had served less than six years.[37] But the majority of murders involve family members, friends, or acquaintances. As noted in Chapter 2, a prior relationship between the victim and the offender lessens the perceived seriousness of the crime. Thus, severe penalties for murder are mitigated by the circumstances surrounding the specific event. The presence of the penalty is symbolically useful, the taking into account of particular circumstances practically necessary. This point is also illustrated by the release figures on rapists. In the same year, 1982, half of all rapists released from prison served less than three years. Forty to fifty percent of forcible rapes involve prior relationships, however. Finally, although the United States has reached a record high in the proportion of the population it imprisons (200 per 100,000), it has reached a record low in the amount of time actually served by prisoners (16 months).[38] Law and order political platforms, "get tough" crime rhetoric, and mandatory sentence legislation may have served useful symbolic purposes. The actual effect, however, was to dramatically increase our prison population without simultaneously increasing the amounts of money necessary to provide space for all the new prisoners. As noted in Chapter 1, prison administrators find room for new arrivals by the early release of those already confined, a practical solution necessitated by the zealous legislative appropriation of a symbol.

Evaluating the Criminal Justice Enterprise: Cost/Benefit Analysis and Summative Evaluation

Part of this chapter has been devoted to discussing one kind of evaluation procedure: cost/benefit analysis. Simply put, cost/benefit analysis poses questions such as, "Is policy X or program Y worth it?" and "Do benefits exceed costs?" It should be clear by now that such seemingly simple questions are extremely difficult to answer. What is a cost and what is a benefit depends upon a series of value-laden criteria. Even what constitutes a cost and a benefit may not be all that clear when the symbolic aspects of a policy are considered. Finally, what is a benefit to one group may be considered a cost by another group in the same policy area. Whose ox is being gored affects the perception of costs and benefits.

The same problems that plague cost/benefit assessments affect other types of evaluations, particularly those aimed at assessing whether a program works or not. Evaluations that attempt to answer the question "Does a program work?" are called summative evaluations.

Modern program evaluation, as a distinctive discipline, began as part of the scientific agriculture movement in the early 1900s. The aim of such research was to determine whether various new techniques affecting agricultural production had the desired outcome, such as better crop yield per acre of land, or fatter cattle, or whatever. Agriculture represents a policy area with clearly defined goals and technologies for achieving the goals. Most social policy areas do not have such clear goals or technologies. Nevertheless, the assessment procedures of agriculture were soon adopted to other social policy areas beginning with education and attempts to measure the effectiveness of different interventions on student progress. The method for determining such effects relies largely on pre-post tests, using experimental and quasi-experimental designs. Groups of students, for example, would be randomly assigned to either an experimental group or a control group. The experimental group is the one that receives the "treatment," such as a new teaching approach, a new kind of book, or whatever the innovation happens to be. The control group is not given the treatment. Each group is then tested prior to the introduction of the treatment and at the conclusion of the experiment. If the experimental group shows significantly more progress than the control group, then the treatment (experiment) can be said to have worked. Eventually this model of evaluation became accepted in still other policy areas, particularly in criminal justice for assessing the impact of various treatment programs on delinquents and other offenders.

The assumptions of this evaluation model include the idea that goals of a policy are clear and technologies for achieving the desired outcomes are well developed. People both know what they want and how to go about getting it. Further, given the model's reliance on experimental or quasi-experimental design, it assumes that the investigator can control all the extraneous variables that might affect an outcome. Such conditions clearly do not exist in criminal justice nor, for that matter, are they present in any other social policy area including education. Finally, the assumptions of the model put the evaluator in a position of judge and jury. If goals are assumed to be clear and the means for achieving them well developed, then a failure in meeting the goals is somebody's fault.[39] The program director, the people who delivered the service, or the clients are not doing something they should be doing. Thus, summative evaluations take on the aura of fault finding, an aura that does not particularly endear the evaluator to the people being evaluated. This is particularly true if a negative evaluation can result in a loss of funding. Program operators are then often put in a position of having to work for good numbers, a goal that may in fact subvert the original intention of the new program or policy. For example, an innovative program for dealing with hard-core delinquents must reduce recidivism among the clients to get continued funding. The temptation is to work only with those youth who have the best chance for success, ignoring those for whom the program was originally designed. Numbers then can look good. They will show that fewer kids went back to a life of crime. Of course selection, not intervention, shaped this outcome.

Formative Evaluation

By the 1960s, many evaluators were questioning the appropriateness of the traditional program evaluation model for public policy. Since goals were often ambiguous and the technologies for achieving the goals unclear, other kinds of evaluation models were suggested. These models were formative rather than summative in their approach to program assessment. Formative evaluations are diagnostic rather than judgmental and seek to answer the question, "What is needed to make a program (policy) work better?" This kind of evaluation has two somewhat distinct goals. First, information is gathered in order to suggest how a program might work more effectively. Second, such information is simultaneously used to increase the knowledge available about a particular social problem or condition. Thus, there is an attempt to ameliorate the situation at hand while at the same time trying to learn more about it. This approach seems much more appropriate to most of the problems that are confronted in areas of criminal justice and crime control.

Process Evaluation

Besides cost/benefit analysis, summative evaluations, and formative evaluations, a fourth type of evaluation seeks to answer the question, "What is occurring in program delivery?" Such evaluations are called process evaluations. These seek to monitor the implementation of a program and deal with such issues as how organizational dynamics affect program delivery. Here, theories from organizational sociology can be quite helpful for understanding how new programs are used to solve organizational problems and enhance organizational structures as well as to provide a new service to clients.

As will be seen, evaluations of criminal justice policies have generally been pessimistic. Numerous authors have suggested, for example, that little now works to rehabilitate criminals. Others suggest that organizational dynamics will prevent major alterations in the process of justice. Much of the evaluation literature assumes, however, that policy goals are clear and mainly seek utilitarian ends. There is a failure to take into account the symbolic nature of much legislation. Further, many evaluations suffer from an overreliance on traditional research methods therefore failing to take into account the unique characteristics of the policy environment. In short, one cannot understand criminal justice policy or evaluation research unless one understands the values and ideology that underpin both. We turn to such ideological issues in the next chapter.

SUMMARY

What Was Said

- The worth of a policy can be assessed symbolically, monetarily or from a combination of these two perspectives.
- The criminal justice wedding cake, consisting of celebrated cases on the top, serious felonies on the next tier, then less serious felonies and finally misdemeanors at the base of the cake, captures both the formal and informal criteria for assessing casework.
- Criminal justice policies are often formed in response to celebrated cases, the least representative kinds of cases in the criminal justice system.
- Criminal justice policies based on celebrated cases may function as symbols of concern but often have no practical effect. Even worse, they may create problems where none existed before.

- Reform of the insanity defense represents symbolic but essentially useless policy change for the day-to-day doing of justice.
- Prison overcrowding and what appears to be a systemically discriminatory application of the death penalty represent policy problems created by policy decisions responding largely to measures of symbolic worth.
- Symbolic policies have real costs.
- Costs of imposing the death penalty after appeals approximate $2 million.
- Cost/benefit analysis and summative program evaluation which asks the question "Did the program work?" assumes clear policy goals, technologies for achieving such goals, and a level of scientific control not possible in the policy arena.
- Formative evaluations which ask the question "What can make this program work better?" and process evaluations which attempt to find out how a program is actually being implemented are necessary for evaluating the full impact of a policy.

What Was Not Said

- Policy makers should ignore symbolism in constructing legislation.
- Costs should be the only consideration in determining the worth of a policy.
- Public officials and academics should not attempt to evaluate program effects since all evaluation procedures contain a number of flaws.

NOTES

1. Coopers and Lybrand, *The Cost of Incarceration in New York City* (Hackensack, NJ: National Council on Crime and Delinquency, 1978). See also, *Report to the Nation on Crime and Justice*, 2nd ed., U.S. Department of Justice, Bureau of Justice Statistics (Washington, DC: U.S. Government Printing Office, 1988), p. 123.

2. Samuel Walker, *Sense and Nonsense about Crime*: *A Policy* Guide, (Pacific Grove, CA: Brooks Cole Publishing Company, 1985), p. 16.

3. *New York Times*, 5, April 1981, p. 22e.

4. Aric Press et al. "The Insanity Plea on Trial," *Newsweek*, 24, May 1982, p. 56.

5. Walker, *Sense and Nonsense about Crime*, p. 120.

6. Press et al. "The Insanity Plea," p. 59.

7. Ibid.

8. Stuart Taifor, Jr., "Psychiatrists Worry over Image in Hinckley Trial," *New York Times*, 24, May 1982, B7.

9. The Vera Institute of Justice, *Felony Arrests*, rev. ed. (New York: Longman Inc., 1977, 1981), pp. 68–86.

10. Ibid.

11. Walker, *Sense and Nonsense about Crime*, p. 21.

12. Ibid., p. 31.

13. Arthur Rosett and Donald R. Cressey, *Justice by Consent* (Philadelphia, PA: J.B. Lippincott Company, 1976).

14. David J. Rothman, "Sentencing Reforms in Historical Perspective," *Crime and Delinquency* (October 1983), pp. 631–49.

15. Ibid.

16. *Sourcebook of Criminal Justice Statistics 1981 and 1986*, U.S. Department of Justice, Bureau of Justice Statistics (Washington, DC: U.S. Government Printing Office, 1982, 1987).

17. *Report to the Nation on Crime and Justice*, p. 114.

18. Ronald C. Kramer, "Corporate Criminality: The Development of an Idea," in *Corporations as Criminals*, Ellen Hochstedler, ed. (Beverly Hills, CA: Sage, 1984), p. 19.

19. Ibid.

20. *Report to the Nation on Crime and Justice*, p. 114.

21. U.S. Department of Justice, *The Nation's Toughest Drug Law: Evaluating the New York Experience*, (Washington, DC: U.S. Government Printing Office, 1978.

22. *Report to the Nation on Crime and Justice*, p. 115.

23. "American Attitudes toward the Death Penalty," in *The Death Penalty in America*, 3rd ed., Hugo Adam Bedau, ed. New York: Oxford University Press, 1982), Chap. 3.

24. U.S. Department of Justice, Bureau of Justice Statistics, *Capital Punishment, 1981* (Washington, DC: U.S. Government Printing Office, 1982).

25. Furman v. Georgia, 408 U.S. 239 (1972).

26. Gregg v. Georgia, 428 U.S. 169 (1976); Woodson v. North, 428 U.S. 280 (1976).

27. McCloskey v. Kemp, 107 S. Ct. 1756 (1987).

28. Richard M. McGahey, "Dr. Erlich's Magic Bullet: Econometric Theory, Econometrics, and the Death Penalty," *Crime and Delinquency*, 26, No. 4 (October, 1980), 485–502.

29. William J. Bowers and Glenn L. Pierce, "Deterrence or Brutalization: What Is the Effect of Executions?" *Crime and Delinquency*, 26, No. 4 (October 1980), 453–84.

30. See Thorstin Sellin, *The Penalty of Death*, (Beverly Hills, CA: Sage Publications, 1980), pp. 35–53, 69–74.

31. See Michael L. Radelet and Glenn L. Pierce, "Race and Prosecutorial Discretion in Homicide Cases," *Law and Society Review*, Vol. 19, No. 4 (1985) pp. 587–621.
     Also, Raymond Paternoster, "Prosecutorial Discretion in Requesting the Death Penalty: A Case of Victim-Based Racial Discrimination," *Law & Society Review*, 18, No. 3 (1984), 437–78.

32. Robert Fitzgerald and Phoebe C. Ellsworth, "Due Process vs. Crime Control: Death Qualification and Jury Attitudes," *Law and Human Behavior*, Vol. 8, Nos. 1/2 (1984), 31–79.

33. Furman v. Georgia, 408 U.S. 358 (1972).

34. Public Defense Backup Center, "Capital Losses: The Price of the Death

Penalty for New York State: A Report to the Senate Finance Committee, the Assembly Ways and Means Committee and the Division of the Budget," (Albany, NY: State Defenders Association, Inc., 1982).

35. Ibid.

36. South Carolina Department of Corrections, "Execution Procedures," Number 1500.31, August 13, 1984.

37. "Prison Time Hits Record Low in 1982," *St. Louis Post-Dispatch*, 3, July 1985.

38. Ibid.

39. Egon Guba, "Perspectives on Public Policy," *Policy Studies Review* (August 1985), 14.

V

A History of Crime Control Perspectives

At the end of this chapter, the student will be able to:

A. Describe the influence of ideology on problem definitions and solutions.
B. Distinguish liberal from conservative crime control philosophies.
C. Discuss the historical influences and major periods of different crime control policies.

ISSUE BACKGROUND

Ideology

The term ideology is a much-debated one in the social sciences.[1] At the close of the eighteenth century, when the term was first coined, ideology referred to an empirically based science, focusing on the study of ideas. Understanding how ideas were formed could then lead to better social arrangements for the development and support of human kind. Napoleon Bonaparte viewed this new discipline as a threat to his political goals and accused its supporters of being dangerous visionaries. Thus, ideology became associated with programs of change more than with the study of ideas. Moreover, it acquired a negative connotation. A person or group acting ideologically is sometimes thought to be acting in a less than rational or scientific manner. Ideologically based programs for change are therefore viewed by their opponents as having little chance for success, since values and subjective beliefs rather than facts and scientific analysis fuel them. Unfortunately, the implied dichotomy between objective and subjective oversimplifies the nature of human understanding. Knowledge is not simply objective, nor are beliefs and values merely subjective. Human understanding is a maddening combination of both the objective and the subjective. At times, therefore, it is extremely difficult to know whether our perception of the world is being influenced more by what is there or by what we want to see there!

This dilemma is nowhere more apparent than in discussions of crime and in policies aimed at controlling it. In fact, the history of crime control illustrates an important policy principle: *Solutions to problems result from the values and ideologies of those who propose them.* Because problems and their solutions are caught in webs of values, points of view, and incomplete knowledge, it is important to understand the role of ideology in shaping the policy process.

Philo C. Wasburn suggests that ideology has a number of characteristics, two of which are particularly relevant for our discussion. He states that an ideology is:

1. A more or less integrated set of explicit beliefs about the nature of man and society which are held to be empirically true by members of some social unit (example, class, status group, political association, nation).
2. The set of beliefs is associated with an explicit program for social action for the unit, that is, defending or challenging the existing distribution of rights and advantages to create, maintain, or change them. (Ideologies are intended to be linked with politically relevant collective behavior.)[2]

Two key phrases are contained in the above definition of ideology. The first is "a more or less integrated set of explicit beliefs." This phrase expresses the nonempirical nature of ideologies. Nonempirical is not, however, the same as false. Ideologies can be based on assumptions that are true or false. The point is that they are assumptions, not tested propositions. The second key phrase, "an explicit program for social action," draws attention to the fact that ideologies include political programs for action, hence their importance for the study of public policy.

The two key phrases also provide a convenient method for distinguishing ideology from social science. Social science itself rests on a set of assumptions, but the assumptions should be testable and falsifiable. If an assumption is shown to be incorrect, the scientist willingly alters or abandons it in light of the evidence. The assumptions of an ideology are not so easily abandoned, and the contrary information rather than the assumptions themselves is likely to be challenged. Further, social science is not thought of as having a program of action. Social scientists like to think of themselves as value-free and apolitical, at least in pursuing their research agendas.

The history of crime control policy illustrates the role of ideology in policy formulation. At the same time, it challenges the easy distinction between ideology and social science. Early American criminologists particularly were advocates of social reform, working for specific programs congruent with the then prevailing assumptions about the nature of crime. Since social science tends to be ahistorical, a brief history of crime control policy can illuminate some of its own ideological blind spots, while simultaneously providing a framework for understanding and critiquing current crime control efforts. Finally, a historical overview provides background for assessing the role of ideology in formulating present-day criminal justice policies.

CRIMINOLOGICAL/CRIMINAL JUSTICE CONSIDERATIONS

Crime Control from a Historical Perspective

It is tempting to think of our own era as the most crime-prone, the most disorderly, the most dangerous. Such a view would, however, be erroneous. The Middle Ages had, for example, far higher levels of interpersonal violence than our own age, and rates of homicide were excessive even by modern standards.[3]

According to Kai T. Erikson, colonial America experienced crime waves.[4] Three major ones consisted of outbreaks of witchcraft, heresy, and the satanic manifestations of Quakerism. While these may appear to be quaint or unimportant incidents, they certainly were not considered so at the time. They were treated as seriously as crime waves today and created just as much fear. To illustrate, 22 persons died in a four-month period during the height of the witchcraft hysteria in Salem, Massachusetts. Nineteen people had been adjudicated as witches and had been promptly executed. One was pressed to death under a rock pile in an effort to overcome the person's reluctance to testify at his trial. Two died in prison.[5] Witches were seen everywhere, and hundreds of people were eventually engulfed in the nets of the justice system trying to cope with this outbreak of crime.

At the beginning of the industrial revolution, many burgeoning urban centers were described as cesspools of crime and violence. Gurr reports that high levels of theft, alcoholism, and interpersonal violence plagued many European urban centers.[6] Fear of crime and riot abounded as did demands for control of the "dangerous classes."

Infanticide and cruelty to children were apparently quite common during both the Middle Ages and the early stages of the industrial revolution. In Philadelphia during the 1800s, a fairly large proportion of infants listed as having died from "unknown causes" were in fact found unburied in the city's streets, lots, and privies.[7]

By the mid-1800s, however, as the social dislocation caused by the new industrial order began to wane, the level of violence in society gradually started on a downward course. Social reformers then turned their attention to the control of vice, immorality, and disorderliness that continued to characterize the urban scene. And they found plenty to keep them busy.

Nineteenth-century America has been described as a "dope fiend's paradise."[8] Opium and its derivatives were widely available and were referred to in medical circles by the initials G.O.M.—"God's own medicine."[9] The Bayer Pharmaceutical Company marketed heroin as a cough suppressant in 1898, a year before they marketed aspirin. Both aspirin and heroin are in fact trade names.[10] Coca-Cola and other soft drinks had cocaine as one of the key ingredients until 1903. The first "new" coke eliminated this ingredient.[11] Given the widespread availability of both opiate and stimulation drugs, the "typical" addict of the day was very unlike the modern counterpart. Most users of narcotics were women.[12] The average age of the addict was around 40, and addiction was thought to be an "aristocratic vice."[13] In other words, narcotic use was associated more with the middle and upper classes, although it was found among all class levels.

The nonmedicinal use of opiates, particularly if it resulted in addiction, was considered a vice by nineteenth-century Americans, but not something that needed to be controlled by law. It was simply one among a number of vices that deserved moral condemnation but not legal sanctioning. Other "immoral" activity included dancing, smoking, theater going, gambling, and sexual promiscuity. But because these were not enthusiastically outlawed, the activities flourished throughout the nineteenth century and provided reformers with plenty of things to reform at the dawn of the twentieth century. Changes in patterns of prostitution further illustrate the point.

Up until 1860, it was common for fashionable theaters to reserve a special section for prostitutes to ply their trade. This was known as the infamous "third tier."[14] Church-going people frowned on theater going not only because of the sometimes bawdy shows on a stage, but because of what went on in the audience as well!

The parlor house was also a fixture in most cities and towns of the nineteenth century. The "madame" ran the house in an economically rational manner to provide prostitution for customers. She usually owned the house and hired cooks, maids, and sometimes musical entertainers. She also procured the "sporting women" for customers.[15]

These houses were often confined to the red light or tenderloin district of a town. Such districts were common in the nineteenth-century American city, providing a central location for the betting parlors, gin mills, houses of prostitution, and opium dens that housed the vices morally frowned upon but legally and socially tolerated. Such tolerance did not, however, last through the twentieth century. Red light districts, parlor houses, tolerance toward drug addiction, and disorder generally have all largely disappeared from the American scene. Vice, corruption, and disorder of course still exist, but it has been argued that both violence and public disorder began to decrease in the mid-1800s and continued in a generally downward direction until the 1950s. And, in the case of public disorder, the downward trend remained in effect throughout the twentieth century, even while crime once again appeared on the increase in the 1960s.[16]

The fluctuation and changes in crime and rates of public disorder pose an interesting issue for those concerned with how public policy affects crime and crime control. Were such changes the result of historical trends beyond the control of policy makers, or were public policies at least in part responsible for such occurrences? It is in attempting to answer this question that the roles of both policy and ideology become highlighted. Their intermingling and mutually causal relationship is nowhere more apparent than in the history of the modern police.

POLICY CONSIDERATIONS: THEORIES/ARGUMENTS/APPLICATIONS

Ideology and the Modern Police

Modern-day police forces were largely formed as a response to the economic and social disruptions engendered by the industrial revolution. But the first professional police department, the London Metropolitan Police, created in 1829 by Sir Robert Peel, represented a *liberal, humanitarian* response to the problems of social disorder and crime. London riots in the early 1800s were met by military force and the repeal of many of the rights to free speech, assembly, and protection from arbitrary incarceration that Englishmen had enjoyed. Such repressive measures underscored the weaknesses of the night watch system and the constabulary system for enforcing public order. Able-bodied men volunteered for night watch in each local community, while constables were elected officials charged with a variety of duties, the least important of which was law enforcement. The concern for public order, however, conflicted with the concern that a centralized, professional, full-time police force generated. If state repression could occur in the absence of such a body, what would the consequences for liberty be of a government-controlled police department? Many feared it would mean even greater repression. Thus, committees of Parliament rejected the idea of the police as incompatible with British liberty in 1816, 1818, and 1822.[17] The dilemma posed by the need for both public order and for liberty was resolved by the writings of Jeremy Bentham and the ideology of utilitarianism.[18]

Utilitarianism and the Founding of the London Metropolitan Police

Utilitarianism assumed that humankind was essentially rational and that individuals seek to enhance pleasure while avoiding pain. Thus, the role of the state and of economic systems was to ensure the greatest happiness for the greatest number. This ideology fit in well with the increasingly dominant economic system of capitalism. The individual in the marketplace, left unencumbered by government interference, would seek to maximize profit. Profit could only be gained if consumers were pleased with the products offered. Otherwise, rational buyers, exercising free will, would seek alternate suppliers of goods and services. Therefore, maximizing profit would entail maximizing the satisfaction of consumer demands, thereby resulting in the greatest good for the greatest number. Adam Smith, the economist, was a utilitarian.

Utilitarianism also affected perceptions of justice and criminal law, largely through the writings of the Italian Cesare Beccaria. Beccaria, whose major interest was the reform of draconian criminal laws inherited from the Middle Ages, thought that punishment need only be severe enough to outweigh any pleasure gained from a criminal act. This pleasure-pain principle formed the basis for a major reconstructing of criminal law in Western Europe and the eventual elimination of most capital crimes. If individuals were rational, they would calculate the pleasure involved in a criminal act and assess the pain received if caught and subject to the law. If the pain were greater than the pleasure, the person would refrain from law violation. Of course, the key term in the equation is "if caught." The haphazard, disorganized system of law enforcement that existed in most urban centers made catching law violators a highly unlikely event. Therefore, some of the utilitarian legal reformers began to also concern themselves with the reform of law enforcement. Beccaria himself, although not a strong supporter of a standing police agency, wrote, "It is better to prevent crimes than to punish them."[19] Bentham, on the other hand, thought that both a reform of law and a police force that concentrated on crime prevention were necessary for achieving the greatest good for the greatest number.

Peel borrowed the ideas of Bentham, as well as those of the utilitarian reformer Edwin Chadwick, who developed a theoretical study of the "science of police," to form his plan for a metropolitan police force. The agency was primarily oriented toward crime prevention. Thus, officers wore distinctive uniforms that made them highly visible in the community. They were unarmed, and they were only to enforce laws acceptable to the community. Therefore, reform of the legal system was viewed as essential to the successful operation of the police. Repressive laws and codes were to be repealed. Finally, people recruited for police work needed to be acceptable to the local community.[20]

The American Experience

Like the British police, the American counterpart came into being because of a concern about public disorder, riots, and crime. In New York City, for example, one of the local papers noted in February of 1840 that in the previous 10 months there had been 19 riots and 23 murders in the city.[21]

Commercialized vice prospered. The night watch and the constable system could not even stop thieves at fires nor brawls that erupted between volunteer fire companies who fought each other more often than they fought fires.[22] Thus, by the mid-1800s most large American cities were ready for a professional, centralized police force. The questions then, as now, were who would control this force and what was to be their primary responsibility.

The riots of New York City and other American urban centers were eclectic. There were race riots, labor riots, antiabolitionist riots, and political riots. Thus, many groups struggled to control the police. Among the multiple elites there were those who wanted the police to close saloons on Sunday, to enforce vice laws, to ignore runaway slaves, and to concentrate on the protection of property and the catching of criminals. It was never clear, even among the elites, whether crime control or control of public disorder was to be paramount. Further, many of the laws that were to be enforced, antisaloon laws, for example, were not popular either among officials or police officers. Nor were elites always in positions of local political power. Police agencies were early on the handmaiden of urban political machines, whose bosses clearly expected the police to keep them in power. Since the American police did not develop from a rational orderly plan influenced by a clear ideological mandate, the development of full-time police agencies was much more haphazard than in England, responding to a variety of often competing pragmatic concerns.

From their beginnings in the mid-1800s until the close of the century, American police agencies performed a vast array of social services. They provided housing in the local police stations for the large army of displaced workers. Tramps were put up for two to five nights before being forced to move on.[23] Some police agencies also dispensed drugs to known addicts and escorted drunks home. At the same time, police forces brutally suppressed riots, clubbing and arresting sympathizers or any other troublemakers, despite the fact that in many instances both officers and rioters shared the same ethnic heritage—Irish. Vice was controlled, but payoffs to police were common. Police departments dispensed both welfare and a brutal form of justice where confessions were beaten out of suspects. Finally, police officers, even in the beginning, performed many heroic deeds to save life and property, despite widespread corruption and brutality within their ranks.

The contradictory expectations, demands, and activities that characterized the beginnings of the police system in the United States might well have been due to the relative lack of a clear ideological influence. There was little guidance, other than the pragmatic problems of the moment, to structure police activity. This ideological vacuum was, however, being filled by the beginning of the twentieth century. The ideology of progressive reformers began to more clearly focus the role of the police, while at the same time creating a supportive environment for social science and professional welfare workers.

Progressivism, Professionalism, and the Control of Crime

Many streams fed the progressive ideology that was to become dominant in many social policy areas from the beginning of the twentieth century well into the late 1950s. There were the utilitarian principles of Bentham and Beccaria, the scientific problem-solving approaches of sociology and psychology, the moral convictions of white, rural Protestantism, the elan of the medical profession, and a dash of Darwin's evolutionary theory. This was all mixed together in a stew that was at once elitist and populist, religious and secular, charitable and punitive. The contradictions and tensions were managed within a framework that can best be termed the ideology of professionalism.

Gail Miller describes eight characteristics of professionalism and their consequences for the delivery of services by a "professional" to a "client."[24] First, professionalism rests on an ethic of individualism. Individualism fosters the notion of a contractual relationship between the professional and the client. Such a relationship is therefore safe from third-party interference. On the positive side, this fosters the notion that the relationship between the two parties is special and private. The negative side, however, shields the relationship from regulation. Further, by stressing the ethic of individualism, professionalism often perceives problems and solutions as residing in individuals rather than as within systems. Thus, unemployment may be viewed as a symptom of a personal inability rather than as the failure of a system to provide a sufficient number of jobs.

A second characteristic of professionalism stresses a division of labor along intellectual lines. This creates an aura of specialized knowledge to which only the professional has access. Thus, the professional not only knows more than the nonprofessional, the professional knows better than the nonprofessional. This leads to a third characteristic.

In a professional relationship the client is expected to be passive, the professional in control. Passive clients mean the professional is not to be challenged regarding problem definitions, strategies for solutions, or the right to tell the client what to do.

A fourth characteristic of professionalism relates directly to public policy. Miller terms this characteristic alarmism. Alarmism means that when a professional defines a problem, society should respond with both its attention and its resources. This element of professionalism encourages the idea that professionals are in the best position to know society's needs. Of course, by claiming the right both to define what are the important social problems and to direct the expenditures of public resources, professionals place themselves in a position to enhance the power, prestige, and resources of their own occupational group. Thus, the stakes in the game of who gets to define a problem are quite high, and it is not always clear whether problem definitions that emerge are in the best interest of the society or the profession proposing them. If I am a teacher, I am inclined to think of most problems in terms of formal education. Crime, unemployment, substance abuse, and unhealthy life styles would all be ameliorated if only education could be given more resources to properly teach and train people. Of course in the process of defining the problem and its solution, I have also enhanced both my profession and quite possibly my own personal fortunes.

By this point it should be evident that professionalism itself faces a potential conflict between altruism and self-interest. Is the good of the public or the good of the profession to be served? This conflict is handled by a fifth characteristic of professionalism, the belief that public interest and professional interest coincide. Thus, what enhances the profession enhances the public and vice versa. When physicians rail against national health care, they do so on the basis that such a scheme would in fact seriously threaten the quality of health care in the United States. True, it might also threaten the financial circumstances of most physicians, but in threatening this you also negatively affect the former. Both public interest and professional interest coincide.

A sixth characteristic of a professional ideology suggests that upward mobility is based on competition and achievement. The history of this particular dimension of professionalism illustrates again the conflict between altruism and self-interest. According to Miller, the modern notion of professionalism developed from a conflict between the nobility and the middle class. The traditional professions, law, medicine, and theology, were often the only choices left to the offspring of nobility who were not first in line to inherit the title and land that went with it. Thus, a professional position was itself often a result of birth rather than aptitude. However, the emerging middle class also saw the professions as an opportunity. By demanding licensing, proper schooling, and professional positions based on achievement, they were able to dislodge the aristocratic grip on the professions. This provided more opportunity for their own mobility. The myth is, however, that meritocracy has totally replaced less rational criteria of professional selection. Thus, only those who are competent and deserving become professional practitioners. Who would want somebody with a "D" in surgery to perform a complicated operation on them? Nobody. Patients like to believe that their doctor is one of the best in the field. Of course not every doctor is, nor do many patients ask what grades their physician received in medical school. The myth that professional mobility is based solely on competition and achievement simultaneously comforts clients while increasing the power of professionals over them.

Professionalism as an ideology tends to support the existing status quo. A seventh characteristic is therefore professional, political, and social conservatism. Since professionals are highly regarded in the existing society, radical social change could only endanger this position. The same is true of radical changes in theories or common practices. Thus, professional innovators are often subject to ridicule and derision when they suggest new approaches to problems. Sigmund Freud was ostracized by his colleagues in Vienna for his radical ideas on sex and the human psyche.

Finally, professionalism involves more than just the practice of an occupation. The social rewards such as money and status that accompany a professional position mean that professionals adopt a particular life style. This life style might best be described as upper middle class and involves certain expectations of decorum, dress, entertainment, and so on. This of course can create tensions and misunderstandings between the professional and clients who may have different standards of behavior.

The emerging ideology of professionalism affected the police directly. By the 1920s police agencies had become relatively specialized, concentrating mainly on crime and traffic control. Social welfare problems were largely removed from police purview, as the emerging professions of social work and child welfare promised solutions rather than simply control of some of the maladies formerly dealt with by the police.[25]

The close of the nineteenth century and the first two decades of the twentieth century might well be considered the period of rapid professional expansion. "Better living through science" became a guiding principal in a host of different social policy areas including public health, crime control, and even homemaking. Police were the experts in crime control, social workers in the problems of poverty and social dislocation, and child welfare workers in the area of delinquency and child abuse. Penologists would cure the criminal once the police caught him. Even the homes of the middle class were not safe from the expanding ideology of professionalism. Home economics developed as a discipline wherein the virtues of scientific housekeeping were extolled. The homemaker who kept the house clean worked shoulder to shoulder with the physician in fighting germs. Ecology became popular just prior to World War I and legislation to clean up streams, ensure mine safety, and establish pure food and drug laws was passed. Professionals in a variety of fields would cure social ills. The police thus lost their broad social mandate and became responsible for a much more narrowly defined set of tasks. The new professionals would take care of the social order, an order that ideally would reflect the decorum of the middle and upper classes as the norm.

What were the results of this professionalizing on the problem of crime and public order and the strategies for dealing with them? As noted, it is clear that both crime and public order offenses began a downward movement beginning about 1850 and continuing through 1950. For the most part, public order offenses have remained low while crime trends began a reversal in the 1950s and 1960s. What is not clear is what caused the fluctuations and the overall increase in public decorum. There are two dominant theories.[26] One suggests that the decreases in crime and the accompanying increases in public decorum are due to the creation of formal control agencies such as the police and, particularly regarding crime, law enforcement's specialization beginning in the 1900s. The increase in crime, starting midcentury, was simply due to a nineteenth-century system being overwhelmed. A second theory suggests that rather than criminal justice agencies being responsible for the decrease in crime, general changes in the social system brought about by industrialization and urbanization were mainly responsible for historical declines in deviance.[27] Industrialization demanded discipline on the part of workers, and an expanding economy could absorb, over time, large numbers of formerly idle or displaced people. Further, urbanization made the observing of crime easier, which in turn acted as a prophylactic on criminal behavior. According to this view, the midcentury increase is due to economic dislocation and technological shifts which again are creating an urban underclass.

Whatever the primary reason for the macro historical trends, three things seem clear. First, the results of a policy innovation are constrained and influenced by larger historical conditions.[28] The police themselves, were, after all, a response to nineteenth-century concerns about disorder and unrest as industrialization at first displaced people faster than they could be absorbed by the new economic system. Thus, a policy effect is always historically conditioned. Second, since policies are historically conditioned, they often reflect the dominant ideology of the age. If people believe that the devil causes crime, policies for dealing with it will be different than if they believe that crime is the result of some type of disease. Strategies are not the only thing affected, however. Ideology also influences who is likely to be viewed as a deviant. Finally, since policy is ideologically anchored, its micro effects have consequences unintended by its proponents. Ideology influences individuals to see the world a particular way, and if the world is not the way it is perceived, ideological remedies have effects not anticipated by those who apply them. This point is illustrated by the history of drug legislation.

America's First War on Drugs

Progressive reformers, influenced by science, rationalism, moral sentiment, and the emerging professional ethic sought to make America strong and morally righteous, a leader among nations. These feelings were reinforced by America's entry into World War I. The need for America and Americans to be strong resulted in a spate of legislation to curb the use of narcotics and alcohol. Prohibition and a series of antinarcotic legislation resulted. Both of these particular policy moves had nativist overtones. Alcohol was associated with the Irish and later on with Eastern Europeans, most of whom were Catholic, and who were seen as a threat to white, Protestant America. Drug use, on the other hand, became increasingly associated with the Chinese and with fear of white slavery. Innocent young girls were being led into prostitution by unscrupulous foreign purveyors of drugs. Actually, there were also international monetary and trade considerations that further influenced the first narcotics control law in the United States.[29] In China itself, where opium was not outlawed, there was great demand for British opium. Many American traders thought the money spent on British opium could be better spent on American products. Further, missionaries in China decried what opium was doing to the Chinese people. All of these factors contributed to the passage of legislation aimed at controlling narcotics at home. In 1914, the Harrison Narcotics Act was passed. By 1918, the United States became a signatory to an international agreement aimed at solving the opium problems being created in the Far East.

The Harrison Narcotics Act was originally intended as a revenue act to control the marketing of drugs. But given the climate in which it was passed, its provisions soon became subject to vigorous law enforcement efforts to eliminate users and suppliers of narcotics. Since the latter were largely physicians, many were arrested when the law was first implemented, even though the law provided that they could supply opiates in the course of professional practices. Dissension within the medical profession concerning this issue prevented medical societies from exerting professional control over the problem and its definition. Law enforcement captured the policy initiative. Law enforcement interests reasoned that addiction was not a disease, addicts were not therefore patients, and thus physicians supplying them with drugs were not doing so in the course of professional practice.

The image of the opiate addict, for example, the heroin user, is one of poor physical health, living in terribly squalid conditions, preying on society by criminal acts to support a vicious habit. While the image may contain some truth, the mistake is to attribute such conditions exclusively to the effect of the drugs. Those conditions may result primarily from the policy of drug control, not from the drugs themselves.[30] The history of drugs in the early nineteenth century shows that while addicts were objects of concern, they did not constitute a social menace. The addict's changed image was the direct result of a policy to control them. By driving up prices, forcing addicts to deal with criminal elements, creating an adulterated, uncertain supply, and subjecting the addict to arrest and incarceration, a "normal way of life" for the drug addict, possible in the nineteenth century, is no longer possible in the twentieth. As a result, both the health of the addict and the health of society have been endangered. As is also clear from the periodic attempts to tighten drug laws and make them more severe, such a policy has been ineffective in stemming drug use. The current move towards encouraging on-the-job drug testing also illustrates the point. The concern with drugs being everywhere may be legitimate. At the same time, it underscores the ineffectiveness of the punitive policies begun in the second decade of this century to control their use. There is also an irony in the move towards universal drug testing. If drug use is so debilitative, its effects should be obvious. Why, then, the need for sophisticated chemical tests to determine if a person is a user? Drug policy may be just as debilitative as the drugs it tries to control.

The Emergence of Other Criminal Justice Professions

The ideology of professionalism affected not only laws and law enforcement, but also a number of new occupations that were ready to "treat" the problems of society. Thus, the ideology of professionalism was even more apparent in the emerging professions of penology, social work, and child welfare. Police agencies, after all, still had to cope with a variety of political and practical pressures. While there were early police reformers who argued the need for professionalization, politicians demurred. Thus, of all the criminal justice components, the police were perhaps the least imbued with the new ideological spirit. As we will discover in Chapter 10, professionalism is still one of the answers posed to solving a variety of police problems.

The professional ideology that pervaded other emerging criminal justice specialities is illustrated by the Declaration of Principles issued in 1870 from the National Congress on Penitentiary and Reformatory Discipline. The Declaration proclaimed, "the supreme aim of prison discipline is the reformation of criminals, not the infliction of vindictive suffering."[31] The Principles proposed a new scientific approach in dealing with those confined to prison. The hallmark of this approach was to be individualized treatment. Sentence should therefore be indeterminate, depending on the prisoner's progress rather than his crime. The prisoner should be able to earn his way back to freedom, and so a mark system was introduced whereby a prisoner was given so many marks for good behavior. When a sufficient number was obtained, the prisoner could be released. Since not all prisoners were to be treated the same, a system of scientific classification should be employed and treatment tailored to the diagnostic category into which the prisoner was placed. Academic and vocational education was to be provided, mild discipline rather than force was to be employed, and a large dosage of religious instruction and positive reinforcement were to be given. Individualized treatment and indeterminate sentences gave a great deal of discretion to the prison authorities. They were now, however, not simply or primarily keepers. They were penologists, scientific experts who could cure prisoners of their crime-prone behavior. Penologists were trained in social work, psychology, sociology, and psychiatry to cure, not to punish. Of course, the practice was often different than the rhetoric would suggest.

While discretion, scientific classification, and reliance on the knowledge of experts were clear manifestations of a professional ideology, the humanitarian aspects of a treatment approach were often overshadowed by a control orientation on the part of prison administrators. This can be illustrated by noting how the "new" penology was in fact implemented at the nation's first reformatory for young male adults, the Elmira Reformatory, at Elmira, New York.

Elmira was opened in 1876, and was hailed as a monument to the new penology. Zebulon R. Brockway was its first superintendent, and since he was largely responsible for crafting the "Declaration of Principles," his superintendency provided an opportunity to put into practice what the document preached. Brockway has traditionally been thought of as one of the greatest prison reformers America has produced. This reputation has been repeated in numerous textbooks on crime and correction. Unfortunately, as recent research by Alexander W. Pisciotta shows, the reputation was not deserved.[32] Brockway in fact used extremely severe corporal punishment in controlling his charges, including burning with a red-hot poker, beating with a paddle, a rubber hose, or fists, and chaining inmates to the wall. Further, the mark system was used arbitrarily. Thus, control again subverted what was to be an essentially therapeutic device. Nevertheless, therapy and the rhetoric of sciences were used to justify even the beatings endured by inmates. Such medical-scientific justification is captured in this quote from Brockway:

> . . . physical shock served to convince [the inmate] that a radical change in his personal behavior was indispensable *and it perhaps made possible such a change by the incident molecular commotion in changing the channels for the flow of nervous energy.*[33] (emphasis added)

The rhetoric of science could now justify the practice of physical abuse carried over from an earlier period of correctional history. Such justifications were not, however, always successful. A New York State Board of Charities investigation found in 1894:

> The charges and allegations against the General Superintendent Z. R. Brockway of cruel, brutal, excessive, and unusual punishment of inmates are proven and most amply sustained by the evidence.[34]

Despite the gap between rhetoric and reality, the professional ideology as manifested in the "new penology" became the dominant reform orientation within criminal justice, and guided the thinking in the field until the 1970s. To understand why this ideology was able to become predominant, it is important to emphasize the level of control it provided practitioners over their work. The expert was in the best position to make decisions regarding those accused of crime or adjudicated criminals. The ideology thus held that discretion was absolutely necessary if the professional was to be able to discharge his responsibilities to the client and the community. Such a powerful justification for discretionary activity answered a very real problem in the criminal justice system, while at the same time it enhanced the occupational position of some criminal justice workers.

By 1870, the relatively recent innovation of the penitentiary was breaking down. Because of fixed sentences, prisons were extremely overcrowded. Moreover, wardens had few means at their disposal to control inmates, since they could not reduce their time based on good behavior. One of the few things wardens could do, however, was to maintain order by the use of physical punishment. As overcrowding increased, order deteriorated, so that reliance on physical punishment grew to truly staggering proportions. Prisoners were hung from their thumbs, beaten, and subjected to the "water crib," a contraption that submerged prisoners in water until they were nearly drowned. David J. Rothman maintains that the period 1870–1900 was probably the most brutal in the history of American prisons.[35] The punishments were often justified as the only way one could control the dangerous Irish (and later on the dangerous Italians and Slavs). But the reform spirit of Beccaria and Bentham and the emerging ideology of professional and scientific treatment were in the air. The punishments were beginning to be viewed as too harsh, "even for the Irish."[36] If wardens had more discretion in the release of prisoners, such barbarity would not be necessary, and new forms of treatment could be employed. Thus, professional discretion was the solution to the very practical problem of overcrowding. At the same time, the humanitarian rhetoric provided reformers with a rationale for eliminating, at least in theory, the brutal excesses of some prison administrations. Discretion also worked its way into the courthouse, so that by 1920 plea bargaining had become a well-entrenched practice for dealing with the overcrowded dockets. The new ideology, by providing a rationale for giving workers more control over their work, was rapidly accepted by criminal justice practitioners. The fact that its treatment principles were not always adhered to or that they were often subverted to the older ethics of control was less important than the leverage it gave a variety of practitioners to claim professional standing and to carry out their activity relatively free from outside interference.

The fact that this ideology held sway for nearly 100 years is a tribute to its appeal for resolving problems of *criminal justice professionals*. That it did less than promised for those caught up in the system did not become an issue until the early 1970s. The contradictions that were part of the professional ideology of corrections and criminal justice were finally brought to light in part because of a general distrust of experts that was beginning to surface in society generally.[37] Government officials, teachers, physicians, social workers, and a wide variety of other assorted experts all came in for their share of criticism as Vietnam, Watergate, and a host of lesser scandals captured the front pages of American newspapers. Ironically, the attack on the liberal, prison reform tradition came first from the left.

The Demise of the Progressive Tradition and the Development of the Justice Model

As David J. Rothman notes, the only coherent policy statements regarding corrections and criminal justice came from the progressive tradition described above.[38] This is what was taught in schools of social work and law, and in departments of sociology and criminology. But, during the 1960s and 1970s, the products of this education were the first to point the finger at the inequalities created by giving correctional professionals too much discretion.

People were serving relatively long sentences, without any clear idea of when they would be getting out. Sentence disparity was widespread. Thus, liberals began the campaign to reduce discretionary power within the system, again a move paralleled in society generally by the distrust of experts.

Fear of rising crime provided conservatives with a rallying point against indeterminacy, and they flayed against the existing system because its rhetoric gave the impression of being soft on crime. The end result was a convergence of both liberal and conservative opinion into a new model of corrections—the justice model.

The justice model, as articulated in the 1976 book, *Doing Justice: The Choice of Punishments* by Andrew Von Hirsch, argues that the goal of sentencing should be punishment. Punishment in turn should be based on the harm done by the offense and the culpability of the offender. The culpability factor would in part be based on the defendant's past record.[39] While these recommendations sound very conservative, the aim of most academic researchers in criticizing indeterminacy and suggesting in its place presumptive sentences was to bring more fairness into what was increasingly viewed as an arbitrary system. Thus, while the purpose of the sentence was presumed to be punishment, prison was thought to be inappropriate for all but the most serious offenses. Alternatives such as fines, periodic imprisonment, and community service were suggested as ways of increasing the range of punishments available. The rhetoric was harsh, but the programming was an attempt to move away from severe sentences.

The components of the justice model go back to the utilitarian principles of Beccaria and Bentham. By making punishment swifter and surer, advocates of this model believed that potential offenders could more accurately calculate the costs and benefits of their illegal activity. This reincarnation of utilitarianism is not, however, overlaid by the ethic of professionalism. As noted, while the treatment model had its critics, its professional ideology enhanced the positions of criminal justice decision makers. Thus, the model was rapidly adopted. Because the justice model, on the other hand, seeks to abolish the discretion of prosecutors, judges, prison administrators, and parole boards, it is unlikely that these entrenched interests will easily give up their power.[40] Each group may want the other groups' discretion limited, while they maintain their own. This conflict among groups of practitioners may prevent the justice model from enjoying the ideological hegemony of its predecessor. The result to date has been a kind of institutional schizophrenia. Demands for longer sentences exist simultaneously with concerns about overcrowding. Demands to end plea bargaining coexist with the desire to speed up case processing. This ideological vacuum has resurrected issues originally confronted in the mid-1800s.

Conclusions

A historical review of crime and crime control suggests that there were three dominant ideological periods. The first, and by far the longest, was the religious period. Within the framework of a religious ideology, crime is viewed as a sin and the individual is seen as a person in need of redemption. Throughout most of its history, religious ideology put a strong emphasis on corporal punishment as a programmatic response to the problem of deviance. The devil was literally beaten out of people. Punishment was severe because it was both a means of salvation and a means for restoring moral order. While a religious ideology provided a unified framework for defining what acts should be considered a crime and what policies should be adopted for coping with them, it did generate its own set of contradictions. After all, Christian charity was as much a religious cornerstone as was justice and punishment. In part, the conflict was handled by dividing institutional responsibilities. Punishment was carried out by the state, not by religious authority. During the Middle Ages, for example, clerics were forbidden to be state executioners. Moreover, given the religious belief in an afterlife, death was not considered in the same light as within a purely secular framework. Death was only a door through which one passed into eternity. If an individual was sorry for what he or she had done, then in a way death was a welcome relief from the trials and tribulations of this life. Within this kind of ideological belief system, death was not necessarily a cruel punishment, even for what might be considered relatively minor crimes.

The second ideological period in the history of crime control was the period of utilitarianism. The human being was thought to be rational and deserving of rational treatment. This period brought about a reform of criminal law, the creation of the first modern police force, and a movement away from corporal and capital punishment to the use of confinement. Thus, the utilitarians helped encourage the founding of the modern penitentiary system. As the name "penitentiary" suggests, ideologies do not simply cease to exist—instead old ideologies influence new ideologies, so that new programs actually reflect both old and new belief systems. Early penitentiaries represented the utilitarian concern with more humane forms of punishment while at the same time institutionalizing the religious view that crime was a sin. Penitentiaries were at first viewed as places to do penance. As we will see, the early penitentiaries were very much modeled on monasteries, with solitude and reflection emphasized. Quakers were very much involved in the establishment of prisons, and this also added to the emphasis early prisons placed on silence and self-reflection.

Elements of utilitarianism eventually became incorporated within the scientific approach to crime and criminology. The two together created the ideology of professionalism which emphasized discretion and treatment. Indeterminate sentences and a social science rhetoric were hallmarks of this approach. And although the practice often fell short of the goal, this approach legitimated a humanitarian view of criminals. They were not sinners but people in need of treatment.

At the present time, criminal justice ideology is in the state of flux. Rather than there being a single, well-thought-out and integrated program for change, there seems to be instead a vaguely liberal and a vaguely conservative approach to the crime problem. According to Samuel Walker, the liberal crime control agenda rests on viewing the world as a large classroom.[41] Thus, what an offender needs is instruction on how to behave correctly. Rehabilitation forms the key solutions for liberals. But given their disillusionment with experts, the specific programs that such an approach would call for remain vague. Further, the rehabilitation approach is not now tied to the emergence of a new class of practitioners, and so liberal rhetoric surfaces in debates rather than in programs of actions aimed at simultaneously enhancing the fortunes of a particular group while solving a problem.

According to Walker, conservatives view the world as a large family. The family is patriarchal, and thus discipline by authority is highly valued. Crime results from a lack of appropriate discipline, and therefore sufficient punishment for wrongdoing will solve the crime problem. Again, however, this conservative world view is not able to maintain consistency in the face of other conservative principles such as economic and fiscal restraint on the part of government. While people demand longer sentences, there is not the willingness to spend tax money to pay for more prison construction. So again a conservative world view is largely articulated at the level of debate rather than at the level of program application. And since it too is not tied to the fortunes of an identifiable group in the society, it has not yet become articulated into a clearly identifiable framework for action. The lack of clear ideological commitment, and its replacement with shifting interest group politics, may in fact be responsible for the apparent chaos in current criminal justice policy.

Clearly, however, ideologies and value positions influence specific policies. Such ideologies and value positions are themselves influenced by historical circumstances. The question of the historical influence on policy innovation is a complex one. On a macro level, ideologies, policies, and fluctuations in crime and deviance are related to larger historical movements. At the same time, specific policies may have hastened the effects of longer-term historical trends. The creation of the Metropolitan Police in London and its imitation to some degree in other European urban centers and in the United States may have contributed to the decrease in crime and public disorder, things that would have declined in any event but perhaps have taken longer to do so.

In terms of specific issues, however, policies clearly do have effects. Unfortunately, as this chapter has shown, they are often not the effects intended by those proposing the policy. This is because policies, caught in webs of values and ideologies, tend to oversimplify extremely complex problems. But as noted in Chapter 1, both scientists and policy makers simplify problems in order to act toward them. Policy makers will use the rhetoric of a prevailing ideology or appeal to a particular set of values in simplifying the problems of crime. These, rather than the theories of science, form the immediate problems and solutions toward which a policy maker directs effort and energy. Yet, as noted, science itself has ideological overtones. Thus, viewing crime through a so-called scientific lens can also distort the picture. Solutions proposed, whether purely ideological or a mixture of ideology and science, only address part of a problem, and address it imperfectly at best. The ideological influences on scientific, criminological theory will be explored in Chapters 6 and 7, together with the consequences of applying various theories to particular policy problems.

SUMMARY

What Was Said

- Solutions to problems result from the values and ideologies of those who propose them.
- Our own era is not the most crime-prone, the most disorderly, nor the most dangerous.
- Utilitarianism was a major ideological component in the founding of the modern police.
- The American police were founded in a kind of ideological vacuum, and thus early law enforcement efforts were directed at diverse problems with diverse groups trying to control police activity.
- The Progressive Movement and the ideology of professionalism affected both the American police and a number of emerging criminal justice occupations.
- The first war on drugs was fought at the beginning of the twentieth century as the United States, in response to a variety of national and international influences, began to move from a medical to a law enforcement strategy for controlling opiate addiction.
- One of the consequences of this change was to make it increasingly difficult for addicts to live a "normal life," as they had throughout the previous century.
- The rhetoric of the Progressive Movement was often more humane than its practice, particularly in criminal justice.
- During the 1960s and 1970s both liberal and conservative disillusionment with the results of discretionary activity on the part of justice professionals led to the development of the justice model of corrections.

What Was Not Said

- Drug abuse is not a problem.
- Science can or should replace the ideological and value base of policy interventions.
- The modern police should not strive for professional standing.

NOTES

1. For an excellent discussion of ideology, see Philo C. Wasburn, *Political Sociology: Approaches, Concepts, Hypotheses*, (Englewood Cliffs, NJ: Prentice-Hall, 1982), pp. 234–67. This chapter forms the basis for my discussion of ideology.

2. Ibid.

3. Ted Robert Gurr, "Development and Decay: Their Impact on Public Order in Western History," in *History and Crime: Implications for Criminal Justice Policy*, James A. Inciardi and Charles Faupel, eds. (Beverly Hills, CA: Sage Publications, Inc., 1980), p. 43.

4. Kai T. Erikson, *Wayward Puritans*, (New York: John Wiley and Sons, Inc., 1966).

5. Ibid., p. 149.

6. Gurr, "Development and Decay," p. 34.

7. Roger Lane, "Urban Homicide in the Nineteenth Century: Some Lessons for the Twentieth," in Inciardi and Faupel, *History and Crime*, p. 94.

8. Edward M. Brecher and the Editors of *Consumer Reports, Licit and Illicit Drugs*, (Boston: Little, Brown and Company, 1972), p. 3.

9. Ibid., p. 8.

10. David Musto quoted in "As American as Apple Pie," *Yale Alumni Magazine* (January 1972), 16.

11. Ibid., p. 17.

12. Brecher et al. *Licit and Illicit Drugs*, pp. 17–18.

13. Ibid.

14. Eric H. Monkkonen, "The Organized Response to Crime in Nineteenth and Twentieth Century America," *Journal of Interdisciplinary History*, XIV: (Summer 1983), 119.

15. Mark H. Haller, "Illegal Enterprise: Historical Perspectives and Public Policy," in Inciardi and Faupel, *History and Crime*, p. 80.

16. Monkkonen, "Organized Response to Crime," p. 117.

17. T. A. Critchley, "The New Police in London, 1750–1830," in *Police in America*, Jerome H. Skolnick and Thomas C. Gray, eds. (Boston: Little, Brown and Company, Inc., 1975), p. 12.

18. Ibid., p. 11.

19. Elio Monachesi, "Cesare Beccaria" in Hermann Mannheim, *Pioneers in Criminology*, 2nd ed. (Montclair, NJ: Patterson Smith, 1972), p. 47.

20. Skolnick and Gray, *Police in America*, p. 3.

21. James F. Richardson, "The Early Years of the New York Police Department," in Skolnick and Gray, *Police in America*, p. 17.

22. Ibid.

23. Monkkonen, "Organized Response to Crime," pp. 127–28.

24. Gail Miller, *It's A Living: Work in Modern Society*, (New York: St. Martin's Press, 1981), p. 101.

25. Monkkonen, "Organized Response to Crime," pp. 126–27.

26. Ibid., p. 124.

27. Gurr, "Development and Decay," p. 46.

28. Ibid.

29. Brecher et al., *Licit and Illicit Drugs*, pp. 48–49.

30. Ibid., p. 33.

31. Alexander W. Pisciotta, "Scientific Reform: The 'New Penology' at Elmira, 1876–1900," *Crime and Delinquency*, 29, No. 4 (October 1983), pp 613–29.

32. Ibid., pp. 614–15.

33. Zebulon R. Brockway, *Fifty Years of Prison Service: An Autobiography*, (Montclair, NJ: Patterson Smith, 1969).

34. New York State Board of Charities, *Report and Recommendation in the Matter of the New York State Reformatory at Elmira* (C. G. Burgoyne, Walker, 1894) pp. 41–42. Quoted in Pisciotta, "Scientific Reform," p. 620.

35. David J. Rothman, "Sentencing Reforms in Historical Perspective," *Crime and Delinquency* (October 1983), pp. 631–49.

36. Ibid., p. 637.

37. Ibid., p. 642.

38. Ibid.

39. Andrew Von Hirsch, *Doing Justice: The Choice of Punishments*, (New York: Hill and Wang, a division of Farrar, Straus, and Giroux, 1976).

40. Paul F. Cromwell, Jr. et al. *Probation and Parole in The Criminal Justice System*, 2nd ed. (St. Paul, MN: West Publishing Co., 1985), pp. 182–83.

41. Samuel Walker, *Sense and Nonsense about Crime* (Monterey, CA: Brooks/Cole Publishing Company, a division of Wadsworth, Inc., 1985), p. 10.

VI

Ideology and Science

Crime as a Product of Individual Predilection

At the end of this chapter, the student will be able to:

A. Describe the general ideological climate in which modern criminological theories developed.
B. Describe how these theories both influenced and were influenced by ideological consideration.
C. Describe the biological, psychiatric, and psychological approaches to explaining crime and list the leading proponents of each approach.
D. Discuss both the scientific and policy limitations of individualistic theories.

ISSUE BACKGROUND

Social scientists, including criminologists, face a rather disheartening situation. They have always wanted to be policy relevant. That is, they have continually sought to have their work used by those in authority to better the state of society. Beccaria, Bentham, and the early penologists were primarily reformers who sought to apply their knowledge and insight to the practical problems of the day.[1] Beccaria, for example, was particularly interested in the reform of criminal law. He believed that legal reforms based on the principles of utilitarianism would ultimately reduce the amount of crime in society. This view formed what has been termed the classical school of criminology. Proponents of the classical school used the insights of philosophy and logic to effect changes in criminal law and jurisprudence. As noted in the last chapter, this approach also contained a theory of human behavior. It stressed humankind's rational nature and a person's ability to weigh the consequences of action.[2]

As criminology increasingly moved from philosophical to scientific approaches of understanding, criminologists' desire to be relevant did not diminish. Albion Small, who chaired the first sociology department in the United States at the University of Chicago, insisted that knowledge gained through the scientific investigation of society should be used to systematically alter social arrangements for the betterment of humankind.[3] But, as with a continually rejected suitor, the desire for marriage with those who make political decisions has resulted mainly in frustration and self-doubt. While there have been moments of bliss, in general these have been outweighed by the difficulties involved in the relationship. Critiquing both their own work and that of other sociologists in terms of its policy relevance, Scott and Shore remark that the research resulted in

> ... the production of a body of findings which, at best, helped to illuminate theoretical questions of interest to academic sociologists, but which appeared to carry policy implications that are nonexistent, trivial, ambiguous, indiscernible or impossibly utopian.[4]

A review of most textbooks in criminology will quickly reveal why suitors from this particular discipline are often rejected by those in positions of power. The typical textbook will review the major theories of crime causation. After each theory is reviewed, a concluding comment will be made as to the deficiencies of the theory for explaining crime. Thus, a dozen or more theories will be presented, analyzed, and then seemingly discarded as inadequate for explaining crime. The policy maker will search in vain for a clear statement of crime causation that (a) every criminologist agrees upon and/or (b) will be useful for structuring a specific program of action.

This traditional textbook approach should not be surprising. If criminology is to successfully claim scientific status, its theoretical suppositions must be testable. This means that any particular statement is potentially false. Science tests propositions by trying to show that they are false. Thus, science tends to be self-critical. The job of the scientist is to be suspicious of statements made by colleagues or oneself hypothesizing causal relationships. As the last chapter noted, it is this critical stance and the emphasis on empirically falsifying that separates science from ideology. But, as discussed in Chapter 1, the procedures of science are not conducive to the solving of policy problems. Policy actors must act and not wait for scientifically adequate answers. What is surprising is that social scientists and policy makers have, at various times, each thought that a trouble-free union was possible. Neither should have expected a marriage made in heaven. Policy makers were the first to realize this. Social scientists have only recently, however, begun to realize that perhaps they are not the perfect mates for those who manage society. Thus, two key questions present themselves. First, how did social science practitioners come to believe that they could provide the information necessary to cure social ills? Second, while a perfect union may not be possible, what kinds of contributions can social science (specifically criminology) make to the policy process? The answer to the first question requires understanding the ideological climate in which modern-day criminological theories were developed. The second question is more complex and addresses theoretical, political, philosophical, and organizational issues. A substantive understanding of the standard criminological theories together with a critique of their explanatory adequacy is necessary.

Ideology and the Growth of Scientific Criminology

The last chapter described the development of a professional ideology among social scientists, social workers, and penal reformers. A major tenet of this ideology was the belief that social scientists and those trained in their discipline could cure social ills. Such a belief, however, required a fundamental alteration in understanding the nature of knowledge. After all, if reformers were going to change the world, they had to first believe that the world is changeable through human intervention. This was a distinctly minority view among intellectuals until the nineteenth century. The dominant intellectual tradition held that knowledge was a static entity, separate from the world of action. It was to be discovered and passed on rather than created and applied for purposes of social change.[5] Two trends, one technological, the other political, led to the eventual demise of this point of view.

Industrialization was completing the breakup of the last vestiges of feudal society. Further, new technology required a complex division of labor. People now gained rather than inherited their status. Nationalism, spurred in part by the Protestant Reformation, had by this time created a Europe of relatively smaller, independently governed units. This led to widespread acceptance of the notion that society exists because people agree to certain standards so that all can live in harmony. The reforms of Beccaria and Bentham, discussed in the last chapter, are a product of this period. Thus, both rapidly advancing technology and new political arrangements increased people's sense of control over their world.

While Beccaria and Bentham can be classified as philosophers, their concern with practical affairs provided a guidepost for the scientific criminology which replaced the classical school. Yet, the belief that individuals could bring about major changes in the social order had to compete with the desire for order and stability. The revolutions, industrial, political, and social, of the eighteenth century and the vast social changes they wrought spurred people to turn back once again and seek refuge in notions of immutable laws and natural order.

In criminology, as with other emerging sciences of the period, early theories, many of them espoused by European intellectuals, had heavy elements of determinism in them. Lombroso, for example, often considered the founder of modern criminology, was greatly influenced by a Darwinian process of selection.[6] Thus, at least initially, the social sciences, including criminology, were not optimistic about the possibilities for large-scale social change. Policy prescriptions arising from the "new" criminology therefore tended to stress the need for control rather than change. A different social philosophy needed to emerge before social science could assume an activist, interventionist role. This philosophy was to emerge in the fertile, nontraditional, often anti-European soil of the United States.

Scott and Shore argue that by the close of the nineteenth century, the United States had lost its feelings of cohesiveness and local control of government.[7] Urbanism, industrialization, and immigration had permanently altered the small-town quality of American life. The centers of population moved from the countryside to the vast, sprawling cities where ward bosses rather than civic-minded townsfolk ran local government. Those displaced by the changes, particularly white, middle-class, Yankee Protestants, sought ways to reassert their values and find their place in this new world. The answer to the seeming chaos appeared to be rational planning.[8]

The rational planning movement in the United States was based on the social philosophy espoused by intellectuals such as John Dewey, Thorsten Veblen, William James, and Oliver Wendell Holmes. These thinkers viewed the world in evolutionary terms. But unlike the evolutionary schemes found in traditional European social thought, these social philosophers made humankind central to the process of evolutionary change. To quote Scott and Shore:

> By *viewing the future as an extension of a continuing process, it led the new social philosophers to conceive of the idea of manipulating the present to alter the future*, an idea which, of course, is prerequisite to conceiving the possibility of social planning itself.[9]

Thus, human beings were not only a product of evolution; they could become the prime architects of their own evolutionary development.

This intellectual shift in understanding combined with the discontent of many middle-class, educated, professional people who needed to reassert some claim to power created the impetus for the planning movement in the United States. Planning in turn required a social science that was less deterministic and oriented far more toward problem solution rather than simply control. Thus, in a very real sense, the planning movement and its ideology helped create a unique American social science. This movement was very much a part of the progressive political agenda discussed in the last chapter. According to Scott and Shore, three ideas of progressivism were especially significant for shaping the assumption of rational, scientific planning and, in turn, the social science it was to utilize. First, there was a belief that every problem could be overcome with proper knowledge and action. Second, social evils could only be eradicated if people got involved. The problems would not solve themselves. Finally, expert, scientific knowledge was needed if social problems were to be solved.[10] The sociologist and other such experts would provide the information necessary to make the world a better place. In this day and age, it may be difficult to appreciate the expectations placed on social science and its practitioners. But faith in rational, scientific progress abounded. Lester Frank Ward, a prominent sociologist of the period, described state legislatures as "laboratories of philosophical research into the laws of society and of human nature."[11] Further, he held that: "Every true legislator must be a sociologist."[12] The philosopher-king of Plato was to be replaced by the sociologist-legislator.

It was within this ideological framework that many of the American theories of criminology developed. Unfortunately, the faith in social science's ability to solve problems led to a blind spot in sociological and criminological practice. Theories and findings were assumed relevant to the needs of policy makers. But there was very little actual understanding of how policy makers functioned and of the kinds of information needed to make policy-relevant decisions. Thus, the desire to be relevant met with increasingly less success. Yet, ideological commitments and assumptions did not change. Concerning criminology specifically, the stage was set for a grand disillusionment on the part of both scientist and legislators. This occurred in the mid-1960s through the 1970s, when vast amounts of criminological expertise was demanded to solve the "crime problem." Theories, practices, and the ideology of progressivism was found wanting. By the 1980s, a control orientation predominated in discussions of what to do about crime. In this sense, the 1980s mirrored the policy thrust of the first school of scientific criminology.

CRIMINOLOGICAL/CRIMINAL JUSTICE CONSIDERATIONS

The Beginnings of Modern Criminology: The Positivists

Intellectual advancement often seems to occur through a process of conflict. In the case of criminology, the classical school of Beccaria and Bentham was attacked by critics who argued (a) the criminal, not the crime, should be the focus of attention, (b) individuals did not have free will and thus penalties based on deterrence theory (that is, the pleasure/pain principle) were useless; and (c) science rather than philosophy was the appropriate means for determining both the true nature of the criminal enterprise and what to do about it. These three ideas formed the basis for the first school of modern, scientific criminology, the Positivist School. Its founder, as noted, is often considered to be the Italian physician, Cesare Lombroso (1835–1909).

Lombroso was very much influenced by advances in the physical sciences and was particularly impressed by Darwin and the theory of evolution. Further, his own studies on degenerative brain diseases convinced him that criminal behavior had a biological base. The criminal was for the most part born, not made. Criminals could therefore be identified by certain physical traits that set them apart from the normal population. These traits, such as a protruding jaw, asymmetrical skull, retreating forehead, and long arms, were viewed as symptoms of evolutionary failure. The characteristics were not themselves the cause of crime, but were indicative of atavism, a condition of reversion to a primitive or subhuman type of individual.

Throughout his life, Lombroso always held that organic factors were of primary importance in understanding criminal behavior.[13] He first estimated that "born" criminals accounted for 65–70% of the criminal population. Near the end of his career he had considerably lowered his estimates of "born" criminals, speculating that they accounted for a third of the criminal population.[14] Thus, he expanded his categories of criminal types beyond the "born" criminal to include those who, in varying degrees, were also influenced by the environment. There were "criminaloids," whose organic tendencies toward crime were slightly less than the born criminal. As a consequence, criminaloids were open to the influences of the environment such as the presence or absence of available opportunities to commit an illegal act. An exceptionally benign environment might therefore inhibit criminal activity among this group. The "habitual criminal" was even less organically abnormal. Criminal activity among this group was largely the consequence of poor education and training. Crime was also thought to be linked to epilepsy in certain instances. Finally, Lombroso has a residual category in which violent crimes without an apparently organic base are included. These are crimes of passion.

Lombroso has often been criticized for being excessively committed to organic, physiological/biological explanations of crime. Given his background as a physician and physical anthropologist, it is not surprising that he sought the explanation for crime in the biological realm. Nevertheless, he did expand his explanations to allow for some influences from the environment. Today, however, Lombroso's specific explanations for criminal behavior are largely discredited. His scientific method was clearly inadequate, with many of his conclusions based upon subjective descriptions rather than accurate and precise measurement. He constructed theories based on very limited samples and then attempted to generalize his findings to populations beyond those he studied. He largely ignored the earlier works of researchers who would cast serious doubt upon his biological explanations. Chief among those whose works he failed to adequately recognize were Lambert Quetelet and Andre Guerry, positivists who emphasized a statistical approach to the study of crime.[15] These researchers predated Lombroso and, using statistical procedures remarkable for the period, carefully correlated criminal occurrences with a variety of social facts external to the individual. The genesis of crime was to be found in institutional arrangements, not in biological predispositions. While Lombroso makes passing reference to these theories, he never seriously uses them to critique his own explanations.

The scientific adequacy of a theory constitutes cnly one criterion for judgment. And, as we have seen, it may not even be the most important one. A theory can also be judged in terms of its appeal and influence. Based on these factors, Lombroso was one of the most influential criminologists of the last two centuries. He decisively moved the study of crime from the classical schools' concern with the nature of law to instead focus on the nature of the criminal. He firmly anchored criminology to the assumptions, procedures, and traditions of scientific empiricism. Speculation about the nature of crime was replaced by an emphasis on the gathering of facts through careful observation and experimentation. Although Lombroso fell short of the ideal he set, he did in fact set it and tried his best to live up to it. Finally, he began a specific tradition of biological explanations for crime, a tradition that has stimulated much research and controversy and still remains very much a part of the criminological scene today. In fact, as we will see, most members of the Positivist School continued to anchor their explanations of crime in biology, even those who criticized Lombroso's specific formulations. The chief exceptions are Quetelet and Guerry, who predated Lombroso.

Among the early researchers to expand on Lombroso's studies were two other Italians, Raffaele Garofalo (1852–1934) and Enrico Ferri (1856–1929). Together with Lombroso, they constitute the three leading proponents of the Italian School, a subdivision of the Positivist School. Garofalo's contribution to the study of crime was his insistence that crime cannot simply be defined in legal terms. Laws and historical circumstances change, while the basic subject matter of the criminologist should remain constant. This subject matter consists of the study of "natural crime," acts which violate innate sentiments of piety and/or innate sentiments of probity. Acts of the former variety involve attacks against human life, while the latter acts involve offenses against property. Such acts are caused by an organic deficiency in the moral sensibilities of the criminal. Organic deficiencies vary, however, among criminals, and thus according to Garofalo a classification of criminal types needs to be developed. This he proceeds to do. Ferri, too, developed a classification of criminal types, and, in fact, it was he who coined the term "born criminal" which he suggested to Lombroso. These various classification schemes are not important for their scientific contribution but for the research they stimulated and, as we shall see, for their policy significance.[16]

Charles Goring (1870–1919) attempted to refute the work of Lombroso and his followers. As we have seen, Goring's book, *The English Convict*, published in 1913, claimed that low intelligence rather than atavism caused criminal behavior. As noted in Chapter 1, Goring's argument that weak-mindedness caused crime was hampered by his research method. The sample upon which he based his conclusions was biased since he only studied incarcerated criminals, that is, those who had been caught and therefore were presumably less intelligent than those who were not caught. Moreover, Goring's procedure for measuring intelligence was sloppy. Rather than using standardized intelligence scales available at the time, he used his own impressions as to whether the criminal was "intelligent," "slightly intelligent," "mentally weak," or "imbecilic."[17] Finally, while Goring disputed Lombroso's explanation of crime as being due to a throwback in evolution which produced easily recognizable criminal stigmata, he did not refute the role of biological factors in crime causation. Both mental and physical deficiencies played a role in Goring's explanation of crime. These deficiencies were largely the result of biological processes. While these biological conditions interacted with certain external environmental factors such as social class, social conditions merely provided greater or fewer opportunities for committing criminal acts. They were not causative in the primary sense.

In the United States, biological explanations received a major boost from the work of Earnest A. Hooten (1887–1954), a Harvard physical anthropologist. Although largely discredited today, he claimed that crime could be traced directly to biological inferiority. His work, published in 1939, raised a storm of protest and controversy, particularly with the suggestion that sterilization represented the most effective form of crime control.[18]

Explanations of crime that link body type, temperament, and illegal behavior are also biologically based. Most famous among these theories is that developed by William H. Sheldon (1899–1977). Sheldon, building upon the work of Ernst Kretschmer who, in the 1920s, argued that physical structure led to certain characteristics of temperament, developed a classification of body types and their respective personality characteristics. The endomorph has a round, soft body and tends toward obesity. In temperament, the endomorph is an extrovert, jolly, comfortable, and relaxed. This type of temperament was termed "viscerotonic" by Sheldon. The ectomorph is the opposite of the endomorph. A lean, fragile, thin body and a tendency toward nervousness and introversion identify the ectomorph. This nervous, introverted temperament was described as "cerebrotonic." The mesomorph is the third body type identified by Sheldon, and this body is muscular with tendencies toward aggression.[19] The assertive personality is classified as "somatotonic." It is this last body type and temperament that is closely associated with crime and delinquency. Sheldon's work in the 1930s and 1940s was continued in the 1940s and 1950s by Sheldon and Eleanor Glueck, who systematically compared 500 persistent delinquents with 500 nondelinquents. They found that 60% of delinquents as opposed to 31% of nondelinquents were mesomorphic.[20]

All of the biological explanations for crime, including those of the 1940s and 1950s, suffer from serious methodological defects. Thus, the case for a biological explanation of crime remains unproven. But again, weak science does not mean weak influence. Lombroso's quest for biological determinants of crime continues today. In the 1970s, for example, certain geneticists attempted to link criminal behavior to chromosomal makeup. A normal male cell contains an X chromosome and a Y chromosome. A normal female cell contains two X chromosomes. The presence of an extra male chromosome has been noted in a small percentage of the population. This XYY pattern seems more prevalent among those confined to institutions (mental hospitals or prisons) than among a "normal" population. Violent crime has therefore been linked to this biological abnormality. Unfortunately, as with most biological theories, the presence of an abnormality such as an extra chromosome is so rare that very little crime can be explained by the factor designated. Moreover, the majority of those with a particular characteristic, mesomorphic body build, for example, never become criminals. Finally, relatively few of those designated as criminals will have the specific characteristic mentioned such as an extra Y chromosome or a pure body type and temperament. But the 1980s has not been immune from these types of explanations. For example, James Q. Wilson and Richard J. Hernstein are once again assessing the influences of biological and physical factors on tendencies to be involved in crime.[21]

Psychological and Psychiatric Theories

Criminological theory can be judged according to three criteria: scientific adequacy, popularity, and policy influence. Most criminological textbooks, naturally enough, place the most emphasis on the first criterion. Unfortunately, at least in terms of the actual history of the development of criminology, this may be the least important aspect of a theory's impact. Biological determinist theories have not proved adequate in a scientific sense. Yet, in terms of initial popularity and policy influence, at least in Europe, they enjoyed considerable success. The lack of relationship between scientific adequacy and the other criteria is also illustrated by the history of the many psychological and psychiatric theories of crime.

Charles Goring can be viewed as a kind of bridge between the heavily biologically deterministic views of the Positivist School and the less biologically deterministic approach of certain psychological and psychiatric explanations. It has already been noted that, in the United States at least, the latter theories have been far more popular. Their popularity and influence, however, often seem to be the inverse of their proven scientific validity.

Goring, while still anchoring his theory in biological determinism, introduced a notion that potentially allowed for the greater operation of environmental factors on behavior and consequently for somewhat greater ameliorative activity. The first formulations of the linkage between mental states and crime were simple extensions of Lombroso's views. Imbeciles and idiots cannot resist criminal impulses, nor can they tell right from wrong. In the United States, however, these deterministic overtones were lessened with the popularity of IQ testing. The concept of IQ provided both a predictive tool and the hope of corrective and preventive measures.

In an excellent review of research on the relationship between intelligence and delinquency, Hirschi and Hindelang describe the short-lived popularity of this linkage and why its day in the sun was so brief.[22] What lessened its subsequent influence was the overenthusiastic reception it received accompanied by certain exaggerated claims of its applicability. During the early 1900s, initial estimates of the number of feebleminded people in prisons in the United States were placed at between 25 and 50%. Such feeblemindedness was estimated to be present in less than 1% of the general population. Thus, the correlation between low intelligence and crime was thought to be quite high. Widely inconsistent findings as to the percentages of low intelligence among various groups of criminals and delinquents and a movement toward more sociological explanations of crime spelled the death knell for the influence of theories linking IQ and crime. By the 1930s "mental testers" were being ridiculed by one of the leading sociologists of the period, Edwin Sutherland. In discussing the fluctuations in the numbers of feebleminded among criminals and delinquents, Sutherland, critiquing a leading proponent of testing, Samuel Goddard, states:

> In those early days of mental testing the influence of Goddard was very great; he had asserted that the more expert the mental tester the larger the proportion of delinquents he would find to be feebleminded. Many of the testers attempted to demonstrate their superiority in that matter. Consequently, . . . psychometric tests of delinquents throw more light upon the intelligence of the mental testers than upon the intelligence of delinquents.[23]

Because sociology eschewed explanations of crime that smacked of either biological determinism or individual, nonsocial differences between the law abiding and the law violating, the link between intelligence and IQ failed to receive much positive attention in most major criminological texts through the 1970s.[24] But there is an irony here. As we shall see, and as Hirschi and Hindelang amply demonstrate, many major sociological theories contain at least an implicit link between IQ and delinquent behavior. Moreover, their review of research in the area seems to clearly establish such a link. But, in fact, it has been the less scientifically defensible propositions of psychiatry and psychology that have been more popular and more policy relevant within the field of criminology.

Psychiatric theories attribute crime to neuroses or psychoses. Although Sigmund Freud (1856–1939) is considered the originator of psychiatric crime-causation theories, the idea of a sick mind causing crime is quite old. Cavemen, for example, scraped a hole in a miscreant's skull to allow evil causing demons to escape. Freud was less drastic in his approach, relying mostly on the exploration of the subconscious through long conversations with patients. This is known as psychoanalysis. The psychoanalytic approach to explaining criminal behavior assumes that such behavior is purposive. The purpose is to relieve subconscious tensions or guilt generated in the psyche. Specific applications of this line of reasoning to crime causation have grown out of Freud's general theory of personality.

Freud asserts that personality is primarily a product of biological processes. The personality consists of three elements, the *id*, the *ego*, and the *superego*. The id constitutes a seething cauldron of biological drives and needs. To satisfy the biological drives of the id, the ego develops to gain necessary satisfaction of these impulses from the environment. The ego operates on a reality principle, managing the specific biological drives of the id so that as much satisfaction as possible can be gained in the face of real world constraints. Freud's overall view of civilization is pessimistic. Civilization necessarily constrains and distorts the natural drives of the id. Thus, individuals always live more or less unfulfilled lives, never being able to fully satisfy their deepest longings. The tensions created are manifest in a variety of ways, with the drives being channeled into either appropriate or inappropriate forms. The person who devotes him or herself to work, for example, may achieve a great deal, but such devotion can be a substitute for basic biological drives such as sexual release. The channels for releasing this biological drive are often severely proscribed by the culture, thus devotion to work becomes an imperfect substitute. Because it is imperfect, further tension can be generated which leads to further devotion to work, which ultimately can become pathological, much like the workaholic syndrome of popular literature. Of course being a workaholic is preferable to being a sexual pervert. But this distinction in fact illustrates one of the difficulties with psychoanalytic theories. The mechanism by which one person comes to relieve tensions constructively and another destructively is not very clear. The concept of superego illustrates the problem.

Superego is the last component of personality to develop. It develops in male children through what Freud termed the resolving of the Oedipal complex. At around the age of five, the male child wishes to possess the mother sexually. Postulating the existence of this drive in a child is a logical extension of Freud's theory of childhood development. After all, in most cultures the mother is the primary nurturer of the child, meeting his basic needs of food, physical stimulation, and emotional comfort from the time of birth. Thus, when the child reaches the beginning stage of sexual development, it is logical to assume that the mother will again be the source of comfort and pleasure. The father, however, presents an obstacle to the fulfillment of this desire. The child fears the father and the consequences of his (the child's) desire for the mother. The dilemma is solved when the child incorporates into his own personality the value system of the father. By becoming like the father, the child can possess the mother vicariously, that is, becoming her "little man." Now, the three parts of personality must attempt a balance among the various needs each seeks to have met. The manager of this system is the ego. Should any part of the personality become dominant, a pathology is manifest.

While the system contains its own inherent logic, it is not easily verifiable empirically. In fact, Freud's initial formulations were based primarily on his own dealing with patients and on self-analysis. Further, similar pathologies can result in very different behavior. An overdeveloped superego can result in repressed drives that then become the basis for substitute behavior, some of it potentially quite bizarre. If my superego does not allow me to express normal sexual drives, I may fulfill the drives in abnormal ways. I could become Jack the Ripper and kill prostitutes. Or I could put in 15 hours a day working and become rich and famous. Again, why I become one or the other is not at all clear. Finally, psychoanalytic theory pays too little attention to environmental factors in the generation of crime. Nevertheless, because it did provide a clear method of intervention, psychoanalysis, the theory has proved quite popular and has been influential in certain areas of crime control policy. We have seen in previous chapters the role of psychiatry in attempting to establish the legal meaning of insanity. We have also discussed the development of sexual psychopathic laws, requiring mandatory commitment to state mental facilities. Bizarre crimes conjure up images of a "sick mind." People who commit mass murder are hopefully very different from the rest of us. Unfortunately, the theories of psychiatry do not clearly pinpoint what those differences are or what should be done about them.

Less esoteric and biologically based, many psychological explanations of crime attempt to trace criminal behavior to interactive linkages between the self and the social environment. Delinquents and criminals are emotionally ill-equipped to deal with the stresses and strains of life. The stunting of emotional development is caused by deficiencies in family life, the school environment, or the peer culture to which an individual is exposed. In this view, general personality problems replace deep seated, subconscious factors as causes of criminal behavior.

While early studies showed a marked association between personality factors and delinquency, later research challenged such findings.[25] Poor conceptualization, research methodology, and sampling procedures have all contributed to the lack of faith in psychological explanations of crime. Sophisticated studies correcting some of the earlier research have failed to clearly separate delinquents from nondelinquents on the basis of personality characteristics.[26] Nevertheless, approaches based on these ideas have dominated the field of corrections. To quote Gibbons:

> Prison programs, probation services, guidance clinics, juvenile courts, and other treatment agencies have considered the lawbreaker as an emotionally disturbed person in need of psychotherapeutic treatment, almost to the exclusion of any other tactic.[27]

A theory does not have to be right to be either popular or policy influential.

POLICY CONSIDERATIONS:
THEORIES/ARGUMENTS/APPLICATIONS

The Policy of Social Defense

Despite their scientific inadequacy, biological explanations have had wide appeal and significant influence on the development of criminology. Surprisingly, such theories have also had a certain amount of direct policy impact, particularly in Europe.

Lombroso, to some extent, and more specifically Garofalo and Ferri were interested in the social policy implications of their research. Sometimes, however, the connection between their view of crime causation and their view of what could be done about it did not logically follow. After all, if the criminal was born and not made, it is difficult to construct a program for the prevention of wrongdoing and the rehabilitation of those involved in misdeeds. Nevertheless, Lombroso, for example, espoused programs of education, controlled work environments, indeterminate sentences, and punishments tailored to fit individual needs. In fact, his writings in this area influenced Zebulon Brockway and the program established in Elmira.[28] Thus, biological determinism was less rigorously applied in policy formulation than in its theoretical statement. The most obvious, direct link between biological determinism and a policy prescription is found in Lombroso's lukewarm endorsement of the death penalty as an aid in natural selection to eliminate extremely antisocial individuals. But even here, Lombroso did not see this penalty as appropriate for the majority of born criminal types. Garofalo, on the other hand, was far more willing to inflict the death penalty.

> In this way, the social power will effect an artificial selection similar to that which nature effects by the death of individuals inassimilable to the particular conditions of the environment in which they are born or to which they have been removed. Herein the state will be simply following the example of nature.[29]

Despite this strong endorsement of the death penalty, however, Garofalo also allowed for the rehabilitation of many types of criminals. His policy theory, and that of Lombroso and Ferri, are based upon notions of elimination and control. According to Garofalo the most efficient form of elimination is the death penalty. But since there are various degrees of criminality, there must also be within penal policy various degrees and forms of elimination. Ferri, who was a Marxist, did not believe in the death penalty at all, but the idea of elimination from the social group tied all three of the Italians together in a policy of what is essentially social defense.

The crime-control policy of social defense can be traced directly to the writings of the Italian criminologists. Five assumptions underlie this policy approach. First, crime is inevitable. Second, the criminal has little control over his or her actions and is therefore not morally responsible for the criminal act. Third, nevertheless, society has a right to defend itself. Thus, fourth, punishment is justified not on moral grounds or grounds of deterrence, but on grounds of defense. Finally, then, eliminating the criminal from the social group provides social protection. For less serious crimes, indeterminate sentences to prison provide sufficient elimination and social protection. As a side effect, such separation might also reform the offender, and therefore the possibility of release must be present. How the reform is to take place is not clearly specified, but elimination from the social group, even for a limited time, serves the idea of protection. Elimination might also be limited to expulsion from a specific social group, such as revoking of a license to practice a particular profession. Policy implications thus range from the draconian (death or life of penal servitude) to the more benign possibility of simply losing the right to engage in a particular livelihood. Lombroso and his followers also suggested fines as a suitable penal practice, and the Italian school generally was quite supportive of the notion of compensation for crime victims.

The first modern, scientific criminologists, steeped as they were in theories of biological determinism, found themselves in a situation faced by many contemporary criminologists trained in the other scientific approaches. The scientific theory adopted for exploration does not always lend itself to clear policy statements. Garofalo, in criticizing his colleague Ferri's classification of criminal types, noted the problem: "Being of no avail to legislation it is consequently without practical interest."[30] And speaking of other efforts at scientific criminology, he states, "But when we come to consider how this theory may be applied to legislation, serious difficulties are encountered."[31] The biological school seems to have solved this problem the same way modern social scientists have. Policies are often argued based on influences other than the purely disciplinary ones. Lloyd Ohlin, commenting on the participation of sociologists on the Commission on Law Enforcement and the Administration of Justice which convened in 1968, highlights the process.

> ... the sociologists serving as consultants to the Commission were reluctant to specify the logical implications of their analyses in the form of action recommendations for the Commission. When they did try to do this, the recommendations were often more influenced by personal ideological conviction than by appropriately organized facts and theories or arguments.[32]

The doctrine of social defense fits admirably with the ideological notions that undergird the biologically deterministic theories of early criminology. Thus, while specific recommendations may have been at odds with the logical implications of such determinism, the overall thrust of the social defense movement gave primacy to the power of the state for controlling individual actions. The state is both supreme and benign. Thus, according to Garofalo, "metaphorically speaking, the individual represents but a cell of the social body."[33] Within this tradition the efficient apprehension and conviction of offenders is paramount, with the method of appropriate removal from society based on a scientific scheme of classification and not on notions of individual rights.

Biological determinism found a less hospitable ideological climate in the United States. The controversy surrounding Hooten's suggestion of forced sterilization illustrates the point. Since ideologically the notion of an impersonal social organism responding to natural laws had been replaced by a belief in the efficacy of the individual, theories of crime causation needed to hold out the hope that intervention would have a positive effect. Reform rather than defense was emphasized. Further, individuals had rights and were morally responsible for their activity. Thus, punishment was to be both limited and based on the Beccarian principle of deterrence. Psychological and psychiatric theories, while having elements of both determinism and biological causation, at least provided for a greater, more direct role on the part of the expert. These theories consequently had greater currency in the United States, and along with sociological theories ended up having a primary place in our intellectual history. Even those theories that remained biologically anchored, such as those of Sheldon and the Gluecks, provided for factors that experts and the state could ameliorate.

The Policy Implications of Individualistic Causal Theories

A number of common threads run through the explanations of crime described above. There is a tendency toward what the nineteenth-century Italian sociologist Pareto called "combinations."[34] People tend to put together or combine like things. Consequently, an undesirable result (crime for instance) is seen as caused by an undesirable or pathological condition.

A second common thread is that of determinism, wherein little attention is paid to the operation of free will. The criminal is viewed as a victim of circumstances, propelled into law-violating behavior by forces beyond his control. The rescuer will of course be the expert who understands such forces. Determinism influenced early behavioral science and the first school of criminological theory founded by Lombroso. In this scheme, experts could tell the state how to best defend itself against those suffering biological abnormalities. The American version of this deterministic viewpoint involved the expert curing individuals of malfunctions over which they had little or no control.

Finally, a third element that unites these various scientific explanations of criminal conduct is the belief in the essentially orderly, understandable nature of human society. The early founders of modern behavioral sciences firmly grounded their new discipline in the techniques of the natural sciences. At the same time, they espoused a deterministic belief in a natural order governed by immutable laws. Such a belief was comforting in the face of the drastic social upheavals of the eighteenth and nineteenth centuries. It nevertheless represented a turning away from the egalitarian philosophy of the classical school whose utilitarian principles encouraged large-scale social reform.

The combination of scientific method with a deterministic world view had both direct and indirect policy effects. In Europe, the direct policy effect was the development of crime control strategies based on a concept of social defense. In the United States, where for ideological reasons, more direct intervention strategies were favored, the cult of the expert was encouraged. As noted, this led to such direct policy consequences as the development of the juvenile court, probation and parole services, and the predominance of the treatment paradigm within correctional institutions. The indirect influence of these formal theories were perhaps even more pervasive.

Although policy makers respond to day-to-day contingencies in both their formulations of policy and its implementation, such practical considerations are influenced by the popular theories of crime causation. This mixture of practical knowledge and theoretical knowledge forms what might be called the "folk wisdom of the educated." Formal theories indirectly impact on policy then by providing legitimacy for particular problem definitions.

The problem definition legitimized by behavioral science theories of crime causation biases subsequent policies in three ways. The tendency to associate bad effects with bad causes creates policy initiatives largely concerned with the crimes of the underclass, or those already seen as being deviant. Although such crimes are less costly than white-collar crime, they generate the majority of policy initiatives in crime control. The tendency toward combinations results in this policy blind spot.

The tendency toward determinism reinforces the power of the professional, often at the expense of those who seek help. The millions of dollars spent by the Law Enforcement Assistance Administration during the presidencies of Lyndon Johnson and Richard Nixon seems mainly to have enhanced the power and resources of professional criminal justice groups. The child-saving movement as described by Platt illustrates the same point.[35] A coalition of emerging social work professionals and women rights advocates called attention to the problem of lower-class delinquency and a need to save these children. The result was an enhanced profession of social work, a public role for upper-middle-class women, and considerable control of immigrant children.

Finally, an overemphasis on rationality has led to inflated expectations about what can be accomplished in the area of crime control and, in combination with the values of professional culture, has generally led to policies that fail to look beyond individual determinants of crime. We have not dealt with some of the simpler explanations of crime that have been a part of biological determinism. For example, phrenology attempted to determine criminal tendencies by examining and measuring cranial bumps, asserting that such skull measurements corresponded to the parts of the brain that were dominant and thus controlling of behavior. Nor have we examined popular psychiatric categories for explaining crime such as sociopath or psychopath. Again, while these may be popular, they have very little in the way of scientific validity to recommend them as cogent explanations of criminal behavior. Yet they share with those biological, psychiatric, and psychological theories that we have discussed a penchant for looking at what is different about the criminal. This leads to the expectation that the solution to crime or at least its control is a relatively straightforward matter of treating or isolating those who possess a certain trait. Little attention has been paid to the notion that crime is generated by a complex set of social structural conditions. America has more crime than most other countries, not because there are more "sick" people here, but because of the complex interaction of values, institutions, and social conditions that make us simultaneously the envy of some and the bane of others. But the theories described in this chapter are unable to satisfactorily account for differential rates between geographical areas. As we have seen, however, scientific adequacy is only one criteria for judging a theory. Its popularity and policy impact will often have little to do with its scientific validity. The simpler the theory, the more it will appeal to both the public and to policy makers. Thus, while the sociological theories described in the next chapter have tried to address the scientific inadequacies of biological determinism and psychological and psychiatric categories, they have not met the ambitious goals of the rational planning movement that shaped their existence in the full expectation that they would solve the problems of society.

SUMMARY

What Was Said

• The adequacy of a criminological theory can be judged by three criteria: scientific adequacy, popular acceptance, and policy relevance.
• Although Lombroso's theory lacks scientific adequacy, it was both popular and policy relevant in Europe.
• The positivist's school of criminology stressed a policy of social defense.
• Biological explanations of crime continued to be developed today. Yet, they have rarely overcome problems of scientific inadequacy that have plagued them from the days of Lombroso.
• Psychological and psychiatric theories have a biological base but allow more intervention by experts.
• Many of these theories also lack scientific verification, but their policy relevance in the United States was particularly strong in the fields of correction and juvenile reform.
• The tendency to associate bad effects with bad causes in positivist and behavioral criminology creates policy initiatives largely concerned with the crimes of the underclass, resulting in a policy blind spot regarding upper-class deviance.

• The tendency toward determinism in positivist and behavioral criminology can reinforce the power of the professional at the expense of those who seek help.

• An overemphasis on scientific rationality has led to inflated expectations about what can be accomplished in the area of crime control and individual reform.

What Was Not Said

• There is no place for rigorous science in policy discussion of crime and criminal justice.

• Theoretical formulations and criminological research have been useless.

• We have no more understanding of crime than we did at the time of Lombroso.

• Scientific formulations were not influenced by the ideological currents of the time.

NOTES

1. Hermann Mannheim, ed., *Pioneers in Criminology*, 2nd ed. (Montclair, NJ: Patterson-Smith, 1972), pp. 2–3.

2. Ibid., pp. 36–49.

3. Robert A. Scott and Arnold R. Shore, *Why Sociology Does Not Apply: A Study of the User of Sociology in Public Policy* (New York: Elsevier, 1971).

4. Ibid., p. IX.

5. Ibid.

6. Mannheim, *Pioneers in Criminology*, pp. 13–16.

7. Scott and Shore, *Why Sociology Does Not Apply*, pp. 92–95.

8. Ibid., p. 95.

9. Ibid., p. 87.

10. Ibid.

11. Scott and Shore, *Why Sociology Does Not Apply*, p. 105.

12. Ibid.

13. Marvin E. Wolfgang, "Cesare Lombroso," in Mannheim, *Pioneers in Criminology*, p. 275.

14. Ibid., p. 268.

15. Charles W. Thomas and John R. Hepburn, *Crime, Criminal Law, and Criminology* (Dubuque, IA: William C. Brown Company Publishers, 1983), p. 132.

16. Francis A. Allen, "Raffaele Garofalo," in Mannheim, *Pioneers in Criminology*, pp. 318–39. Thorsten Sellin, "Enrico Ferri," in Mannheim, *Pioneers in Criminology*, pp. 361–83.

17. Edwin D. Driver, "Charles Buckman Goring," in Mannheim, *Pioneers in Criminology*, p. 441.

18. Earnest A. Hooten, *The American Criminal, An Anthropological Study* (Cambridge, MA: Harvard University Press, 1939).

19. William H. Sheldon, *Varieties of Delinquent Youth* (New York: Harper and Row, 1949).

20. Sheldon Glueck and Eleanor Glueck, *Physique and Delinquency* (New York: Harper and Row, 1956).

21. James Q. Wilson and Richard J. Hernstein, *Crime and Human Nature* (New York: Simon and Schuster, 1985).

22. Travis Hirschi and Michael J. Hindelang, "Intelligence and Delinquency: A Revisionist Review," *American Sociological Review*, 42 (August, 1977), 571–87.

23. Edwin H. Sutherland, "Mental Deficiency and Crime," in *Social Attitudes*, Kimball Young, ed. (New York: Holt, Rinehart and Winston, 1931).

24. Ibid.

25. Karl F. Schuessler and Donald R. Cressey, "Personality Characteristics of Criminals," *American Journal of Sociology*, 55 (March 1950), 476–84. Gordon P. Waldo and Simon Dinitz, "Personality Attributes of the Criminal: An Analysis of Research Studies, 1950–1965," *Journal of Research in Crime and Delinquency*, 4 (July 1967), 185–202. D.J. Tennebaum, "Research Studies of Personality and Criminality: A Summary and Implications of the Literature," *Journal of Criminal Justice*, 5 (3:1977), 1–19. Don C. Gibbons, *Society, Crime and Criminal Behavior*, 4th ed. (Englewood Cliffs, NJ: Prentice-Hall, Inc., 1982), p. 170.

26. Gibbons, 1982.

27. Gibbons, *Society, Crime, and Criminal Behavior*, p. 164.

28. Marvin E. Wolfgang, "Ceasare Lombroso," in Mannheim, p. 278.

29. Francis A. Allen, "Raffaele Garofalo," in Mannheim, *Pioneers in Criminology*, p. 329.

30. Ibid.

31. Ibid., p. 318.

32. Lloyd E. Ohlin, "The President's Commission on Law Enforcement and Administration of Justice," in *Sociology and Public Policy*, Komarovsky, ed. (New York: American Elsevier Publishing Co., 1975), pp. 93–116.

33. Garofalo, *Criminology*, p. 224; and Allen, "Raffaele Garofalo," p. 338.

34. Vilfredo Pareto, *The Mind and Society*, (New York: Harcourt, Brace and Company, 1935).

35. Anthony Platte, *The Child Savers*, (Chicago: The University of Chicago Press, 1969).

VII

Ideology and Science

Crime as a Product of Social Factors

At the end of this chapter, the student will be able to:

A. Describe the main tenets of six major sociological schools of crime causation.

B. Name the key proponents of each school.

C. Discuss the strengths and weaknesses of the various approaches.

D. Discuss and describe approaches that attempt to combine various theories.

E. Define the phrase "ideas in good currency" and discuss its relevancy to public policy.

ISSUE BACKGROUND

The Planning Ideology

In the United States, the ideology of planning provided fertile ground for the development of sociological explanations of crime. Sociology was less deterministic than the biologically anchored theories developed by European thinkers. Therefore, it provided even more opportunity for experts to ply their trade.

The concept of "expert" was the linchpin of the whole planning movement. Its importance lay not only in the technical know-how the trained scientist could supposedly provide the policy maker; more importantly, perhaps, the concept of expert solved a philosophical/political problem faced by middle-class reformers. They wanted to reassert their authority amid rapidly changing social conditions, which gave rise to big city machines, government by bosses, and corruption.[1] They wanted to return government to the people, albeit their kind of people. A national planning agenda to accomplish this, however, required a strong centralized government. Yet a strong centralized government was susceptible to the very things the reformers were trying to correct: corruption and lack of middle class professional influence in its workings. The solution to this dilemma was the idea of a neutral state guided in its decision making by disinterested experts.[2] Even then, however, the concept of expert did not entirely alleviate concerns about control of government. What exactly was the role of the expert to be? Teddy Roosevelt envisioned a situation where, based on scientific evidence, the expert would determine the best course for society to take.[3] This elitist view of the expert was challenged by a populist notion of the expert as someone who would find out what people wanted and would figure out the best way to implement their will. Woodrow Wilson was an advocate of this approach.[4] Public opinion, the will of the people, was to be the ultimate policy guide. Overlying this conflict was the question of whether the expert was to also be an advocate for particular positions. Sociology generally and criminology specifically were eclectic enough in their theoretical development to accommodate the various views on what experts should do. And, more importantly, they provided a rationale for the expert to do something, and to do it on a grand scale.

Sociology's focus on aggregates of people paralleled nicely with the idea that government policy could affect the lives of large segments of the population. The planning movement was aimed at a better society, not simply better individuals. Thus, as we have seen, while certain psychological approaches affected specific agency responses to crime and corrections, sociology, both directly and indirectly, influenced broader government policy aimed at alleviating problems of crime and poverty. It was compatible with the notion of government responsibility for large-scale social planning.

Sociology's ability to accommodate the various ideological shades of the planning movement was in part due to its origins in both scientific method and a deterministic ideology. The first school of sociology was Positivistic Organicism. Positivism stressed the idea that you could only know what was experienced directly. This led to an emphasis on empirical testing. At the same time Organicism assumed that society developed much like a biological organism and that natural laws were there to be uncovered. The assumption, of course, was not based on an empirical demonstration. Thus, sociology contained an odd amalgam of objective and subjective approaches to understanding. These contradictory elements, however, allowed it to develop theories that could accommodate some of the contradiction in the planning movement itself. In the course of its development in the United States, therefore, criminology, as a subfield of sociology, moved from a concern with broad impersonal social forces to the notion of individuals creating their own social reality. Along the way, various conceptions of crime and its solution were espoused and various government policies formulated and/or legitimated.

CRIMINOLOGICAL/CRIMINAL JUSTICE CONSIDERATIONS

Social Disorganization: The Early Chicago School

As noted, American criminology owes its intellectual origins to a European tradition of social thought. The influences of such sociologists as Emile Durkheim (1858–1917) and Gabriel Tarde (1843–1904) can be seen throughout the history of American criminology, which in this country was largely anchored in the discipline of sociology.

Emile Durkheim wrote on a wide variety of sociological issues including religion, the division of labor in society, and suicide.[5] In the area of deviance and crime, he noted that all societies produced aberrant behavior. He therefore reasoned that crime was both normal and functional for a social group. This insight placed him in opposition to those who argued that crime was abnormal. Since all societies had examples of deviance, it must somehow be a necessary component of collective living. It helped societies avoid stagnation so that they could change and progress. Punishments of crime clarified the social norms of a group, which were often general or vague. Further, by punishing deviance, society indirectly rewarded those who kept the law. Thus, crime and punishment could not be separated from the total dynamic of a society. In a way, society got the kind of crime it both needed and deserved. For Durkheim, then, crime was a social fact. Its cause as well as its solution was to be found in the way society was structured. While crime was functional, however, a society could produce such an abundance of deviance that the overall effect on the collective good was dysfunctional. Understanding the social forces that produced it was therefore necessary to avoid crime's negative effects.

Gabriel Tarde also emphasized the social origins of crime.[6] In fact, his attacks upon Lombrosian theory considerably lessened its influence in Europe. Tarde, unlike Durkheim, did pay attention to both social and personal factors in criminal careers. The blending of sociological and psychological insights can be found in his theory of imitation. People learned to be criminals like they learned everything else; that is, they learned through imitation in close association with others. The closer the contact, the greater the imitation. In large cities, where there are rapid changes, imitation takes the form of fashion. In smaller, stable societies imitation becomes custom. But customs can change or new fashions develop, and these fashions in turn have the prospect of themselves becoming customs. Imitation generally follows a pattern from the superior to the inferior. Thus, crime was originally found primarily among royalty (poisoning and drunkenness, for example) and later spread to the lower classes. Great cities become centers for certain fashions in crime, and later these spread throughout a region. Tarde illustrates his point by noting that a "fashion" of cutting corpses into pieces began in Paris in 1876 and then spread to other parts of France.[7] Finally, when fashions compete with one another, the newer one will often win out. Tarde noticed, for example, that murders by knifing decreased while murders by guns increased.[8]

The Chicago School comprised the first school of both sociology and criminology in the United States. In 1892 the University of Chicago established the first department of sociology in the United States. Indeed, it was the first department of sociology in the world![9] The influence of both Durkheim and Tarde can be seen in the Chicago School's theories of crime. Like Durkheim, early students of criminology emphasized a concern with social order and conversely, with the dysfunctional elements of disorganization brought about by rapid social changes. There was a tendency to attribute crime to impersonal social forces. Nevertheless, early Chicago sociologists also recognized the influences of socialization that occurred in particular kinds of crime-prone groups, particularly juvenile gangs that developed in the slums of large cities. Further, the Chicago School added a heavy dose of American pragmatism to its European intellectual heritage. These researchers were interested in helping solve the problems evident in the sprawling city of which they were a part. Crime, poverty, poor housing, and poor nutrition were all focal points of concern. Funding for much of their research was provided by welfare agencies and criminal justice groups, who expected them to develop specific policies to alleviate the problems they encountered.[10] Thus, the social science that developed in response to the ideology of planning combined practical urban concerns with certain currents of European social thought.

The first fruits of this marriage were found in the ecological theories of crime developed by the Chicago researchers. In 1925, Robert E. Park, Earnest W. Burgess, and Roderick D. McKenzie, all at the University of Chicago, published *The City*.[11] In their book, Park and Burgess expounded their notion that the city can be conceptualized as a series of concentric zones. The growth of the city was likened to an ecological process in which plant and animal life interact with their physical surroundings, bringing about changes in both themselves and the environment. By processes of invasion and succession, the city grew out from a central core. Zone I, the core, contains the central business district. Zone II, a zone of transition, is an area of physical and social deterioration which is being invaded by business and light manufacturing from Zone I. This in turn causes those who are able to to move to Zone III, an area of working men's homes. Zone IV is an area of high-rent buildings or single-family houses. Zone V is a commuter zone of dormitory suburbs. The process of invasion begins when a new land use is introduced into an area, for example, a formerly residential area begins to change to an area of manufacturing. Succession is when the new land use completely replaces the former land use. The physical changes that such expansion causes in an area are obvious. The social changes were also obvious, but the reasons for them were less clear. The insight provided by the Chicago School was the linking of physical deterioration and change with social deterioration and change.

Many Chicago researchers noted that various kinds of social problems were consistently higher in the zone of transition than elsewhere. High rates of promiscuity, divorce, mental illness, delinquency, and crime were concentrated in the zone surrounding the central business district.[12] Moreover, it appeared to make little difference which ethnic group predominated in this area. Building on the work of Park and Burgess, Shaw and McKay developed a delinquency area theory.[13]

Because zones of transition lacked stable community institutions, cracks or fissures developed in the social structure of the community. Disorganization resulted from the constant movement of people in and out of the area. Cheap housing was available for newcomers to the city in these zones because the housing stock was allowed to deteriorate in the expectation that a new land use was eventually going to replace these residences. Those who could move out did, those who couldn't shared the increasingly dilapidated housing with other less economically advantaged people. Institutions of control, including family, school, and church, could not function effectively with such mobile populations, and the value conflicts that emerged as newcomers confronted those already there. A social vacuum was created because stable norms of conduct could not develop in the face of ecological growth patterns. A youth confronted with conflicting norms and the absence of clear controls was naturally drawn to delinquency, particularly in the form of gang behavior. The gang was the substitute family, church, and school.

The juvenile gang soon became the focus of attention for early criminologists. For many in the Chicago school, the juvenile gang was a result of the social disorganization caused by the physical growth of the city. Criminal behavior was learned in the gang as a result of imitation by younger members of older gang leaders. Frederic Thrasher's work on the gang represents this brand of criminological research and theory.

In 1927, Thrasher published *The Gang: A Study of 1313 Gangs in Chicago*.[14] His ecological base and his concern with disorganization is evident in the most important conclusion of the study:

Gangland is an Interstitial Area[15]

The most important conclusion suggested by a study of the location and distribution of the 1,313 gangs investigated in Chicago is that *gangland represents a geographically and socially interstitial area in the city*. Probably the most significant concept of the study is the term interstitial—that is, pertaining to spaces that intervene between one thing and another. *In nature foreign matter tends to collect and cake in every crack, crevice, and cranny—interstices. There are also fissures and breaks in the structure of social organization. The gang may be regarded as an interstitial element in the framework of society, and gangland as an interstitial region in the layout of the city.*

The gang is almost invariably characteristic of regions that are interstitial to the more settled, more stable, and better organized portions of the city. The central tripartite empire of the gang occupies what is often called "the poverty belt"—a region characterized by deteriorating neighborhoods, shifting populations, and the mobility and disorganization of the slum. Abandoned by those seeking homes in the better residential districts, encroached upon by business and industry, this zone is a distinctly interstitial phase of the city's growth. It is to a large extent isolated from the wider culture of the larger community by the processes of competition and conflict which have resulted in the selection of its population. Gangland is a phenomenon of human ecology. As better residential districts recede before the encroachments of business and industry, the gang develops as one manifestation of the economic, moral, and cultural frontier which marks the interstice.

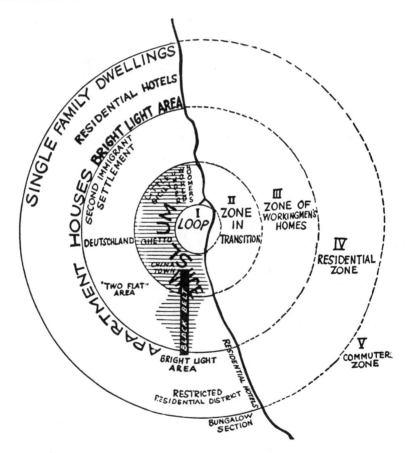

Figure 7-1

Shaw and McKay, Thrasher and others from the early Chicago school set the agenda for much of the later research on crime and delinquency. Their emphasis on social disorganization and ecology contained seeds for a variety of different theoretical approaches. In the fashion of science, these developments occurred through challenges to some of the basic premises of the original approach.

While the data from studies of the zone of transition clearly show a high correlation between area and delinquency, such correlations are not necessarily causal. This was recognized by the original researchers, and they did not in fact argue direct causality. Other factors, such as differential law enforcement, could account for the variation in delinquency rates between different areas of the city. Nevertheless, the ecological approach was criticized, often unfairly, for overemphasizing the contribution of geography to crime. However, contrary to what the authors did argue, different ethnic groups in the zone of transition did have different rates of delinquency. Chinese and Jewish populations, for example, had low rates of delinquency despite their location in poor neighborhoods.[16] Moreover, because there was little attempt to treat hypothetical relationships, variations in the data were left unexplained.[17] Thus, Thrasher's description of gang dynamics appears at times contradictory. He describes gang members as tightly bound by codes of conduct and feelings of loyalty and, later on, describes gangs as social units with tendencies toward instability and social disintegration.[18] Finally, the central concepts of disorganization appeared to shoulder too great an explanatory burden. The descriptive data often suggested that it was organization around a different set of values, not disorganization, that led to high rates of deviance. This insight formed the foundation for a second major approach in the sociology of crime and delinquency, an approach that emphasized the role of subculture in generating delinquents and/or criminal behavior.

Social Organization: The Subcultural School

In 1943, William Foote Whyte published *Street Corner Society.*[19] This study refuted the then standard theory of lower-class criminal behavior. Whyte believed that middle-class people misunderstood the dynamics of lower-class neighborhoods. Their information was often based on the spectacular events that made headlines, such as gangland shootings or indictments for political corruption. From this perspective, the slum appeared to be chaotic and disorganized.[20] This popular perception was supported by much of the sociological research of this period, and thus middle-class reformers were intent upon bringing order to the neighborhood. But the day-to-day activity of racketeers, politicians, and street corner boys turned out to be a far different reality than either headlines or social workers suggested. Whyte, who spent four years living in and studying an Italian slum community, "Cornerville," documented the highly organized nature of the disorganized" lower-class neighborhood.

Values such as loyalty to the neighborhood and suspicion of outsiders formed the base for the organization of Cornerville. Since the larger society lacked a sufficient number of jobs for immigrants and their children and was sometimes less than hospitable toward these newcomers, illegal enterprises provided an alternative source of income and prestige. Politics, on the other hand, was simply a method for getting along with a hostile dominant society. Local law enforcement and neighborhood politicians worked together to protect Cornerville from too much outside interference. The emphasis was on the control rather than the elimination of criminal enterprises. Thus, political corruption, criminal racketeers, and a seeming lack of interest in social mobility were indicative of a complex organizational structure and not signs of disorganization. In this kind of environment, the settlement house was an alien force, and those locals who participated in its programs were viewed as traitors to the neighborhood.

Other researchers, following Whyte's lead, further developed the notion of lower-class subculture as a generating milieu for delinquent and criminal behavior. Albert Cohen combined the notion of subculture with the psychological concept of reaction formation to explain lower-class juvenile gang delinquency.[21] In this view the juvenile gang forms among lower-class boys as a novel solution to the problem of status degradation. Lower- or working-class boys do not have the advantages of education and social contacts enjoyed by their counterparts in the middle class. They therefore cannot compete effectively for middle-class jobs and status. One solution to this problem would be to change the situation. But, obviously, it is not possible for the lower-class male to change the social order. Further, self-improvement through education requires making it in a middle-class institution for which he is ill prepared, that is, the school. Besides, to become middle class means turning one's back on friends and neighborhood. Therefore, some lower class boys chose instead to change their frame of reference. Since middle-class values and their rewards seem unobtainable, their worth is denied. This is a process of "sour graping." Like the fox in the Aesop fable who couldn't reach the grapes, the lower-class boy says the grapes, or in their case the values, are no good anyway.[22] But to reject values such as ambition, individual responsibility, deferred gratification, respect for property, and the control of physical aggression and violence requires group support. Thus, sour graping and a rejection of middle-class values occurs, according to Cohen, through group interaction. Boys feeling rejected by society tentatively test with each other a new frame of reference that supports behaviors and values opposite those of the larger society. What emerges is a set of subcultural values that stand middle-class norms on their head. The juvenile gang as described by Cohen is nonutilitarian, engaging in behavior that apparently serves no purpose. Shoplifting for fun rather than for profit or use of the items illustrates this characteristic. Stolen merchandise is discarded after it is taken. The behavior tends to be malicious, with the juveniles enjoying the discomfort they give to others. There is little or no criminal specialization, and acts are committed on the spur of the moment without planning. The contempt for and rejection of middle-class values was symbolized for Cohen by an incident report of a boy defecating on a teacher's desk.[23]

Walter Miller is another researcher who used a cultural framework for explaining crime.[24] Miller argued that the behavioral norms of the juvenile gang were not simply a product of the gang's own group dynamics. Rather, they represented norms common to lower-class society. Lower-class society is a culture unto itself organized around a set of focal concerns. Lower-class people expect trouble in their environment. The concern with trouble causes a posture of hostility when dealing with the world and a value placed on being tough. Another focal concern is smartness, the ability to put one over on somebody and to get away with "conning" people. There is a search for excitement, for easy money, for daring, for showing one's manhood. The focal concern for excitement is accompanied by a belief in fate. What happens to a person is a matter of luck rather than a matter of personal control. Finally, there is a desire for autonomy, for independence from the daily hassles of the straight society. The focal concerns of trouble, toughness, smartness, excitement, fate, and autonomy create a situation in which violence is both expected and accepted. Gang boys are simply participating in a larger cultural phenomenon of their class.

At this point, we have covered a great deal of conceptual territory. The image of crime and criminals that emerges is far from clear, but that is hardly surprising. Neither the ecological approach nor subculture theories present clear pictures of the phenomena they address. Instead they form a montage of kaleidoscoping images. Thrasher's view of the juvenile gang appears almost romantic, with gang membership a result of youthful exuberance rather than criminal tendencies. Cohen's description is less benign, with the gang described as malicious and negativistic. Even less clearly focused is the nature of the criminal or delinquent subculture. For Shaw, McKay, and Thrasher, where the early seeds of a subculture explanation lurked, the delinquent subculture is a means of coping with the lower-class physical and social environment characterized as disorganized. Whyte, on the other hand, describes a highly organized lower-class culture. Here the gang is simply one part of a complex organizational setting. Miller seems to agree with Whyte, at least in terms of focusing on lower-class culture rather than on a specific group such as a gang, but his view of lower-class life is far less complimentary. Finally, Cohen, who focuses narrowly on the lower-class juvenile male gang, paints an idealized picture of the middle class in order to emphasize the status degradation faced by lower-class males.

While many theorists have either implicitly or explicitly used the notion of subculture as a part of their explanatory base for deviant behavior, the concept is really not adequately defined. As a result, it means different things to different people. Further, use of the concept often leads to tautologies. The work of Wolfgang and Ferracuti on the subculture of violence illustrates this point.[25] They note that high arrest rates for assault may indicate allegiance to the values of violence, and then they explain violent crimes by adherence to such subcultural values. Subcultural explanations of crime and delinquency have also focused on lower-class crime to the exclusion of crime in other parts of the social system. In doing so, subcultural explanations of crime and delinquency may assume much more isolation between groups than actually exists in modern-day society.

These problems with the concept are underscored when empirical data testing the subcultural framework are examined. Cohen's theory would lead one to expect that gang boys would evaluate so-called middle-class values such as "hard work" lower than their opposite. Gordon and colleagues tested this assumption on black and white populations consisting of lower-class gang, lower-class nongang, and middle-class nongang samples.[26] They found that all populations evaluated images representing salient features of a middle-class style of life equally. Delinquents ordered behaviors as to their goodness much the same as did nondelinquents. This finding fails to support the notion that delinquents have a distinct set of values that replace the dominant values of society. Reiss and Rhodes operationalized each of Cohen's characterizations of delinquent values. Contrary to expectations, no delinquent group could be identified that had a nonutilitarian, malicious, and negativistic emphasis.[27]

Miller's distinct set of lower-class values has been challenged by Matza and Sykes.[28] These authors conclude that such values are found in other sectors of society, notably in the leisure classes. As the authors state, "we must be struck by their [the values'] similarity to the components of the code of this 'gentleman of leisure' depicted by Thorsten Veblen." Veblen was referring to the upper strata of European society who because of inherited wealth had no need to work. Their days were spent primarily in the pursuit of pleasure. Thus, it appears doubtful that delinquents are marked by an adherence to a distinct and deviant set of values or that they fail to incorporate the values of the dominant society. Middle-class values are not themselves homogeneous but instead can support a wide range of behaviors, the rightness or wrongness of which are judged in specific context. Stealing is wrong, but stealing a loaf of bread when you are starving may be permissible. Stealing from the government in the form of income tax evasion or from large impersonal concerns (taking towels from hotels, for example) may be permitted. A single hotel chain has reported an annual loss of $3 million in towels alone.[29] It is hard to imagine that these are being taken by lower-class males in delinquent gangs. Similarly, the government has lost $25 billion in a single year because of income tax evasion.[30] Again, such crime is not likely to be that of juvenile gangs with distinct values. Major retail outlets lose more through employee theft than through shoplifting, and in the construction industry it is estimated that between 1 and 6% of the net worth of a contractor's equipment is stolen each year.[31] A broader framework for understanding crime is needed, one that can account for white-collar crime, street crime, and the crime of ordinary middle-class folks. The work of Edwin H. Sutherland provides this wider perspective.

Social Learning Theory and Crime

Science proceeds through a process of negation, elaboration, and at times revolution. We have already seen that criminology, in its beginning stages, developed largely through the process of negation. Thus, Lombroso's explanations were attacked by Goring and others, and these negations of his theory resulted in new explanations of crime. Subcultural explanations of crime developed in part by challenging the assumptions contained in the early statements of social disorganization. Sutherland's work, on the other hand, represents an elaboration of early theories and includes elements of both disorganization and subcultural views of crime. It also incorporates notions borrowed from social psychology and learning theory. Obviously, to accomplish such integration and elaboration, Sutherland had to develop concepts that were general enough to subsume the specific explanatory factors of the individual theories. In this way, he could move beyond the narrow preoccupation with lower-class crime that plagued these theories. Sutherland's explanation of crime can thus be viewed as a large box that contains within it a number of smaller boxes. The fact that it could incorporate various explanations of crimes made the theory quite popular. Because it had to be very general in order to achieve such a synthesis, however, it was also vulnerable to a wide range of criticisms.

Sutherland's personal intellectual history exposed him to a variety of competing frameworks. He began his work at the University of Chicago in 1906.[32] He was very much influenced by the Chicago School, both in terms of theoretical orientation and in terms of the desire to be practical by contributing to criminal justice reform. In 1924, he published the first edition of his criminology text, a text that has gone through nine editions and has been a significant force in shaping American criminology. Sutherland began work on this text in 1921, when theories of environment and theories of heredity competed for dominance in the field.[33] Sutherland, who must have been a synthesizer by nature, wanted to utilize the sociological concepts with which he was familiar to explain crime while, at the same time, pinpointing specific, concrete causes for crime. He sought to combine the general theoretical concepts of sociology with the concrete conditions for criminal activity found in some hereditary explanations. He soon abandoned the latter part of this quest. Most crime is committed by males. Yet, as Sutherland saw, this specific, concrete association has no explanatory power since sex is not a cause of crime[34] He therefore sought explanations for crimes in more general, theoretical constructs. The work of W. I. Thomas, who stressed the importance of cognitive processes in the formation of social reality, provided the broad framework of understanding that Sutherland sought. Crime could be understood as a result of learning particular social definitions.

The full exposition of this theoretical insight took almost 26 years to develop. Since the main assertion was that criminal definitions are learned, the first problem was to account for the development of such definitions. To do this, Sutherland used the insights gained at Chicago. Deviant definitions of appropriate conduct are possible when a society is characterized by heterogeneous rather than homogeneous standards of conduct. In a complex society, different organizations permit or require differing standards of conduct.[35] Modern society can be understood as disorganized in the sense that an individual is faced with competing rather than harmonious sets of standards. Thus, Sutherland avoids the trap of thinking that only the lower-class experience conflicting conduct norms. Instead, Sutherland recognized that the norms and values of the middle class were not homogeneous. Sharp business practices may be encouraged in tough economic times, even though organizations such as churches continue to condemn stealing or taking advantage of people. The notion of differential organizations with differential norms of behavior set the stage for the full expression of Sutherland's ideas, the theory of differential association. By 1947, the theory had nine propositions:

1. Criminal behavior is learned. Negatively, this means that criminal behavior is not inherited, as such; also, the person who is not already trained in crime does not invent criminal behavior, just as a person does not make mechanical inventions unless he has had training in mechanics.

2. Criminal behavior is learned in interaction with other persons in process of communication. This communication is verbal in many respects but includes also "the communication of gestures."

3. The principal part of the learning of criminal behavior occurs within intimate personal groups. Negatively, this means that the impersonal agencies of communication, such as movies and newspapers, play a relatively unimportant part in the genesis of criminal behavior.

4. When criminal behavior is learned, the learning includes (a) techniques of committing the crime, which are sometimes very complicated, sometimes very simple; (b) the specific direction of motives, drives, rationalizations, and attitudes.

5. The specific direction of motives and drives is learned from definitions of the legal codes as favorable or unfavorable. In some societies an individual is surrounded by persons who invariably define the legal codes as rules to be observed, while in others he is surrounded by persons whose definitions are favorable to the violation of the legal codes. In our American society these definitions are almost always mixed, with the consequence that we have culture conflict in relation to the legal codes.

6. A person becomes delinquent because of an excess of definitions favorable to violation of law over definitions unfavorable to violation of law. This is the principle of differential association. It refers to both criminal and anticriminal associations and has to do with counteracting forces. When persons become criminal, they do so because of contacts with criminal patterns and also because of isolation from anticriminal patterns. Any person inevitably assimilates the surrounding culture unless other patterns are in conflict: a Southerner does

not pronounce "r" because other Southerners do not pronounce "r." Negatively, this proposition of differential association means that associations which are neutral so far as crime is concerned have little or no effect on the genesis of criminal behavior. Much of the experience of a person is neutral in this sense, for example, learning to brush one's teeth. This behavior has no negative or positive effect on criminal behavior except as it may be related to associations which are concerned with the legal codes. This neutral behavior is important especially as an occupier of the time of a child so that he is not in contact with criminal behavior during the time he is so engaged in the neutral behavior.

7. Differential associations may vary in frequency, duration, priority, and intensity. This means that associations with criminal behavior and also associations with anticriminal behavior vary in those respects. "Frequency" and "duration" as modalities of associations are obvious and need no explanation. "Priority" is assumed to be important in the sense that lawful behavior developed in early childhood may persist throughout life. This tendency, however, has not been adequately demonstrated, and priority seems to be important principally through its selective influence. "Intensity" is not precisely defined, but it has to do with such things as the prestige of the source of a criminal or anticriminal pattern and with emotional reactions related to the associations. In a precise description of the criminal behavior of a person these modalities would be stated in quantitative form and a mathematical ratio be reached. A formula in this sense has not been developed, and the development of such a formula would be extremely difficult.

8. The process of learning criminal behavior by association with criminal and anticriminal patterns incorporates all of the mechanisms that are involved in any other learning. Negatively, this means that the learning of criminal behavior is not restricted to the process of imitation. A person who is seduced, for instance, learns criminal behavior by association, but this process would not ordinarily be described as imitation.

9. While criminal behavior is an expression of general needs and values, it is not explained by those general needs and values since noncriminal behavior is an expression of the same needs and values. Thieves generally steal in order to secure money, but likewise honest laborers work in order to secure money. The attempts by many scholars to explain criminal behavior by general drives and values, such as the happiness principle, striving for social status, the money motive, or frustration, have been and must continue to be futile since they explain lawful behavior as completely as they explain criminal behavior. They are similar to respiration, which is necessary for any behavior but which does not differentiate criminal from noncriminal behavior[36]

Because Sutherland's theory is so general, it is difficult to provide empirical verification for the assertions that he made. Thus, words and phrases like "excess of definition" and "vary in frequency, duration, priority, and intensity" are difficult to operationalize. Further, some of the specific statements that have been tested have not been verified. When Cressey studied embezzlers, for example, he found that these occasional criminals had learned the appropriate techniques and rationalizations, but had not had the direct socialization into criminal patterns suggested by the theory.[37] The theory's popularity was at times matched by the vehemence of its critics. Sheldon Glueck, writing in 1956, stated that the theory "adds nothing but the excess baggage of confusing terminology to what is already well known and explainable without the benefit of the theory."[38]

The theory's generality also inhibited its usefulness for formulating social policy. How could policy makers change definitions available in the culture? On the other hand, it drew academic attention and perhaps ultimately the attention of policy makers to a previously neglected area of crime. As Sutherland noted:

> We have no reason to think that General Motors has an inferiority complex or that the Aluminum Company of America has a frustration-aggression complex or that U.S. Steel has an Oedipus complex, or that the Armour Company has a death wish or that the Duponts desire to return to the womb. The assumption that an offender must have some such pathological distortion of intellect or the emotions seems absurd, and if it is absurd regarding the crimes of businessmen, it is equally absurd regarding the crimes of persons in the lower economic class.[39]

Sutherland's interest in white-collar crime, "a crime committed by a person of respectability and high social status in the course of his occupation," was spurred by the exclusive research focus on crimes of the lower class.[40] Since "respectables" commit crime, the causes of such deviance cannot be all that different from that which contributes to lower-class crime. Yet, when many of the theories that purport to explain lower-class crime are applied to the crimes of the upper class, they appear ridiculous. What was needed was a conceptual framework that could explain both kinds of crime. For Sutherland, his theory of differential association fit the bill.

Ironically, efforts to improve evaluation research, a very practical, applied kind of information gathering, may serve to verify some of the abstract principles of differential association. Traditionally, evaluation research has been atheoretical, asking such straightforward questions as whether or not a program worked. For example, did a program aimed at reforming delinquents in fact reform them? If rates of recidivism were reduced below that of a similar population that did not have the particular intervention, the answer would be yes. If, on the other hand, rates between groups getting the program and those not getting it were the same or if the treatment group had higher rates, it could be concluded that the program did not work. At least traditional evaluations would draw this conclusion. But whether that conclusion is in fact true hinges in part on how similar the two comparison groups are. Often groups getting treatment and those not getting it are matched on such things as age, race, sex, and, sometimes, type of delinquency. Since Sutherland in the early 1920s, and sociologists both before and since, have rejected biological and hereditary causes of criminal behavior, it seems strange that social scientists involved in evaluation research would match groups largely on the basis of characteristics they have rejected as significant in the generation of crime to evaluate programs aimed at crime reduction. It makes more sense to match groups based on characteristics thought significant to the cause of crime. Daniel Glaser reevaluated certain delinquency programs that were based on individual or group therapy "talk" models of intervention. Youth would meet singly or in small groups with a counselor to talk about their past and to discuss what their future could become. In an attempt to improve both evaluation and criminological theory, Glaser based his reassessment on hypotheses he developed from Sutherland's differential association theory. According to Glaser:

> If evaluation of the recidivism reduction capacity of individual or group psychotherapy or counseling were guided by differential association theory, two principal working hypotheses derived from it might be phrased as follows:
>
> Hypothesis One.
>
> The recidivism reduction achieved by these talk programs will vary directly with the extent that they produce intimate personal relationships between anticriminal staff and criminal clients, thus fostering the offender's learning anticriminal definitions.
>
> Hypothesis Two.
>
> The recidivism reduction achieved by these talk programs will vary inversely with the prior criminal learning of the offenders.[41]

When different "talk" programs were reevaluated using theoretical dimensions to construct comparison between treatment and control groups, formerly "ineffective programs" in fact did show an effect. For example, as predicted by Hypothesis One, individual counseling and psychotherapy were most effective for young adults whose criminal careers were not well advanced, particularly when such programs fostered anticriminal definitions through vocational guidance.[42] Hypothesis One would also suggest that size of a probation officer's case load would be related to recidivism rates: The larger the case load, the less chance a personal relationship could be developed with the client. In turn, the chance an offender would have of learning anticriminal definitions would be lessened. Research by Lipton et al. in fact supports this notion. For young probationers, recidivism rates varied directly with the size of the case load.[43] It made little or no difference with older probationers or with most parolees regardless of age. This is what would be expected given Hypothesis Two.

Glaser's work is valuable in that it demonstrates the importance of theory for the practical exercise of program evaluation. At the same time, theory itself can be improved by a concern with testing it in the cauldron of public policy.

Social Structural Approaches to Crime Causation

When Emile Durkheim began his work, sociology was attempting to establish its unique identity, thereby securing for itself a place in the academic community. Unlike philosophy, it was an empirical science based on data collection and the positivistic method. Unlike psychology, it was concerned with how society as a collective phenomenon affected the human condition.

In numerous works, Durkheim brilliantly mapped out the special place of sociology. Its concern was with the social fact, both external to the individual and encountered as a coercive force. According to Durkheim, social facts could only be explained by reference to other social facts and were not reducible to simple psychological, individual explanations.[44] One way Durkheim illustrated this idea was through his study of suicide.[45]

At first glance, suicide seems to be an entirely personal, individualistic phenomenon. Yet, it appeared that suicide rates varied systematically among particular groups. Married men had lower suicide rates than single men, Catholic countries lower rates than Protestant countries, and enlisted men lower rates than army officers. Further, suicide rates seemed to go up whenever there was a sudden downturn or upturn in the business cycle. These systematic differences and fluctuations could not be explained by reference to individual psychological states. The social fact of suicide rate variation had to be explained by variations in the state of society. According to Durkheim, variations in social organization accounted for variations in the suicide rate. Thus, for example, when society was organized around a strong ethic of individualism, with few mediating structures between the individual and the consequences of his or her action, individual success or failure was not a shared phenomenon. A person was seen as captain of his own ship, responsible for what befell him. In such a social system, failure was an entirely individual burden. Other societies, however, stressed the collective, and thus both success and failure were shared burdens. This explained the higher suicide rate in Protestant countries and among single men. The institutional structure of family life or of the Catholic Church lessened the need for individuals to assume life's burdens alone. On the other hand, some organizations stress the life of the group at the expense of the individual. In this kind of social arrangement, the individual is expected to put the group's welfare above his own. The army is one such institution, and thus officers, who are more socialized into its values than enlisted men, will voluntarily sacrifice themselves more quickly for group interests than will those who are serving only short periods of time, often against their will. Finally, a society that is disorganized and offers no clear indication of success or failure will produce high suicide rates since external controls to regulate behavior are lacking. When there is an economic depression or an economic boom, the traditional standards by which a person judges himself or herself in relation to others are absent, and thus a person is set adrift without the social moorings to guide him or her. Personal fulfillment becomes increasingly difficult in this state of normlessness or, as Durkheim termed it, the state of anomie.

As we have seen, notions of anomie are contained in the writings of the early Chicago School. The gang is an outgrowth of a disorganized, anomic social situation. The concept of anomie and the place of the social structure in generating deviant behavior was further developed by Robert K. Merton.

Merton developed an elegant yet simple schematic for portraying society's role in the generation of various kinds of behavior.[46] Society dictates the appropriate goals that a person should strive to achieve. At the same time society also dictates the means one should use for obtaining the goals. If there are not a sufficient number of socially approved means available for achieving socially desired goals, a situation of anomie is created and deviant adjustment to the situation encouraged. The goals and means schema with behavioral adaptations are as follows:

	Goals	Means
Conformist	+	+
Innovator	+	−
Ritualist	−	−
Retreatist	−	−
Rebel	±	±

A person who accepts both the goals and the means for obtaining them is a conformist. An individual who accepts the goals of a society—money, material possession, and so on—but uses means not approved by the society to obtain them—burglary rather than a job in the straight world—would be an innovator. Obviously, this kind of adaptation would be of interest to the criminologist. Merton argued that innovative behavior is encouraged when society fails to provide the legitimate means necessary to obtain a goal. Further, those people on the margins of a society, the economically dispossessed, for example, are more likely to be socialized into deviant means. The ritualist is a person who does not accept the goals of a society, but who goes through the motions that would be expected to lead to a particular goal. The person who has a nine-to-five job but is not really interested in its rewards and simply performs a task because there is nothing better to do would exemplify this adaptation. Systems, too, can become exercises in ritual. As we will see, courtroom procedures are sometimes gone through for appearance sake rather than to actually obtain the goal of justice. A retreatist is one who accepts neither the goals nor the means of a society. The dropout, the beat generation of the 1950s, the hippies of the 1960s, would exemplify this mode of adjustment. Substance abusers would also represent a retreatist adaptation. Finally, the rebel would be the individual who does not accept the current goals and means of a society, but at the same time actively seeks a substitute for these new goals and new means.

Merton's scheme is compelling from a number of perspectives. It sounds true. Its essentials can be easily grasped. And it provides a rather clear policy mandate. Legitimate means must be expanded if deviant, innovative behaviors are to be curtailed. Thus, it shifts the focus from crime being the fault of individuals to crime being the fault of inadequate social systems, systems that create anomie because of a dysfunction between goals and means.

Is the scheme, however, scientifically valid? The answer is no. It would be difficult to prove the assertions of the theory. For one thing, as we have already seen, there is not a simple, unified value set in American society. People are simultaneously exposed to competing values, which support a variety of goals and a variety of means to obtain them. Moreover, there is a strong suggestion that joblessness, or more specifically poverty, causes crime. Yet most poor people do not become criminals. To make matters even more confusing, most unemployed people are not poor, nor are most poor people unemployed.[47] Many poor people work, but work in positions that do not provide more than a subsistence level of wages. On the other hand, people who are unemployed may be covered by insurance or be members of families where other wage earners cushion the economic impact of loss of a job. Thus, the link between poverty and crime is complex and by no means straightforward. Moreover, crime is not an unknown entity among people who hold very good jobs and have considerable economic resources, a point underscored by Sutherland. Again, however, the theory does seem to offer a policy prescription. This prescription was further developed by Cloward and Ohlin.

In 1960, Richard A. Cloward and Lloyd E. Ohlin published *Delinquency and Opportunity: A Theory of Delinquent Gangs*. The book is dedicated to Robert K. Merton and Edwin H. Sutherland.[48] The dedication is significant because it highlights the book's attempt to integrate two distinct theoretical traditions. Merton, following Durkheim, attempted to account for the societal pressures that lead to deviance. Sutherland and people such as Shaw and McKay focused on how certain features of the social structure led to the selection and evolution of particular forms of deviant behavior. Thus, lower-class boys and businessmen can both experience pressure toward deviance, but the specific form such deviance will take will vary according to the social conditions in which each one finds himself. Further, among gang boys themselves there appear to be different deviant traditions and adaptations.

Cloward and Ohlin postulate two opportunity structures, one legitimate and one illegitimate. If the legitimate structure is either inaccessible or if its rewards are not sufficiently attractive, the illegitimate opportunity structure becomes a viable alternative. But part of this variation can be explained by the norms and traditions of particular geographical areas within the city. Some areas are characterized by stable criminal subcultures. Whyte's Cornerville, where the rackets existed alongside of and in mutual cooperation with legitimate enterprise, represents a particular kind of illegitimate opportunity structure. Gang behavior lends itself to organization and goal orientation. Thus, theft, extortion, and so on become a systematic way of securing income. Some areas, however, do not have such stable criminal patterns and tend to be disorganized. In this kind of environment, conflict subcultures develop wherein gang activity tends to involve violence to secure turf and status. Gangs fight each other for symbolic rewards rather than for income. Finally, individuals can be double failures, unable to make it in either the legitimate or illegitimate opportunity structure. The deviant adaptation in this case tends to be retreatist, and individuals become members of gangs that stress the consumption of drugs.[49]

Labeling Theory

Since the days of W. I. Thomas, Charles Horton Cooley, and George H. Mead, there had been the suspicion that the social structural approach was inadequate for understanding human behavior.[50] Durkheim had been criticized for reifying society, that is, creating a concept which then took on a reality independent of the action and beliefs of individual people. In the view of the opposition, society had no existence independent of the people who made it up. Thus, sociology should concentrate on micro questions, questions of how people construct meaning in their everyday life. This view, which had always constituted a distinctly minority position in the field, found the climate of the late 1960s and early 1970s ideal for growth and development. Suspicion of the federal government, dismay at the control orientation of criminal justice implementers, and disaffection from the general status quo of the discipline led to this minority position asserting itself. In criminology, this development became known as labeling theory.

Labeling theory began as a rather mild reform to then current criminological theory with Edwin M. Lemert's 1951 book, *Social Pathology*.[51] In this work, Lemert proposes two forms of deviance, primary and secondary. Primary deviance is situationally induced through exposure to conflicting norms and the choice of one set of norms over another because of the immediate pressures within the situation. In this formulation, Lemert follows the tradition of Sutherland and others who attribute pressure toward deviance to norm conflict. Thus, there may not be clear rules for a particular situation, or the usual rules may be less satisfactory than an alternative set of norms in certain circumstances. While everybody finds themselves in such situations occasionally, certain groups within society find themselves more often in circumstances where there is pressure to adopt alternative sets of norms.

Such situational deviance is primary in the sense that it is in response to an immediate situation. The individual is not likely to see himself or herself as deviant, but to separate the self from the act. However, primary deviance can excite a social response. Others recognize the act as deviant and respond to it in a negative manner. Further acts of deviance may then be met with even harsher societal or group responses. These responses eventually isolate an individual causing defensive, hostile behaviors on his or her part. These behaviors are examples of secondary deviance. According to Lemert:

> When a person begins to employ his deviant behavior or a role based upon it as a means of defense, attack or adjustment to the overt and covert problems created by the consequent societal reaction to him, his deviation is secondary.[52]

Lemert's work drew attention to the role of control agencies in the creation and perpetuation of deviant careers. By the 1960s, the notion that control agencies were themselves responsible for many of the problems then facing society had currency in the academic community. By then, some scholars were arguing that deviance itself had no existence independent of its being recognized and labeled by those in authority. Howard Becker's view summarizes this more radical stance:

> Social groups create deviance by making the rules whose infractions constitutes deviance, and by applying those rules to particular people and labeling them as outsiders. From this point of view, deviance is not a quality of the act the person commits, but rather a consequence of the application by others of rules and sanctions to an "offender." The deviant is one to whom that label has been applied, deviant behavior is behavior that people so label.[53]

Other theorists such as Schur and Erikson continued to challenge not only the notion that deviance is inherent in certain behaviors but also the objective reality of the concept.[54] Simply put, deviance exists only in the eye of the beholder. Under this conceptual scheme, government was no longer the agency of problem solution but was itself the problem. This formulation reflected the political tenor of the times. Like other theoretical frameworks we have discussed, the labeling perspective gained adherents and popularity because it fitted in well with certain ideological viewpoints that were then current. As with previous theories, its ideological elements were at times more important than its scientific rigor. While labeling theory provided stimulating ideas and research that illuminated the workings of criminal justice agencies, its central concepts were not routinely subject to vigorous testing. When they were, the research evidence, at best, cast suspicion on some of the theory's major tenets.[55] At worst, the evidence seemed to refute key concepts of the labeling perspective. To complicate matters even further, interpretation of the data often depended upon the theoretical stance of those doing the interpreting. Black and Reiss, for example, found that police officers routinely based their decision to arrest juveniles on the seriousness of the offense and not on factors such as the juvenile's race. The only exception to this was when legal evidence was unclear.[56] Then demeanor of the juvenile became an important determinant of the decision to arrest. Labeling theory holds that those who are already perceived as having negative social traits are more likely to be labeled deviant. The perceived nature of the individual rather than the objective nature of the act is the key variable. How are the Black and Reiss data to be interpreted? Those holding the labeling perspective viewed the data as supportive of their position.[57] Demeanor did predict outcome in cases where legal evidence was ambiguous. Those holding other theoretical perspectives concluded that the data refuted labeling theory.[58] The objective characteristic of the act, particularly when this was apparent, determined the legal categorization of the event. What this example clearly illustrates is the need for labeling theorists to be more precise in both their conceptual categories and in their description of the relationship among act, actor, and perceiver of the act. Ironically, it may also illustrate that, among criminologists at least, the label they attach to each other predicts their assessment of and reaction to "objective" data sets.

Conflict Theory from a Marxist Perspective

We saw in Chapter 2 that a variety of interest groups attempt to shape the law, its interpretation, and its administration. In a pluralistic society, it is difficult to pinpoint a single, overriding power center. Yet, this is the major thrust of a Marxist perspective on crime and criminology. Laws serve the interest of the capitalist or ruling class at the expense of the proletariat or working class. Given this orientation, two questions must be confronted when applying a Marxist-oriented framework to the understanding of crime. First, is there a ruling elite? Second, how would such a group be able to exercise power in a complex heterogeneous society? Unfortunately, the answers to these questions are neither simple nor straightforward.

Evidence clearly suggests that there is an elite in this society. At the beginning of the 1970s, the top 1% of the population owned over 40% of the wealth in the United States.[59] By 1983, the income gap between rich and poor had widened. The poorest one fifth of families with children had a lesser share of the national wealth than they had in 1968. The richest one fifth had increased its share. Between 1980 and 1984, the richest one fifth of American families increased their disposable income by $25 billion. The poorest one fifth lost $7 billion. Those who manage society, corporate executives, high-level politicians and state administrators, military commanders, and those in the judiciary are overwhelmingly drawn from the upper middle, professional, and propertied classes.[60] Further, economic power seems concentrated in a relatively few major corporations. In 1965, of the 340,000 industrial corporations in the United States, the biggest 500 had 60.2% of the industrial sales and accounted for 71% of the industrial profits. Similar concentrations of economic resources existed in other areas of the economy including banking and utilities. A relatively small number of companies accounted for a major share of economic assets and profits.[61] By 1986 this concentration too seemed to have increased. As Chapter 10 will show, the corporate mergers and acquisitions of the mid-1980s further consolidated economic power.[62]

While there may clearly be an elite in this society, however, the question of whether it *rules* is more complex. Laws respond to interest group pressure. Thus, particular laws do serve the interest of the haves. But, again as was noted in Chapter 2, criminal statutes have the assent of the majority of the population. Further, research suggests that interest groups are formed in response to specific issues.[63] Thus, such groups are relatively unstable with a certain collection of groups coalescing around one issue at one time, but given another issue these same groups may find themselves at odds. The presence of an elite therefore does not automatically mean that a tiny, readily identifiable group can or does exercise power exclusively or in its own interests. Elite interests may not themselves be unified, nor may representatives of elite groups have the technical knowledge necessary to exercise control. The history of nineteenth- and early twentieth-century criminal justice reform efforts discussed in Chapters 5 and 6 illustrates these points. Different elites expected the police to respond to different problems. And, as the last chapter noted, social science was to provide the technological know-how decision makers (political elites) lacked.

Marxist scholars such as Dahrendorf have recognized that in a highly complex technologically advanced society, technicians and administrators wield a great amount of influence and power.[64] The issue is clouded, however, by the meaning of the word rule. This brings us to the second question.

Marx wrote:

> . . . the ideas of the ruling class are in every epoch the ruling ideas: i.e. the class which is the ruling material force of society, is at the same time its ruling intellectual force. The class which has the means of material production at its disposal, has control at the same time over the means of mental production.[65]

Marxist criminology does not require that the elite exercise control directly through a monopoly of offices or the exclusive use of a legislative process. Control can mean the ability to dictate what constitutes legitimate knowledge and therefore the legitimate definition of problems. The import of this for the study of criminology is captured by Jeffrey H. Reiman, who applies a Marxist perspective to the criminal justice system:

1. Society fails to protect people from the crimes they fear by refusing to alleviate the poverty that breeds them.
2. The criminal justice system fails to protect people from the most serious dangers by failing to define the dangerous acts of those who are well off as crimes and by failing to enforce the law vigorously against the well-to-do when they commit crimes.
3. By virtue of these and other failures, the criminal justice system succeeds in creating the image that crime is almost exclusively the work of the poor, an image that serves the interests of the powerful.[66]

Reiman offers the provocative thesis that the so-called failures of the criminal justice system are really not failures at all. The criminal justice system works the way it does to perpetuate a particular image of crime and the criminal. This keeps efforts to control crime focused on the poor, leaving the rich to define their own activity in noncriminal terms. The end result is the title of Reiman's book, *The Rich Get Richer and the Poor Get Prison.*

It was noted in Chapter 1 that applying the term "crime" is essentially a judgment or evaluation of a situation. It was further pointed out that definitions change over time and that formerly noncriminal activity can come to be seen as criminal. The process by which this occurs brings us back to interest groups. Those who can capture the engines of public opinion can greatly affect the definition of what is considered criminal. But are these always the same people, a distinct elite forging the image of legitimate knowledge to suit their own ends? In a highly complex society like our own it would be naive to believe that a small cadre of people continually, consciously manipulate public opinion, knowledge, and law in such a simplistic, conspiratorial manner. Nevertheless, it would also be naive to believe that certain groups do not have an advantage in shaping public opinion. It was Sutherland who early on recognized that white-collar crime is less stigmatized than street crime and that indeed the former is often not even considered to be a crime. Marxist criminologists are correct to draw attention to societal dangers posed by "respectables." They have a tendency, however, to oversimplify the nature of the elite, associating it with a simple class dichotomy, the ruling elite or capitalist class. Everybody else, the workers, are subject to exploitation by this class.

Yet Marxist scholars, as opposed to Marxist criminologists, have begun to move away from a simple class dichotomy to describe modern society. Indeed Marx himself recognized that a professional-bureaucratic class existed, and that this class would become increasingly important as society advanced technologically.[67] Thus, while Marxist criminology has contributed provocative ideas to the study of crime, further research and work needs to be done so that the various subtleties of Marx's original thought can be appreciated. This is not an easy undertaking, as the many commentaries on Marx suggest. Marx himself never specifically dealt with crime, and his own economic thought changed over time.

A Combination of Perspectives: Control and Bonding Theories

Some perspectives have tried to combine various elements of particular approaches. Notable among these is Walter Reckless's containment theory.[68]

Reckless viewed people as being controlled by both inner (psychological) and outer (sociological) containments. Outer containments consist of community norms and values that exact pressure toward noncriminal behavior. Included here would also be social roles that conform to society's expectations. Thus, being a student, a worker, a spouse, and so on all exact an external force on an individual to perform certain activities in certain ways. Inner containments are the result of socialization or the internalization of societal expectations. Another word for internal containment might be "conscience." Reckless has developed five indicators of internal containment: a healthy self-image, goal directedness, a realistic level of aspiration, the ability to tolerate frustration, and an identification with lawful norms. The absence of any of these types of containments, inner or outer, will make deviance more likely.

Containment theory forms the foundation for much modern probation and parole practice, particularly assessment of a person's chances for success on probation. Thus, this theory will be discussed more fully in the chapter on corrections.

Another attempt at integrating the diverse understandings of crime can be found in David Matza's theory of delinquency and drift. Matza struggles with an issue that has haunted much criminological theorizing since the time of Lombroso. In their efforts to understand crime, criminologists have often tended toward a deterministic view of human behavior. Even sociological theories, while not as deterministic as biological and psychological views, have paid little attention to the operation of free will. Ultimately, most individuals make a conscious choice to behave one way or another. The only exception to this would be in cases where an individual is so pathologically debilitated that such choices are absent. As we have seen, most crime is not of this variety.

Matza's concept of value stretch attempts to incorporate free will within the sociological dynamics of mainstream perspectives.[69] Conflicting values transmitted through the socialization process combined with situational exigencies can cause juveniles to stretch the boundaries of what is considered acceptable behavior. Such stretching puts the individual in a state of drift, making the decision to engage in deviant behavior possible. Delinquents exist, therefore, in a transient state between conventional and unconventional values. In certain circumstances, the conventional values can be neutralized so that unconventional behavior can be engaged in while maintaining the view that such behavior is not really wrong. Sykes and Matza identified five techniques of neutralization. These are denial of responsibility ("I got in with the wrong crowd" or "My parents misunderstand me"); denial of injury ("The guy's losses are covered by insurance"); denial of victim ("The store owner deserved to be ripped off since he cheats people"); condemnation of the condemners ("The cops are the real crooks"); and appeal to higher loyalties ("The needs of friends are more important than the demands of the law").[70]

As we will see in discussing alternatives to traditional case processing, many of these views are in fact reinforced by the routine handling of cases. The criminal justice system is not set up to challenge many of these assumptions.

Notions of drift and containment are found in one of the more popular integrated theories, Travis Hirschi's social bond theory.[71] Our behavior is controlled in large measure by the bonds we form with others. This webbing of social commitment can be gauged by the strength of four separate but interrelated strands. Attachment refers to the sensitivity shown to the opinions of others. It is the ability to empathize and consider how one's behavior will affect relationships with other people. Commitment refers to the time and energy devoted to constructive pursuits. Involvement, which develops as a result of commitment, enmeshes people in a particular way of life, thereby restricting possibilities for other ways of life. If your daily routine involves working from nine to five, cooking dinner for the family, and then doing household chores, your opportunities for a walk on the wild side are severely restricted. Finally, belief refers to acceptance of social norms and legal rules and assent to their legitimacy for guiding behavior.

Hirschi's own studies, using self-report data, show that delinquents and nondelinquents vary according to their degree of agreement with items measuring each of these four dimensions. Nondelinquents show greater respect for law, more involvement in conventional activities, and greater attachment to parents and teachers than do delinquents.[72]

As is clear from the above discussion, integrated theories incorporate a number of different sociological and social psychological explanations of crime. Their foundation, in fact, can be found in the classical notions of Beccaria and Bentham that recognized the choice-making behavior of individuals. People are not simply forced or propelled into deviance. Rather, they choose a particular course of behavior. The presence or absence of internal or external controls, strong, unchallenged social norms, and bonds to conventional people and institutions make the choice of deviant behavior either unlikely or probable.

The eclectic nature of these theories is both a strong and a weak point. On the one hand, the theories appeal to a wide variety of researchers and practitioners, and there is a body of research that can support individual elements of the general approach.[73] On the other hand, since the theories are broad in their scope, the various component parts are not well defined and thus not easily verifiable. For example, a particular level of social bonding is assumed. There is little discussion of why people maintain or fail to maintain social bonds, how weak or strong such bonds have to be to either encourage or discourage deviance, and, finally, whether certain elements of a bond are more important than others.

Critics of these approaches also note that proponents fail to describe the link between bondedness and motivation.[74] A weakening of social bonds does not automatically result in deviance. Why not? Without answers to this and the other questions raised above, the theories can easily slip into the unsatisfactory conclusion that people are deviant because they choose to be.

POLICY CONSIDERATIONS: THEORIES/ARGUMENTS/APPLICATIONS

The Policy Impact of Sociological Criminology

The theories discussed in this chapter, despite their scientific limits, were not without policy impact. Indeed, as noted, most of the theorists assumed and desired that their theories would be useful to those making policy decisions. And the theories did in fact influence the way agencies carried out their programs of delinquency and crime reduction. Detached workers, who went out on the street to work with delinquent gangs rather than stay in the settlement house, were responding to the research of the Chicago School and to the insights of Cohen and others on delinquent subcultures. And while Sutherland may have been less influential on the development of specific programs, the recent work of Glaser suggests that for program evaluation, and thus ultimately for program innovation, Sutherland may yet have something to teach us.

To understand the various policy impacts of the theories discussed thus far, it is useful to review Guba's three levels of policy, originally discussed in Chapter 2. Policy-in-intention refers to the desires and goals of policy makers when they formulate a particular plan of action. Policy-in-implementation is the program that is formulated to achieve the goal of the particular policy. Finally, policy-in-experience is how a particular policy is received by those who are supposed to benefit from it.[75] As noted, many theorists contributed to policy-in-implementation. Their theories were used either to design or to legitimate specific types of intervention. Evaluation research, at least if it is well done, is useful in understanding how the people who are subject to a policy intervention view what is happening, in other words policy-in-experience. But it was not until the 1960s that sociology and criminology were able to contribute to policy-in-intention on a national scale. Two things had to occur before this could take place. First, crime, poverty, and social ills generally had to find a place on the national federal agenda. Second, a theory had to be developed that would suggest how the federal government, through legislation, could affect crime and poverty on a large scale. Such a theory had been in the works since the time of Durkheim and came to policy fruition in the work of Cloward and Ohlin.

Clearly, a policy that the federal government could adopt to combat delinquency would be one that would expand legitimate opportunities while at the same time providing the necessary training to compete successfully within this structure. Cloward and Ohlin's book contained a key idea leading to Lyndon Johnson's War on Poverty and the development of the Office of Economic Opportunity.[76] Poverty had become a national issue because of muckrakers such as Michael Harrington who, in his book *The Other America* pointed out that in the land of opportunity one third of the nation was ill-housed and ill-fed.[77] The civil rights movement further pointed to systemic inequities in the availability of legitimate opportunities. Poverty and what was assumed to be one of its major consequences, crime, had become national issues at a time when sociology seemed to provide for a national solution.

At one level, the war on poverty was a success. The number of those living below the poverty line decreased.[78] Whether it was cost-effective was a question of the 1980s. In the 1960s and 1970s this did not occupy the attention of policy makers. But another issue related to poverty increasingly took center stage in the national policy arena. Contrary to expectations, the crime rate, rather than decreasing, appeared to increase. Moreover, as legitimate opportunities seemed to expand, the demand for even greater opportunity increased. Some of these demands were made in the streets, and urban riots became a commonplace spectacle on the nightly news. Thus, concern about law and order replaced the more general concern about the plight of the poor. As already discussed, Lyndon Johnson, reacting defensively to Barry Goldwater and the Republican's effort to make crime an issue of the 1964 election, created the Law Enforcement Assistance Administration. Criminologists were now called upon to provide specific, concrete answers to the problem of crime, answers that would result in immediate solutions. Long-term structural change was no longer a fashionable approach. Sociology, and the standard criminology that flowed from it, had enjoyed a brief moment in the sun. Its time was now eclipsed by a demand to be practical and immediate.

The criminological community was generally suspicious of the law and order rhetoric that predominated in so much of the political discourse of the mid-1960s through the early 1970s. A generally liberal community, it reacted negatively to the control-oriented strategies that were being encouraged at the federal level. Further, disaffection with the federal government and its ability to solve problems began to pervade the social science community as the war in Vietnam continued to rage. Protest seemed the order of the day. In the streets, in changing life styles, and even in social science theory, the status quo was under attack. In the last arena, that of social science theory, there had always been a loyal opposition to the dominant orientation of the field. Labeling theory seemed to fit the critical stance adopted by many social scientists toward the criminal justice system.

When assessing the policy impact of labeling theory, it is tempting to view movements such as deinstitutionalization, diversion, and decriminalization as direct outgrowths of this perspective. It is also wrong, at least as far as criminal justice is concerned. As Lemert himself noted in a 1981 article assessing the impact of diversion in juvenile justice, diversion is an old rather than new concept.[79] The juvenile court itself was an effort at diversion. Further, in its modern reincarnation, diversion programs have more often been a response to pragmatic concerns such as budgetary constraints and overloaded court dockets than to the theoretical tenets of labeling theory. Moreover, it is far from clear, at least in juvenile justice, that true diversion has actually taken place. As Lemert notes, diversion has often meant a simple change in the location of social control as, for example, a diversion from the juvenile court to a private treatment agency. In many cases, such "diversion" has resulted in more rather than less social control and, from the labeling perspective, a therefore greater chance for the development of secondary deviation. Finally, it might have been naive to think that the labeling perspective would have had a great deal of policy impact, particularly at the level of implementation. Research from this perspective tended to be highly critical of those responsible for carrying out criminal justice policies, the police, the lower courts, and correctional personnel. This tendency was described by Howard Becker in a seminal piece, "Whose Side Are We On?" Becker argued that the criticism of lower-level policy implementers was functional. It allowed criminologists to be liberal and well funded at the same time.[80] The policy makers, who also distributed the research funds, were not the subject of labeling critiques. This lacuna, however, was probably due less to crass materialism than to the problem labeling focused on. How do the decisions of control agents affect the adoption of deviant careers by those responding to such control? Nevertheless, there was clearly a need to look, with a critical eye, at those who set policy in the first place. This need was filled by a more macro perspective: social conflict theory.

The policy relevance of conflict theory is difficult to ascertain. Obviously, a theory that suggests a radical reorientation of an entire society would not be welcome by policy makers, who after all represent the existing status quo and are by nature incrementalist. Many of the policy suggestions that have been made by Marxist criminologists—gun control, a more equitable distribution of wealth and income, less reliance on prison, recognition of white-collar and industrial crime—are policy suggestions flowing from a variety of theoretical paradigms including the traditional sociological ones discussed in this chapter. Nevertheless, despite problems of conceptual, scientific, and policy adequacy, Marxist criminology has served to remind researchers that it is often too easy to accept the definitions and assumptions prevalent in a society and thereby to perpetuate injustice and exploitation. The contribution of Marx to criminology can potentially increase, if proponents of this view develop or delve into the writings of Marx himself and combine advances in Marxian scholarship with advances in criminological understanding.

Finally, the policy impact of social control theories can be seen in many programs designed specifically for juvenile offenders and, as noted, in the administrative rationales justifying certain probation and parole practices. Almost any program that seeks to strengthen family ties, commitment to law, or involvement in "wholesome" religious or civic activities can be legitimated by control theories.

Have We Influenced Policy?

Have criminologists been successful in their attempts to contribute to public policy? A review of criminological theory suggests that the answer is a straightforward yes and no.

Most often, it seems that criminological theory and public policy develop simultaneously, each responding to the dominant ideological current of the time. Thus, while it is certainly true that criminology has been used by the policy community, its use has been primarily to legitimize programs of intervention that have come about in response to broader social trends and ideas. To be sure, academic knowledge helps formulate the ruling ideas of the times, but this knowledge is boiled down and transformed in the cauldron of immediate needs, problems, prejudices, and administrative activity. Programs and theory have therefore often been mutually reinforcing, and criminologists have participated in the policy arena more as informed citizens than as scientists. It is little wonder that a theory's popularity is not dependent upon its scientific adequacy.

Scientific understandings of crime must compete within the marketplace of ideas for influence. Public policy is shaped by what has been termed "ideas in good currency."[81] These are ideas that for a time structure both the problems and the solutions within a policy arena. Such ideas hold center stage for only a limited time, since other ideas are constantly attempting to become ideas in good currency. The history of criminological theory illustrates this same dynamic. Certain ideas for a time command attention and resources, only to be replaced by new theories. The lesson for public policy is that general ideas in good currency and specific theories of crime are incomplete. They are like metaphors that highlight certain aspects of the problem but ignore others. To say that crime is like a disease is useful for a time, but it becomes dysfunctional when the metaphor becomes a myth, i.e. crime is a disease.[82] Scientists, policy makers, and policy implementers therefore must exercise skepticism regarding ideas in good currency and recognize that they are metaphors that can be useful for understanding some parts of a problem, but not all of the problem.

Such skepticism comes easily for a scientist when working in a laboratory, a library, or a classroom. It becomes much more difficult when attempting to influence a policy maker or a policy implementer, who wants solutions, not more questions and problems. And so the dilemma remains. How can a scientist influence policy, *as a scientist*? How can scientific knowledge be best utilized by those governing society? To answer these questions, it is necessary to understand how organizations work, and how those within them utilize information in their daily job activity. We turn to these issues in the next chapter.

SUMMARY

What Was Said

- In the United States, the ideology of planning provided fertile ground for the development of a sociological explanation of crime.
- The early Chicago School, influenced by the writings of Durkheim and Tarde, emphasized an ecological approach to explain crime and delinquency. Differential rates of deviance in urban areas was due to social disorganization, which in turn was caused and/or exacerbated by urban land use patterns.
- The subculture explanations of crime and delinquency stress the organized nature of deviance around a value set at odds with the larger society. The works of Whyte, Cohen, and Miller illustrate the different facets of this approach.
- Social learning theory is developed in the work of Edwin Sutherland and his theory of differential association.
- Social structural explanations of crime and delinquency emphasize

Durkheim's concept of the independent nature of the social structure on human activity. The works of Merton and Cloward and Ohlin illustrate this view.

• Labeling theory has a more micro orientation and forces attention on how the action of control agents may encourage further deviance.

• Marxist criminology or conflict theory stresses the role of macro structures in creating an underclass and a definition of deviance favorable to maintaining the position of the powerful.

• Integrated theories stress the need to develop and maintain social bonds as a check for delinquent activities.

• Sociological theories have a number of scientific inadequacies and yet have contributed to the process of social policy.

• Such contributions seem, however, to be more indirect than direct: A theory's ability to influence social policy is directly related to its appeal based on larger social trends and influences. It is therefore often used to legitimate programs or policies formed in response to broader societal pressures.

What Was Not Said

• Improving the scientific rigor of criminological theory will enhance its policy relevance.

• Scientific rigor should be ignored.

NOTES

1. Robert A. Scott and Arnold R. Shore, *Why Sociology Does Not Apply: A Study in the Use of Sociology in Public Policy*. (New York: Elsevier, 1979), p. 94.

2. Ibid., p. 100.

3. Ibid., p. 101.

4. Ibid.

5. Emile Durkheim, *The Elementary Forms of the Religious Life*, trans. Joseph Ward Swain (Glencoe, IL: The Free Press, 1954); George Simpson, *The Division of Labor in Society*, trans. (Glencoe, IL: The Free Press, 1933); *Suicide, A Study in Sociology*, trans. John A. Spaulding and George Simpson (Glencoe, IL: The Free Press, 1951).

6. Margaret S. Wilson Vine, "Gabriel Tarde" in *Pioneers in Criminology*, Hermann Mannheim, ed. (Montclair, NJ: Patterson Smith, 1972), p. 292–304.

7. Ibid., p. 295.

8. Ibid.

9. Nicholas C. Mullins, *Theories and Theory Groups in Contemporary American Sociology*, (New York: Harper and Row, 1973), p. 41.

10. Ibid., p. 45.

11. Robert E. Park, Ernest W. Burgess, Roderick D. McKenzie, *The City*, (Chicago: The University of Chicago Press, 1925).

12. Ibid., p. 150.

13. Clifford R. Shaw with Frederick M. Zorbaugh, Henry D. McKay, Leonard S. Cottrell, *Delinquency Areas* (Chicago: The University of Chicago Press, 1929).

14. Frederic M. Thrasher, *The Gang* (Chicago: The University of Chicago Press, 1927).

15. Ibid., pp. 22–24.

16. Sophia M. Robison, *Juvenile Delinquency: Its Nature and Control* (New York: Holt, Rinehart and Winston, 1960), pp. 166–72.

17. Ibid., p. 94.

18. Thrasher, *The Gang*, pp. 194–213, and 214–27.

19. William Foote Whyte, *Street Corner Society* (Chicago: The University of Chicago Press, 1943).

20. Ibid., p. xvi.

21. Albert K. Cohen, *Delinquent Boys: The Culture of the Gang* (New York: The Free Press, 1955).

22. Ibid., p. 54.

23. Ibid., p. 28.

24. Walter B. Miller, "Lower Class Culture as a Generating Milieu of Gang Delinquency," *Journal of Social Issues*, 14, No. 3 (1958), 5–19.

25. Marvin E. Wolfgang and Franco Ferracuti, *The Subculture of Violence: Towards an Integrated Theory in Criminology* (London: Tavistock, 1967).

26. Robert A. Gordon, James F. Short, Jr., Desmond S. Cartwright, and Fred L. Strodtbeck, "Values and Gang Delinquency: A Study of Street Corner Groups," *American Journal of Sociology*, 69 (September 1963), 109–28.

27. Albert J. Reiss and Albert L. Rhodes, "The Distribution of Juvenile Delinquency in the Social Class Structure," *American Sociological Review*, 26, (October 1961), 720–32.

28. David Matza and Gresham M. Sykes, "Juvenile Delinquency and Subterranean Values," *American Sociological Review*, XXVI, 5 (October 1961), 712–19.

29. "People, etc." *St. Louis Globe-Democrat*, March 8–9, 1980, p. 12.

30. Joseph F. Sheley, *Understanding Crime—Concepts, Issues, Decisions* (Belmont, CA: Wadsworth Publishing Company, Inc., 1979), pp. 37–38.

31. Gwynn Nettles, *Explaining Crime*, 2nd ed. (New York: McGraw-Hill Book Company, 1978), p. 79.

32. Karl Schuessler, in *On Analyzing Crime*, Edwin H. Sutherland (Chicago: The University of Chicago Press, 1973).

33. Sue Titus Reid, *Crime and Criminology*, (Hinsdale, IL: The Dryden Press, 1976), p. 211.

34. Ibid., p. 213.

35. Edwin H. Sutherland, *Principles of Criminology*, 3rd ed. (Philadelphia: Lippincott, 1939).

36. Edwin H. Sutherland, *Principles of Criminology*, 4th ed. (Philadelphia: Lippincott, 1947), pp. 6–7.

37. Donald R. Cressey, *Other People's Money*, (New York: Free Press, 1953).

38. Reid, *Crime and Criminology*, p. 214.

39. Herbert A. Bloch and Gilbert Geis, *Man, Crime and Society* (New York: Random House, 1962), p. 380.

40. Edwin H. Sutherland, *White Collar Crime*, (New York: Holt, Rinehart and Winston, 1971), p. 9.

41. Daniel Glaser, "The Interplay of Theory, Issues Policy, and Data," in Malcolm W. Klein and Katherine S. Teilmann, *Handbook of Criminal Justice Evaluation* (Beverly Hills, CA: Sage, 1980), p. 127.

42. D. Lipton, R. Martinson, and J. Wilks, *The Effectiveness of Correctional Treatment: A Survey of Treatment Evaluation Studies* (New York: Praeger, 1975), pp. 172–79, 207–14.

43. Glaser, "Interplay," p. 129.

44. Emile Durkheim, *The Rules of Sociological Method*, trans. S. A. Solovay and John H. Mueller, G. E. G. Catein, ed. (Glencoe, IL: The Free Press, 1938).

45. Durkheim, *Suicide*.

46. Robert K. Merton, *Social Theory and Social Structure*, enl. ed. (New York: The Free Press, 1968), pp. 190, 192–193.

47. Michael Harrington, *The New American Poverty* (New York: Holt, Rinehart, and Winston, 1984), p. 110.

48. Richard A. Cloward and Lloyd E. Ohlin, *Delinquency and Opportunity: A Theory of Delinquent Gangs* (New York: The Free Press, 1960).

49. Ibid., p. 150.

50. Charles Horton Cooley, *Social Organization* (New York: Charles Scribner's Sons, 1909, 1937). George H. Mead, *Mind, Self, and Society from the Standpoint of a Social Behaviorist*, Charles W. Morris, ed. (Chicago, IL: University of Chicago Press, 1934). W. I. Thomas and F. Znaniecki, *The Polish Peasant in Europe and America* (New York: Knopf, 1927).

51. Edwin M. Lemert. *Social Pathology*, (New York: McGraw-Hill Book Company, Inc., 1951), p. 75.

52. Ibid., p. 76.

53. Howard S. Becker, ed. *The Other Side* (New York: The Free Press, 1964), p. 9.

54. Kai T. Erikson, "Notes on the Sociology of Deviance," *Social Problems*, 9 (Spring 1962), 307–14. E. M. Schur, *Labeling Deviant Behavior* (New York: Harper and Row, 1971), p. 25.

55. Charles W. Thomas and John R. Hepburn, *Crime, Criminal Law, and Criminology* (Dubuque, IA: Wm. C. Brown, 1983), pp. 251–53.

56. D. Black and A. J. Reiss, Jr. "Police Control of Juveniles," *American Sociological Review*, 35 (1970), 63–77.

57. E. M. Lemert, "Response to Critics: Feedback and Choice," in *The Uses of Controversy in Sociology*, L. Coser and D. Larsen, eds. (New York: Macmillan, 1976).

58. T. Hirschi, "Labelling Theory and Juvenile Delinquency," in *The Labelling of Deviance*, 2nd ed., W. Gove, ed. (Beverly Hills, CA: Sage Publications, 1980), p. 2.

59. Marshall E. Blume, Jean Crockett, and Irwin Friend, "Stock-ownership in the United States: Characteristics and Trends," *Survey of Current Business*, 54, No. 11 (November, 1974), 17.

60. Ralph Miliband, *The State in Capitalist Society* (New York: Basic Books, 1969), pp. 49–67. Also see Miliband as quoted in Richard Quinney, *Criminology, Analysis and Critique of Crime in America* (Boston/Toronto-Little, Brown and Company, 1975), p. 289.

61. Richard Pelton, "Who Really Rules America?" *Progressive Labor* (February, 1970), 16–17. Richard Quinney, *Criminology*, (Boston: Little, Brown and Company, 1975), p. 286.

62. Barbara Ehrenreich, "Is the Middle Class Doomed?" *New York Times Magazine*, September 7, 1986, p. 44.

63. David B. Truman, *The Governmental Process: Political Interests and Public Opinion* (New York: Alfred A. Knopf, 1962).

64. Ralf Dahrendorf, *Class and Class Conflict in Industrial Society* (Stanford, CA: Stanford University Press, 1959).

65. Marx, *The German Ideology*, in *The Marx-Engels Reader*, Robert C. Tucker, ed. (New York: W.W. Norton, 1972), p. 136.

66. Jeffrey H. Reiman, *The Rich Get Richer and the Poor Get Prison*, 2nd ed. (New York: John Wiley & Sons, 1984), p. 7.

67. Dahrendorf, *Class and Class Conflict*.

68. Walter Reckless, "Containment Theory," in Marvin E. Wolfgang et al., *The Sociology of Crime and Delinquency*, 2nd ed., (New York: Wiley, 1970), p. 402.

69. David Matza, *Delinquency and Drift* (New York: Wiley, 1964).

70. G. M. Sykes and David Matza, "Techniques of Neutralization: A Theory of Delinquency," *American Sociological Review*, Vol. 22 (December 1957), 664–70.

71. Travis Hirschi, *Causes of Delinquency*, (Berkeley, CA: University of California Press, 1969).

72. Ibid., pp. 203–11.

73. See Thomas and Hepburn, *Crime, Criminal Law, and Criminology*, p. 225 for a review of specific research literature that supports elements of bonding theory.

74. For a general critique of the approach, see Donald R. Cressey, "Fifty Years of Criminology," *Pacific Sociological Review* 22 (1979), 457–80.

75. Egon C. Guba, "What Can Happen as a Result of a Policy?" *Policy Studies Review*, Vol. 5, No. 1 (August 1985), 11.

76. James L. Sundquist, "Origins of the War on Poverty," in *On Fighting Poverty*, James L. Sundquist, ed. (New York: Basic Books, Inc. 1969), pp. 11–12, 29–30.

77. Michael Harrington, *The Other America* (Baltimore, MD: Penquin Books Inc. 1962).

78. Laurence E. Lynn, Jr., "A Decade of Policy Developments in the Income Maintenance System," in *A Decade of Federal Anti Poverty Programs*, Robert H. Haveman, ed. (New York: Academic Press, 1977), pp. 55–117.

79. E. M. Lemert, "Diversion in Juvenile Justice: What Hath Been Wrought," *Journal of Research in Crime and Delinquency*, 18 (1981), 34–46.

80. H. S. Becker, "Whose Side Are We On?" *Social Problems*, 14 (1967), 239–47.

81. Donald Schon, *Beyond The Stable State* (New York: Random House, 1971).

82. Theodore R. Sarbin, "Schizophrenia Is a Myth, Born of a Metaphor, Meaningless," *Psychology Today*, 6 (1972), 18–27.

VIII

Organizing Around Crime

At the end of this chapter, the student will be able to:

A. Distinguish the elements of traditional and nontraditional organization theory.
B. Describe how organizational dynamics can affect the implementation of criminal justice policy.
C. Note the problems with interpreting current data on criminal justice reform efficacy.
D. Discuss which of the organizational paradigms presented seem most appropriate for understanding the criminal justice system.

ISSUE BACKGROUND

Importance of Metaphors

The last chapter introduced the notion of metaphor. In order to understand a complex phenomenon such as crime, it is helpful to define it in relationship to something that is already familiar to us. Thus, in the history of thinking about crime, we have seen law-violating behavior compared to sin, to disease, or to violations of contract. This metaphorical approach to understanding is really quite common. Both scientists and policy makers use it, often without a great deal of thought. Metaphorical understanding can therefore precede the formal steps of problem simplification. When a metaphor is used without reflection to initially define a problem, the metaphor can easily become a myth.[1] Instead of highlighting certain problem elements, the myth and the problem are viewed as identical. But then the metaphor turned myth no longer highlights, it falsifies. Crime may be like a disease but it is not a disease. The myth that it is, has, as we have seen, misled both researchers and policy makers.

Metaphor and myth making is not confined to criminology nor criminal justice policy. Metaphor and myth also pervade the literature on organizational theory.

CRIMINOLOGICAL/CRIMINAL JUSTICE CONSIDERATIONS

Organizations and Organizing:
The Organization as Machine

It should be clear that a student of criminology and public policy needs to have an understanding of organizational dynamics. Gaining such an understanding is not, however, an easy task. Peter K. Manning remarks that organizational analysis is in a period of turbulence.[2] If anything, the term "turbulence" understates the degree of ferment in the field. Battles are being waged over basic understandings of organization, research methods, and metaphors for capturing organizational complexity. How did a field that was once relatively tranquil become such a hotbed of competing ideas? The answer is to be found in the shifting currents of ideology.

The last chapter noted that the bulk of modern-day criminological theory was the product of a planning ideology. The political and ideological milieu of the late nineteenth and early twentieth century also influenced the view of organizations. Thus, there was a tendency to emphasize their rational nature. The reigning view stressed such concepts as the division of labor, formal communications, chain of command, efficiency, and measurable output, which can be evaluated empirically. The metaphor this perspective adopts for understanding organizations is the machine. Each part of the organization is seen as working in conjunction with a rationally ordered whole. Change is considered a technical problem which can be brought about rather quickly through the hierarchical chain of command.[3]

This approach to organizations has been termed the functionalist perspective. Although not generally considered a functionalist, German sociologist Max Weber and his writings on the nature of bureaucracy and the development of rational-legal authority laid the foundation for this perspective.

Weber was concerned with the growth of rationalism in Western society. He dealt with this theme in a number of different ways, including studies on religion (*The Protestant Ethic and The Spirit of Capitalism*, 1948) and authority (*Theory of Social and Economic Organizations*, 1947). For Weber, authority consisted of the probability that an order would be carried out because the person who received it believed in the legitimacy of the command and the person giving it. The use of power, on the other hand, requires coercion because an individual does not grant the order or the order giver the right to exercise domination.[4]

Weber postulated three bases for authority; tradition, charisma, and rational-legal criteria. Traditional authority rests on a belief in unchanging rules for conducting one's life and the legitimacy of those exercising dominance under these rules. Kings and popes exercise traditional authority. Charismatic authority rests on an emotional commitment of a follower to a leader who excites devotion. Adolf Hitler, John F. Kennedy, and Ronald Reagan were leaders who could exercise charismatic authority. Rational-legal authority is based upon meeting the criteria of office. Thus, a person who has graduated from an accredited medical school and has passed state-required examinations is legally entitled to assume the position of physician. In Weber's view, rational-legal authority predominates in Western society and is closely tied to the growth of bureaucracy.[5] Bureaucracy represents the most efficient, rational way of coordinating large numbers of people. Its growth in Western society is tied in with the growth of capitalism, which requires the rational coordination of large numbers of workers. Bureaucrats who do not own the means of production occupy positions of authority within organizations because they meet formal, impersonal qualifications for office.

The notion that systems are rational fits in nicely with the overall ideological view of the planning movement. The assumptions that knowledgeable people, experts, could be efficacious and that the causes of social problems were mainly systemic rather than personal were joined by a basic belief in organizational rationality. Thus, if a system malfunctioned, thereby producing a social evil, it was a straightforward process to repair it and get it to function appropriately.

Shifting Assumptions

As noted previously, the optimism and faith of the planning ideology lasted until about the mid-1960s and early 1970s. But then events of the period made it difficult, if not impossible, to hold simultaneously all three assumptions of the planning ideology—that systems are rational, knowledgeable people can be efficacious, and social problems are mainly systemic rather than personal.

Massive programs of social improvement did not have the dramatic effects anticipated. The war on crime seemed to make the problem worse; the war on poverty was accompanied by the increasing discontent of the poor; the war in Vietnam did not make the world safe for democracy. The good intentions of experts and those in charge were challenged by the sometimes brutal and illegal repression of dissent, the events of Watergate, and again the Vietnam War. Alternative life styles dramatically challenged the assumptions of a rationally ordered world. The hippie movement seemed to offer a chemical escape from an increasingly complex, impersonal, unmanageable world. Eastern religion and Western fundamentalism offered an otherworldly escape, while consumerism provided a hiding place in this world. The right toothpaste, the right car, or the right jeans could shield one from the trials and tribulations of modern life.

If large-scale social planning did not work, it was because at least one of the previously taken-for-granted assumptions about the world was faulty. The result of rejecting one of the assumptions while accepting the other two was ideological turmoil, which in turn affected the theories and disciplines that grew out of the planning movement.

Some policy makers and academics began to deemphasize the systemic nature of social problems and instead focus on individual responsibility. Knowledgeable people were still viewed as efficacious and systems were still rational, therefore program failure was blamed on the clients. Crime and poverty were the fault of the criminal and the poor. Theories and research dealing with biological and psychological determinism reemerged and gained new adherence. Government policies favoring individual entrepreneurs who succeeded while severely penalizing individual failure, either economic or social, became popular. In criminal justice this meant longer sentences and an emphasis on punishment rather than treatment.

Not everyone chose this mix of assumptions. A kind of populist philosophy reemerged which held that people were basically good and systems were rational but experts didn't know what they were talking about. While people holding this view supported many of the policy initiatives of the individualists, they diverged in significant ways. Thus, the political referendum became popular. Many of these referenda were aimed at limiting the ability of government to provide large-scale social services. In some states the power to raise taxes or to impose new sources of government income was severely limited by requiring a popular vote each time a governing unit wanted more money.

Finally, some groups began to suspect that systems rather than people were not what they were thought to be. Maybe systems were not as rational as had been maintained. Actually, the dominant view never did argue that bureaucracies were totally rational. Weber's description of bureaucracy is an ideal type. Weber used ideal types as a research method. The method involved taking the key elements of a phenomenon and using these to construct a typical instance of comparison. Thus, while there is no such thing as the typical American, certain traits associated with the American personality can be combined to form the ideal type. This can then be compared to, say, the typical Frenchman (another ideal type) to advance the understanding of each specific culture.[6]

Researchers after Weber explored in more detail the informal rule of the workplace and the need to sometimes bend the rules if an organization is to work.[7] But even in these studies, the image of the rationally ordered bureaucracy prevailed. Informal work rules, social-emotional leaders not pictured on the company flowchart, and nonproductive job activity were considered ultimately to be in the service of the bureaucracy. They were the safety valves in an essentially rational, goal-directed enterprise. By the 1970s, however, a substantial minority of theorists were questioning the essential rationality of the organization. This view has been designated the interpretive perspective.[8]

Organizations and Organizing: The Organization as Rose-Colored Glasses

The interpretive perspective views organizations as systems of meaning. People actively structure their organizational reality. Thus, organizations act primarily as interpretive lenses through which people assign meaning both to their own activity and to the activity of others. The implications of this assumption stand traditional organizational theory on its head. Activity occurs first. Then the meaning of the activity is negotiated and made to fit into a perceived pattern. Solutions come before problems, action before planning, and goal designation after goal attainment.[9] Organizations act irrationally as often as they act rationally and resist change in spite of overwhelming "factual" evidence that change is required for survival.[10] Moreover, the consequences of organizational action are uncertain and/or accidental.[11]

Chapter 2 showed that the outcomes of organizational activity in criminal justice are sometimes ambiguous. Thus, routines become substitutes for clear results. From an interpretive perspective, then, members of an organization create an environment in which they can act out their typical routines. Notice the radical shift this implies for the understanding of organizations. Organizations do not simply respond to objective situations present in the world around them. Instead, they create an environment that allows them to do what they have always done. Through selective interpretations of events and situations, organizations respond to a world of their own making, a world that reinforces what it is they already do. The goals, plans, strategies, and problem analogies of the rational, functional organization are turned into cultural artifacts that support routines. Actions come before analogies and planning, and, as shown in Chapter 2 noted, problem solutions are available prior to problem designations.

The interpretive perspective also suggests that organizations create the very hurdles they sometimes fall over. By misjudging the environment, by confusing constructed reality with objective reality, by uncritically accepting metaphors as empirical descriptions of events, that is, by inventing myths about the environment, organizations can, in the words of one author, trip and fall right on their artifacts.[12] As we shall see, the world of criminal justice provides numerous examples of organizations attempting to enhance their routines, sometimes in ways that cause them to fall over their own creations.

The interpretive paradigm has shed light on the whimsical nature of the organization. Whimsy, however, is not the only characteristic of created meaning.

Organizations and Organizing: The Organization as Power Talk

What has been termed the radical-humanist paradigm acknowledges that individuals create their own environments.[13] But rather than stressing the whimsical nature of such creations, this perspective underscores the role of power, authority, and coercion in creating and maintaining certain systems of meaning. One method of using power to control the meaning of a given situation is to deny a person the opportunity to talk.

Numerous studies have shown that people have different access to interpretive procedures while talking because the rules of conversation vary among groups. Molotch and Boden review the relevant literature on this issue.[14] Taking a turn to talk is problematic for women when conversing with men,[15] for students when conversing with teachers,[16] for patients when conversing with doctors,[17] for witnesses when being questioned by interrogators.[18] Denial of a turn in talking is more than simple rudeness. The person so denied is unable to participate equally in the structuring of the reality being created through talk. Controlling talk about a phenomenon determines the shape of that phenomenon.

In this perspective an organization does not exist independently of how it is talked about. The perception that an organization has an objective reality, independent of the people who make it up, is a trick of language. Examine the statement, "The company has always done it this way." While the term "company" appears to have a clear meaning, we really do not know to what it refers. Does it mean the president, the board of directors, or are we to understand the term in its most literal sense, to include everybody who is a member of the organization? We really do not know what the term means. Yet it appears to make sense. That is because we habitually grant an objective reality to language terms that are in fact abstract. This process is called reification. But while the term "company" may not have a reality independent from the use of the term, such an abstract category makes certain action both called for and legitimate. If the company has always done it this way, then we had better do it this way too. The "company" has thus exercised control over our action, even though it is our language use that created the reality in the first place! As the radical humanist perspective also notes, we create the lines of our reality, but often trip over what we've drawn.

Organizations and Organizing: The Organization as Dialectic

The notion of reification is also found in Marxism. The systems that exploit people are human creations. In the Marxian view, however, such systems take on a much more objective reality than in the radical humanist approach, and therefore Marx is much more structuralist in orientation.

Marxist social analysis has generated a body of organizational theory that has been termed radical structuralist.[19] This perspective emphasizes the contradictions and tensions that exist in society as a whole and in organizations that both incorporate and attempt to transcend such problems. Thus, organizations are viewed as reflecting deeper societal concerns. For example, the profit motive and the concern for the common good are values that can and do conflict with one another. The response to this conflict has been the creation of a large number of regulatory agencies that function to simultaneously regulate the unrestrained pursuit profit and to maintain the credibility of an overall capitalistic economy. At one level, therefore, conflict between government and business is good for the entire economic system since it allows society to simultaneously hold the values that emphasize the unique worth of individuals and those that emphasize the importance of the bottom line in human transactions. "Let the buyer beware" and "Love thy neighbor" are norms that can each find organizational embodiments. The tensions created by these conflicting norms, however, provide the energy for organizational and societal transformation. Like the general conflict perspective discussed in the last chapter, therefore, tensions and contradictions are viewed as positive for organizations helping them avoid stagnation. Organizations and whole societies change by transcending such problems. To borrow a phrase from the world of bodybuilding, this organizational perspective would argue, "No pain, no gain."

Of course, after a certain level, pain signals a threat to the integrity of the body. The same is true of conflict within and between organizations. One of the tasks of the radical structuralist perspective is to sort out those conflicts that are functional from those that are debilitating within the organized environment. Another task is to determine which conflicts maintain the status quo and which signal a significant societal change. Underlying these tasks is the assumption that attempts to manage conflict create new conflicts in a dialectical process. Like the radical humanist perspective, therefore, this perspective acknowledges the role of the human actors in creating an environment which they then must respond to and manage. Its view, however, is on reification writ large than on the reification of everyday life.

Differences in the perspectives discussed above can be illustrated by noting how each approach can be applied to the study of criminal justice policy.

POLICY CONSIDERATIONS: THEORIES/ARGUMENTS/APPLICATIONS

Functionalist and Interpretive Perspectives Applied

In the functionalist perspective, the environment external to an organization presents objective problems that lend themselves to rational analysis and logical solutions. This is the perspective adopted by most police management texts. The police manager must gather the objective facts and information from the external environment to aid objective decision making inside the organization. Leonard and More's text on police organization and management illustrates this approach:

> Police problems involving crime, delinquency, vice and traffic occur and reoccur in time and place with such a high degree of regularity that administrative predictions are possible. The curves of yesterday and today can be projected into tomorrow in terms of what and how much is going to happen, when and where. Accurate estimates of the situation can be prepared and from them short-term, long-term, and special plans can be formulated.[20]

As we have seen, the nature of the external environment is more problematic within the interpretive frame of reference. From this perspective, an organization creates its own environment and then responds to this creation. An important concept, therefore, is the notion of occupational culture. The environment created supports the activity dictated as appropriate by those performing particular occupational tasks. Two examples will clarify the point.

The War on Drugs, Again

In 1986, the federal government began another battle in its war on drugs. It allotted $1.7 billion for the efforts.[21] The first skirmishes fought, however, were not against drug dealers. The first shots of the battle were those fired in bureaucratic conflicts between agency heads. The various organizations concerned with drug abuse wanted their share of the money to do more of what they were already doing. Of course, what they were already doing had not been particularly effective. Hence the need for the "new" assault on drugs.

One such skirmish was between the head of the Customs Service, the agency which attempts to curb smuggling, and the commandant of the Coast Guard. In the original legislation, the Customs Service was to receive four Navy E2-C radar planes. But the Coast Guard felt it should get the planes. Congress compromised by giving each agency two planes, a solution that left Customs officials bitter.[22]

When President Reagan signed the bill, he went out of his way to emphasize that the legislation was not simply for law enforcement enhancement. Squabbles over airplanes aside,

> This legislation is not intended as a means of filling our jails with drug users. What we must do as a society is identify those who use drugs, reach out to help them, help them quit, and give them the support they need to live right.[23]

Yet old ways of doing things die hard, and "typical" solutions seemed to win the day. The Drug Enforcement Administration, in addition to the $412 million dollars they had already been provided, was authorized an additional $60 million to hire 400 more agents. The U.S. Attorney's Office, funded at

$320 million in the regular budget process, received another $31 million to hire approximately 200 new assistant attorneys general. The U.S. Marshal's Service, budgeted at $142 million, received $17 million more for new positions. The Coast Guard got an extra $128 million and the U.S. Customs Service an additional $44.1 million. This was over and above $93.1 million allotted for the "air interdiction" of drugs. The money given for research was $75 million, while education and prevention were given $200 million.[24] Law enforcement strategies seemed to have once again prevailed in the battle of the budget.

To quote Yogi Berra, this seemed "like déjà vu all over again." We saw in Chapter 3 LEAA's impact, which seemed mainly to consist of increasing the fortunes of law enforcement. Certain officials of the Justice Department also noticed the parallel.

> I'm afraid it looks like we're just throwing money at them again. . . . We still have helicopters sitting around that were bought with LEAA money. There's still an armored personnel carrier that was bought with LEAA money. . . .[25]

The recipients of this new pot of gold were not totally sanguine about its effects on their agencies. A senior drug enforcement official was quoted in the *New York Times* as saying:

> I've been hearing from Congressmen who'd never shown any interest in the drug issue before and don't know much about it. Now all of a sudden they're telling us what we're supposed to accomplish. This is raising everyone's expectations unreasonably.[26]

In the same article an official of the Immigration and Naturalization Service, which houses the U.S. Border Patrol, was quoted as saying:

> There's going to be pressure to get bigger and bigger drug seizures every year. But what's going to happen if our alien arrests fall off as a result?[27]

Finally, the head of the Drug Enforcement Administration stated:

> Law enforcement cannot, did not, and will not solve the appetite for drugs in this country.[28]

He went on to note the disappointment that would develop if law enforcement was expected to solve the problem. The agency did not, however, turn down the money.

Finally, the ironic thing about this war on drugs was that it began several years after drug use began to decline in this country. Social scientists predict that drug use will decline through the 1990s regardless of enforcement activity![29]

Scenarios such as the one described above underscore the nonrational aspects of organizational activity. Nonrational is not, however, inconsistent. Each organization consistently pursues strategies that have failed in the past in order to gain the resources needed to carry out these same strategies in the future.

The Occupational Culture of Police

Jerome Skolnick's book *Justice without Trial* is an in-depth study of the police occupational culture. Skolnick notes that police officers develop a perceptual shorthand for spotting people likely to give them trouble. Skolnick terms the category used by police to identify such people as the "symbolic assailant."[30] From past experience, officers know the traits of those likely to cause them harm. Such traits can include style of hair, style of walking, race or ethnicity, area of the city, and so on. From the point of view of the police officer, such categorizing can be justified on the grounds that it increases the officer's margin of safety. Knowing who is likely to cause harm before an actual encounter can help one be appropriately cautious. Of course, approaching a subject in a brusque or threatening manner can cause that person to react with hostility. This actually decreases the officer's safety. But in either event, the officer is able to confirm the reality of his or her world, a world that calls for the authoritative action supported by police occupational norms. If a person thought to be a symbolic assailant responds meekly to an authoritative command, such as "show me some I.D.," the officer has demonstrated the effectiveness of the approach. If the person gives a smart remark or makes a threatening gesture the officer is able to confirm the view of the world that says certain people will cause trouble. He or she is then justified in exacting even more authority. What is clear here is that police officers participate in the structuring of their external environment. They respond to their own images of the world in ways that call forth from the environment actions that reconfirm the essential rightness of both their behavior and their world views.

The Radical Humanist and Radical Structuralist Perspectives Applied

The radical humanist perspective suggests that one of the key methods for structuring our social worlds is conversation. Criminal justice processes seem particularly filled with speech categories that warrant action based on abstract categories. Sentences are then given based on the category of person, not on the individual's unique circumstances or qualities.[31] Plea negotiations have also been examined in this framework,[32] as have the reality construction of police officers when dealing with suspects.[33] The scenario below illustrates this last example.

In the following exchange, a police officer and a suspect each attempt to define the nature of their encounter.[34] The officer has already discovered track marks on the individual's arm, indicating that he is a narcotics user. However, the encounter began as a traffic incident.

SUSPECT: How come you guys stopped me?

OFFICER: No brake lights.

SUSPECT: No brake lights? I just had the car in the shop. I can show you the bill of sale for getting it fixed.

OFFICER: We can make it hard on you if you want to go that route. We don't stop you for nothing.

SUSPECT: You going to write me a traffic ticket for it? It's a traffic offense.

OFFICER: We'll write you a traffic ticket for it. Also take you to jail for not having a valid operator's license—you want to get heavy.

SUSPECT: Not having a valid license?

OFFICER: You want to play the game that's fine. You want to get heavy, that's fine too. It makes no difference to us.

SUSPECT: Well, wait a minute, man, you can't take me in. I'm working for Martinson. You know, he's a detective in narcotics. He wants me out on the street.

OFFICER: Well maybe you can work for us.

SUSPECT: Hey, no man, I can't. I already work for Martinson.

OFFICER: We'll see.

In the above exchange, it is clear that each participant is trying to negotiate the reality of the situation. The suspect would like the situation defined as simply a traffic encounter and himself as merely a traffic offender. The officer obviously is defining the situation as something else. For the officer, the individual is a narcotics user who can possibly be used as an informant.

It is equally clear that the two participants do not come to the exchange with equal amounts of power. The police officer's definition of the situation is the one finally adopted, after some not-so-subtle reminders that if the suspect doesn't "play the game," the officer can make it even worse for him.

The use of abstract categories rather than situationally specific ones reifies social structures. From this perspective organizations are not external realities that exert pressure, rather they are created and reproduced in particular situations. To quote Maynard and Wilson in regard to sentencing:

> . . . reification is not some pre-existing quality of the criminal justice system that is somehow imposed externally on particular occasions. Rather, the systematic reification of categories is produced in concrete interaction which in turn reproduces the institutional context.[35]

Finally, the conflict perspective discussed in the last chapter illustrates the radical structuralist approach applied to criminal justice. The tension caused by the conflicting norms of society becomes regulated through organizational structures. Therefore, organizations must be viewed in terms of deeper societal concerns. At one level an organization can appear to fail. The criminal justice system is unable to control street crime. At another level, however, this failure can contribute to the maintenance of particular social forms. Focusing on the crimes of an underclass diverts attention from the economic system that may encourage greed and exploitation.[36]

Which Approaches to Apply

Which of the various organizational approaches is most appropriate for understanding policy innovations? The answer depends on the nature of the problem the policy addresses. Policy effects will vary according to two factors: (a) degree of change desired, and (b) the degree of knowledge. These two dimensions can be displayed in a four-cell table.[37]

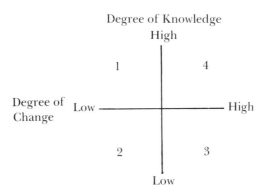

Policy directed at problems that have a high degree of technical knowledge associated with them and will result in a low level of change are best understood in the context of functional theory. A police agency decides to join an already existent regional crime information network to increase its data base on local felons. In this scenario, the rational model can be used to guide policy makers. Specific problems can be anticipated and resolved. Cost and benefit projections will be made, clear contractual obligations spelled out, rules governing personnel access to the information formulated, and equipment purchases balanced against budgetary constraints. Cell 1 simply requires careful planning prior to a policy implementation.

Cell 2, indicating both low knowledge and a low degree of change, describes certain reform situations that occur in criminal justice. As we have seen, it is difficult to bring about a great deal of change in the justice system because of institutional resistance to the alterations of routines. The interactionist perspectives are quite helpful in understanding this dynamic by drawing attention to how such routines create and maintain particular world views. Since such definitions of reality provide both benefits and costs to those who hold them, an interactionist perspective can suggest both the degree of change to be expected and methods for maximizing a policy impact. Computerization can provide another example for illustration.

A department introduces electronic tracking of police vehicles. Dispatchers can now determine which available car is closest to a call by simply checking light blips on a large computer screen overlayed with a map of the city. At first glance, this may seem to be a relatively minor innovation associated with a high degree of knowledge. Such technology has been available for over 20 years. Police officers are already in contact with dispatch through radio. Electronic tracking represents a simple incremental change in an already established communications link with headquarters. But administrators often proceed with such plans ignorant of their symbolic significance. Knowledge of work-group norms and values is low. When such contextual knowledge is low, a seemingly minor change can produce nasty surprises for an administrator. Police officers may interpret the new electronics as a method of increasing administrative control while reducing worker autonomy. The change may be seen as another example of "Big Brother" attempting to regulate all facets of work life. A seemingly straightforward technological innovation becomes a labor relations issue, a symbol of distrust, an object of sabotage. A failure to appreciate the multiple meanings of a situation can result in resistance to change, increased inefficiency, and the eventual failure of a policy innovation.

Cell 3 is a high-risk/high-gain cell. No one is quite sure of what the outcome will be. In 1973, Jerome B. Miller closed all of the state training schools in Massachusetts. As director of the State Department of Juvenile Justice, he took a major risk. The training school was replaced by privately run community residential and nonresidential programs. Critics charged that the crime rate would rise dramatically. The state legislature was furious because Miller waited until they were in recess for the summer before carrying out his action. The end result, however, was considerable savings for the state, a model program of community corrections, and no appreciable change in the rate of delinquency. The gamble seemed to pay off. Unfortunately, because of the criticism Miller's actions engendered, he felt it necessary to leave his job a year or two later, and other states have been slow to adopt the Massachusetts approach.[38] The radical structuralist perspective helps us understand the resistance to such large-scale reform by underscoring the vested interests that benefit from things as they are. In the case at hand, the jobs of correctional officials, the power of legislators, and a juvenile justice system that depended upon a particular definition of crime were all undermined. Such vested interests can therefore be designated as likely sources of reactionary response to reform and their arguments anticipated and countered.

Cell 4 is a change situation seldom if ever encountered in the criminal justice system. We do not deal in areas where there is a great deal of knowledge to carry off large-scale reforms. That does not prevent people from trying, however. In the history of criminal justice reform, prisons, juvenile justice, drug wars, and so on were embarked upon with an optimism and sense of knowledge that were hardly justified. The end result was what has been termed a "panacea phenomenon."[39] People are convinced they have the answer to the problem. They raise their expectations only to have their hopes dashed. The resultant frustration makes acceptance of a new panacea more likely, and the cycle starts all over again. Panaceas can be avoided by applying all of the organizational approaches that have been described and by not letting one of them become the sole lens through which a policy maker or an analyst views the organization of interest.

With these cautions, we are ready to proceed to the actual study of the criminal justice system.

SUMMARY

What Was Said

- Both scientists and policy makers use metaphors when attempting to gain some understanding of complex problems and situations.
- The use of metaphor involves relating something new or complex to something that is already familiar or more simple.
- The statement, "Crime is like a disease," is an example of a metaphor.
- If the statement were interpreted to mean crime is a disease, the metaphor would have become a myth, that is the metaphor and the problem would be viewed as identical.
- A metaphor turned myth no longer highlights, it falsifies. Crime may be like a disease but it is not a disease.
- Metaphors and myths are found in both criminology and organizational theory.
- Organizational theory is in a state of turmoil in part because of shifting ideological currents.
- The major metaphors guiding organization theory are:
  —The organization is like a machine (functionalist perspective)
  —The organization is like rose-colored glasses (interpretive perspective)
  —The organization is like power talk (radical humanist perspective)
  —The organization is like a dialectic (radical structuralist perspective)
- Criminal justice policy analysis can benefit from multiple organizational perspectives, depending upon the degree of knowledge and the degree of change appropriate within a given situation.

What Was Not Said

- Metaphors are an inappropriate means for understanding complex issues.
- There is one correct organizational theory.
- Organizations should be rational.

NOTES

1. Theodore R. Sarbin, "Schizophrenia Is a Myth, Born of a Metaphor, Meaningless," *Psychology Today*, 6 (1972), 18–27.

2. Peter K. Manning, "Organizational Work: Structuration of Environment," *The British Journal of Sociology*, 33, No. 1 (March 1982), 118.

3. Gareth Morgan, "Opportunities Arising from Paradigm Diversity," *Administration & Society*, 16, No. 3 (November 1984), 306–327.

4. Clifford I. Nass, "Bureaucracy, Technical Expertise, and Professionals: A Weberian Approach," *Sociological Theory*, 4, No. 1 (Spring 1986), 61–62.

5. Ibid.

6. W. Richard Scott, *Organizations: Rational, Natural, and Open Systems*, 2nd ed. (Englewood Cliffs, NJ: Prentice-Hall, Inc., 1987).

7. George Homans, *The Human Group*, (New York: Harcourt Brace Jovanovich, 1950).

8. Gareth Morgan, "Opportunities Arising from Paradigm Diversity," *Administration & Society*, 16, No. 3 (November 1984), 313.

9. Karl Weick, *The Social Psychology of Organizing*, 2nd ed. (Reading, MA: Addison-Wesley, 1979).

10. William H. Starbuck, "Congealing Oil: Inventing Ideologies to Justify Acting Ideologies Out," *Journal of Management Studies*, 19, (1982), 3–27.

11. M. D. Cohen, J. G. March, and J. P. Olsen, "A Garbage-Can Model of Organizational Choice," *Administrative Science Quarterly*, 17, (March 1972), 1–25.

12. H. Achuman, "Artifacts Are in the Mind of the Beholder," *American Sociologist*, 17, (1982), 21–28.

13. Morgan, "Paradigm Diversity," p. 317.

14. H. Molotch and D. Boden, "Talking Social Structure," *American Sociological Review*, 50 (1958), 273–88.

15. Don H. Zimmerman and Candace West, "Sex Roles, Interruptions, and Silences in Conversation," in *Language and Sex: Difference and Dominance*, Barrie Thorne and Nancy Henley, eds. (Rowley, MA: Newbury House, 1975).

16. Hugh Mehan, *Learning Lessons: Social Organization in the Classroom* (Cambridge, MA: Harvard University Press, 1979).

17. Sue Fisher and Alexandra Dundas Todd, eds. *The Social Organization of Doctor-Patient Communication* (Washington, D.C.: Center for Applied Linguistics, 1983).

18. Molotch and Boden, "Talking Social Structure," in J. Maxwell Atkinson and Paul Drew, *Order in the Court: The Organization of Verbal Interaction in Judicial Settings* (Atlantic Highlands, NJ: Humanities Press, 1979).

19. Morgan, "Paradigm Diversity," p. 320.

20. V. A. Leonard and Harry W. More, Jr., *Police Organization and Management*, 5th ed. (Mineola, NY: The Foundation Press, 1978), p. 293.

21. Joel Brinkley, "Drug Law Raises More Than Hope," *New York Times*, November 2, 1986, Sec. E, p. 5.

22. Ibid.

23. "Drug Enforcement," *Criminal Justice Newsletter*, 17, No. 21 (November 3, 1986) 2.

24. Ibid.

25. Ibid., pp. 3–4

26. Brinkley, "Drug Law."

27. Ibid.

28. Ibid.

29. Ibid.

30. Jerome Skolnick, *Justice without Trial* (New York: John Wiley and Sons, Inc., 1966).

31. Douglas W. Maynard and Thomas P. Wilson, "On the Reification of Social Structure," in *Current Perspectives in Social Theory*, Scott G. McNall and Gary N. Howe, eds. (Greenwich, CT: JAI Press, Inc., 1980), p. 287.

32. D. Sudnow, "Normal Crimes: Sociological Features of the Penal Code in a Public Defender's Office," *Social Problems*, 12, (Winter, 1965), 255–76.

33. James F. Gilsinan, *Doing Justice: How the System Works as Seen by the Participants* (Englewood Cliffs, NJ: Prentice-Hall, 1982) pp. 41–62.

34. Ibid., pp. 53–54.

35. Maynard and Wilson, "On the Reification of Social Structure," p. 306.

36. Jeffrey Reiman, *The Rich Get Richer and The Poor Get Prison* (New York: John Wiley & Sons, 1984).

37. Donald P. Sprengel, mimeographed paper, St. Louis University.

38. Lloyd E. Ohlin, Alden D. Miller, Robert B. Coates, *Juvenile Correctional Reform in Massachusetts: A Preliminary Report of the Center for Criminal Justice of the Harvard Law School* (Washington, DC: U.S. Government Printing Office, 1976), p. 21.

39. James O. Finckenauer, *Scared Straight! and the Panacea Phenomenon* (Englewood Cliffs, NJ: Prentice-Hall, 1982).

IX

Crime Victims

At the end of this chapter, the student will be able to:

A. Discuss the contingent nature of criminal victimization.
B. Describe the demographic characteristics of certain types of crime victims.
C. Describe the location of certain types of victimization.
D. Discuss various policies aimed at improving the plight of the victim.

ISSUE BACKGROUND

Is the Criminal Justice System a System?

The criminal justice system has often been accused of being a nonsystem. It does not operate as a unified entity, but rather as three separate units: police, courts, and corrections. When conceptualized as a single system, it does not appear to operate in a clearly consistent, rational manner.

As noted in the last chapter, most organizations fail to operate consistently in a totally rational way. Much of what goes on in and between organized entities involves symbolic manipulations, value displays, ritual activity, and unreflective responses to the perceived environment. Organizations are driven by myths as much as by rational planning. And, as we have seen, myth can also pervade our understanding of and expectations for organized entities. Thus, the charge that the criminal justice system is in fact a nonsystem perpetuates the notion that rational, bureaucratic planning is the solution to the myriad of problems faced by the criminal justice enterprise. Rational management is the panacea of many criminal justice reformers and administrators. It is a panacea because it both oversimplifies a very complex phenomenon and holds out hope for an ultimate solution.

As noted, the criminal justice system is not a single entity but a collection of different groups, each with its own beliefs, values, symbols, interests, and strategies. Further, the groups that should be considered part of the system can vary. Chapter 1 argued that there are specific, long-lasting social concerns in our society around which regular governmental coping strategies have developed. The institutions that implement these strategies form the core institutions of the policy area. In criminal justice, people will readily agree that police, courts, and corrections constitute core institutions of the system. Yet for certain purposes various legislative bodies can also be considered central to the criminal justice system, since they are, after all, responsible for the formulation and passage of our criminal statutes. Victims and criminals are also elements of the system. And, depending upon the circumstances, these categories of actors manifest differing degrees of organization. Thus, the so-called system can vary both as to the groups within it and the degree of organization of those groups.

The Different Myths of Criminal Justice Policy: Due Process vs. Crime Control

Different myths also compete for dominance within the criminal justice policy area. Two have traditionally held center stage of the policy debates within the field. These are the crime control model of criminal justice and the due process model. The crime control model argues that the primary responsibility of the criminal justice system is the enforcement of substantive criminal law. This model sees many of the procedural safeguards that have been established as stumbling blocks to fulfilling the primary purpose of the system. Search and seizure laws, Miranda warnings, and so on, are viewed as interfering with the apprehension, prosecution, and incapacitation of the criminal element. On the other hand, the due process model of criminal justice suggests that individuals need protection from government coercion and interference in their lives. Thus, the government must prove a person guilty of a crime and do so according to certain procedural rules.

At first, the due process model was operative only in federal criminal cases. The founders of our country, when articulating the Bill of Rights, were mainly concerned about a too powerful federal government. Most criminal statutes, however, were and are enforced by the states. Thus, at least initially, important protections against unreasonable search and seizure (the Fourth Amendment), self-incrimination (the Fifth Amendment), arbitrary convictions (the Sixth Amendment), and cruel and unusual punishment (the Eighth

Amendment) had little bearing on the bulk of criminal cases. At the state level then, the crime control model flourished. Unfortunately, so too did the abuse of individual rights. Eventually, such abuses shocked the conscience of the nation. A long series of court battles ensued that ultimately resulted in the incorporation of the due process model within state criminal codes.[1]

The stage for these battles was set by the passage of the Fourteenth Amendment after the Civil War. The Fourteenth Amendment holds that "no State shall make or enforce any law which shall abridge the privileges or immunities of citizens of the United States, nor shall any State deprive any person of life, liberty, or property, without due process of law; nor deny to any person within its jurisdiction the equal protection of the laws."

The Supreme Court, however, did not immediately use the Fourteenth Amendment to review state criminal proceedings. In fact, it was not until the 1920s that the Court began to apply federal procedural safeguards to the states, and then only in a very limited way.[2] A decisive shift did not occur until 1961 in *Mapp* v. *Ohio*, when the Court declared that the entire Bill of Rights applied to the states through the Fourteenth Amendment.[3]

Dolly Mapp was convicted by the State of Ohio of possessing obscene material. The Cleveland police initially entered her home looking for a suspect in a bombing. Although the officers claimed to have a search warrant, none was ever produced at her trial. At the time of the incident, when she demanded to see a search warrant, she was shown a piece of paper. She grabbed it and tucked it in her bosom. The officer retrieved it and handcuffed Miss Mapp. The allegedly obscene material was found in a trunk in the basement of her apartment. Although the Ohio Supreme Court upheld the conviction, the United States Supreme Court overturned it, and in doing so ushered in an era of procedural rulings that protected individuals from the arbitrary exercise of power by the state government. Some of the procedural safeguards that developed during this period were the exclusionary rule, which prohibits the use of illegally obtained evidence in a trial (*Mapp* v. *Ohio*), the right to an attorney when police activity changes from investigation to accusation (*Escobedo* v. *Illinois*),[4] and the right to be informed of the protection against self-incrimination and the right to counsel (*Miranda* v. *Arizona*).[5]

It is important to remember that the Supreme Court's activity in this area was in response to some flagrant abuse on the part of police agents. Danny Escobedo, for example, was moved from station house to station house by the Chicago Police Department every time his lawyer appeared and demanded to see him. The lawyer was told that his client was not there. Meanwhile, Danny was simultaneously hustled out the back door to another police station where his interrogation could continue without the interference of a lawyer. Thus, the due process model of criminal justice emphasizes the fact that the defendant is or can become a victim of the state.

The series of procedural rulings issued by the Warren Court during the 1960s and early 1970s were attacked by advocates of the crime control model. The attack took two forms. First, the rulings were portrayed as handcuffing the police. Second, the rulings were viewed as advocating the rights of the defendant at the expense of the crime victim. The first of these arguments will be dealt with in Chapter 11, when policies affecting the police are discussed. The second issue forms part of the subject matter of this chapter.

At the outset, it should be clear that neither model historically paid a great deal of attention to the crime victim. The due process model tended to view the defendant as a victim or potential victim of government excess. The crime control model also focused not only on the defendant, but on his capture and removal from the community. Thus, the actual victim of a crime got little consideration in either model.

The recent interest of criminal justice policy makers in crime victims can be attributed to a number of factors. First, the plight of the victim became a kind of symbol used by advocates of the crime control model to attack the procedural reforms of the Warren Court. Second, victims and/or victim advocates began to organize and exert pressure on legislators to do something for crime victims. In short, victim interest groups emerged as part of the criminal justice policy area. Finally, a new model was fighting for dominance in the area of criminal justice. The model might best be described as the administrative control model.

The New Myth: Administrative Control

The previous chapter noted that advocates of rational management have a long history in criminal justice. It is only recently, however, that the shift in problem definition that this approach implies has taken hold among various components of the criminal justice system. Decreased resources, increased demands for accountability, and crime rates stubbornly resistant to law enforcement strategies have led criminal justice managers to emphasize problems they have some control over and a reasonable expectation of solving. The administrative control model emphasizes efficiency over effectiveness. We may not be able to stop crime, but we can stop waste and manage our resources wisely. Within this context, the problems of crime victims are appealing. As will be seen, such problems have often resulted from procedures that administrators control and can change. Crime victims, therefore, present problem solvers with problems they might actually be able to solve.

Criminal justice policies are influenced by three models: crime control, due process, and administrative control. The first two models are anchored in the purpose and nature of the criminal law. The third model is anchored in organizational theory and flows from the functionalist paradigm discussed in the last chapter. Its concern is the purpose and nature of the organization. While some criminal justice policies represent tradeoffs among the three approaches, many can be seen as coming primarily from one or another of the models. Policies affecting the plight of crime victims illustrate these points.

CRIMINOLOGICAL/CRIMINAL
JUSTICE CONSIDERATIONS

Who and What Is a Crime Victim?

There is a tendency to think of victim and offender as distinct roles. Such a dichotomy, however, tends to oversimplify a complex reality. First, the term "crime victim" is a contingent one. Whether it will be applied depends upon a number of factors. The nature of the incident, the relationship between the victim and the offender, and the characteristics of the person claiming the label are some of the factors considered in its application.[6] Second, while the term is often viewed as describing single individuals, large, impersonal social entities can also be crime victims. As noted in Chapter 6, the federal government can lose as much as $81 billion yearly because of income tax evasion.[7] Recall the hotel chain with its $3 million loss due to towel theft.[8] Third, there are levels of victimization. While the term "victim" is often restricted to an individual directly hurt by a criminal act, there are two other levels of victimization. A secondary level includes spouses, siblings, parents, and others who share a close relationship with the primary victim. These people, too, are affected by a criminal act. A tertiary level includes co-workers, friends, neighbors, and even those who do not know the victim but reside in the same community. At this level, fear and emotional distress can result from the primary victimization.[9] Fourth, given the fluid nature of social interaction, the roles of victim and offender can switch over the course of an incident. Research has shown that some aggressors end up being victims when the person attacked fights back.[10] As Marvin E. Wolfgang has noted, some homicides are victim-precipitated.[11] Finally, a person's status as a victim can undergo transformation at various stages of the criminal justice process. For example, the only legal standing a crime victim has in court is as a witness. He or she is not a victim but someone who is subject to cross-examination and to having his or her version of events challenged.

Like the term "crime," the term "victim" is evaluative rather than descriptive. Thus, a host of factors influence the decision as to whether or not to apply the term. Unfortunately, research in the area is not at the level where all the complexities of such decisions are adequately understood. The criminal justice system has historically concentrated its data-collection efforts on reported crime and arrested criminals. This, ironically, also underscores the place of the victim in much of criminal justice thinking. The whole system is geared toward the arrest of the offender and the processing of the case. Yet, the definitional and conceptual problems raised by the term "victim" are not without direct policy consequences. For example, 44 states and the District of Columbia have victim compensation programs to help victims of violent crime.[12] While laudable, most programs do not compensate victims in incidents where they are related to the offenders.[13] This is understandable, since many compensation programs developed at least partially in response to fears of attack by strangers. Yet, Bureau of Justice Statistics estimate that at least half of the 20 million violent crimes committed in 1982 through 1984 were committed by someone the victim knew. Eight percent, or over 1.5 million of these crimes, involved people related to one another.[14] As we shall see, fear of attack by strangers is not without some empirical base. But home is not the safe haven we ordinarily think it is. Moreover, the likelihood of sustaining injury in a criminal incident appears to increase the more intimate the victim–offender relationship.[15] Victim compensation programs that exclude victims of family violence do nothing for a substantial number of victims and, indeed, may discriminate against a group that needs the most help. Recent federal legislation has recognized this fact by denying federal victim assistance monies to states whose compensation statutes exclude victims of non-stranger crimes.

Crime Victim Characteristics: Street Crime

The need for adequate data is clear, and information gaps are slowly being filled. Thus, it is possible to pinpoint the specific characteristics of certain kinds of crime victims. The greatest amount of data center on the crimes most feared by the public; personal crimes of violence including rape, robbery, and assault and personal crimes of theft including larceny without contact, purse snatching, and pocket picking. Description of victim characteristics can help in the assessment of risk factors and the development of social policies that will lessen the likelihood of criminal encounters.

Table 9-1 highlights some interesting facts about street crime victimization.[16] First, victims of these kinds of crime are more often men than women, younger rather than elderly, and lower income rather than higher income. Second, looking at violent crimes, blacks are more likely to be victims than whites or members of other racial groups. But regardless of race, young males have the highest violent victimization rates, while elderly females have the lowest.

These data suggest that fear of crime and actual risk of victimization do not coincide. Those least likely to be victimized seem to fear crime the most. A number of factors can account for this discrepancy. Fear of crime among the elderly, for example, together with an actual lessening of victimization risk may be due to life-style changes associated with aging.[17] Berg and Johnson have argued that the elderly are more likely to see the victim role as self-defining, that is, they are more predisposed to see themselves as victims or potential victims.[18] This is because in their other relationships, the elderly also experience an increasing lack of power. They experience less mastery of the world around them than they did when they were younger and, consequently, have greater feelings of vulnerability. Many elderly, therefore, appear to be tertiary victims, feeling fear and emotional distress at any victimization in the community. These feelings in turn are reinforced by the overall changes in

Table 9-1 Victimization Rates per 1,000 Persons Age 12 and Older

	PERSONAL CRIMES OF . . .	
	Violence	Theft
Total (U.S.)	30	69

Sex

	Violence	Theft
Male	39	75
Female	22	65

Age

	Violence	Theft
12–15	54	108
16–19	67	122
20–24	60	108
25–34	37	83
35–49	20	63
50–64	10	40
65 and older	5	19

Race and origin

	Violence	Theft
White	29	70
Black	38	63
Other	25	73
Hispanic	30	60
Non-Hispanic	30	70

Marital status by sex

	Violence	Theft
Males		
Never married	72	112
Divorced/separated	57	102
Married	19	52
Widowed	10	31
Females		
Never married	38	102
Divorced/separated	51	84
Married	11	50
Widowed	7	21

Family income

	Violence	Theft
Less than $7,500	52	68
$7,500–$9,999	34	63
$10,000–$14,999	32	65
$15,000–$24,999	28	68
$25,000–$29,999	29	69
$30,000–$49,999	22	76
$50,000 or more	25	90

Education

	Violence	Theft
0–4 years	13	23
5–7 years	35	59
8 years	34	57
9–11 years	39	71
High school graduate	27	60
1–3 years college	34	87
College graduate	22	89

Employment status (1984)

	Violence	Theft
Retired	5	20
Keeping house	14	35
Unable to work	17	25
Employed	32	81
In school	45	110
Unemployed	76	90

Residence (1984)

	Violence	Theft
Central city	43	85
1,000,000 or more	45	80
500,000–999,999	45	92
250,000–499,999	37	88
50,000–249,999	44	81
Suburban	30	77
Rural	22	54

Race, sex, and age summary

	Violence	Theft
White males		
12–15	73	111
16–19	92	134
20–24	78	116
25–34	44	87
35–49	23	66
50–64	11	42
65 and older	5	22
White females		
12–15	39	116
16–19	47	129
20–24	42	103
25–34	28	78
35–49	15	62
50–64	8	39
65 and older	3	17
Black males		
12–15	68	81
16–19	69	74
20–24	67	103
25–34	60	113
35–49	31	60
50–64	27	48
65 and older	*	21
Black females		
12–15	19	74
16–19	46	54
20–24	58	70
25–34	48	68
35–49	20	54
50–64	10	33
65 and older	*	12

Note: Personal crimes of violence include rape, robbery, and assault. Personal crimes of theft include larceny without contact, purse snatching, and pocket picking.

* Too few cases to obtain statistically reliable data.

Source: BJS *Criminal victimization in the U.S. 1984* and *1985.*

their lives. The fear, however, may also result in life-style restrictions that in fact reduce the overall chances of being victimized. Paradoxically, however, increased isolation seems to be accompanied by increased fear.[19] Fear may continue going up as risk of victimization decreases.

On the other hand, when the elderly do experience an actual criminal incident, such incidents tend to be more serious in a number of ways and perhaps more frightening than crimes committed against young people.[20] Elderly violent crime victims, for example, are more likely to be confronted by an offender armed with a gun than are younger victims, and the offender is more likely to be a stranger.[21] About 45% of the violent crimes committed against the elderly between 1980 and 1985 were robberies, compared to 18% of the violent crimes committed against those under 65.[22] Robbery is considered a more serious crime than assault, the most common violent crime, since it involves both force and theft. Thus, when the elderly actually become crime victims, it may be more difficult for them to recover from the experience. The crime may be more serious, and factors associated with aging may reinforce the victim role.

Women, too, may have greater feelings of vulnerability than men, since in other relationships they may also experience a relative lack of power. Primary victimization among both the elderly and women is more serious because it tends to be more self-defining.[23] In other words, they may carry the role of victim with them into other situations. Thus, the aftermath of victimization may last longer among these groups, making the resumption of a normal life style a more difficult enterprise. And, as noted, tertiary effects may also be greater, explaining the higher degree of fear in populations least likely to be victimized.

Berg and Johnson argued that the same dynamics operate among blacks. They would have a harder time dealing with primary victimization and express greater fear about crime. This proved not to be the case. Young black males, the most vulnerable group in terms of violent crime, express the least amount of fear. The authors suggested that the discrepancy may be due to the fact that, after a point, victimization becomes an accepted way of life. Adjustments are made in the form of simply accepting one's fate or pretending, in spite of the evidence, mastery over the world (the "cool" role).[24]

Interestingly, male crime victims, while constituting the most victimized group, have received little attention in the research literature. They appear to be the least fearful group prior to victimization. Thus, the tertiary effects of victimization appear negligible. Nevertheless, due to the still pervasive stereotype of male strength and aggressiveness, secondary victimization may be much more traumatic for males than for females. When a man's wife or family is victimized by a crime, feelings of inadequacy at being unable to protect one's home and loved ones may be pervasive.[25] When men themselves are primary victims, rage, feelings of impotence, and inability to express the need for help may complicate male recovery from crime victimization.[26]

It seems important for policy makers to distinguish between problems caused by fear of crime and those caused by actual risk of victimization. Some elderly seem to suffer a decline in quality of life primarily as a response to fear. Young black males, on the other hand, are the ones who face grave risk. In fact, this risk remains higher throughout their lives than the risk in the general population. The Bureau of Justice Statistics estimates that a black man's chances of being a victim of a homicide during his life are one in 21 compared to one in 133 for the general population.[27]

The table pinpoints a number of other factors concerning victimization risk. While theft rates are high for people with low incomes, those rates begin to pick up again at the higher income level (more than $25,000 per year) and are highest for those who earn $50,000 or more. It is also clear that rural residents are less often crime victims than are people living in the cities.

As noted previously, individuals are not the only crime victims. Table 9-2 displays characteristics of households associated with various kinds of property crime.[28] This table shows that larceny is the most common property crime; motor vehicle theft is the least common. Hispanics are more often victims of household crimes that non-Hispanics. Renters have higher rates of victimization than homeowners, and households in central cities have higher rates than suburban or rural households.

Crime Victim Characteristics: Family Violence

Data on "typical" street crime victims are the most abundant. Data on other kinds of victimization are less well developed. Included here would be violence involving intimates. While the data clearly show that over half of all homicides are committed by someone known to the victim, with at least 18% committed by relatives, the dynamics leading to this outcome are less clear.[29] As noted, some research suggests that who becomes a victim and who becomes an offender in such incidents is often a matter of chance. Almost half of all assaults are committed by relatives or acquaintances.[30] Excluding homicides, however, most violent crime appears to be committed by strangers.[31] Robbery is the violent crime most committed by strangers (75%).[32] Yet appearances may be deceiving. Many researchers believe that a very large proportion of crimes committed by relatives are not reported to the police or revealed in crime surveys.[33] This may be due in part to the fact that victims of assault by friends or relatives may not think of themselves as crime victims. And, indeed, for certain kinds of assaults, the individual may not legally be considered a victim. Up until quite recently, a woman would not be given the status of crime victim if she were assaulted by her husband, and in most states a wife is still not legally a rape victim if her husband is the offender. For many years children were not considered crime victims if they were assaulted by their parents. In areas such as these, where perceptions of crime victimization are relatively recent, data are scarce. Nevertheless, that which is emerging is not comforting. Two thirds

Table 9-2

	RATES PER 1,000 HOUSEHOLDS		
	Household Burglary	Larceny	Motor Vehicle Theft
Age of household head			
12–19	213	224	18
20–34	83	137	21
35–49	69	110	15
50–64	48	75	13
65 and older	33	41	5
Race or origin of household head			
White	60	95	13
Black	83	120	22
Other	45	88	17
Hispanic	85	127	23
Non-Hispanic	62	96	14
Income			
Less than $7,500	86	98	11
$7,500–$9,999	60	101	15
$10,000–$14,999	67	101	14
$15,000–$24,999	59	104	14
$25,000–$29,999	54	95	13
$30,000–$49,999	58	99	16
$50,000 or more	56	104	21
Number of persons in household			
One	53	62	10
2–3	61	92	14
4–5	75	136	18
6 or more	78	173	17
Form of tenure			
Home owned or being bought	50	83	11
Home rented	84	123	19
Place of residence (1984)			
Central city	87	129	22
1,000,000 or more	85	97	35
500,000–999,999	81	138	20
250,000–499,999	90	144	22
50,000–249,999	91	142	13
Outside central city (suburban)	56	97	16
Nonmetropolitan (rural)	53	76	8

Source: BJS *Criminal victimization in the U.S., 1984* and *1985.*

of all assaults on divorced and separated women were committed by acquaintances and relatives. Half of all assaults on women who have never been married and 40% of assaults on married women were committed by nonstrangers. More than half of all assaults on women, but only a third of those on men, were committed by relatives or acquaintances.[34]

Definitional problems confront those trying to assess the extent of child abuse. The biblical story of Abraham and Isaac illustrates the point. In the story, God asks Abraham to sacrifice Isaac, his only son. Abraham proceeds with the preparations, taking Isaac to a high mountain and tying him to a makeshift altar surrounded by straw. As Abraham is about to kill his son, God intervenes to save Isaac and praise Abraham for his faithfulness. Does this story portray a man's adherence to the will of God or the actions of a parent who at very least is guilty of the psychological abuse of his child?

What qualifies as child abuse has both theoretical and policy consequences. Many mental health professionals argue that physical abuse is equally present at all levels of society. Others argue that such abuse is more prevalent among the economically disadvantaged. The debate may well hinge on definition. Physical punishment is used widely throughout society. When such punishment crosses the line and becomes abuse may, at the margin, be a matter of debate. On the other hand, most data seem to show that serious physical abuse involving injury is more prevalent among those who experience the stresses associated with poverty: low income, unemployment, and feelings of hopelessness. Mental health professionals, by claiming child abuse as a universal phenomenon, can demand a significant proportion of social welfare resources for their own professions. According to Leroy Pelton, however, such a claim may direct resources away from programs that would deal more directly with the economic circumstances that seem associated with child abuse.[35] Thus, direct economic aid to lessen the frustration of poverty may be more beneficial than a program of psychological counseling aimed equally at all levels of society.

Because of such definitional debates, numbers of victims and their respective characteristics are not well established. The term "estimate" appears with greater frequency when describing these victims than when describing the victims of street crime. Nevertheless, the equally or perhaps even more serious nature of the problem seems clear. During, the 1980s, it was estimated that there were 1.5 million battered children.[36] These batterings resulted in 50,000 deaths and 300,000 permanently injured children in the United States.[37] One of the leading causes of death among American infants between 6 and 12 months of age has been killing by a parent.[38]

Sexual abuse of children within the family also appears to be a serious problem, but again one on which data are just beginning to be developed. In 1982, there were 48,000 cases of reported incest.[39] Estimates of sexual abuse in the home, however, range as high as 250,000 cases a year in the United States.[40] According to Diana Russell, daughters are at a much greater risk if they live with a stepfather than if they are with their biological father. In her

San Francisco study, she found that one out of six women raised by a stepfather as compared to one out of 40 living with the biological father was molested.[41]

Women are far less likely to be perpetrators of sexual abuse. Mother-son incest is estimated to be very low. Father-daughter incest accounts for 75% of reported cases.[42] The results of such victimization can include guilt, promiscuity, and suicide.[43] In one study, the average age of incest victims was nine.[44]

Crime Victim Characteristics: Economic Crime

Victimization from illegal economic activity is also difficult to measure. Included in this category of criminal activity would be computer-related fraud, arson for profit, embezzlement, and a number of types of underground economic activity including the manufacture, distribution, and sale of illegal substances. Chapter 2 indicated that the cost of this type of crime substantially exceeds that of other crime categories. In 1980, for example, the estimated income for the underground economy was somewhere between $170 and $300 billion.[45] There are also social costs including lost tax revenue, higher insurance premiums, and the loss of productivity in the work force.

Crime Victim Characteristics:
The Urban and Rural Environments

Finally, cities can be considered crime victims. Fear of crime has contributed to the migration from cities and to the generally poor reputation cities have had since the 1800s. In fact, the image of the city as a hotbed of vice and danger is what led early reformers to place juvenile facilities in rural areas, thus removing the delinquent from the sin and corruption of the urban area. The city may be the quintessential tertiary victim. Yet, the data on both actual crime occurrences and attitudes toward various urban areas do not provide a clear picture of the dynamics of such victimization. Thus, while crime tends to be higher in central areas of cities and to decrease as one goes to suburbs and then to rural areas, crime rates are not the same throughout all parts of the city. Moreover, regarding household victimization, cities of a million or more appear likely to have fewer of these types of crimes than smaller cities (see Table 9-2) Household crimes are not, therefore, directly related to city size. Regarding fear of crime, public opinion polls show that most people feel safe in their own neighborhood and think that their neighborhood is less dangerous than others, regardless of the actual amount of crime in an area.[46]

To summarize, data on victimization, victim characteristics, and criminal justice system response to victims are less well developed than data dealing with offenders. As might be expected, however, lack of data has not deterred the formulation of policies. Such policies, therefore, tend to be anchored in one of the three models discussed previously: the crime control model, the due process model, or the administrative model. The ideological content of these approaches fill in the gaps left by the lack of empirical fact. Results of such policy interventions have unfortunately, then, been decidedly mixed.

POLICY CONSIDERATIONS: THEORIES/ARGUMENTS/APPLICATIONS

The Crime Victim and Public Policy

Much of the rhetoric of the victim's movement has been captured by those on the political right. As noted, this approach decries the constitutional protection given to defendants and demands that rights of victims supersede those accused of a crime. The recommendations for federal and state action listed below, taken from the *President's Task Force on Victims of Crime, Final Report,*[47] illustrate this approach:

1. Legislation should be proposed and enacted to ensure that addresses of victims and witnesses are not made public or available to the defense, absent a clear need as determined by the court.
2. Legislation should be proposed and enacted to ensure that designated victim counseling is legally privileged and not subject to defense discovery or subpoena.
3. Legislation should be proposed and enacted to ensure that hearsay is admissible and sufficient in preliminary hearings, so that victims need not testify in person.
4. Legislation should be proposed and enacted to amend the bail laws to accomplish the following:
   a. Allow courts to deny bail to persons found by clear and convincing evidence to present a danger to the community;
   b. Give the prosecution the right to expedited appeal of adverse bail determinations, analogous to the right presently held by the defendant;
   c. Codify existing case law defining the authority of the court to detain defendants as to whom no conditions of release are adequate to ensure appearance at trial;
   d. Reverse, in the case of serious crimes, any standard that presumptively favors release of convicted persons awaiting sentence or appealing their convictions;
   e. Require defendants to refrain from criminal activity as a mandatory condition for release; and
   f. Provide penalties for failing to appear while released on bond or personal recognizance that are more closely proportionate to the penalties for the offense with which the defendant was originally charged.
5. Legislation should be proposed and enacted to abolish the exclusionary rule as it applies to Fourth Amendment issues.
6. Legislation should be proposed and enacted to open parole release hearings to the public.
7. Legislation should be proposed and enacted to abolish parole and limit judicial discretion in sentencing.
8. Legislation should be proposed and enacted to require that school officials report violent offenses against students or teachers, or the possession of weapons

or narcotics on school grounds. The knowing failure to make such a report to the police, or deterring others from doing so, should be designated a misdemeanor.

9. Legislation should be proposed and enacted to make available to businesses and organizations the sexual assault, child molestation, and pornography arrest records of prospective and present employees whose work will bring them in regular contact with children.

10. Legislation should be proposed and enacted to accomplish the following:
    a. Require victim impact statements at sentencing;
    b. Provide for the protection of victims and witnesses from intimidation;
    c. Require restitution in all cases, unless the court provides specific reasons for failing to require it;
    d. Develop and implement guidelines for the fair treatment of crime victims and witnesses; and
    e. Prohibit a criminal from making any profit from the sale of the story of his crime. Any proceeds should be used to provide full restitution to his victims, pay the expenses of his prosecution, and finally, assist the crime victim compensation fund.

11. Legislation should be proposed and enacted to establish or expand employee assistance programs for victims of crime employed by government.

12. Legislation should be proposed and enacted to ensure that sexual assault victims are not required to assume the cost of physical examinations and materials used to obtain evidence.

Several things about this list merit comment. First, recommendations 1 through 9 are primarily aimed at defendants and seek swifter, more severe punishment while reducing the rights of the accused. Thus, crime control, not victim assistance, appears to be the main focus of the recommendations. Second, an ironic consequence of demanding due process for victims appears to be a subversion of the due process model. As noted, however, there is no necessary conflict between the rights of victims and those the due process model seeks to protect. In fact, as discussed in the first chapter, reforms aimed at procedural safeguards, while sold as helping the victim, can in fact make the victim's plight worse. Because any evidence having bearing on the crime is deemed admissible, victims as witnesses become subject to intensive examination about their lives. Bad debts, past sexual practices, and so on are fair game for defense lawyers to exploit.

Finally, notice that the recommendations dealing directly with the crime victim (parts of numbers 10, 11, and 12) are extremely modest reforms. Some of the suggestions are more symbolic than substantive. For example, 10b, concerning the protection of victims and witnesses from intimidation, is already covered by the substantive law in most states. In 10c, which seeks victim restitution, a mechanism allows the court to avoid imposing the restitution requirement. In 10d there is merely a pious affirmation. Eleven and 12 are limited proposals, requiring little expenditure of funds. As Samuel Walker has noted, at best these guidelines offer symbolic assurances, and at worst they complicate the life of the victim and increase the trauma of victimization.[48]

Again, the California experience of modification of the exclusionary illustrates the point. The victim's past life can now be made public and held up to ridicule.

Compare the recommendations of the President's Task Force with the "Crime Victims' Bill of Rights," promulgated by the International Association of Chiefs of Police:

> The association declares the following to be incontrovertible rights of all crime victims and urges the establishment of procedures and training of personnel with these rights in mind. In addition to rights and privileges presently observed, crime victims are entitled:
>
> 1. To be free from intimidation;
> 2. To be told of financial assistance and social services available and how to apply for them;
> 3. To be provided a secure area during interviews and court proceedings, and to be notified if presence in court is not needed;
> 4. To a quick return of stolen or other personal property when no longer needed as evidence.
> 5. To a speedy disposition of the case, and to be periodically informed of case status and final disposition; and when personnel and resource capabilities allow, to be notified in felony cases whenever the perpetrator is released from custody;
> 6. To be interviewed by a female official in the case of rape and other sexual offenses, when personnel and resource capabilities allow.

These suggestions, while modest, for the most part represent changes in administrative procedures that can be accomplished with relative ease. Number 1, demanding freedom from intimidation for the victim, and number 5, extolling speedy case dispositions, are the exceptions.

This list illustrates the kinds of suggestions that flow from an administrative model. Generally, they represent areas of concern over which criminal justice managers, in this case, chiefs of police, have some control. If implemented, they can also result in considerable improvement in the way victims are treated by the system. This approach is not, however, without drawbacks. The needs of the administrator and the needs of the victim are not in fact the same.

The interest of criminal justice managers in the plight of the victim is due, at least in part, to the fact that administrators are convinced that by improving the victim's plight, they will also improve organizational goal attainment. Number 6, suggesting female officials interview victims of sexual offenses, provides a method for the police organization to get the best information possible so that an offender can be apprehended. The more comfortable the victim is with the interviewer, the more cooperative that person will be. The same point can be illustrated by victim-witness assistance units in the office of the prosecutor.

Some prosecuting attorney offices have established victim-witness assistance units to help crime victims recover emotionally, physically, and financially from their trauma. Particularly in cases of child sexual abuse, such offices can help relieve the trauma of testifying in open court by familiarizing the victim-witness with both the courtroom and its procedures. In cases of sexual abuse, counselors simultaneously help the child psychologically cope with the event and legally perform correctly as a witness. The use of anatomically correct dolls when preparing the child for testimony is an effective strategy to achieve the latter goal. Such offices also provide clothing for victim-witnesses to improve their appearance in court. The thrust of these programs is to help the crime victim become an effective witness. Again, this fits in with the organizational goal of the prosecutor's office to produce convictions. Unfortunately, however, a large number of crime victims will not have such services available to them. Most crimes are not reported to the police.[49] Of those that are, most do not end in an arrest. And of those that do end in an arrest, relatively few get beyond the stage of initial processing.[50] Victim-witness assistance units are there to serve victims who will become witnesses, not victims in general.

To take care of the majority of victims who do not fully pursue a case, a number of volunteer associations have developed. Counseling, monetary assistance, and advice on how to deal with the criminal justice system are services that can be offered through volunteer groups. The last function is particularly important since administrative needs do not always coincide with the needs of the victim. Thus, even in states where victim compensation is available, the reporting requirements to obtain assistance sometimes present formidable barriers to victims who can use the aid. The form in Figure 9-1 is four pages long and can appear complicated to people not used to forms or unskilled at either reading or writing. Notice also the eligibility requirement in Section VI. If any item is answered yes, the individual is excluded from compensation. The large number of victims of intrafamily violence are therefore not eligible for compensation in Missouri or in 39 other states. Only five of the 45 states with victim compensation laws permit reimbursement to victims of family crime.[51] Hopefully, as noted, recent federal legislation may encourage states to modify this exclusion. And volunteer groups can provide an important service by helping people wind their way through the bureaucratic maze of state and local governments to procure needed services.

In part, the effort of criminal justice managers to focus on the crime victim can be explained by their inability to affect or radically change either crime rates or offenders. The administrative control model directs the administrator's attention to those things that can in fact be controlled. Many of the problems faced by crime victims can, fortunately, be administratively resolved. It is a mistake, however, to think that system needs and victim needs automatically coincide. The downside of the administrative control model for victims is that in the event of a conflict between efficiency and victims' rights, we might

File No. _____

STATE OF MISSOURI

Division of Workers' Compensation
722 Jefferson Street
Jefferson City, Missouri 65101

Application for Crime Victims' Compensation

Mailing Address: For this application and all correspondence:

Division of Workers' Compensation, Crime Victims' Unit
P.O. Box 58, Jefferson City, Missouri 65102

Telephone: (314) 751-4231

Claimant's Name and Address: _____

You are filing this application because you are/were: (Check one)

1. ☐ The victim of a crime
2. ☐ Trying to help a crime victim or police officer
3. ☐ The survivor of a crime victim or person administering the victim's estate
4. ☐ The parent/guardian of a crime victim under 18
5. ☐ The guardian of a crime victim who is incompetent

Section I — Claim Information

1.	Is or was the victim a resident of the State of Missouri?		☐	Yes	☐	No
2.	Did the injury occur in the State of Missouri?		☐	Yes	☐	No
3.	Was the Crime reported to the proper authorities within 48 hours? (if no, explain why not.)		☐	Yes	☐	No
4.	Are you filing this claim within: 1 year of the crime?		☐	Yes	☐	No
	90 days after death of Victim? (If no, explain why not.)		☐	Yes	☐	No
5.	Did you suffer a minimum out-of-pocket loss of $200?		☐	Yes	☐	No
	OR, did you lose at least two continuous weeks of earnings or support? Number of days lost earnings or support: _____		☐	Yes	☐	No
	Are you retired by reason of age or disability? (If yes, explain disability or give age) _____		☐	Yes	☐	No

6. This is an application for: (Check one)

☐ Personal Injury Benefits   ☐ Survivor's Benefits   ☐ Funeral Benefits only

7. Person applying for compensation is: (Check one)

☐ Victim - Injured directly from a crime.   ☐ Survivor - Victim died as a result of a crime.

8. Describe injuries resulting in this claim:

Victim's _____

_____

_____

_____

_____

MO 625-0302 (3-86)   CV-1 (3-86)

Figure 9-1

expect the former to win out. Such a conflict may well be developing over the issue of victim impact statements. Requiring a victim impact statement and, in some cases, victim testimony prior to sentencing can create a delay in the smooth functioning of the courthouse, where cases are disposed of in assembly-line fashion. As noted in Chapter 2, the wedding cake model of criminal justice describes a system where cases are settled based on a going rate. The "worth" of a case is known by all who work in the courthouse, and such knowledge allows for the routine, efficient handling of the bulk of cases. Introducing the victim's impact statement may well slow down the process of justice and introduce an inefficiency not appreciated by those charged with the administration of the system. Victim advocacy groups can, however, help mediate tensions that arise between the needs of victims and the needs of systems.

Section II — Claimant Information

9. Victim — Complete all the following information about the victim.		
Victim's Name	Social Security No.	Telephone No.
Complete Address (No. & Street, City, State, Zip Code		Birthdate

Sex
□ Male   □ Female

Marital Status:
□ Single   □ Separated   □ Widowed
□ Married   □ Divorced

Race/Ethnic (Check One)
□ 1. White   □ 2. Black   □ 3. Hispanic
□ 4. American Indian/Alaskan Native □ 5. Asian/Pacific Islander □ 6. Other

Are you a U.S. citizen?   □ Yes   □ No

If no, give nationality. _____

Handicapped?
□ No
□ Yes (Prior to crime)
□ Yes (Permanently as result of crime)

10. Survivor —Complete all the following information about the survivor if victim died.

Survivor's Name	Social Security No.	Telephone No.
Complete Address (No. & Street, City, State, Zip Code)		Birthdate

Sex
□ Male   □ Female

Marital Status:
□ Single   □ Separated   □ Widowed
□ Married   □ Divorced

11. Your relationship to the Deceased Victim
□ Spouse
□ Parent
□ Child
□ Other ____

12. Are (Were) you dependent on the deceased victim for:	No	Yes	If Yes, How Much - How Often
Principal Support?			
Child Support?			
Alimony?			

13. Will dependent(s) receive any accident or life insurance? □ Yes □ No   If yes, complete the following:
Name of Company _____   Amount $ _____

Will dependent(s) receive benefits from the following? □ Yes □ No   If yes, complete the following:
□ Social Security $ ____   □ Workers' Compensation $ ____   □ Other $ ____

Section III — Crime Information (Obtain the following from Law Enforcement Agency)

14. Date Crime Occurred	Place of Crime: Street ____ City: ____ County: ____
Date Crime Was Reported	Police Agency Involved
Brief Description of Crime	

Name of Defendant	Complaint or Incident Number	Docket Number

Figure 9-1   (continued)

Preventing Victimization

Police managers, as well as court managers, have expressed interest in programs that provide both visible change and concrete results. Specifically, in regard to victims, some police agencies have begun to emphasize prevention rather than simply apprehension and prosecution. This has a twofold advantage for those who espouse an administrative control model. First, crime prevention programs utilize law enforcement officers in the role of consultant. The officers deliver specific, concrete advice on how to set up a neighborhood crime watch program or a secret witness procedure whereby citizens can provide anonymous tips concerning a given incident. They can recommend the most effective target-hardening procedures, including the best locks to buy and advice on

Section IV — Out-of-Pocket Expenses: Enter below all expenses for services rendered as a result of this crime. (Attach all bills.)

15. Name of Doctor, Hospital, or Other Provider of Service	No.	Street	City	State	Zip Code	Telephone No./Area Code

Section IV (Continued)

16. Indicate below, if any sources will pay any of your expenses listed.	
Name of Source of Payment	Your Claim or Policy No.
☐ Social Security	
☐ Health Insurance ☐ Workers' Compensation	
☐ Veteran's Administration	
☐ Public Assistance	
☐ Medicaid ☐ Medicare	
☐ From or on Behalf of the Offender	
☐ Other	

Section V — Loss of Earnings or Support

17. Is this claim for loss of earnings or support? ☐ Yes ☐ No	Note: If self-employed, attach your Federal Income Tax Return, and any Estimated Returns for this year.
Name of Employer	Name of Your Supervisor
Address of Employer Zip Code	Employer's Phone No.

Section VI — Eligibility

18. Is Applicant:				
1. An offender in this case?		☐ Yes	☐ No
2. An accomplice of the offender?		☐ Yes	☐ No
3. A member of the family of the offender?		☐ Yes	☐ No
4. A person living with the offender?		☐ Yes	☐ No
5. A person maintaining sexual relations with the offender?		☐ Yes	☐ No
6. Additional comments:			

Figure 9-1   (*continued*)

whether an alarm system will be cost-effective. In this role, the police officer interacts with the citizen as an advisor and helpmate rather than as disciplinarian or law enforcer. Public relations is enhanced while, at the same time, a specific service is being delivered. Second, and perhaps more importantly, police administrators are able to shift the burden of responsibility for crime control to the community. Many police administrators have become aware of the fact that the police can do little to affect the overall amount of crime in a community. Yet they confront expectations that their job is to stop crime. If they appear not to be doing it, they are subject to criticism, budget cuts, and perhaps short tenures as administrators. By emphasizing the neighborhood or community role in crime prevention, the police executive can deflect criticism back to the community. Instruction in crime prevention makes the police officer an expert

Section VII — Income: Enter below all sources of your income. (Complete all items)

19. Description of Income	Income Amount	Paid How Often
Employment		
Interest or Dividends		
Rent or Land Contracts		
Alimony, Child Support		
Veteran's Benefits, Military Allotment		
Social Security, Pensions		
Public Assistance		
Workers' Compensation		
Unemployment Compensation		
Disability or Sick Benefits		
Other:		

Additional Comments

Consent to Pay Providers: I do hereby consent and agree that, if an award is made, money due and owing to any provider of medical services and due to any other qualified person or entity, including any attorney's fees allowed to my attorney, may be paid direct to said provider, entity or attorney by the agency and need not be paid to me.

Date _____   Claimant's Signature X _____

Authorization: I hereby authorize any hospital, physican or other person who attended or examined (Name of victim) _____ ; any funeral director or other person who rendered services, any employer of the victim; any police or other local governmental agency including state and federal revenue services; any insurance company; or organization having knowledge, to furnish to the Division of Workers' Compensation or its representative, any and all information with respect to the incident leading to the victim's personal injury or death, and the claim made herewith for compensation. A photo copy of this authorization is as effective and valid as the original.

Date _____   Claimant's Signature X _____

Declaration: I understand that any recovery of my losses through legal action shall entitle the State of Missouri to reimbursement to the extent of any compensation awarded me. I declare, under penalty of perjury, that I have read all the questions in the claim form and to the best of my knowledge and belief, all of my answers are true, correct and complete.

Date _____   Claimant's Signature X _____

Figure 9-1 (*continued*)

who can help the community do a better job for itself. Failure to do a better job then becomes a community responsibility, not a police one.

Evaluation of various crime prevention programs has shown mixed results. There have been some dramatic successes, particularly in terms of what has become known as environmental criminology. Environmental criminology stresses physical design as a potential inhibitor of crime. When airplane hijacking became a serious cause of concern in the early 1970s, the initial policy response was one based on the crime control model. Air marshals were trained and randomly placed aboard aircraft. Should a hijacking incident begin, the air marshal was responsible for apprehending the perpetrator and aborting the incident. How this was to be done 20,000 feet in the air with a plane full of passengers was not well thought out. A shoot-out with the hijackers, on reflection, seemed ludicrous. Passengers as well as the physical integrity of the airplane were at risk. Waiting to land in some unknown country and then commencing arrest procedures likewise seemed fraught with difficulty. If the country landed in was hostile to the United States, the air marshal would find him or herself in an untenable position. Environmental criminology suggested that the physical design of airports could be altered so as to prevent security risks from boarding an airplane. In the United States, passengers are now all subject to luggage checks and checks of person in order to prevent someone from boarding an airplane carrying a weapon. The results have been dramatic. Airplane hijacking has become a very rare occurrence.

Defensible Space

Perhaps best known among the environmental criminological approaches is Oscar Newman's concept of "defensible space."[52] Based on his research of varying crime rates in adjacent public housing projects, Newman argues the necessity of physically showing that space is cared for and that watchers are available to watch for violations within certain areas. As Newman maintains:

> Defensible space is a model for residential environments which inhibit crime by creating the physical expression of a social fabric that defends itself.[53]

According to Newman, the physical design of many public housing projects discourages either the development or the maintenance of a community, that is, a sense of common enterprise, social ties, and concern for a shared territory. Thus, crime flourishes since responsibility is only taken for the self and not for others with whom space may be shared. The physical arrangement of certain public housing projects provides both social cues and physical opportunities that encourage criminal actions. Isolated stairways and high-rise towers create too much separation between living and recreational areas. A lack of demarcation between public space and private space physically and culturally signals a no-man's-land where crime will be tolerated. Housing projects that have these characteristics tend to have higher crime rates than those where the physical characteristics permit and portray residential concern for the area. Low-rise buildings, where apartments face one another and where there is a clear demarcation between the development and the surrounding area allow residents to distinguish between neighbors and intruders and to develop a sense of responsibility for the entire project. The physical design symbolizes an area cared about and watched. These physical attributes, according to Newman, discourage criminal activity.

Research evaluating defensible space concepts has been mixed. The opportunity to observe outside public space does not seem strongly related to crime occurrence in that space.[54] On the other hand, public areas inside apartment buildings (hallways, etc.) do seem to benefit from defensible space concepts, particularly regarding limiting access and providing opportunities for residents to observe such space.[55] These findings cast some doubt on whether large public expenditures should be made to redesign elements of outdoor neighborhood areas.

Concern with physical design as a crime control factor is best expressed prior to construction. Unfortunately, opportunity for such considerations is rare in older cities. Nevertheless, there have been attempts on the part of city governments to implement some of these ideas on a limited scale. Thus, in some urban neighborhoods city mayors and/or administrators have encouraged blocking off streets as a crime prevention measure. By discouraging access to residential streets, it is hoped that residents will become familiar with cars that belong there and become wary of strange cars.

Routine Activity Approaches

A number of researchers and theorists have begun to focus on differences in routine activities to explain the differences in victimization rates among groups of people.[56] In their original articulation of this approach, Cohen and Felson suggest that three elements must come together for a direct-contact, predatory violation to occur. The three elements that must converge are a) motivated offenders; b) suitable targets; and c) the absence of capable guardians.[57] Thus, certain categories of people more often find themselves, because of their life styles (that is, routine activities), in locations where these three circumstances come together. This would explain the higher street crime victimization rates among males, youth, and blacks when compared to females, the elderly, and whites.

Evidence for this essentially ecological approach often lacks sufficient demonstration of a connection between life style and place. Life style differences are often assumed because of differences in demographic characteristics.[58] Moreover, risk is not assessed based upon differences in the amount of time spent in various locations.[59]

Recent research by Sherman, Gartin, and Buerger suggests that the focus on the routine activities of people be shifted to a focus on the routine activities of places. They found that in Minneapolis, 3% of places (defined as intersections or addresses) produced 50% of calls to the police, and that for the predatory crimes of robbery, rape, and auto theft all calls came from less than 3% of the places in their study. Thus, less than 3,500 "places" out of approximately 115,000 "places" to which a police car could be dispatched accounted for the majority of predatory crime. Given these data, the authors ask, "Are places the cause of crime?"[60]

This question is an intriguing one and will provide future direction for research in crime victim studies. Despite the lack of a clear answer to this question, however, the concept does provide policy options. A criminal "hot-spot" might be made less criminal by either increasing the number of guardians or decreasing the number of potential targets or offenders. Baggage checkpoints at airports represent an effort to decrease the number of potential offenders in a given area. Closing all-night food shops reduces the number of potential robbery targets. Requiring an armed guard at certain locations increases guardianship. As Sherman and his colleagues conclude, it may be easier to change the routine activities of places than the routine activity of people.[61] What remains unanswered is whether this approach will actually lower crime or simply displace it to a less-well-guarded, more vulnerable location. The problem of displacement is evident when considering crime prevention measures as well.

Other Crime Prevention Strategies

Target hardening has also had an example of seemingly dramatic success. The addition of ignition and steering locks to automobiles together with design features that make unlawful automobile entry more difficult have resulted in a decrease in auto thefts, particularly by juvenile perpetrators.[62] The Bureau of Justice Statistics reports a 20.2% decline in auto theft victimization rates between 1973 and 1984.[63] Similarly, the Insurance Information Institute shows a decline in motor vehicle thefts known to the police from 800 per 100,000 motor vehicle registrations in 1968 to 600 per 100,000 registrations in 1983.[64] From 1973 to 1982 arrests for motor vehicle theft declined for all age groups by 22.3%, but by 48.9% for those under the age of 18.[65] While the overall decline in the proportion of juveniles in the population can account for some of this decrease, it also seems clear that the amateur auto thief, the joy rider, has been discouraged by the increasingly security conscious design of automobiles.

Less clearly successful have been large-scale neighborhood programs that have encouraged either greater watchfulness or more adoption of physical security on the part of residents. While neighborhood watch–type programs have encouraged the cooperation of police and citizen and have resulted in some decrease in criminal activity in certain neighborhoods, their overall effect is unclear.[66] Neighborhoods that adopt such strategies may be simply displacing crime to adjacent locations rather than preventing it. This same dynamic may occur when individuals adopt target-hardening procedures, such as better locks, or security protection, such as marking valuables with an identification number and posting a window sticker on the door advertising the fact to would-be miscreants. The potential burglar may simply go on to a house or a neighborhood where he or she feels less vulnerable. Programs that encourage witnesses to provide secret information to local media outlets in exchange for a reward if a particularly difficult case is solved have been shown to result in increased cooperation between police, media, and certain citizens but have had little effect on overall crime rates.[67] Such crime stopper or secret witness programs were specifically developed to handle dead-end cases of some notoriety (the top tier of the wedding cake). Thus, while successful for these type of felonies, they have had little effect on the bulk of crime.

Citizen crime prevention programs raise a number of interesting policy issues. To this point, it has been argued that the encouragement of such activity fits in with an administrative control model of criminal justice. Both budgetary and political pressures encourage police administrators to be most active in those areas where they can show some demonstrable effect. Such pressures increase as shrinking dollars for urban services require a decrease in personnel costs. Personnel must be used sparingly, and services formerly routinely provided may have to be scaled back. Thus, in some jurisdictions now, police only respond to auto accidents with injuries or to burglaries where loss exceeds a particular amount. In all other cases, reports are taken over the phone or in person at the police station. From an administrative standpoint, it makes sense to encourage citizen involvement for obtaining services and outcomes previously thought to be the sole responsibility of the agency.

Models of Citizen Public Service Involvement: Equity and Other Considerations

Such citizen participation in public service delivery has been described as taking three forms.[68] Co-production involves cooperation and interaction between individuals or groups and official representatives of government agencies. Operation I.D., neighborhood watch programs, and other activities that bring police officers together with citizens so that the former can help the latter procure a safer environment represent co-production. Ancillary production is more indirect. Citizens teach their children to obey the law. They also pay taxes and participate in required civic activity such as jury duty and voting. Finally, there is parallel production. Citizens, acting as individuals, take responsibility for acquiring a particular public good or service. Thus, someone who installs a new lock because they are fearful of crime in the neighborhood illustrates parallel production. The action to secure a safe environment is not in response to working with the police or to the dictates of good citizenship but to individually perceived needs.

Research has suggested that co-production activity is most likely to be engaged in by "community"-minded individuals, a small minority in any community.[69] Parallel activities in crime prevention are also more likely to be engaged in by younger, higher-income citizens, or by previous crime victims.[70] In short, there appears to be differential involvement in attempting to secure urban services, and often the involvement favors those with less need. Thus, as public service delivery meets administrative control demands and therefore requires greater citizen participation, those most in need of such services may be least able to provide them for themselves. Equity considerations become a key policy concern within the administrative control model.

There are other considerations. If parallel production is the primary way citizens deal with threats to safety, particularly if public service agencies are perceived as becoming less active, Newman's concern about the fabric of social life in a community is brought to the fore. Newman argues that when people begin to defend themselves as individuals and not as a community, they are doomed to lose the battle against crime. Again, the weakest become the most vulnerable.

This raises a final consideration within the administrative control model. What should be the response of an individual victim when confronted with a crime and what is the role of public policy in encouraging or discouraging certain responses?

Police agencies have generally counseled that victims offer no resistance in crime situations. In this regard, at least, the passive citizen is the preferred model. The reasons for this stance are apparent. First, an agency that counsels resistance may be liable if such resistance results in serious injury or death. Second, there is concern of vigilante activity among citizens and the resulting disorder this would bring. The legal use of force is reserved to police agencies, and it's a monopoly they do not want to relinquish. Finally, the police traditionally have responded in a reactive way to crime and its victims. It is the attempted or completed victimization that activates the system. Actual or attempted victimizations are crimes, and it is here, following a crime control model, that the police are most comfortable. They expect to act and have the citizen not act.

Data on the effects of resistance to a crime are mixed.[71] Resistance to criminal attacks seems to be associated both with greater likelihood of injury and less likelihood that the criminal will successfully complete the act. The quandary for those who articulate public policy is obvious. By publicly supporting a passive response to criminal attacks, agencies may encourage criminal activity.[72] The robber, the rapist, the burglar have gained an ally, since a passive public is precisely what is desirable from the perpetrator's point of view. On the other hand, an agency that encourages resistance may contribute to increased injury. Thus, this may be one area beyond the limits of effective public policy action.[73]

Crime situations vary too much to develop a standard of appropriate behavior. Ironically, however, police agencies and other units of the criminal justice system may be unable to refrain from conveying some message in this regard. Even if they choose to make no public statement on how to respond to victimization, administrative actions that encourage parallel production may result in actions that increase the potential for harm. If the administrative model dominates criminal justice, those responsible for law enforcement need to consider how citizens can best participate in the procurement of services for a safe community. If this is left to chance, emphasis on administrative efficiency and resultant cost saving may result in a community that becomes its own worst enemy, developing a social fabric that encourages rather than discourages criminal acts.

The Due Process Model and the Crime Victim: The Neighborhood Justice Center Movement

The due process model may seem to have little direct relationship to the crime victim. Yet those on the political left need to consider the crime victim and not leave the debate in this area to those on the right and those responsible for criminal justice management. The liberal response to crime victims has been to encourage reconciliation through the use of court alternatives. The model is integrative, stressing the idea that the rights of victims and the rights of defendants are not antithetical. Both have rights and needs that can best be met in a nonadversarial proceeding. One of the results of this view has been the development of neighborhood justice centers. Neighborhood justice centers have been defined as "facilities . . . designed to make available a varying of methods of processing disputes, including arbitration, mediation, referrals to small claim courts, as well as referral to courts of general jurisdiction."[74] This movement will be thoroughly discussed and evaluated in the last part of this book, which deals with the privatization of justice services. At this point, suffice it to say that in regard to victims, the neighborhood justice center movement holds that victim rights include:

—The right to information from the offender:
  —Were they being watched?
  —Was the crime random or planned?
  —Why was the particular individual chosen as victim?

—The right to express anger
—The right to compensation

The offender, on the other hand, has the right:

—To take responsibility for his or her action
—To have an opportunity to make up for a misdeed
—To humane and effective treatment in the criminal justice system[75]

Both can expect the community to be more cognizant of the needs of victim and offenders and to provide opportunities for each to improve their condition.

The impetus for many neighborhood justice centers can be found in the religious traditions of particular groups. Mediating disputes outside of the formal legal system has a long history. Various religious and ethnic communities have often avoided the civil or criminal system for dispute settlement, choosing to rely instead on their own community mechanisms. Orthodox Jewish communities still maintain their own form of courts for working out disputes among their members. Less formally, certain Hispanic and Italian communities rely on their neighborhood church for third-party adjudication in a family or community altercation. Specifically in criminal justice, many programs have been spearheaded by the Mennonites. These efforts have resulted in the development of the Victim-Offender Reconciliation Program. The emphasis is on bringing the victim and the offender together so that the latter can help the former through a restitution program that is worked out between the two. This approach is said to help in the reform of the offender by making him or her take responsibility for the harm done. At the same time, if the victim and the offender can be reconciled, the overall community is strengthened making future criminal activity more difficult. Paradoxically, this approach is sold as a crime prevention approach using some of the rhetoric of the crime control model, just as the notions of victims rights is sold using the rhetoric of the due process model.

Conclusion

The attention of policy makers and criminal justice administrators is now focusing on the plight of the crime victim. The focus, however, is somewhat blurry, and as a result, policy outcomes can be expected to be mixed.

Current data have not kept pace with interest. Added to this has been the definitional problem of who is a crime victim. The role of victim is contingent, depending upon the nature of the event, the social status of the participants, and the needs and pressures faced by those involved in case processing. As will be seen in the next chapter, these same factors affect the application of the term "criminal." And so the victim and the criminal are reluctant partners in a definitional game, the status given to one affecting the description of the other. This chapter has suggested, however, that while participants in the game fight for control of definitions of situations, their respective rights may not be antithetical to one another. The chapter has also suggested, however, that ideological rather than factual considerations form the basis for many policy initiatives in the area of crime victims. Thus, the needs of victims get caught up in organizational, administrative, and political imperatives with policies at times reflecting these rather than what is most appropriate for the victim. Ironically, then, victims and offenders share another similarity. Their fate is often decided on grounds of what is organizationally and symbolically best, not on what they think is best for themselves. It is little wonder that in surveys of victims and offenders that assess their attitudes toward the criminal justice system, both express highly negative feelings toward the system that has processed their case.[76] Two people who start as antagonists both end up disillusioned with the system of justice, and once again become reluctant partners of a shared experience. The next chapter discusses this paradoxical duet from the point of view of the offender.

SUMMARY

What Was Said

• The reaction of certain citizens and politicians to the expansion of the due process model, the development of victim interest groups, and the desire of problem solvers to have solvable problems has led to increased attention on crime victims.

• The due process model of criminal justice suggests that individuals need protection from government coercion and interference in their lives and thus stresses the importance of procedural law, while the crime control model argues that the primary responsibility of the criminal justice system is the enforcement of substantive criminal law.

• An administrative control model, which stresses efficiency rather than effectiveness, is competing for dominance in the criminal justice policy arena.

• The term victim, like the term crime, is contingent and evaluative rather than descriptive.

• Fear of crime and actual risk of victimization do not coincide.

• While data on typical street crime victims are most abundant, victims of domestic violence represent at least as serious and perhaps a more serious problem.

• Many so-called crime victim programs primarily serve the symbolic needs of policy makers and the production needs of managers rather than the needs of victims.

• Some programs that stress environmental changes to prevent victimization have been successful.

• Because of differential citizen involvement in public affairs, administrative programs that seek greater citizen participation in crime prevention activities raise issues of equity and fairness in the delivery of public service.

• The liberal response to crime victims has been to encourage reconciliation through the use of court alternatives such as the Neighborhood Justice Center.

What Was Not Said

• The rights of victims and criminals are antithetical.
• Improving certain administrative procedures will not help victims.
• Conservatives are the only ones concerned about victims.

NOTES

1. For a discussion of some of the cases that marked the battle of due process see George F. Cole, The *American System of Criminal Justice*, 4th ed. (Monterey, CA: Brooks/Cole Publishing Co., 1986), p. 92–96.

2. Ibid., p. 93.

3. Mapp v. Ohio, 367 U.S. 643 (1961).

4. Escobedo v. Illinois, 364 U.S. 478 (1964).

5. Miranda v. Arizona, 384 U.S. 436 (1966).

6. James F. Gilsinan, *Doing Justice* (Englewood Cliffs, NJ: Prentice-Hall, Inc., 1982), pp. 212–225.

7. Patsy A. Klaus, Carol G. Kaplan, Michael R. Rand, and Bruce M. Taylor, in *Report to the Nation on Crime and Justice*, 2nd ed., U.S. Department of Justice, Bureau of Justice Statistics, (Washington, DC: U.S. Government Printing Office, March, 1988), p. 114.

8. "People, etc.," *St. Louis Globe-Democrat*, March 7–8, 1980, p. 12.

9. Crime Victimization Task Force, *Crime Victims In the St. Louis Region: Their Rights—Our Responsibilities* (St. Louis: Confluence, 1986).

10. Harold R. Lentzner and Marshall M. DeBerry, Crime Statistics Analysis Staff, Bureau of the Census, "Intimate Victims: A Study of Violence Among Friends and Relatives," for U.S. Department of Justice, Bureau of Justice Statistics (Washington, DC: U.S. Government Printing Office, January 1980), p. 9.

11. Marvin E. Wolfgang, "Victim Precipitated Criminal Homicide," *Journal of Criminal Law, Criminology, and Police Science*, 48, No. 1, (June, 1957) p. 1–11.

12. *Report to the Nation on Crime and Justice*, p. 37.

13. Patsy A. Klaus, Michael R. Rand, and Bruce M. Taylor, in *Report to the Nation on Crime and Justice*, U.S. Department of Justice, Bureau of Justice Statistics (Washington, DC: U.S. Government Printing Office, October, 1983), p. 26.

14. Anita D. Timrots and Michael R. Rand, "Violent Crime by Strangers and Nonstrangers," U.S. Department of Justice, Bureau of Justice Statistics (Washington, DC: U.S. Government Printing Office, January, 1987), p. 1.

15. Ibid.

16. Klaus, Rand, and Taylor, *Report to the Nation*, p. 22.

17. Ibid., p. 19.

18. William E. Berg and Robert Johnson, "Assessing the Impact of Victimization: Acquisition of the Victim Role among Elderly and Female Victims," in *Perspectives on Victimology*, William H. Parsonage, ed. (Beverly Hills, CA: Sage Publications, Inc., 1979).

19. Nancy Ashton, "Senior Citizens' Views of Crime and the Criminal Justice System," in *The Elderly Victim of Crime*, David Lester, ed. (Springfield, IL: Charles C. Thomas, 1981), p. 18.

20. Catherine J. Whitaker, "Elderly Victims," *Bureau of Justice Statistics Special Report*, U.S. Department of Justice (Washington, DC: U.S. Government Printing Office, November, 1987), p. 1.

21. Ibid.

22. Ibid., p. 2.

23. Berg and Johnson, "Assessing the Impact of Victimization."

24. Ibid.

25. Dean G. Kilpatrick and Melissa J. Himelein, "Male Crime Victims, the Most Victimized, Often Neglected," *National Organization for Victim Assistance Newsletter*, Vol. 10, No. 12 (December, 1986).

26. Ibid.

27. Patrick A. Langan and Christopher A. Innes, *Bureau of Justice Statistics Special Report*, U.S. Department of Justice (Washington, DC: U.S. Government Printing Office, May 1985) p. 2.

28. Klaus, Kaplan, Rand, and Taylor, *Report to the Nation*, 2nd ed., p. 27.

29. Ibid., p. 32.

30. Ibid.

31. Ibid.

32. Ibid.

33. Ibid., p. 33.

34. Klaus, Rand, and Taylor, *Report to the Nation*, p. 21.

35. Leroy Pelton, "Child Abuse and Neglect: The Myth of Classlessness," *American Journal of Orthopsychiatry*, 43, (1978), pp. 608–17.

36. Philip G. Ney, "Infant Abortion and Child Abuse: Cause and Effect," *Child & Family*, 19, No. 2 (1980), 139–49.

37. Ibid.

38. Ibid.

39. Elizabeth Stark, "The Unspeakable Family Secret," *Psychology Today* (May, 1984), 42.

40. Ibid.

41. Ibid.

42. Ibid.

43. Ibid.

44. Ibid.

45. Klaus, Rand, and Taylor, *Report to the Nation*, p. 22.

46. Ibid.

47. President's Task Force on Victims of Crime, Final Report (Washington, DC: U.S. Government Printing Office, 1982), pp. 17–18.

48. Samuel Walker, *Sense and Nonsense About Crime*, (Monterey, CA: Brooks/Cole Publishing Company, a division of Wadsworth, Inc., 1985), pp. 139–45.

49. U.S. Department of Justice, Bureau of Justice Statistics, *Criminal Victimization in the United States* (Washington, DC: U.S. Government Printing Office, 1985), p. 8.

50. Walker, *Sense and Nonsense*, pp. 26–27.

51. *Nova Legislative Directory*, U.S. Department of Justice, 1987.

52. Oscar Newman, *Defensible Space: Crime Prevention through Urban Design* (New York: Macmillan, 1972).

53. Ibid.

54. Alan Booth, "The Built Environment as a Crime Deterrent," *Criminology*, Vol. 18 (February, 1981), 557–570.

55. Ibid.

56. Cohen, Lawrence E. and Marcus Felson, "Social Change and Crime Rate Trends: A Routine Activity Approach." *American Sociological Review* 44, 1979, pp. 588–608; and Felson, "Routine Activities and Crime Prevention in the Developing Metropolis," *Criminology* 25, 1987, pp. 911–32.

57. Cohen and Felson, *Ibid*.

58. Miethe, Terance D, Mark C. Stafford, and J. Scott Lang, "Social Differ-

entiation in Criminal Victimization: A Test of Routine Activities Life Style Theories," *American Sociological Review* 52, 1987, pp. 184–94.

59. Sherman, Lawrence W., Patrick R. Gartin, and Michael E. Buerger, "Hot Spots and Predatory Crime: Routine Activities and the Criminology of Place," *Criminology* 1, February, 1989, pp. 27–55.

60. *Ibid.*

61. *Ibid.*

62. United States Senate, Committee on Commerce, Science, and Transportation, Report 98-478, "Motor Vehicle Theft Law Enforcement Act of 1984."

63. Timothy J. Flanagan and Edmund F. McGarrell, eds., *Sourcebook of Criminal Justice Statistics—1985*. U.S. Department of Justice, Bureau of Justice Statistics (Washington, DC: U.S. Government Printing Office, 1986), p. 292.

64. Ibid.

65. Edmund F. McGarrell and Timothy J. Flanagan, eds., *Sourcebook of Criminal Justice Statistics—1984*. US. Department of Justice, Bureau of Justice Statistics, (Washington DC: U.S. Government Printing Office, 1985). p. 464.

66. Arthur J. Lurigio and Dennis P. Rosenbaum, "Evaluation Research in Community Crime Prevention: A Critical Look at the Field," in *Community Crime Prevention: Does It Work?* Dennis P. Rosenbaum, ed. (Beverly Hills, CA: Sage Publications, 1986), pp. 19–44.

67. Dennis P. Rosenbaum, Arthur J. Lurigio, and Paul J. Lavrakas, "Crime Stoppers—A National Evaluation," U.S. Department of Justice, National Institute of Justice, September, 1986.

68. Robert Warren, Mark S. Rosentraub, and Karen S. Harlow, "Coproduction, Equity, and the Distribution of Safety," *Urban Affairs Quarterly*, Vol. 19., No. 4 (June, 1984), 447–64.

69. Fred Dubow and Aaron Podolefsky, "Citizen Participation in Community Crime Prevention," *Human Organization*, 41 (1982), 307–14.

70. Warren et al., "Distribution of Safety," p. 455.

71. Eduard A. Ziegenhagen and Delores Brosnan, "Victim Responses to Robbery and Crime Control Policy," *Criminology*, Vol. 23, No. 4 (1985), 675–95.

72. Ibid., p. 675.

73. Ibid., p. 693.

74. Daniel McGillis and Joan Mullen, *Neighborhood Justice Centers, An Analysis of Potential Models* (Washington: DC: U.S. Government Printing Office, 1977), p. i.

75. Howard Zehr and Kathy Makinen, *Victim Offender Reconciliation Program Volunteer Handbook*, 2nd ed. (Akron, PA: Mennonite Central Committee, U.S., 1980).

76. James F. Gilsinan, *Doing Justice* (Englewood Cliffs, NJ: Prentice-Hall, Inc., 1982).

X

Criminals and Crime Control Policy

At the end of this chapter, the student will be able to:

A. Note some of the various ways to categorize crime and criminals.
B. Describe some of the demographic characteristics of "typical criminals."
C. Describe different policies that emerge from different crime classifications.
D. Discuss the utility of such concepts as the "career criminal" and of various policies flowing from different images of who the criminal is.

ISSUE BACKGROUND

The Contingent Nature of the Term Criminal

Since the application of the legal definition of crime to a particular act is contingent on a number of factors, the definition of a criminal is by no means straightforward. This point was underscored in Chapter 2.

From a policy perspective, a number of factors contribute to the way legislators, law enforcement officials, and court and correctional personnel classify crime and criminals. As noted in Chapter 6, the combination of these factors make up what might be conveniently labeled "the folk wisdom of the educated." Such folk wisdom is formed in the cauldron of practical experience, as theoretical and empirical facts mix with a host of subjective elements. Included among the latter are personal history, the particular role played in the criminal justice system, and the political and administrative pressures faced in the day-to-day application of the law.

This chapter will explore the empirical and theoretical elements that contribute to our understanding of who the criminal is. It is possible to define criminals by the types of acts they engage in, the length of criminal involvement, the volume of crime committed by particular cohorts of individuals, the concern specific acts cause among the populace, and the amount of money the acts cost society. Choosing one or another of these dimensions has certain implications for the type of crime control policy developed. The connection between various definitions of who the criminal is and policies of control will also be explored in this chapter. Beginning in Chapter 11, the experiential elements that influence how the criminal is recognized and treated will be analyzed.

CRIMINOLOGICAL/CRIMINAL JUSTICE CONSIDERATIONS

The Typical Street Criminal Isn't

The terms "crime" and "criminal" often refer to a very select group of acts and people.[1] When used in everyday discussions, these terms most often denote street crimes and offenders that have readily identifiable characteristics. Street crimes include homicide, rape, robbery, aggravated assault, burglary, theft, drug violation, and auto theft. These crimes are the ones that generate the most concern among the population. Further, since these crimes are readily detectable, their commission is more likely to end in arrest, conviction, and sentencing than is the commission of other crimes such as violation of the Pure Food and Drug Act.[2] Therefore, our understanding of who the criminal is is often incomplete. It is based on a biased sample—those who are more often arrested and processed through the system. Moreover, those who go to jail or prison are likely to be repeat offenders. Again, those we have the most data on are not representative of the total criminal population, but of a select sample, often repeat offenders involved in typical street crimes.[3]

Street crime is a young man's endeavor. Arrests for property crime peak at age 16. Violent crime arrests peak at age 18.[4] Almost 90% of the arrestees for violent crime in 1985 were males. In the same year, arrestees for property crime were 76% male.[5] Of convicted jail inmates, 93% are male, the same percentage found among federal prison inmates.[6] Ninety-six percent of state prison inmates are male.[7]

The majority of those arrested for both violent and property crime are white, 52% and 68%, respectively. Nevertheless, blacks account for 47% of those arrested for violent crime and 30% of those arrested for property crime.[8] These percentages are astoundingly high, considering that blacks make up only 12% of the general population.[9]

In many ways, the image of the street criminal mirrors the image of the victims of these crimes. Both victim and criminal tend to be predominantly young and male and disproportionately black. Thus, it should be evident that these characteristics do not cause people to commit crime. Rather, they seem to be associated with other factors that are crimeogenic. What these factors are, however, and how exactly they cause crime is the subject of considerable debate.

The Relationship Between Poverty and Crime

Chapters 6 and 7 discussed the various theories of crime causation. These chapters underscored three points about criminological theory development. First, such development does not take place in a vacuum. Instead, scientific theories are influenced by prevailing ideologies. Second, by its very nature, scientific explanations of crime are incomplete. In simplifying the world, scientists narrow problem definitions to explore specific hypotheses. Thus, the relationship between poverty and crime is complex, involves only certain types of crime, and will change depending upon both the definitions of crime and of poverty employed by the researcher. Therefore, evidence adduced to support a specific hypothesis about economic standing and crime will be applicable only to a relatively narrow range of behavior. The point can be illustrated by noting recent research efforts to explore the link between poverty and violent crime.

David Brownfield has reviewed various studies about the relationship between social class and violent behavior.[10] His conclusion is that depending upon the definition of social class used, the link between class and violence is nonexistent, moderate, or relatively strong. If a Marxist definition of class is used, the relationship between class and violent behavior is nonexistent. The criteria of class placement in the Marxist approach are not simply economic, but stress more the worker's relationship to the productive processes. Does the worker own the means of production, control the work of others, and have control over his or her own labor? Using these criteria, sons of working-class fathers have a slightly lower rate of self-reported violent behavior than sons of semi-autonomous employees (for example, professionals) and nearly identical rates of such behavior when compared to sons of supervisors (foremen or self-employed merchants).[11] On the other hand, if the definition of poverty is limited to include only the "disreputable poor," the association between poverty and violent behavior appears quite strong.[12] The disreputable poor, the "Lumpenproletariat" in Marxist terminology, are those who experience chronic unemployment and a lack of social ties. Family life is chaotic or nonexistent, and there are few if any institutional affiliations such as with a church, a neighborhood or community group, etc. Finally, if social rank is defined by gradational measures which place people along a continuum based on a combination of factors such as income, education, and occupation, or if it is defined by ecological means such as location in a particular area of the city, the relationship between social class and violent behavior is moderate.[13]

Since the association between poverty and certain kinds of crime is not clearly understood and since the linkage itself is dependent upon how terms are defined, scientists must proceed in a piecemeal fashion, with each research project addressing a relatively narrow set of concerns. Policy making, however, does not seem to proceed in a careful, step-by-step manner. Nor does it ordinarily attempt to be piecemeal. Policy is addressed to the big picture and the big solution.

Criminological Theory and Public Policies for Controlling Criminals

Chapters 6 and 7 underscored a third point about criminological theory: It does contribute to the policy process. Given the differences among theories, how does this contribution occur? The answer is straightforward. The cauldron of experience that produces the folk wisdom of the educated reduces the complexities of scientific theories to a few common themes. The themes distilled from theory influence the policy actor's view of who the criminals are and what should be done about them.

At first glance, the various theories about crime causation may seem entirely dissimilar. Closer examination will reveal that, despite such apparent differences, the theories share, to a remarkable degree, a similar world view. Specifics aside, there are certain common themes that run through the various scientific accounts of criminal behavior. These themes were discussed briefly in Chapter 6. The tendencies toward combinations, determinism, and rationalism are reviewed below. Against this background, a currently popular criminal justice policy is then analyzed to illustrate the influence of these tendencies on crime control efforts.

An example from the advertising annals of the recent past highlights the tendency toward combinations. A couple of years ago, a popular mouthwash advertised that it killed germs that caused bad breath. You could tell it was effective because it tasted bad. Bad-tasting liquid got rid of bad germs which caused bad breath. At least that was the association that the advertising attempted to establish. In the public mind, a bad-tasting concoction that attacked germs was like medicine, which also usually tasted bad but got rid of bad things in the body. The Federal Trade Commission put a stop to these advertisements since there was no evidence that the bad-tasting liquid killed germs or even that germs caused bad breath. Despite the lack of evidence, the notion that something that tasted bad was good for you seemed to contain a certain inherent logic. This demonstrates what the Italian sociologist Pareto, writing in the nineteenth century, called the tendency toward combinations.[14] People tend to put together or combine like things. Consequently, an undesirable result (bad breath or crime, for example) is seen as caused by an undesirable or pathological condition. Most of the theories previously discussed exhibit this tendency toward combinations, or the combining of like with like. Crime is accounted for as something caused by bad physique, weak intelligence, psychiatric disability, or those social conditions associated with poverty: pathological causes for pathological effects.

Determinism suggests that given a certain preexisting condition, crime will almost inevitably result. As previously noted, such determinism is most evident in the biological, psychological, and psychiatric approaches to criminal behavior, but it also lurks in the sociological explanations of illegal conduct. Except for social control theories, there is little attention paid to the operation of free will in the face of adverse social conditions. The criminal is viewed as a victim of circumstance, propelled into law-violating behavior by forces beyond his control. Even the labeling perspective which, according to Howard Becker, takes the position of the underdog or the outsider, contains a heavy dose of determinism. Individuals are labeled, accept the label, and then act accordingly. The people labeled are seen as passive, that is, as uncritical, uncomplaining acceptors of labels.

The belief in the essentially orderly, understandable nature of human society is the third element that unites the various scientific explanations of criminal conduct. Social life is viewed as rule governed. Deduce the rules from an appropriate theoretical construct, and it is possible to understand and predict human behavior. This third thread tying together the various theories is the thread of rationalism. We have seen that the early founders of the modern behavioral and social sciences firmly grounded their new disciplines in the rhetoric and images of the physical sciences. Human behavior, while extremely complex, was ultimately reducible to mathematical formulae. Given factor X, Y will result.

While scientific explanations of crime are constrained by the ideological climate in which they are articulated, the relationship is circular. Scientific explanations reinforce particular world views. The reason the terms "crime" and "criminal" most often denote street crime and offenders that have readily identifiable characteristics can be partly explained by the fact that the folk wisdom of the educated emphasizes certain common themes from the scientific literature. Those already on the margins of society and who experience other forms of pathology are thought to be more prone to criminal activity, which is a tendency toward combinations.

Determinism translates into viewing the offending population as powerless. This in turn suggests that criminal activity is more the result of individual pathology rather than social pathology. Policies mostly seek the control of individuals, not the restructuring of the society. Control can be benign, such as through therapy and counseling, or penal, as through the increased use of prison. Even sociological theories fail to escape this trap. Except for Marxism, most sociological theories suggest more efficient systems, not new systems, as a crime remedy. Educational systems can be improved, more job training can be provided, police, courts, and corrections can be better managed. At most, midlevel bureaucrats end up being the targets of change and criticism, not whole systems or the powerful upper level functionaries that run them.[15]

The effects of scientific rationality on policy actors have already been discussed. This theme provides policy actors with both a rationale and a mandate for doing something about crime. Further, it provides the populace with the hope that with just a little more time and a little more money, the problem can be solved.

The results of these influences are not difficult to see. Most crime policies end up focusing on the criminal activities of the lower class and tend to emphasize strategies of control rather than radical social change. Yet it is clear that crime exists in the corporate board room as well as on the street.

White-Collar and Corporate Crime

White-collar crime includes crime committed by a person of high status in the course of his or her occupation and/or illegal behavior designed to increase corporate, as opposed to personal, wealth. It is immediately apparent that this definition obscures as much as illuminates. Terms like "high status" and "illegal behavior" are vague. Does this behavior include the low-level clerk who steals petty cash? Does "illegal" necessarily mean criminal, or does it include regulatory violations that do not carry criminal sanctions? The answer to these questions depend upon the particular researcher's point of view. Like the term "street crime," the phrase "white-collar crime" often tells more about the person applying it than about the phenomenon to which it is applied. Nevertheless, street crime and white-collar deviance can be distinguished in at least two ways. Perpetrators tend to be older, well established, white males, and, as already noted, this type of crime tends to be the most expensive in terms of loss to the economy.[16]

A review of research literature suggests that a fair number of Fortune 500 companies fit the definition of persistent offender. Marshall Clinard and his associates, reviewing enforcement actions against large corporations in the 1970s, discovered that 60% had at least one such action initiated against them in a two-year period. Forty percent of the manufacturing corporations had been repeat offenders, and about one fifth of them had five or more offenses.[17] These findings mirror those of Sutherland 30 years previously. He studied the corporate histories of the 70 largest manufacturing, mining, and mercantile corporations in the United States and discovered that the 70 corporations had been involved in over 980 legal violations in their organizational lifetimes, which averaged 45 years.[18] While some of these involved violations of civil rather than criminal codes, these data underscored the fact that crime was not simply a street phenomenon.

White-collar and corporate crime cover a wide variety of behavior. Included are such things as the manufacturing of defective and dangerous products, the manufacture and sale of impure drugs, price fixing, Medicare and Medicaid fraud on the part of physicians, fraudulent sales tactics, violation of worker safety standards, and more common forms of individual activities like embezzlement.[19] The amounts of money involved can be staggering.

When the U.S. House of Representatives investigated the billing practices of defense firms in 1982, they found that some firms had overcharged the government tens of millions of dollars.[20] Two firms even billed the government for legal expenses incurred while defending themselves against charges brought by the government! In one instance the legal fees charged amounted to $67,685. Another company charged the government $93,474 for legal costs in fighting warranty claims by commercial customers. The company offered the warranty, but the government was going to pay for it.[21]

Although white-collar and corporate crime involve a far greater loss to the economy than street crime, and in many instances greater threat to physical safety for a larger number of people, the issue does not have the salience for citizens and policy makers that street crime does. The relatively light penalties given corporate and individual offenders is a reflection of this. Many violators are simply fined, often in an amount far less than the illegal act reaped its perpetrators. Occasionally, a relatively short jail or prison sentence might be imposed, but generally those who steal less, the street criminals, get a proportionately higher share of the punishment.

Theories of White-Collar and Corporate Deviance

Numerous explanations for white-collar and corporate crime have been proffered. Much of the literature, like that dealing with lower-class crime, puts the blame on individual factors. Yet recent research suggests that systems rather than individuals are the locus for most crimeogenic factors. In other words, because of particular legal, organizational, and economic arrangements, white-collar and corporate deviance are encouraged. Three such system models are currently being researched.

The oldest model describes crime-coercive systems. As the name implies, the organization of particular markets by those at the top of an industry pyramid force lower-level employees into corrupt practices. The model has been used to explain white-collar and corporate crime in the automobile industry,[22] the heavy electrical equipment industry,[23] and the wholesale and retail liquor business.[24] Common to all three of these industries are highly organized, hierarchical markets, where a few manufacturers control product supply to franchisers.[25] Such manufacturing oligopolies can force sales quotas and low profit margins on retailers, who in turn are forced to engage in corrupt business practices to stay solvent. Thus, car dealers may fake repairs, add unwanted options to cars at inflated prices, bill excessive finance charges, switch engines, and so forth in response to economic pressures created by a legally established market. Needleman and Needleman refer to such systems as being pervaded by "Godfatherism":

. . . high ranking corporate officials set up conditions that, in effect, confront lower-level system members with an "offer they can't refuse," leading them to break the law for the system's (and incidentally their own) economic benefit.[26]

The Needlemans, however, criticize this model for its limited applicability and for its deterministic overtones, which have not stood the test of empirical analysis. They cite Farberman's research, which shows that almost half of the auto dealerships he studied did not use kickbacks to obtain a supply of used cars.[27] Clearly, there are pockets of resistance to market pressures, and these must be more clearly understood. Also, relatively few markets are organized in the tight fashion required by the crime-coercive model. A less deterministic model is required to understand white-collar and corporate deviance in looser market structures. The Needlemans suggest a crime-facilitative model to fill this considerably large gap.

If crime is a part of doing business in a crime-coercive model, it is an unwelcome but unavoidable cost of doing business in the facilitative model. Conditions encourage deviant activity, while the cost of correcting abuses is viewed as too great given other organizational goals.

In describing the crime-facilitative model, Needleman and Needleman use an example from the stock market. They demonstrate that securities theft and fraud are made easier by structural conditions that encourage a continuous flow of commerce unimpeded by cumbersome mechanisms of cross-checking security issues. Moreover, legal codes remove a bank's liability for trading in counterfeit securities. If a bank did not know the securities traded were bogus, they do not have to make up the cash lost by the purchaser. Of course, the system discourages banks from closely checking such securities. Again, while money can be lost because of such transactions, the cost of system reform is viewed as greater than the cost of maintaining the existent system. Such systems are thus crime facilitative.[28]

Another example of how industries can facilitate the commission of criminal acts can be found in the reluctance of some corporations to expose and prosecute embezzlers. Companies are sometimes reluctant to pursue prosecution because to do so would undermine public confidence in the organization. After all, if an employee over a period of years can divert large amounts of money to his or her own use without being detected, the competence of those minding the store can be called into question. In 1987, an employee of a California bank was charged with embezzling $44.9 million from the bank and conducting almost $1 billion in fraudulent transactions to cover up the scheme. The prosecutor who brought the case claimed that the bank in question had urged him not to prosecute, despite the large sums of money involved. According to the prosecutor, the bank preferred to handle the matter internally. The prosecutor acknowledged that companies prefer that such information not become public since it calls into question the adequacy of an institution's financial control.[29] At the same time, however, reluctance to prosecute such activity facilitates the commission of the crime. Potential embezzlers may not be caught, and, if caught, may not be prosecuted. Embezzlement obviously does not serve the corporation, but the cost of vigorous correction is viewed as too high. Of course, if the embezzler is caught and prosecuted, the penalties he or she faces may not be all that severe. In the case cited, the person upon conviction would face a maximum penalty of a $10,000 fine and six years in prison.

A third model to explain corporate deviance is proposed by Szasz. He suggests that some environments can be represented by an externalizing model.[30] Criminogenesis, factors related to crime causation, is externalized so that legal liability and social blame is transferred away from the corporation and onto another entity, such as organized crime.

Organized Crime and Criminals

Clearly, all three system models for explaining white-collar and corporate deviance call into question the easy distinction between legitimate business and organized crime. Given the illegal activity among Fortune 500 corporations and the dependency, whether intended or unintended, of legitimate business on organized crime activity, the boundary between the two types of economic activity can be reasonably challenged. A number of authors have in fact suggested that such distinctions are arbitrary.[31]

Historical evidence would also seem to indicate that our current view of organized crime overstresses its exotic, foreign characteristics, that is, its distinctiveness. As Chapter 4 pointed out, certain criminal and vice activities, including prostitution and drugs, were organized, at least on the local level, in the eighteenth century. Often control of these enterprises was in the hands of Irish and Jewish ethnics. Gambling was similarly organized, and indeed criminal organizations seem to go back to colonial times when smuggling, controlled by Yankee Protestants, flourished.[32] The Volstead Act of 1919 which outlawed the sale of beverages containing more than one half of one percent alcohol is credited with spurring the development of our current day mob, Mafia, or Cosa Nostra.[33] Organized crime on a large scale was needed to meet the demand for illegal beverages. This demand was met by a variety of ethnic criminal gangs, the best organized being the Italian gangs that operated primarily in their own communities. Controlled largely by second-generation Italians, these gangs victimized their fellow ethnics through extortion and other means. Prohibition provided the opportunity to move out of their neighborhoods and to expand their criminal enterprises.

Current debate about the nature of organized crime centers around three issues. First is the issue of organization itself. Exactly how organized is organized crime? Second is the issue of Italian domination of the rackets and the link to foreign criminal cartels in Sicily and other Italian regions. Finally, there is debate about the reasons for organized crime. Does it flourish despite public desires or because of public desires that can only be met by an illegal enterprise?

Within the popular press, entertainment media, and academic research, two different pictures of the mob emerge. One portrays an efficient, highly organized criminal cartel with a central management structure. Decision making is largely based on a rational model, although family ties and tradition do assert their influence. According to the President's Commission on Law Enforcement and the Administration of Justice, the core group within organized crime consists of 24 "families" located in large cities in the United States. These groups are exclusively Italian but control other gangs within local jurisdictions that are comprised of various ethnic groups. Each of the 24 families are organized hierarchically, with the greatest number of employees being street-level operatives. The families stay in frequent contact with one another. Disputes are settled by a commission located in New York. The commission is made up of 9–12 men representing the nation's most powerful families. The commission's will is enforced by tradition and persuasion. Penalties for disobedience can range from relatively mild reprimands to beatings and ultimately death.[34]

A second picture suggests that organized crime is not nearly as organized as some have argued. The notion of Mafia has been portrayed as more a state of mind than an actual organization.[35] While there are clearly organized criminals in the United States and Italian Americans have been overrepresented in their ranks, there is no central authority or clear link among the various cartels. Further, some of the organized criminal groups that identify with the Mafia are, in fact, made up of relatively incompetent individuals who are a far cry from the image of the Godfather. Jimmy Breslin, the columnist, social commentator, and novelist has captured this picture of the mob in his book, *The Gang That Couldn't Shoot Straight*.[36]

Chapter 8 shows that organizations are both rational and irrational, organized and disorganized. Thus, the seemingly contradictory pictures of the Mafia are probably both correct. Criminal trials of organized crime leaders in the mid-1980s in New York City provided evidence supporting the view of a central management commission. The leaders of five New York families, the Gambinos, the Genoveses, the Luccheses, the Colombos, and the Bonannos, are among the most powerful members of the commission. The extent of the commission's influence beyond the East Coast, however, was not clear. Evidence suggests a second commission operating out of Chicago, with influences extending to the western part of the United States. Law enforcement officials believe, however, that the New York Commission is the supreme authority throughout the United States. The mob apparently does have global contacts and makes use of top financial and legal advisors.[37]

In the 1980s drugs became a major commodity for organized crime. According to news accounts, evidence showed that between 1979 and 1984, the Mafia smuggled tons of heroin and cocaine into the United States, using Turkey and Sicily as bases of operation and processing.[38] Other foreign connections included Switzerland and Bermuda, where large-scale money laundering operations took place. Side by side with this international corporate image, the trials demonstrated the existence of groups fractured by generational conflict and self-interest. Older mobsters, in secret recorded conversations, complained about a lack of respect among younger members and the difficulty of controlling them. Moreover, the successful prosecutions themselves were made possible by a breaking down of the tight control supposedly exercised by the commission and/or erosion of the code of secrecy that had been central to the older members' style of life.[39]

Death, prosecution, and ongoing assimilation will continue to change the ethnic face of organized crime in the United States. The Italian influence, dominant since the 1920s, will wane. But like corporations in the legitimate sectors of the economy, global crime networks will probably increase in importance. In this regard, it is interesting to note that the Sicily connection probably represents an exporting rather than an importing of a criminal phenomenon. While some traditions of organized crime hark back to the family traditions of Italian peasants, the current mob is clearly an American creation. Its current form arose in response to the American characteristic of legislating morality while tolerating and even encouraging corruption. Its influence and activity is aided and abetted by legitimate enterprise. And finally, its structure mirrors some of the central elements of corporate America. Excessive competition is frowned upon, and loyalty is apparently being replaced by an ethic of self-interest and focus on the bottom line.

It has been noted that much of our popular literature stresses the foreign nature of organized crime. In part, this helps maintain the illusion of a clear distinction between legitimate and illegitimate business activities. Yet it seems clear that organized crime exists because of the cooperation of citizens with its activities. At times this cooperation is overt and conscious. Thus, organized crime provides goods and services that are illegal, but are also in great demand. Gambling, prostitution, and narcotics flourish because citizens want these commodities.

The Crimes of Good People

The connections between white-collar, corporate, and organized crime suggest the cooperation of a far larger segment of the population in criminal activity than would a single focus on street crime. Such cooperation is even more apparent in the activities of people who do not consider themselves to be criminals. The last chapter noted, for example, that corporations can be victims. Often, they are victims of criminal activities, the perpetrators of which would be insulted if they were called criminals. There are no demographically distinguishing characteristics of criminals in this category. We are the perpetrators. Because of the widespread acceptance of some of these activities, losses can be quite extensive. Remember the hotel chain that reported an annual loss of $3 million in towels alone. As noted, employee theft is a serious problem for many organizations. Also included in these types of crimes are social order deviances. Typically, such crimes include behavior dealing with sex, gambling, and drugs or alcohol. Because of society's ambivalent attitudes towards this category of crime, both acts and typical perpetrators change over time (see Chapter 5). A host of other activities of a criminal nature are also committed by "ordinary," "law-abiding" citizens. Cheating on income tax is apparently widespread. Government losses because of income tax evasion have been estimated to be as high as $81 billion.[40] Crimes of the masses also include violence, as the previous chapter's discussion on intrafamily violence illustrates.

Because of public ambivalence toward these types of activities, policy efforts tend to be sporadic and largely symbolic. Periodic crackdowns occur but with little long-term effect.

Indeed, the criminal justice system focuses primarily on that segment of crime toward which the least ambivalence is shown. They are aided in this narrow focus by the folk wisdom of the educated. Thus, street crime constitutes the major concern of the criminal justice system. This can be illustrated by reviewing the concept of the career criminal and the policy of selective incapacitation that flows from it.

POLICY CONSIDERATIONS: THEORIES/ARGUMENTS/APPLICATIONS

The Career Criminal and Selective Incapacitation

The concept of the career criminal is not particularly new. Since the turn of the century, criminal justice practitioners and policy makers have been interested in the "habitual" offender, the "chronic" offender, the "career" criminal. The concept, however, received new life with the publication, in 1972, of Wolfgang, Figlio, and Sellin's research, *Delinquency in a Birth Cohort*.[41] The concept was restored to such vigor that it now enjoys an almost unchallenged existence within the folk wisdom of the educated.

Wolfgang and colleagues traced the official records of all the males born in Philadelphia in 1945 through to their eighteenth birthday in 1963. Of these, 34.9% were considered delinquent, that is, having had one or more officially recorded contact with the police. The fascinating thing about the findings, however, was that a small percentage of youth, 6.3%, were responsible for over half of the total offenses committed by the group, 51.9%. Six hundred twenty-seven youth committed 5,305 officially recorded criminal offenses and averaged the highest number of contacts with the police—five or more. Moreover, these chronic offenders were responsible for the bulk of serious street crime among the sample. They committed 71% of the murders, 73% of the rapes, and 82% of all the robberies. This research indicated that a relatively small number of offenders were responsible for the bulk of the crime. The policy implications were clear. Arrest and incapacitate this group, and a significant reduction in crime could occur without a concomitant increase in expenditures to house large populations of offenders.

The birth cohort research of Wolfgang and his colleagues and the policy conclusions it stimulated received an added boost with the 1982 study, *Selective Incapacitation*, by Peter W. Greenwood of the Rand Corporation.[42] After interviewing prisoners from three states and cross-checking official records to determine the volume of crime committed by inmates between arrests, the Rand report reached the following conclusions. Inmates generally were responsible for a high number of offenses, although criminal activity varied significantly among states, with two states apparently already practicing some form of selective incarceration. Imprisoned robbers in Texas averaged nine robberies per year. Those in California and Michigan, however, averaged 53 and 77, respectively, apparently indicating a policy of only locking up the most persistent offenders. Moreover, it was apparent that criminals do not specialize; instead they are generalists—committing robberies, burglaries, thefts or frauds, and drug offenses all in the course of a given year! Finally, it appears that there is a hard core among the hard core. Among inmates surveyed, the median number of robberies for 90% of the sample was five per year. But for the remaining 10% of the group, the median number of robberies per perpetrator per year was 87.

While the Rand Study concluded with a specific caution about the applicability of the study to sentencing policy, and pleaded the need for more research before any conclusions were drawn, such cautions were generally not heeded by the policy community nor, for that matter, by a fair number of criminologists. In the folk wisdom of the educated, locking up those who committed the most crimes, the career criminals, was a way to both lower the crime rate and to lower correctional costs. The concept of the career criminal and the policy of selective incapacitation which flowed from it offered hope to a community frustrated with crime. Unfortunately, both the concept and the policy are seriously flawed.

In an essay reviewing the concept of the career criminal, Gottfredson and Hirschi note a number of difficulties.[43] First, the concept refers to different things depending upon who is using it. The concept has been used to refer to a state of mind, the kinds of acts committed, the number of acts, and the number of arrests and convictions. Second, the concept fails to take into account research which shows that involvement in street crime in no sense conforms to the conventional meaning of the term "career." There is no specialization, no advancement in skill or knowledge, and no increasing monetary gains. As already noted, incarcerated offenders commit a wide variety of crimes, but these crimes require no special skill or knowledge. Many burglaries, for example, simply involve taking advantage of an opportunity (an open door) or breaking a window to gain access. Monetary gain is usually low and does not change over the course of criminal activity. To quote Gottfredson and Hirschi, "his career starts at the bottom and proceeds nowhere. . . ."[44] Third, the notion of career criminal fails to address adequately the age-related circumstances of street crimes. After peaking at the age of 16 or 17, street crime activity drops off dramatically in subsequent age groupings. The relationship between age and crime holds regardless of sex, race, county, time, or offense.[45] This fact leads to the major problem with a policy of selective incapacitation. The habitual or career offender is identified with 20/20 hindsight. That is, the label of career offender is based upon past activity. Thus, incarceration is most likely to occur after criminal activity has peaked. We incarcerate those ready to retire. Their places are filled by young offenders, 13 and 14, who have not yet reached their peak.

The above discussion raises the problem of prediction. This particular problem has plagued the social and criminological sciences from their beginning. Simply put, their theories are not developed to the point where they can adequately predict the likelihood of a given behavior, particularly criminal activity. Attempts to do so have continually resulted in high numbers of false positives and false negatives. False positives mean that people have been incorrectly identified as likely to exhibit a particular behavior. False negatives refer to people who have not been identified as likely criminals, who then subsequently engage in criminal activity. The Rand study used very sophisticated analysis of criminal histories to try to predict behavior but did no better than chance. Thus, even with very advanced techniques, we would end up incarcerating a large number of people who do not need to be incarcerated and releasing people who will subsequently commit new crimes.[46] While notions such as the career criminal and selective incapacitation seem to solve the dilemma of high costs for relatively little safety, it is clear that they do not. Finally, the notions create serious dilemmas for due process.

Should people be sentenced based upon a vague notion of what they might do? An affirmative answer undermines notions of Western jurisprudence as these have been developing since the time of Beccaria. A person is punished according to the harm done society by being given a penalty statutorily mandated. While it is true that the law considers an incapacitation effect, that is, the prevention of future crime, this is a secondary rather than a primary consideration. To reverse the order would be to punish a person primarily for something he has not yet in fact done. While this is troublesome enough, some of the criteria for predicting future law-violating behavior involve activity that is not itself criminal. For example, the Rand study uses unemployment as a predictive criterion. This is weighted the same as a prior conviction. Use of this formula penalized the unemployed! The due process problems with this should be obvious, and as Walker notes it returns us to the era of debtor prisons.[47] We are not moving forward, but backward in an attempt to deal with crime. And as discussed at the beginning of this section, we are orienting our crime policies toward the control of the most vulnerable members of our community. The image of crime and criminals provided by a focus on street crime justifies and perpetuates this control orientation. This is not to say, however, that the concept of a career criminal cannot be made applicable to other forms of crime.

A White-Collar Criminal Career: Insider Trading

The reason for the low salience of white-collar and corporate crime may have to do in part with their complexity and seeming lack of victims. They are thus not easily translated into mass media events. The disposal of hazardous waste is, on its surface, a less exciting issue than a daring, daylight robbery. Similarly, insider trading, while of interest to government prosecutors trained in high finance, may seem an arcane issue to those not directly involved in the management of corporate stocks and bonds. Yet as an examination of these two issues will show, the average middle-class citizen is more likely to be affected by criminal wrongdoing in these spheres than by street crimes.

Insider trading refers to the illegal practice of using knowledge gained by one's position as an insider in a corporation or as a person entrusted with sensitive corporate information, to trade on that company's stocks and securities.[48] Thus, federal law would prohibit me as a stock and bond manager of a large corporation from buying or selling the company's stock for myself if I knew the company was about to be bought by another concern. Of course, if somebody paid me for my insider information and then that person bought or sold stock based on my tips, that too would be illegal. That is exactly what occurred in the Wall Street scandal of the mid-1980s.

Dennis B. Levine, a company merger specialist, passed insider information on impending company takeovers to Ivan F. Boesky. Boesky would then buy large blocks of the company's stock. Once merger plans become public, the company's stock prices generally rose and Boesky made large profits, a portion of which he shared with Levine. When the scheme become known, Levine and Boesky implicated a large number of other people, some of whom worked for the most respected brokerage houses on Wall Street.[49] In return for his cooperation, Levine was fined $362,000 and sentenced to two years in prison.[50] While this sentence may appear fairly harsh, it is estimated that Mr. Levine made $12.6 million in five years by using his insider knowledge in stock transactions.[51] Boesky was fined $100 million.[52] This too seems like a harsh penalty, but it is estimated to be only about half of what Boesky actually made on his illegal schemes.[53]

While the amounts of money involved in this situation make for interesting reading, it still may be difficult to see how such goings on affect the average citizen. Actually, the effects are both long term and short term.

Many times a company will attempt to buy back large blocks of its own stock in order to fend off hostile takeovers by other companies. The prices for these stocks become inflated when the arbitrager, a specialist in corporate mergers, accumulates a large amount of stock through insider information. He or she is then in a position to sell to the highest bidder, be it the original company or those interested in acquiring it. Regardless of the final outcome, the company, either in its original form or in its merged version, is forced to assume a heavy debt.

Paul M. Hirsch reports that large corporations have diverted more than $300 billion since 1980 to repurchase their own stock or to acquire other companies.[54] That is money not being spent on research, development, and innovation. In the long run, companies faced with such debt will not function as well as they might have, and thus long-term earnings to stockholders will be depressed. Since many people's retirement funds are tied up with the operation of the stock market, this state of affairs can have long-term direct economic impact on a wide variety of people and institutions. In the short run people lose their jobs.

Hirsch reports that one million or so midlevel managers were fired or forced to take early retirement during the 1980s because of the debt incurred by companies trying to avoid takeovers.[55] Company takeovers and merges are not of course illegal. Stock prices in such situations usually rise as a result of increased demand. Worker dislocation is perhaps inevitable in a climate that encourages company acquisition. Some argue that the enormous number of takeovers during the 1980s was in fact good for the economy, as inefficient companies were swallowed up and either restructured or dismantled by a more efficient concern.[56] Others, however, suggest that the image of the corporation has changed from one of a living resource providing jobs, goods, services, and civic contributions to being simply a cash cow.[57] Thus, greed is encouraged. In any event, it seems clear that insider trading exacerbates the dislocation of workers associated with merges. Again, Hirsch notes that Martin A. Siegel, an admitted inside trader, probably made the restructuring of one company a much more expensive proposition. The company in question had to take on a debt of $4 billion to avoid a takeover. As a result, they spend $2 million a day just on interest payments. The chairman of the company is quoted by Hirsch as saying, "Think what that would have done for the U.S. if it had been put into job creation."[58] Not only were jobs not being created because of the debt load, but jobs were in fact being eliminated at the company to service a debt inflated by illegal activity.

An Application of the Externalizing Model of Corporate Deviance: The Case of Hazardous Waste

The disposal of hazardous waste periodically becomes a salient issue in the minds of some. As Andrew Szasz reports, the general concern with environmental issues in the 1970s caused a focusing on the byproducts of modern manufacturing techniques.[59] Traditionally disposed of in rather haphazard fashion, these wastes were eventually perceived as a potential environmental and public health hazard. By the mid-1970s, it was clear that disposing of these chemical byproducts by pumping them into lakes or by mixing them with ordinary municipal garbage in landfills could create massive problems of health and safety. Nevertheless, there is little association in the public mind between this problem and criminal activity. Yet, as Szasz clearly shows, the regulatory environment created to deal with this hazard encouraged an expansion of organized crime activity.

In attempting to regulate the disposal of hazardous waste, Congress faced three problems. First, disposal·technology was not well developed, nor were structures in place that would permit the safe, efficient, economical removal of such material. Second, the major industries responsible for producing these byproducts resisted any attempts to regulate production decisions. Through lobbying efforts, Congress was persuaded not to force companies to reevaluate their production techniques so less hazardous waste would be produced. Finally, generators insisted that they not be held responsible for what finally happened to the waste products. This responsibility, they argued, should be born by the waste hauler. As a result of industry lobbying efforts and structural and technological constraints, a regulatory structure emerged that facilitated the entrance of organized crime into the hazardous waste disposal business.[60]

Organized crime had had a history of involvement with the garbage business. Since thorough investigations of potential hazardous waste haulers would have created a system backlog and thus literally drowned industries in their own waste products, Congress was forced to allow for an interim licensing procedure. This favored already established haulers, many of whom had organized crime connections. Since lobbyists had persuaded Congress that haulers and not businesses should be responsible for final disposal, companies were under no obligation to investigate the reputability of the firms hired to haul their chemical byproducts. Nor did they feel pressure to reevaluate production techniques so as to produce less waste. Thus, organized crime could expand into a new and lucrative area of garbage disposal. Because they were not closely regulated, hazardous waste was in fact disposed of in a very unsafe manner, often continuing to be mixed in with regular garbage. This obviated the need for special disposal sites and technologies, keeping costs down. At the same time, corporate customers could be charged more, since after all, the wastes were hazardous. As Szasz notes, everybody profits by this. Companies, while they pay more, still keep costs within a reasonable range, and organized crime reaps greater profits. The only losers are those potentially affected by chemical contamination. As Szasz writes:

> Improper management (of hazardous waste materials) may result in explosions, fires, pollution of water resources, and other uncontrolled releases that put surrounding communities at risk and may result in physical harm ranging from

skin irritation to increased incidence of cancer, lung disease, birth defects, and other serious illnesses.[61]

The consequences of improperly disposed of hazardous wastes was starkly illustrated in Times Beach, Missouri. This town of 2,041 was literally forced to dismantle when it was discovered that dioxin-contaminated oil had been used to coat road surfaces.[62] Everybody was forced to move and the town no longer exists. Victims of burglary complain that they feel invaded when their homes have been broken into. A private space has been violated, and thus, like rape victims, they feel extremely vulnerable. Imagine that feeling multiplied and extended to a whole town. Hazardous waste disposal may not seem appropriate material for a criminology text, but as this example illustrates, its mismanagement can have far more serious effects for far greater numbers of people than typical street crime. And, as Szasz cogently shows, it is a fit subject if you are interested in organized crime or in how the policy process can result in entirely unintended consequences.

Conclusion

The general public ambivalence toward many types of crime and its control forms an ever-present backdrop to the "doing of justice." Criminal justice policy, in the end, becomes a method of conflict resolution between competing interests and visions of who is the criminal and what is a crime. Each vision in turn is affected by the job problems criminal justice functionaries face. Many of these are created in the first instance by previous policies. Thus, criminal justice policy is both a result of and a cause of the different images of crime. These points will become clear in the following chapters.

SUMMARY

What Was Said

- The application of the term criminal is contingent on a number of factors.
- Street crime is a *young man's* endeavor.
- The relationship between poverty and crime is complex, involves only certain types of crime, and will change depending upon both the definition of crime and poverty employed by the researcher.
- The reasons the terms "crime" and "criminal" most often denote street crime and offenders that have readily identifiable characteristics can be partly explained by the fact that the folk wisdom of the educated emphasizes certain common themes from the scientific literature: the tendencies toward combinations, determinism, and scientific rationality.

- White-collar and corporate crime involve a far greater loss to the economy than street crime and in many instances greater threat to physical safety for a larger number of people.
- There are three dominant models that attempt to explain white-collar or corporate deviance: the crime-coercive model, the crime-facilitative model, and the crime-externalizing model.
- The boundary between legitimate and illegitimate business practices, including organized crime, can become quite vague.
- Our current view of organized crime overstresses its exotic, foreign characteristics; in other words, its distinctiveness.
- Both the concept of the career criminal and the policy of selective incapacitation that flows from it are seriously flawed.
- Insider trading can affect a wide variety of people including retirees and middle-level managers.
- At times, a regulatory structure formed in response to competing demands can encourage the activities of organized crime.

What Was Not Said

- Street crime is not a problem.
- The public condemns all crime equally.
- Organized crime only serves the interest of a few.

NOTES

1. Mimi Cantwell, "The Offender," *Report to the Nation on Crime and Justice*, U.S. Department of Justice, Bureau of Justice Statistics, (Washington, DC: U.S. Government Printing Office, October 1983), p. 30.

2. Ibid.

3. Ibid.

4. Ibid., p. 32.

5. Katherine M. Jamieson and Timothy Flanagan, ed., *Sourcebook of Criminal Justice Statistics—1986*. U.S. Department of Justice, Bureau of Justice Statistics (Washington, DC: U.S. Government Printing Office, 1987), p. 298.

6. Ibid., pp. 394, 417.

7. Cantwell, "The Offender," p. 32.

8. Jamieson and Flanagan, *Sourcebook*, p. 300.

9. Ibid., p. 302.

10. David Brownfield, "Social Class and Violent Behavior," *Criminology*, 24, No. 3 (August, 1986), 421–48.

11. Ibid., p. 425.

12. Ibid., p. 427.

13. Ibid., pp. 429–34.

14. Viffredo Pareto, *The Mind and Society* (New York: Harcourt, Brace and Company, 1935).

15. For an expanded version of this argument, see Alvin W. Gouldner, "The Sociologist as Partisan: Sociology and the Welfare State," *The American Sociologist*, 2 (May 1963).

16. Edwin H. Sutherland, *White Collar Crime* (New York: Dryden Press, 1949).

17. Marshall Clinard, Peter Yeager, Jeanne Bussette, David Petrasher, and Elizabeth Harrias, *Illegal Corporate Behavior* (Washington, DC: Law Enforcement Assistance Administration, 1979), pp. XIX and XX.

18. Sutherland, *White Collar Crime.*

19. Embezzlement is often excluded from the list of white-collar crimes, which are sometimes limited to regulatory violations. As the chapter goes on to show, their exclusion seems arbitrary.

20. Edward W. O'Brien, "Defense Firms Overcharge Pentagon Tens of Millions, Study Finds," *St. Louis Globe-Democrat*, October 11, 1982, p. 1A.

21. Ibid., p. 8A.

22. Harvey A. Farberman, "A Criminogenic Market Structure: The Automobile Industry," *The Sociological Quarterly*, 16 (Autumn 1975), 438–57. William N. Leonard and Marvin Glenn Weber, "Automakers and Dealers: A Study of Criminogenic Market Forces," *Law and Society Review*, 4 (February, 1970), 407–24.

23. Gilbert Geis and Robert F. Meier, eds., *White Collar Crime*, rev. ed. (New York: Free Press, 1977).

24. Norman K. Denzin, "Notes on the Criminogenic Hypothesis: A Case Study of the American Liquor Industry," *American Sociological Review*, 42 (December, 1977), 905–20.

25. Martin L. Needleman and Carolyn Needleman, "Organizational Crime: Two Models of Criminogenesis," *The Sociological Quarterly*, 20, (Autumn 1979), 520.

26. Ibid., p. 518.

27. Ibid., p. 520.

28. Needleman and Needleman, "Organizational Crime," pp. 521–25.

29. Richard W. Stevenson, "$44 Million Embezzling Is Charged," *New York Times*, February 20, 1987, p. 204.

30. Andrew Szasz, "Corporations, Organized Crime, and the Disposal of Hazardous Waste: An Examination of the Making of a Criminogenic Regulatory Structure," *Criminology*, 24, No.1 (February, 1986), pp. 1–27.

31. For a review, see the following: Jay S. Albanese, "What Lockheed and La Cosa Nostra Have in Common: The Effect of Ideology on Criminal Justice Policy," *Crime and Delinquency*, 28 (1982), 211–32.
William J. Chambliss, *On The Take: From Petty Crooks to Presidents* (Bloomington, IN: University Press, 1978). Thomas C. Schelling, "Economics and Criminal Enterprise," *The Public Interest*, 7 (1967), 61–78. Dwight C. Smith, Jr., "Paragons, Pariahs, and Pirates: A Spectrum-Based Theory of Enterprise," *Crime and Delinquency*, 26 (1980), 358–86. Dwight C. Smith, Jr. and Richard D. Alba, "Organized Crime and American Life," *Society* 3 (1979), 32–38.

32. William E. Masterson, *Jurisdiction in Marginal Seas with Special Reference to Smuggling* (New York: The Macmillan Co., 1929), pp. 175–80.

33. Don C. Gibbons, *Society, Crime, and Criminal Behavior* (Englewood Cliffs NJ: Prentice-Hall, Inc., 1982).

34. The President's Commission on Law Enforcement and Administration of Justice, "The Challenge of Crime in a Free Society" (Washington, DC: U.S. Government Printing Office, 1967), pp. 192–95.

35. Dwight C. Smith, Jr., *The Mafia Myth* (New York: Basic Books, 1975).

36. Jimmy Breslin, *The Gang That Couldn't Shoot Straight* (New York: Viking, 1969).

37. Robert D. McFadden, "The Mafia of the 1980's: Divided Under Seige," *New York Times*, March 11, 1987, p. 1.

38. Ibid.

39. Ibid.

40. *Report to the Nation on Crime and Justice*, 2nd ed., United States Department of Justice, Bureau of Justice Statistics (Washington, DC: U.S. Government Printing Office, 1988), p. 114.

41. Marvin Wolfgang, Robert M. Figlio, and Thorsten Sellin, *Delinquency in a Birth Cohort* (Chicago: University of Chicago Press, 1972).

42. Peter W. Greenwood, *Selective Incapacitation* (Santa Monica, CA: The Rand Corporation, 1982).

43. Michael Gottfredson and Travis Hirschi, "The True Value of Lambda Would Appear to Be Zero: An Essay on Career Criminals, Criminal Careers, Selective Incapacitation, Cohort Studies, and Related Topics," *Criminology*, 24, No. 2 (May, 1986), 213–34.

44. Ibid., p. 218.

45. Ibid., p. 219.

46. Samuel Walker, *Sense and Nonsense About Crime* (Monterey, CA: Brooks/Cole Publishing Company, A Division of Wadsworth, Inc., 1985), pp. 56–59.

47. Ibid., p. 63.

48. Marybeth Nibley, "Scandal Raises Legal, Ethical Question," *St. Louis Post-Dispatch*, November 23, 1986, p. 1E.

49. James Sterngold, "Levine Sentencing Scheduled Today," *New York Times*, February 20, 1987, p. 29Y.

50. *New York Times*, February 22, 1987, p. 5E.

51. Ibid.

52. "SEC Gets Tough on Insider Trading," *St. Louis Post-Dispatch*, February 22, 1987, p. 1E.

53. Ibid.

54. Paul M. Hirsch, "So Much for Managers' Loyalty," *New York Times*, February 27, 1987, p. 354.

55. Ibid.

56. James K. Glassman, "Crap Shooters on Wall Street," *St. Louis Post-Dispatch*, November 21, 1986, p. 3C.

57. Hirsch, "So Much for Managers' Loyalty," p. 354.

58. Ibid.

59. Andrew Szasz, "Corporations, Organized Crime, and the Disposal of Hazardous Waste," pp. 1–27.

60. Ibid., p. 4.

61. Ibid.

62. "FEMA Proposes Plan for Dioxin Clean Up in Times Beach," *St. Louis Post-Dispatch*, January 3, 1983, pp. 1–2A.

XI

The Police

At the end of this chapter, the student will be able to:

A. Define the term generative metaphor and discuss the significance of this concept for public policy.
B. Describe the different policies that have been suggested for controlling the exercise of police discretion.
C. Distinguish between law enforcement efficiency and effectiveness.
D. Discuss a variety of policing alternatives and some of the policy experiments that relate to them.

ISSUE BACKGROUND

Is Policy a Problem-Solving Enterprise?

Chapter 1 began with a definition of public policy. It described public policy as what governments choose to do or not do about a particular problem. This definition underscores a theme that pervades much of the literature on policy making, policy administration, and policy analysis. Policy is a problem-solving enterprise.[1]

By this time, it should be clear that if policy is largely a problem-solving enterprise, it is an enterprise that often fails. The reasons for such failure should also be clear. Problems are in the eye of the beholder. Chapter 1 went on to describe the policy arena as a place where solutions often come before problems. The former shapes the latter, rather than the reverse. Thus, policy is heavily influenced by ideology as facts are filtered and molded through sieves of subjective meaning. Chapter 5 noted that knowledge is always knowledge from some point of view. The objective fact, immaculate cognition if you will, is not the stuff of social policy. Policy actions, therefore, are often a response to incomplete or even erroneous understandings of situations. Problems are not ameliorated by such responses and can at times be made worse.

This rather dismal picture suggests that the policy process might be better understood as something other than problem solving. Donald A. Schon asserts that social policy has more to do with problem setting than with problem solving.[2] The implications of this go back to another theme introduced in the first chapter. Policy and its analysis must be concerned with the formulation of "good" problems—that is, problems about which both something should and can be done. But how is this task to be accomplished? The ideology of American social science, including criminology, has stressed problem solving, the determination of optimal means to an end. The ends themselves were viewed as beyond the scope of science. Whether an end or goal was good, bad, or indifferent was a political, ethical, or religious question, not one that a scientist as a scientist could answer. Social science was to be "value-free."

Such demurring is not possible for the person engaged in the policy process. As we have seen, crime, for example, is always encountered in the policy arena as an issue. People disagree on its nature, its causes, its solution. Such disagreements are enmeshed in value-laden webs, wherein ends (goals and solutions) dictate the structuring of the phenomenon. Even at a very general level, goals are a source of disagreement. Is a zero crime rate desirable? At first glance, this may seem a universally agreed-upon end. Further reflection will, however, cast doubt upon the desirability of such a state. What kind of society would it be where no deviance is present? Would repression of individualism have to be absolute? Could such a community even exist, or was Durkheim correct in saying that society needs deviance in order to function? Since policy debates often center around the desirability of particular goals, the policy analyst must attempt to systematically examine various goals and the consequence of pursuing one or another of them. But he or she cannot stop there. Goal conflicts are seldom, if ever, resolved by facts or logic. The history of crime control testifies to the futility of such an approach. Policy analysts must therefore develop methods for bringing together seemingly irreconcilable positions so that new understandings can be generated. Questions must be framed so that new problem perspectives can emerge. In short, problem setting must assume at least an equal place with problem solving. To get good answers you need to ask good questions.

The Importance of Generative Metaphors

Schon suggests that the development of good problems requires an understanding of the stories people tell about troublesome situations. He demonstrates that such stories often contain generative metaphors, that is, ones that frame both a problem and its solution.[3] Such metaphors generally remain hidden and therefore not available for analysis. We have already seen the consequences of this for criminological theory and for theories of organization. If crime is like a disease, then the "patient" should remain incarcerated until a cure is effected. If crime is like sin, then the sinner needs punishment and redemption. If crime is like a physical-biological characteristic, then society needs to be concerned with social defense. Similarly, if an organization is seen as like a machine, workers are simply parts to be replaced when they malfunction. If organizations are compared to rational organisms, they are capable of analyzing an objective reality and planning accordingly. If they are like cultures, however, they shape their own reality and plan, after they have already acted toward a future.

Beginning with this chapter, we will analyze the stories various criminal justice functionaries tell about the reality they encounter. We will discover that stories vary among and between these groups of officials. Thus, the criminal justice system is composed of groups of people, addressing different problems in different ways with different results. As we probe their stories and bring to light the metaphors that generate various problem frames, the importance of appropriate problem setting for criminal justice policy will become even more apparent. At the same time, it may be possible to suggest new problem frames that can incorporate the seemingly contradictory goals of criminal justice system participants. Better problems and questions might then emerge. We begin this quest with police stories.

CRIMINOLOGICAL/CRIMINAL JUSTICE CONSIDERATIONS

Police Stories: How Is the Use of Force to Be Controlled?

A commission appointed by New York Governor Mario M. Cuomo has concluded that the state's law enforcement officers generally show restraint in using physical or deadly force, that race is not a significant factor in decisions to apply force, and that police agencies respond vigorously to complaints of abuse.

. . . the [Hindlelang] researchers concluded that "patrol officers do not have an opportunity to be terribly clever in most conflict situations." The nature of the situation—in particular, whether violence already is occurring when police arrive at the scene—determines whether police are likely to use force, not the tactics of particular officers, the researchers said. "Police training should be directed at avoiding obvious errors—haste, prejudice, insults, provocative threats," they said. "Further fine-tuning of tactical training appears unjustified."

"We were flabbergasted at the findings," said Norman Siegel, Executive Director of the New York Civil Liberties Union. The report "doesn't mirror the reality that we have seen," he said. Siegel criticized the commission's methodology, especially its reliance on police reports and other official sources of information. . . .[4]

These stories are about a troublesome situation, the use or misuse of force by the police. The stories also hint at another dilemma, namely, who controls the police? Each story presents a different view of the situation and is a part of larger stories that have been told and retold least since 1816 when the British Parliament first rejected the idea of the police as incompatible with British liberty (see Chapter 4).

Police Force as a Rational Organism:
The Police Officer as Employee

The first story suggests that police violence is not a problem and that a major source of control on the use of force by the police is the administrative structure of the department. The generative metaphors operative in this story are those of the machine and the rational organism. Police agencies can replace or retool unruly officers. Rational administrative procedures thus can be used to control police abuse. It was the complete version of this story that convinced the British public to finally accept the notion of a standing police force. Supported by the ideology of utilitarianism, early British police administrators used their administrative powers to the fullest. The greatest good for the greatest number required the fledgling police to adhere strictly to the rules and procedures of the department. Being abusive to the public, sloppy in dress, and/or uncooperative and lazy could jeopardize this grand utilitarian experiment in crime control. Therefore, officers were routinely fired for any of these infractions. In the first eight years of its existence, the London Metropolitan Police Force had a turnover of 11,000 "bobbies" through dismissals or resignations, many of them forced.[5]

The Police Force as an Army

The generative metaphor of the last story is not without irony. The police as a standing army of repression was the dilemma British reformers sought to avoid. But the idea of the police as being like the military became the metaphor adopted by American police reformers. As noted in Chapter 4, early American police forces were plagued with problems of brutality and corruption. Local political interference hindered the ability of administrators to control their employees. To gain control of their departments and to create a more favorable public image, reform-minded American police officials began to speak of a war on crime as early as 1890.[6] The police were an army engaged in domestic battle against internal forces of evil. Carl B. Klockars, in his book *The Idea of Police*, discusses the advantages of adopting this metaphor.[7] First, it associated the police with military heroes, thereby raising their status in the eyes of the public. Second, using the war analogy turns out to be a good way to get funds from sometimes reluctant local governments. Failure to vote such funds puts one on the side of criminals, communists, or other assorted miscreants, not the place to be if one wants to stay in office. Third, and according to Klockars most important, it gave police administrators a rationale for asserting day-to-day control of the troops. Politicians decide the broad parameters of the war, but the actual confrontation and battles are planned and fought by those commanders who are in the field. This was a powerful metaphor for removing the police from the daily interference of local politics. Unfortunately, the metaphor was taken over and changed slightly by those subject to police force, particularly the minority communities of the 1960s. The police were not fighting an internal enemy, but were becoming the enemy by repressing legitimate dissent and grievances. The army or military metaphor thus became more starkly shaded in the ominous tones that have lurked in stories of the police since their founding. The fears of nineteenth-century British reformers were realized in the epithets hurled at the American police in the 1960s when they were viewed by some as repressive armies of occupation in minority communities.

Police Force as a Situational Response: The Police Officer as Peacekeeper

The Hindelang researchers suggest that neither police administrators nor the racial or political dispositions of patrol officers determines the use of force in most situations. Rather, the situation itself is determinative. What kinds of situations do police officers encounter? Egon Bittner has given the definitive answer: "Something ought not to be happening about which something ought to be done—NOW!"[8] The comments of a police instructor to a class of recruits illustrates the varying content of such situations:

> Most requests for police service come from citizens who telephone headquarters. The types of calls you'll have to respond to are unlimited. It'll go all the way up to a homicide or kidnapping or one of the biggies, down to helping some old invalid go to the bathroom. You can draw the line at wiping their butt. Why do we get all these off-the-wall calls? Because people don't know who else to call.[9]

This story of the police instructor, that of Bittner, and the story of the Hindelang researchers make one thing clear: the police are expected to take charge, to return a situation to a normal state. If violence is required, the police will use it to accomplish this task. Most situations do not, however, involve or require violence. As Bittner makes clear in other research, police officers spend most of their time in either peacekeeping or clerical functions, not in crime control or tasks that require the coercive use of force.[10] The police are mostly peacekeepers. Yet, precisely because the situations they respond to are so varied, peacekeeping requires a great deal of discretion be given the police. Neither administrators nor individual officers are entirely free to predetermine how a situation should be approached.

"Employees," "occupying army," "peacekeeper"—the different labels structure the different stories about the police. The stories in turn suggest different remedies to different problems. Good management prevents or limits problems caused by a few workers. A radical restructuring of the police and policing is required to secure justice for oppressed people. The police use coercive force when the task of normalization requires it, but mostly it does not require it, and the police need a great deal of discretion to meet situational contingencies. How can these different stories be reconciled? In part, the answer requires a search for a new generative metaphor that provides different, more inclusive stories of police activity. This search can start with a common, troublesome situation the variety of police stories address themselves to, one that is itself more inclusive than the use or misuse of police authority. That troublesome situation is the dilemma of who does or should control the police?

Who Will Watch the Watchers?

The dilemma of who should control the police goes back much further than the founding of the British police. As the Psalmist wondered over 3,000 years ago, "Who will watch the watchers?" Concern with what the watchers actually do has centered on two issues, the potential abuse of authority and the productivity of those assigned to "guard" society. Unfortunately, the two issues are inexorably intertwined. Thus, the history of the police has been one of constant tension among goals of efficiency, effectiveness, and, in modern Western society, democratic values.

A fully effective police force would be one that comes close to achieving 100% compliance with all the laws they are charged with enforcing. Leaving aside for the moment the issue of whether such effectiveness is possible, is the goal itself desirable? Phrased this way, the full compliance, full enforcement issue looks suspiciously like the notion of a society with little or no deviance. The goal would require the creation of a police state with a major share of societal resources devoted to the repression of the individual. Literally, there would have to be a police presence everywhere: home, business, school, and church.

The only way such a presence could be obtained is through the use of a variety of quasi-police roles, "informants," "agent provocateurs," and "thief takers." As Klockars shows, however, these roles have generally been despised throughout history.[11] The informant is traditionally associated with efforts at political repression. Informants give information to the police on matters that, while technically illegal, have the support of at least a minority of the population. Judas Iscariot might be considered the prototypical informant. Agent provocateurs are those who encourage, aid, and abet violations of the law for personal, political, or financial gain. Their typical mode of operation is to surreptitiously infiltrate groups thought to be opposed to particular government actions in order to encourage outright violation of the law. This accomplished, the group members can then be incarcerated and the dissent repressed. Thief takers were a form of law enforcement that preceded the modern-day police force. For a fee, private individuals would attempt to apprehend those who violated the property or person of another. Of course, if the criminal had more money than the person paying for his apprehension, the thief taker might be inclined to have the thief pay his fee in exchange for letting him go. Thus, this system was associated with corruption and the widespread feeling that thief takers were no better than the thieves themselves. The early British founders of the police took great pains to distinguish their new force from these less than reputable characters. As we've seen, the new police were to be uniformed, highly visible, and charged with enforcing those laws that had the support of the general population.

Although efforts to separate the new police from the historically negative images of their predecessors were not entirely successful in Britain, the architects of this police force achieved greater separation than occurred in the United States.[12] Police history in this country has been laced with periodic scandals that have resurrected one or another of these historically despised images. In part, this is because the police occupation has been much more politicized in this country than in Britain. Initially, the police job was a patronage position whose incumbent owed allegiance to the local alderman, not the police supervisors. Given the heterogeneity of American cities like New York and Boston, individual police officers represented very narrow local groups and interests. The end result was near chaos, as police officers refused to obey superiors, wear common uniforms, or enforce general laws. Officers would release other officers' prisoners and were susceptible to corruption since there was no universal agreement on which laws should be enforced. Given the low pay, officers would sometimes imitate the thief takers, dispensing justice according to who could pay the most, victim or thief. Officers were used to infiltrate "undesirable" groups, often labor coalitions seeking radical changes like fair wages and one day a week off.

Under what conditions will a society tolerate the such quasi-police roles, thereby letting effectiveness criteria threaten other values? Historical analysis suggests that fear is the main engine that drives a society toward seeking total law enforcement effectiveness regardless of the cost. The point can be illustrated by the "Red Scare" of 1919–1920.

The Red Menace

On April 2, 1917, Woodrow Wilson asked a joint session of Congress for a declaration of war against Germany. The day before, he had commented on what such a war would mean for the domestic policies of the United States:

Once lead this country into war . . . and they'll forget there ever was such a thing as tolerance. To fight you must be brutal and ruthless, and the spirit of ruthless brutality will enter into every fiber of our national life, infecting Congress, the courts, the policeman on the beat, the man on the street. Conformity would be the only virtue . . . and every man who refused to conform would have to pay the penalty.[13]

By 1919, American citizens had an opportunity to test their need for conformity and the limits of their tolerance. Unfortunately, Wilson's prophecy proved all too true.

As industry adjusted to a peacetime economy, workers experienced a brief but debilitating depression. Jobs were lost, and prices were rising faster than wages. As a result there was considerable labor unrest. The year 1919 saw over 3,600 strikes involving over 4,000,000 workers.[14] More workers struck in this single year than in the 10-year period from 1923 to 1932.[15] The strikers were seeking redress of economic grievances. However, labor unrest in this country coincided with an outpouring of radical literature from Europe. This literature demanded the overthrow of the capitalist class. Thus, in the minds of many Americans, labor unrest, Eastern European immigration, and calls for the violent communist overthrow of the United States were joined into a single fear—the Red Scare.

The major law enforcement responsibility for dealing with "Bolshevism" and the "Red Menace" fell to the federal government and the Attorney General, A. Mitchell Palmer. At first, Palmer was a reluctant participant in the hysteria that affected the nation. But a number of incidents coincided to make him a fervent convert to the cause of repression and deportation of the "dangerous immigrant classes."

On May 1, 1919, the nation learned that a number of mail bombs had been intercepted by the Post Office due to insufficient postage. These bombs were addressed to prominent Americans including Oliver Wendell Holmes and John D. Rockefeller. The New York City police asserted that the plot was due to Bolsheviks in the labor movement. Across the country, mob actions were directed at any group or individual thought to be disloyal to the United States. In the District of Columbia a few days later, an individual refused to rise when the "Star Spangled Banner" was played at a rally. After the anthem, a sailor shot the person three times in the back. A news account of the incident claimed that the crowd clapped and cheered when the body fell.[16]

On June 2, Palmer himself became a victim of a bomb attack when the downstairs of his house was demolished as he and his wife were preparing for bed upstairs. Finally, Palmer's presidential ambitions were threatened by criticism that the Justice Department was not doing enough to curb radicalism.

When Palmer acted, he did so with a vengeance. On August 1, he created the General Intelligence Division within the Justice Department. Its first director was the 24-year-old J. Edgar Hoover. He in turn set up an index file of over 450,000 cards on radical leaders, their publications and organizations.

He also built up a network of informers and agent provocateurs.[17] As a direct result of the information Hoover gathered, Attorney General Palmer invoked the wartime Sedition Act, which led to the infamous "Red Raids."[18]

On January 2, 1920, federal agents in cooperation with local police departments conducted a nationwide dragnet. More than 4,000 suspected radicals were rounded up in 33 major cities. The raids covered 23 states. It is hard to underestimate the massive assault on civil liberties the raids involved. People were held without being charged, denied the right to counsel, and brutally treated if they resisted. Homes were searched without the benefit of search warrants and papers and property confiscated. Truckloads of immigrants were removed from neighborhood pool halls and saloons, and weeks passed before family members found out what happened to them.[19]

If Palmer's Red Raids illustrate the excesses of enforcement effectiveness in terms of assaults on civil liberties, the Knapp Commission of New York underscores the problem of corruption in situations of heterogeneity and ambivalent attitudes toward certain laws. The former example raises the specter of informants and agent provocateurs, the latter, the specter of the thief taker.

The Problem of Police Corruption

In 1972, the Knapp Commission issued a report on police corruption in New York City:

> We found corruption to be widespread. It took various forms depending upon the activity involved, appearing at its most sophisticated among plainclothesmen assigned to enforcing gambling laws. In the five plainclothes divisions where our investigations were concentrated we found a strikingly standardized pattern of corruption. Plainclothesmen, participating in what is known in police parlance as a "pad," collected regular biweekly or monthly payments amounting to as much as $3,500 from each of the gambling establishments in the area under their jurisdiction, and divided the take in equal shares. The monthly share per man (called the "nut") ranged from $300 and $400 in midtown Manhattan to $1,500 in Harlem. When supervisors were involved they received a share and a half. A newly assigned plainclothesman was not entitled to his share for about two months, while he was checked out for reliability, but the earnings lost by the delay were made up to him in the form of two months' severance pay when he left the division.[20]

The Commission also found organized corruption in narcotics enforcement. Other research has also suggested that most major police scandals are likely to begin in vice and narcotics bureaus, those units assigned to enforce laws about which people feel the most ambivalent. Yet the Knapp Commission went on to distinguish between this kind of large-scale, organized corruption and the more garden variety kind that occurs in incidents of traffic enforcement, small gambling operations, and so forth.

... the meat-eaters are those policemen who ... aggressively misuse their police powers for personal gain. The grass-eaters simply accept the payoffs that the happenstances of police work throw their way.[21]

The "meat-eaters" got the huge payoffs and made headlines. But the Commission felt "grass-eaters" posed a greater problem.

Their great numbers tend to make corruption "respectable." They also tend to encourage the code of silence that brands anyone who exposes corruption a traitor....[22]

POLICY CONSIDERATIONS: THEORIES/ARGUMENTS/APPLICATIONS

Policies for the Control of Police Discretion

What remedies exist for the control of the police when the goals of effectiveness overshadow other considerations? The traditional method for controlling such tendencies has been to place legal or administrative restrictions on the activities of the watchers. The use of such control can take four forms: criminal law, procedural law, tort law, and administrative regulation.

Control through Criminal Law

One of the chief functions of internal affairs bureaus in police departments is to prevent the violation of criminal law by the police. Often, criminal law will be applied in situations dealing with corruption. But criminal law can also be applied when unnecessary force is used by an officer, and at times, if this is associated with a person's skin color, federal criminal law can be brought to bear.

Control through Procedural Law

Besides the application of substantive criminal law to the police, police activity is controlled by the body of law known as procedural law. As previously discussed, the major procedural guidelines developed from celebrated cases. *Mapp* v. *Ohio* (search and seizure), *Terry* v. *Ohio* (search and seizure), *Escobedo* v. *Illinois* (right to counsel), and *Miranda* v. *Arizona* (right of notification to have counsel present) ushered in an era of judicial policy making, filling in what was perceived to be a vacuum in agency efforts to control police abuse of citizen's rights.[23] Agency policies in these matters, if they existed at all, were generally weak or not enforced. An analysis of these laws and their impact shows that while they have had some affect on day-to-day policing, precisely because they are based on celebrated cases, the effect on most police activity has not been dramatic.[24] Many police agencies seem to have been able to incorporate the procedural guidelines with little disruption of their daily activity. Thus, Miranda can be used to get a suspect to confess by giving the warnings as a friend who would like to help the individual being questioned. In the context of police interrogation, the psychological effect of the good guy–bad guy roles is well understood. A suspect is often more than willing to cooperate with the "good" guy, who is seen as a friendly protector in a generally hostile environment.

Control through Tort Law

Tort law can also be used in the face of police excesses. Tort remedies involve bringing civil suit for any wrongful act, damage, or injury done willfully or negligently. Such remedies, however, put the burden for correcting these wrongs on the person who might have been the victim of police abuse. Tort law also assumes that the individual has the resources to pursue such a remedy. This is often not the case with police "clients," and so many are not in a position to use this method of control.

Drawbacks of Legal Remedies

Using legal remedies to control the police has a number of drawbacks. Those that rely on the criminal law face the hurdle of "the code of silence" that the Knapp Commission alluded to. The reason for the code is explained in part by the officer below:

> Remember, patrolmen are the public symbols of their organization. You represent the organization. If Officer X makes a mistake or looks like a slob, they don't say Officer X is a jerk, they say the Police Department is a bunch of jerks.[25]

Because people look upon all police officers as the same and use the mistakes of a few to criticize the entire force, it seems best to hide rule violations from both the public and the command staff. Police officers become a self-protecting group. As Skolnick notes, isolation from civilians is further enhanced by two police occupational characteristics.[26] The element of danger in police work develops a strong sense of comradeship among its practitioners, since one may have to rely on one's colleagues to limit the potential for harm. This "pull" factor causes police officers to associate with one another off duty as well as during working hours. The authority of the police, on the other hand, constitutes a "push" factor toward isolation. Civilians can often feel uncomfortable around the police and vice versa, even when the latter are off duty. If an individual drinks too much at a party, becomes rowdy, and a police officer is present, will the officer invoke his or her formal role? If the officer drinks too much and then drives off, will he or she be labeled a hypocrite for violating those laws he or she has enforced on others? At a social gathering, will an officer have to hear about all the "unfair" traffic tickets that have been given? For many reasons then, officers may prefer to socialize with "their own kind."

The codes of silence and police cohesiveness also limit the ability of procedural law to control police behavior. Moreover, procedural remedies to the abuse of police power carry the added burden of having to overcome the ingrained notion of local control. Municipal and county politicians, as well as police officials, can view the procedural rulings of federal courts as undue interference in local law enforcement agencies. This attitude, of course, further hampers attempts to control incidents of police misconduct.

Control by Administrative Remedies

The planning ideology and the functionalist perspective of organizations suggests that the most effective form of control would be that exercised by administrators. Departments vary, however, in terms of the interest, creativity, and ability of police managers to use rule making effectively for the control of misconduct. Some states have attempted to bring some degree of uniformity into the rule-making process by mandating statewide standards for both training and conduct. Thirty-seven states use or have available a decertification process whereby an officer can lose his or her right to "practice" law enforcement within the state.[27] A state agency, often termed the Peace Officers Standards and Training Board (POST), can revoke the certificate or license of an officer for certain kinds of misconduct, which are specified by state law or administrative regulations.[28] An officer whose license is revoked cannot get a job as a police officer in that state. Such licensing and decertification processes are attempts to use administrative law, that is, the regulatory power of the state, to control police behavior. It is an alternative to the use of procedural law and the court management of police conduct. The use of decertification procedures to control police behavior is relatively new and untested. However, it does seem to avoid some of the problems associated with other forms of legal control. Its application is much broader than the criminal law. While its administration is statewide rather than local, the regulations are a product of the deliberations of police managers throughout a given state. In this sense the regulations are a product of the police and not of "outsiders." Finally, a statewide licensing approach avoids the problem of the "gypsy cop," that is, the officer who, when fired from one department, simply moves on to another department to resume both a career and a pattern of conduct that may be detrimental to the overall cause of law enforcement.

The use of administrative law to control the police fits in with the increasing emphasis on management techniques as the key to effective regulation of employee activity. Thus, not only law, but organizational mechanisms can constitute a controlling force on the exercise of police power.

As we have seen, the history of law enforcement in the United States has in part been one of struggle between politicians and police managers over the question of to whom the police are responsible. The paramilitary form of organization was a weapon in this struggle as it was used to justify the proposition that the day-to-day control of the police should be in the hands of police administrators. Its actual effectiveness is, however, far from certain.

The paramilitary form of organization assumes much closer physical proximity between the commander and the commanded than actually exists in police work. Police officers perform most of their duties outside of the purview of supervisors. This form of management therefore puts a great deal of stress on external conformity. Shined brass, polished leather, and appropriate hair length can form the major criteria for judging effectiveness. Looks rather than substance become important. And, as noted previously, the look is decidedly military. But as also discussed, the notion that the police fight a war on crime is misleading. There is much research to document the fact that the majority of police time is spent in responding to noncriminal activity.[29] In light of this, it has been said that in a sense the police in America are all dressed up with no place to go. This, combined with the emphasis on external conformity, can easily lead to cynicism among officers. Most calls are looked upon as "bullshit" calls and administrators are accused of enforcing "chicken shit" regulations. The paramilitary structure may therefore actually impede rather than enhance administrative control.

The Ethic of Professionalism as a Check on Police Discretion

The notion of professionalism has been introduced into police agencies in recognition of the fact that officers often act quite independently of close supervision. As described in Chapter 5, however, an ethic of professionalism is not without its own conflicts and tension. On the one hand, professionals are given wide latitude in the discretion they are able to exercise. Such discretionary decision making is supported by social norms because professional status is only granted after a long period of training and rigorous licensing procedures. As we have seen, the authority of the professional to make decisions based on his or her "expertise" with a minimum of outside interference was established only after a period of struggle. Schooling, licensing, and so on were ways to ensure that society would not be victimized by charlatans. But who could judge the competence of experts? The answer has been other experts. Therefore, professional peer review has been a hallmark of professional control. This brings us to the "other hand" of professionalism. Even in the struggle to upgrade professional practice, altruism and self-interest clashed. Licensing could protect the public, but it also created a monopoly for the delivery of certain services to the obvious economic betterment of practitioners. Professional peer review could be used to control the professionals subject to it or the consumers of professional services by denying them access to and information about remedies to professional malpractice. Thus, the issue of professionalism and control of the police raises two questions. Is it possible and is it desirable?

Mandating training standards, licensing procedures and decertification controls are attempts to incorporate some trappings of the professional model into law enforcement. At this point, one would have to say that the extent of required training in some states and licensing standards have not yet reached the professional level. Professional training takes years rather than months and is always associated with postbaccalaureate training at a university. In theory, however, there is no reason why such a program of advanced university education for police officers is not possible. In practice, though, a number of nitty-gritty political and moral issues would have to be resolved. First, by mandating extensive higher education for police recruits, the policy maker would be closing off a traditional method of social mobility for a variety of groups. The Irish, Italian, and Jewish immigrant populations often used government service, and particularly the police and fire departments, as a vehicle for gaining an economic foothold. Are blacks, Hispanics, and women to be denied this avenue of opportunity? Second, what would a professional police curriculum look like? During the 1960s and 1970s, the Law Enforcement Assistance Administration funded a variety of educational efforts aimed at the police. The results of the Law Enforcement Education Program were decidedly mixed. Some "college" courses merely replicated what was being done in police academies. These became known as the infamous "Handcuffs" or "Nightstick" 101 courses. As Klockars remarks, many officers were not exposed to higher education but to the illusion of higher education and to an academic form of white-collar crime as programs attempted to get large grants of government monies.[30] Other curriculums were heavily oriented toward the liberal arts but were criticized for being too removed from the day-to-day problems police officers encountered. In response to this, some have suggested a curriculum not unlike that found in business schools, with a combination of practical and theoretical training. The struggle over curriculum points to a third unresolved issue. Are police problems solvable through the application of science? At the beginning of this chapter, it was noted that science cannot answer the question of ends. And yet, the issue of crime, like most issues of public policy, involves a struggle over ends, and is therefore ultimately political and moral. Unfortunately, there has been a tendency to blunt political and moral debate by claiming that science has answered the question.[31] Therefore, claims of science and professionalism can be used to control rather than to enlighten, ultimately to the detriment of public policy. More important perhaps than the issue of whether professionalism is possible for the police is the issue of whether it is desirable. The answer may well be no, since an ethic of professionalism could be used to insulate the police from the process of public debate and scrutiny. The history of the FBI under J. Edgar Hoover and the periodic abuses of authority in the operations of the CIA testify to the dangers of removing law enforcement too far from the political process.

The Professional Police Manager

A professional ethic has developed most rapidly among police managers. This specific professional ethic is infused with a highly rational view of the organization and stresses modern management technique as a tool for controlling the police. Two features of this approach are of interest in the context of the current discussion. First, modern management within law enforcement tends to stress efficiency over effectiveness. In other words, attempts at 100% effectiveness are not only doomed to failure, they are costly as well. Therefore, in order to obtain the most for the law enforcement dollar, emphasis should be put on those crimes that can be solved. Less emphasis should be placed on those crimes police have little chance of solving. The second feature of interest is the fact that professional status is granted to managers. The end result is a move toward less discretionary authority granted to the patrol officer. This deprofessionalizing of patrol has increased intraorganizational tension.

A number of targeted patrol experiments illustrate the impact of scientific management and efficiency criteria applied to street-level law enforcement. The Repeat Offender Project (ROP, Washington, DC), Location Oriented Patrol (LOP, Kansas City), and Perpetrator Oriented Patrol (POP, Kansas City) are based on a premise similar to the policy of selective incapacitation. A majority of crime occurs because of the activity of a few people, therefore these individuals should receive the specific attention of the police. ROP and POP are essentially programs of intensive surveillance of individuals suspected of regularly committing multiple crimes. An immediate issue raised by this approach is constitutional. When does intensive surveillance of individuals not judicially accused of crime become unconstitutionally intrusive? It may also hark back to the historical specter of the need to use informers. These issues have yet to be fully explored. On the cost/benefit side, however, these programs seem marginal at best. The man-hours and money required to keep targeted individuals under surveillance have not resulted in appreciably better conviction rates or crime decreases.[32] Location Oriented Patrol, which focuses on likely crime targets rather than likely perpetrators, has had similarly disappointing results. Thus, procedures aimed at enhancing police efficiency through the use of targeted manpower allocation have not to date been successful. Moreover, the process has raised a number of constitutional issues.

Other management efficiency strategies have had equally marginal results. Success at decreasing response time of patrol officers to a crime scene has had little or no effect on the prevention of crime or the apprehension of perpetrators. Since many people do not call the police until a few hours after the crime has been discovered, and the discovery itself may be long after the crime actually occurred, there is little reason for the police to respond rapidly to most calls for service. Obviously, if a call for service involves a crime in progress, rapid response is important. Since most requests for police service are not of this type, a general policy of rapid response is not necessary or cost-effective. Different strategies for managing the time of detectives, management by objectives, increased use of civilians in technical, management, and clerical positions, and other management improvements have also been ineffective in changing the basic patterns of crime in society.[33] Further, they have not noticeably reduced the cost of efforts at crime control. In an organization where technical solutions to problems are lacking, symbolic activity takes on greater importance.

The Two Cultures of Policing

Studies of police culture have increasingly recognized that the movement toward scientific management in law enforcement has in effect created two police subcultures.[34] The management culture, populated by civilians and police officers infused with the scientific management ethic, stresses bureaucratic and public relations values. The "street cop" culture stresses the enforcement of substantive law and getting "the bad guys" off the street regardless of the effect on public relations that are a concern downtown. It also stresses things like sticking together, being tough, not making waves, and not trusting the bosses.[35] Thus, the positive symbols of management that are important for the administrative cop culture become negative symbols of control and manipulation in the street cop culture. Ironically, then, within police departments themselves there is increasing emphasis on the question of who should control the police, and specifically their activity and discretionary decision making when they deal with the public "on the street."

It should be evident by now that the delivery of law enforcement services in this society is in large part controlled by the work-group norms of street level officers. Research on the subculture of the police can be summarized by noting that the norms and values of this occupational group tend to be heavily pragmatic. Police officers develop rules of thumb for dealing with job "hassles," whether these are generated from their own bureaucracy, from citizens, from likely suspects, from the court system, or from the political structure. While much of the research tends to show the police as a relatively isolated group, pragmatic approaches to problem solving require taking into account the needs and expectations of other stakeholders in a particular situation. Ironically, therefore, the citizen does exercise a great deal of control in how the police handle a given incident. The citizen decides whether or not to call the police in the first place. As we have seen, most of the time, even when incidents are serious, citizens decide not to involve the police. Even when citizens do call the police, however, they do not give up total control of a situation. Research by Donald Black has shown that whether or not an arrest is made is partially dependent on the desires of the complainant.[36] Thus, police officers and citizens often find themselves together in situations where they share the power to structure an event's meaning and thereby determine what course of action is most appropriate. The answer to the question of who controls the police is not straightforward. Police officers exercise a wide degree of discretion. However, they do so by responding pragmatically to the characteristics of the situation and people they encounter. But these characteristics are themselves negotiable, and therefore citizens can and do influence police decision making. The determinative factor of police control, therefore, might well be the metaphors used to structure our understanding of the police and their role in society. Since there is conflict about what constitutes appropriate law enforcement activity, this suggests the need for new metaphors that can encompass a variety of views about what the police should be doing.

Toward a New Understanding of the Police

Although science cannot tell us what the police should do, it can help in the structuring of a new metaphor to understand the complex task of policing in this society. Science does this by showing us what it is the police actually do and its effects on our communities. Police officers spend a great deal of time in random motorized patrol, but this kind of activity has no effect on crime rates.[37] Foot patrol lowers the fear of crime, but it too has no effect on crime rates. Nevertheless, people feel better about their communities and officers express greater job satisfaction with foot patrol.[38] Domestic violence seems most amenable to a law enforcement solution. The arrest of the perpetrator lowers the likelihood of repetition.[39] Team policing, where beat officers are given more responsibility for solving problems within their area of patrol, also prove to be an effective alternative to the traditional methods of organizing patrol work.[40] Team policing gives not only responsibility to an officer but authority to handle many problems without needing a supervisor or a special unit such as a detective or finger print technician. And interestingly, when the efficiency and safety of one- and two-person patrol units are compared, the former does much better.[41]

What lessons can we draw from these diverse findings. First, police officers are not primarily crime fighters. Second, law enforcement solutions, such as an arrest, are an appropriate problem-solving solution in some situations. Third, when officers are given increased authority to handle problems in their area of assignment, they respond well. Fourth, the community feels better about itself and its surroundings when a police officer is physically present and not simply encapsulated in a patrol car. Fifth, the norms of the police subculture can at times increase rather then decrease police occupational problems. The reason two-person patrol cars appear less safe is because officers feel they have to prove to their partners that they are tough and able to handle a situation. The tendency therefore is to escalate a situation. In a single-person unit, diplomacy rather than aggressiveness is the first tactic most likely to be used.

The Police Officer as Community Problem Solver

A metaphor which seems able to capture the diverse images of the police is that of "community problem solver." Authority, diplomacy, law enforcement, peace keeping, paramilitary images, and community worker are descriptions and roles that can be useful in this very complex set of tasks. And while crime fighting can clearly be a part of this image, it is not the central motivating activity. In this image of the police officer, crime is simply one of a complex of community issues, and to solve it a variety of other community problems must be addressed. Finally, the metaphor of "community problem solver" breaks down the isolation between the police and the public. Each begins to recognize their dependency on the other. For the community this means increased feelings of safety, for the officer increased job satisfaction.

Experiments with this broader definition of the police task have already occurred. Initial results seem to hold a great deal of promise for this new imagery. The method is termed problem-oriented policing.

Problem-oriented policing involves the breakdown of isolation on a number of different levels. A call for service is viewed as having a history and a future. Thus, it is not necessarily an isolated event that can be handled in 15–30 minutes. Instead, problem-oriented policing emphasizes the analysis of groups of incidents to develop solutions that draw upon a wide variety of public and private resources. Therefore, the police become a kind of coordinator of service and are not considered an isolated government agency dealing with a unique problem.[42] While the full potential of this approach still needs to be assessed, results to date have been impressive. This approach involves four steps. The steps described by the National Institute of Justice are as follows:

1. Scanning. Instead of relying upon broad, law-related concepts—robbery, burglary, for example—officers are encouraged to group individual, related incidents that come to their attention as "problems" and define these problems in more precise and therefore useful terms. For example, an incident that typically would be classified simply as a "robbery" might be seen as part of a pattern of prostitution-related robberies committed by transvestites in center-city hotels.

2. Analysis. Officers working on a well-defined "problem" then collect information from a variety of public and private sources—not just police data. They use the information to illuminate the underlying nature of the problem, suggesting its causes and a variety of options for its resolution.

3. Response. Working with citizens, businesses, and public and private agencies, officers tailor a program of action suitable to the characteristics of the problem. Solutions may go beyond traditional criminal justice system remedies to include other community agencies or organizations.

4. Assessment. Finally, the officers evaluate the impact of these efforts to see if the problems were actually solved or alleviated.[43]

The following case study, also presented by the National Institute of Justice, illustrates the steps in practice.

Burglaries in the New Briarfield Apartments

Built as temporary housing for shipyard workers in 1942, the 450 wood-frame units called the New Briarfield Apartments remained in use during the postwar housing shortage—and into the present.

By 1984, New Briarfield was known as the worst housing in the city. It also had the highest crime rate: burglars hit 23 percent of the occupied units each year. The task force assigned Detective Tony Duke of the Crime Analysis Unit to study the problem.

Duke had patrol and auxiliary officers survey a random one-third sample of the households in January 1985. The residents confirmed that burglary was a serious problem, but they were equally upset by the physical deterioration of the complex. Duke then interviewed employees of other city departments and found that the burglaries were related in part to the general deterioration of the housing.

The Fire Department called New Briarfield a firetrap. Public Works worried about flooding; the complex had no storm sewers. Standing water rotted the floors, noted the Department of Codes Compliance. Cracks around doors and windows made it easier for burglars to force their way in. Vacant units, unfit to rent, sheltered burglars and drug addicts.

Officer Barry Haddix, responsible for patrolling the area, decided to clean up the grounds. Working with the apartment manager and city agencies, he arranged to have trash and abandoned appliances removed, abandoned cars towed, potholes filled, and streets swept.

Detective Duke meanwhile learned that the complex owners were in default on a loan and that the U.S. Department of Housing and Urban Development (HUD) was about to foreclose. Duke wrote a report describing the crime problem, the tenants' discouragement, and the views of other city agencies.

Police Chief Stephens used the report to enlist other departments in a joint recommendation to the city manager: Help the tenants find better housing and demolish New Briarfield. The city manager approved. In June 1986, he proposed replacing New Briarfield with a new 220-unit complex, a middle school, and a small shopping center. Negotiations are underway with HUD.

The long-range solution will take time to implement. For now, the police force assigned Officer Vernon Lyons full-time to organize the neighborhood residents. Since January 1986 the New Briarfield Community Association has been persuading residents to take better care of the neighborhood and lobbying the resident manager and city agencies to keep the complex properly maintained.

Visibly better living conditions have resulted—and the burglary rate has dropped by 35 percent.[44]

Problem-oriented policing recognizes the tremendous discretion exercised by patrol officers. At the same time, it provides for a structuring of this discretion by the creation of agency policy, with significant input from street-level officers who have to cope with the actual community issue. Because officers tend to be pragmatic, they in turn solicit community input on how best to cope with particular difficulties. This approach makes creative use of the variety of roles police officers play while avoiding the tendency to let one particular role be determinative as to how a situation should be handled.

To date, the test of this approach has been in a medium-size department. Its applicability to very large or very small departments remains to be tried.

You Are Sure: The Manufactured Crises in Evaluation Research," *Policy Sciences*, 17 (1984), 179–91.

32. Samuel Walker, *Sense and Nonsense about Crime* (Monterey, CA: Brooks/Cole Publishing Co., A Division of Wadsworth, Inc., 1985), p. 113.

33. Ibid. See also Gilsinan, *Doing Justice*; Elizabeth Reuss-Ianni, *Two Cultures of Policing* (New Brunswick: Transaction Books, c. 1983).

34. Reuss-Ianni, *Two Cultures of Policing*.

35. Ibid., pp. 13–16.

36. Donald Black, "The Social Organization of Arrest," *Stanford Law Review* 23 (June 1977).

37. George L. Kelling et al., *The Kansas City Preventive Patrol Experiment: A Summary Report* (Washington, DC: Police Foundation, 1974).

38. *FBI Law Enforcement Bulletin*, Vol. 55., No. 11 (November, 1986), 6.

39. Ibid., p. 7.

40. Ibid.

41. Ibid., p. 5.

42. William Spelman and John E. Eck, "Problem Oriented Policing," National Institute of Justice, *Research in Brief*, January, 1987.

43. Ibid. p. 2.

44. Ibid. pp. 5–6.

XII

Processing the Case
The Criminal Courts

At the end of this chapter, the student will be able to:

A. Describe the typical case processing that occurs in our court system.
B. Discuss the pros and cons of plea bargaining.
C. Analyze various policies aimed at "improving" the operation of the court.
D. Discuss and compare juvenile case processing.

ISSUE BACKGROUND

The Creation of Accounts

Throughout this book we have talked about the importance of understanding myth, metaphor, and ideology if one is to understand the creation and implementation of public policy. In the public arena, there is no "truth" waiting to be discovered and acted upon. Instead, there are events that are interpreted and made sensical through the stories participants tell about what occurred. These stories are fictions because "making sense" is an act of constructing meaning rather than observing it in the empirical world.

We have also seen that the criminal justice system is largely a reactive one. Its personnel generally respond to a scene after something has happened. Part of what a police officer does is the sorting out of stories. He or she takes statements from witnesses, who reconstruct for the officer what happened. These reconstructions or stories need to be assessed for their credibility, and, if there is disagreement among the storytellers, a judgment made about which story is probably the most accurate. Police officers, in turn, write reports on some incidents, but this too is a reconstruction process. Report writing is not a value-free enterprise. A host of factors operate on police officers that lead to the emphasizing of certain factors and the disregarding of others in reconstructing and interpreting an event. As a case moves through the legal system, different pressures operate on different people at different times to further alter original reconstructions and interpretations. From the various reconstructions and interpretations of events, a final reconstruction (an account of an account) is decided upon and then used to justify a decision on how best to handle the case. The important point in all of this is that the decision is based upon a reconstruction of events, not cold, hard, fast, concrete, indisputable facts. To assume that the legal account constitutes the only possible reality is to have an overly rationalistic view of the law and how it operates. The whole process can be compared to a wonderful description of how Dashiell Hammett's famous detective, the Continental Op, went about solving a case. The following description is from Steven Marcus's introduction to Dashiell Hammett's *The Continental Op*:

> The Op is called in or sent on a case. Something has been stolen, someone is missing, some dire circumstance is impending, someone has been murdered—it doesn't matter. The Op interviews the person or persons most immediately accessible. They may be innocent or guilty—it doesn't matter; it is an indifferent circumstance. Guilty or innocent, they provide the Op with an account of what they know, of what they assert really happened. The Op begins to investigate; he compares these accounts with others that he gathers; he snoops about; he does research; he shadows people, arranges confrontations between those who want to avoid one another, and so on. What he soon discovers is that the "reality" that anyone involved will swear to is in fact itself a construction, a fabrication, a fiction, a faked and alternative reality—and that it has been gotten together before he ever arrived on the scene. And the Op's work therefore is to deconstruct, decompose, deplot, and defictionalize that "reality" and to construct or reconstruct out of it a true fiction, that is, an account of what "really happened."[1]

Of course, what the Op ends up with is simply another account, one constructed by himself, but no more "real" than the other accounts he has encountered. In many ways, the process is the same in the criminal justice system. Events are reconstructed by a variety of actors, the accounts are compared and negotiated, and a compromise account that seems most reasonable and presents the most coherent view of the world is accepted as "reality." Yet, to a greater or lesser extent, it is always a fictionalized reality, a reconstructed view of the past.

CRIMINOLOGICAL/CRIMINAL JUSTICE CONSIDERATIONS

The Criminal Courts

The major stage for comparing, negotiating, and structuring stories about crime is in the criminal courts. As Chapter 2 pointed out, these courts are divided according to the responsibilities each has. Called by a variety of names, police courts, magistrate courts, associate circuit courts are at the bottom rung of the formal case processing ladder. Yet these courts have an important gatekeeping function. Depending upon the specific jurisdiction, these courts will often be the place where decisions are made about whether to proceed with a case. These courts can also decide cases of a less serious nature, leveling fines or short jail sentences against those found guilty.

State trial courts, called district or circuit courts, hear evidence regarding serious criminal cases (felonies). The bulk of criminal cases are disposed of on these first two rungs of the judicial ladder. Again, as noted in Chapter 2, state courts of appeal and the federal courts, which form a separate ladder, handle relatively few criminal cases. Those that make it to the appeals level will, however, become the source of various criminal justice judicial policies and will affect the structuring of stories that come after. Unlike the Continental Op, then, the court system and its functionaries already possess a set of preconstructed accounts or stories. The stories criminal courts' people tell each other are influenced by their day-to-day experience, limited resources, bureaucratic strain, legal precedents, and rules of procedure. Notice that "legalities" are simply one element among many that influence the accounts of the court system. Therefore, to understand the routine doing of justice in our society, it is necessary to understand the court house subculture, the web of symbols, meanings, and ideologies that encase the day-to-day application of the law. Events and people that come before the criminal courts are fitted into these preconstructed meanings. The process begins when a police action becomes a case.

The Elements of a Case

The criminal justice system has relatively little to do with crime. As Chapter 2 showed, most crime goes unreported. Of that which is reported, one fourth of the incidents or fewer will result in an arrest. Over a third of those arrested will be juveniles and will not be dealt with in the adult criminal courts. Since these cases are not "typical," we will review juvenile courts case processing later in the chapter.

Estimates vary widely as to the number of eligible cases actually prosecuted. The highest estimate is 73%,[2] the lowest 25%.[3] Research in New York and St. Louis suggests a midpoint of between 30 and 40%.[4] What is clear is that prosecutors exercise a great deal of discretion in determining what events will be legally considered as crimes and what people will be prosecuted as criminals. They have been called the single most powerful figures in the criminal justice system.[5]

At the local level, prosecutors are elected officials. They run for office in either partisan or nonpartisan elections on a countywide basis. They represent the government in all criminal matters covered by state law, and they have almost total discretion in deciding whether or not "to make a case." Police officials, victims, or the general public cannot bring a case before the court without the prosecutor's participation.

The prosecutor's office is legally powerful and politically sensitive. Therefore, there is a distinction in the way various kinds of cases are handled. Celebrated cases (see Chapter 3) are handled by the prosecuting attorney. Those on the lower tiers of the wedding cake are handled by assistant prosecuting attorneys, men and women hired to staff the office. The prosecutor has a vested interest in making the office look good. Reelection or higher political office may be at stake, therefore the importance of high visibility in celebrated cases. But the bulk of cases do not excite much public interest. Thus, bureaucratic values and the ability to use limited resources efficiently predominate in the handling of cases by staff attorneys. To understand this routine handling, it is necessary to look at the elements of a typical case.

A case is a collection of pieces of paper that proceed from one part of the system to another, triggering various segments of the criminal justice process into action. In its infant stage, the case consists of the police report of the incident and an arrest slip indicating the specifics of the suspect's physical description, the charge he or she is being held on, and a prisoner number. These pieces of paper must be taken by the arresting officer to the prosecuting attorney's office. Here, they will be reviewed by an assistant prosecuting attorney assigned that function. In this capacity, the attorney's job is one of initial screening, weeding out those cases which, in his or her judgment, are either too weak to pursue or too petty to waste time on.

If the assistant prosecutor decides to pursue a case, he or she will seek a warrant. An individual may be held only a limited time by the police acting on their own authority. The actual time a person may be held solely on police authority varies from jurisdiction to jurisdiction but is generally between 20 and 48 hours. To hold somebody beyond the time set by the state legislature (or, if none is set, beyond a "reasonable time"), a judicial officer must issue an arrest warrant, which certifies that there is probable cause that the individual being confined or sought committed a crime. This procedure is mandated by Fourth Amendment guarantees against unreasonable searches and seizures.

Procedurally, this amendment is carried out by the prosecuting attorney who reviews the case. He or she takes the file, to which prosecutorial forms have been added, before an officer of the court. The whole process is rather bureaucratic. If the prosecuting attorney who reviewed the case agrees with the police that a warrant should be issued, the actual issuance of the warrant by a judicial officer is almost automatic. In fact, in some jurisdictions, a clerk of the court may be assigned the function of judicial review and issuance, a practice that raises some knotty constitutional questions, since a clerk is not a judicial officer.

Since the initial review by an assistant prosecuting attorney is essentially to decide whether to seek a warrant, the attorneys assigned to this screening process are often termed warrant officers. Obviously, they play a key gatekeeping function in the criminal justice process. Their decisions determine the flow of cases to the rest of the system. Interestingly, however, this screening function is often assigned to the least experienced attorney on the staff. Court appearances and trials are the prerogative of the more senior staff members. How do warrant officers learn to screen cases? What decision rules do they use? The prosecuting attorney must grapple with these questions:

> You learn about this by osmosis. Nobody ever comes in and sits down and says you can't win this, you can't do that.

> You learn from doing it yourself and listening to other people talking about their experiences.

> If you're around the courthouse long enough, you see what juries do, you see what judges do, you see what cases have what appeal and how strong your evidence is and you just pick all that up through experience.[6]

It is clear from the comments above that the phrase "strong evidence" does not denote a simple empirical reality. The evidence is only as strong as a jury or, more accurately, the constructed image of a jury says it is. The notion of "jury appeal," therefore, is key in understanding the case screening process of the prosecuting attorney's office.

Notice the reasons listed on the Warrant Refusal Form shown in Figure 12-1 for refusing a case. Evidentiary issues appear equally weighted with far more ambiguous concerns such as victim-witness credibility. Notice particularly number 38 under the "credibility heading." Clearly, extralegal factors influence the case screening process.

The form also underscores the bureaucratic nature of the warrant issuance or refusal process. Yet, if a warrant is issued, the document that allows for the longer detention of an individual is a piece of paper that is very formal and official-sounding and which helps maintain the legal niceties of an unfolding play that will increasingly have little to do with the individual's actual circumstances. A typical warrant reads as follows:

> To Any Peace Officer of the State: You are hereby commanded to arrest the above named defendant on the above named charge, alleged to have been committed within the jurisdiction of this court and in violation of the laws of the state, and to bring him forthwith before this court to be here dealt with in

WARRANT REFUSAL FORM

SUSPECT NAME: LAST	FIRST	M.I.	LB NUMBER	ARREST REGISTER

On the right, check the proper box for the disposition, then from the code list on the left give the reason(s) for this action

EVIDENCE

SCIENTIFIC
01 Results Unavailable
02 Results Negative
03 Results Inconclusive

PHYSICAL
05 Essential Evidence Absent
06 Insufficient Connection to Defendent
07 Lack Sufficient Value
08 Lacks Proscribed Character

TESTIMONIAL
11 No Identification
12 Insufficient Connection
13 Element of Offense Not Established
14 Corroboration
15 Identification Not Persuasive
19 Other Evidence Problems

WITNESS/VICTIM

ATTENDANCE
20 Victim Refuses to Assist
21 Victim Unavailable
22 Police Officer Unavailable
23 Essential Witness Refuses to Assist
24 Essential Witness Unavailable

CREDIBILITY
31 Witness Character is Suspect
32 Witness Not Competent to Testify
33 Witness Information is Confused
34 Expert Witness Not Qualified
35 Witness Privileged
36 Police Witness Conduct
37 Witness Testimony in Conflict
38 Jury Won't Like Victim At All
39 Other Witness Problems

INTEREST OF JUSTICE

DEFENSES
40 Alibi
41 Provocation by Victim
42 Self Defense
43 Inadvertance or Accident

INTEREST OF JUSTICE (Cont.)

DEFENSES (Cont.)
44 Lack of Specific Intent
45 Affirmative – VMCSL
46 Affirmative – Other
47 Statute of Limitation
48 Prior Connections Need Investigation

GENERAL PROBLEMS
74 Defendants Personal Data
75 Trivial or Insignificant
76 Not suitable for Criminal
      Justice System

JURISDICTION
61 Refer to City Counselor
62 Refer to U.S. Attorney
63 Refer to Juvenile Court
64 Lack of Venue
69 Other Jurisdicton Reasons

VIOLATIONS OF DUE PROCESS
50 Insufficient Probable Cause for Search
51 Unlawful Search and Seizure –
      Warrant Problems
53 Inadmissible Confession
54 Procedural Delay
      (not timely brought)
55 Improper Identification
59 Other Due Process Problems

CONSOLIDATION/REDUCTIONS
80 Charges Insignificant
      (other warrants issued/refused)
81 Charges Merged
      (other warrants issued/refused)
82 Charge is Surplus
      (other warrants issued/refused)
85 Defendant Convicted –
      Other Offenses
93 Case Arises from Same Evidence
      No Conviction Previously
97 Additional Police Work Requested
98 Other Consolidation
99 Other Reduction

Disp.	Reasons (maxium of 4)			
Ref.				
Uav.				
Ref.				
Uav.				
Ref.				
Uav.				
Ref.				
Uav.				
Ref.				
Uav.				
Ref.				
Uav.				
Ref.				
Uav.				

COMMENTS/REMARKS:

Attorney:	Date	Atty. Code	Entered by:

ATTACH COMPLETED FORM TO WARRANT DISPOSITION FORM AND POLICE REPORTS.
RETURN THIS PACKAGE TO WARRANT OFFICE CLERK.

Figure 12-1

accordance with law, and you, the officer serving this warrant, shall forthwith make return hereof to this court.

From the sound of the official arrest warrant, it seems that the individual is not yet in custody. In certain cases, of course, the actual sequence of events is first the issuance of a warrant and second, the actual apprehension of the individual. But in the majority of cases handled day in and day out by the criminal justice system, the person is detained first and later "arrested" under authority of a warrant. The peace officer (the police officer who made the arrest in the first place) receives a copy of the duly authorized warrant back from the assistant district attorney who was the warrant officer for the case. Looking around the police lockup (at least figuratively), he or she finds that, lo and behold, the person named is already in custody. The piece of paper demanding that the person incarcerated be arrested and brought to court contains the first of many fictions that will be encountered as the process of justice proceeds.

The next step in the process is known in many jurisdictions as the "first appearance." It must take place within a reasonable amount of time. Although "reasonable amount of time" is a relative term, in most jurisdictions it is operationalized to mean that a suspect must be brought before a magistrate within 48–72 hours of his or her initial detention.

Before we leave the screening function of the prosecutor's office, it would be worthwhile to summarize the decision rule used to determine what cases go further in the system. The rule is easily stated. It is a "probable win" test. As discussed previously, bureaucratic values are important to consider at this level of processing. Limited resources, time, money, and personnel, demand that cases be prioritized. Further, political values create a bias toward taking those cases that can be won. Prosecutors routinely gain guilty pleas or win at trials, and this makes the office look good. It makes neither bureaucratic nor political sense, therefore, to expend a lot of effort on "losers." Only those cases that are strong, in other words, likely to be won, are processed to the next stage. A strong case, however, does not refer only to the state of physical evidence. It also can refer to witness-victim credibility and to a general notion of "jury appeal." The prosecutor quoted previously summarizes these points:

> Property crimes to our juries, on the one hand, outrage them. That's our biggest type of crime here. But on the other hand, if you do get a sympathetic defendant, they are reluctant to hit him too badly and they will spend a lot more time arguing over the fine points of the case because they feel at the same time it's no big deal if we let him go on this. With our juries, on a sloppy case you are more likely to get a conviction if it's a rape, or a robbery, or a murder, than if it's a burglary or stealing an automobile. They hold you to much higher standards then. Or if I'm looking and it's marijuana, say the sale of marijuana as opposed to the sale of heroin or almost any other drug, you really want to make sure it's a lot tighter. On a sale of marijuana case we're much more likely not to issue the warrant because the police have screwed up

or left something out of the case. Because that's the kind of case that jurors get so particular about. See that's always in the back of your mind.[7]

Preliminary Court Appearances: The First or Initial Appearance

If the decision is made to pursue a matter, the essential elements of a case are usually in place by the time of an individual's first appearance in court. More paper will be added to the file, more evidence secured, but as a general rule the essential elements of a potential win for the prosecutor are already in the folder. If the prosecutor needs more evidence, he or she can order the police to get additional information and the warrant will be "taken under advisement." This means that the prosecutor will delay making a decision until such time he or she knows whether there is enough evidence to proceed.

The stage of first or initial appearance does not generally include the arresting officer, again despite the official wording of the warrant commanding the peace officer to bring the said individual before the court. In large cities the process is a highly structured group activity. All the people arrested within a given time period are transported to the court en masse.

The first day in court, including a conference with a defense lawyer, will take approximately 10 minutes. A magistrate, after briefly reviewing the folder containing the case to this point, will publicly read the charges as the defendant stands before him or her. The person will again be informed of the right to remain silent. Bail will be set. The individual will be asked if he or she can afford an attorney. If the answer is no, and typically it is, a public defender will approach and, after the formalities, have a hurried conference with the person introducing him or herself as the individual's lawyer.

Most individuals processed through the criminal courts are economically marginal. During the first or initial appearance, some will be able to arrange bail or release on their own recognizance. This last form of release means that the person simply promises to appear for further court processing. Such nonmonetary forms of release, however, usually require the individual to show strong community ties; home ownership, long-term employment, and/or family in the community. Those at the bottom of the economic ladder are often unable to meet such criteria. Those who cannot arrange pretrial release either by posting a money bond (bail) or gaining a personal recognizance release will be taken to the county jail to await the further processing of their case. And again, most of the accused will probably be relying on the services of a public defender.

The Public Defender

Until 1962, states were only required to provide counsel for indigent defendants if a case involved a possible death sentence. But in 1960, when Earl Gideon was convicted of burglary in Florida, a trumpet was about to sound that would bring down the prison walls for many poor defendants found guilty without the benefit of counsel. Gideon, in a direct, handwritten appeal to the Supreme Court of the United States, declared that his Sixth Amendment right to counsel had been violated by the State of Florida. The Court agreed, and in *Gideon* v. *Wainwright* announced that the state had to provide counsel when a poor person was charged with any felony.[8] Ten years later in *Argersinger* v. *Hamlin*, the right to counsel was extended to any crime for which imprisonment was a possible outcome.[9]

Most larger cities provide indigent defendants with counsel through the office of the public defender. Other methods of providing legal services to the poor are through legal aid societies, which are often privately funded, and through systems of appointing private counsel. In the latter instance, private attorneys either request an indigent case load for which they then charge the local government unit or are given a case load and expected to provide services for free as part of their public responsibility. The most common method is, however, a public defender system.

Public defenders have the burden of meeting the constitutionally and judicially mandated responsibility of doing their best for their client. As with other criminal justice roles, however, there are a variety of obligations and responsibilities, besides the formal, publicly recognized one, that compete for primacy.

The public defender is a government employee, not an independent knight who can give his or her all to one case. There are many cases that must be processed. Caseloads can range from 300 to 900.[10] Further, the public defender finds his or her position filled with dilemmas. He or she is a middle-class lawyer who deals mostly with lower-class losers who often are guilty. Granted, in some cases it is not all that clear exactly what the clients are guilty of, but in others it is uncomfortably clear what the clients have done. In any event, it is hard for someone with eight or so years of higher education and middle-class dreams and values to relate either to those who are guilty of simply being poor and unlucky or to those who are guilty of being burglars, rapists, and so on.

A public defender, then, faces a variety of problems in relationship to his or her clients. He or she may find it hard to identify with their impoverished state. Further, it will be hard for the defender to identify with the actions of some of the clients, regardless of what circumstances resulted in a particular crime. Somehow, bragging about getting a burglar or a rapist set free does not fit in with the image of the knight in shining armor protecting the poor and downtrodden. Finally, a public defender will discover that his clients do not particularly like or trust him. The phrase, "Shit man, I didn't have no attorney, I had a public defender," sums up the feeling of many of the individuals served by that office. Add to these problems the further difficulty of low prestige among fellow attorneys, and the dilemmas of the position become even more apparent.

In most jurisdictions, the routine handling of criminal cases is a prosecutor-dominated process, since it is that office that does the initial screening and has the greater investigatory resources to build its cases. As one public defender noted, "Most cases we get are pretty hopeless—really not much chance of an acquittal."[11]

Given this, many public defenders become primarily educators to, rather than advocates for, their clients. They inform the client of the options and attempt to convince him or her that within the unique social world of the courthouse, the individual is getting the best deal possible.

Despite problems with the public defender system, it is not clear that a person is better off with a private attorney, particularly if the lawyer does not specialize in the criminal law. Private attorneys also face dilemmas when confronted with a criminal case. They develop their own "rules of thumb" to deal with such dilemmas.

Private Attorneys vs. Public Defenders

A number of authors have noted that private defense attorneys, because they are in business, have to be concerned with collecting their fee.[12] There are, therefore, rules relating to this necessity. For example, a lawyers' manual suggests that the private attorney not go to visit a client in jail unless a relative can be contacted who will provide a retainer. Such precautions can, however, be waived if the individual is an old client.[13] Abraham S. Blumberg has argued that the need to collect a fee even affects the swiftness with which a case will be brought to a conclusion.[14] By asking for delays in court proceedings, the defense lawyer wields a powerful tool to ensure that his or her efforts are appropriately compensated. Relatives often want to get family members out of jail as quickly as possible, and certainly the accused want to get out. But for attorneys the rule is, "Do not proceed with a case until you have been compensated for the work you have done or will do. Once the guy gets off, there is little you can do to collect."

There are also rules for convincing an individual that the attorney deserves his or her fee. Lawyers sometimes have difficulty convincing a client that he or she really benefited from professional legal assistance. After all, the accused may be found guilty or convinced to plead guilty by the attorney. If the client ends up in jail or is currently in jail awaiting trial, it might be difficult to persuade the client that he is getting his money's worth. The same lawyers' handbook suggests that attorneys explain to their clients exactly what will take place as their cases sojourn through the ways of justice. If this is done at each stage of the proceedings, the defense lawyer is able to justify his or her retainer and convince clients that everything is being done on their behalf.[15]

Since the courthouse does form a subculture, with its own way of doing things, private attorneys may in fact be less effective than public defenders in representing the interest of their clients. A prosecutor illustrates this point:

Who the defense attorney is. If you go to trial, how good is he? Then there are a lot of [defense] lawyers who, subconsciously, are considered more reasonable. . . . But some other guy comes in who still may be a very good lawyer, and maybe you wouldn't want to go to the mat with him, who is just a complete jerk. Subconsciously you recommend those a little higher. There is almost a sense of challenge—I want to get you in the court.

Cases go more smoothly with public defenders than with private lawyers. But there is a handful of private attorneys who do mostly criminal work. They understand the system and know what a case is worth.[16]

For the indigent defendant charged with a felony, the key event to take place during the initial hearing is the assignment of counsel. If an individual is accused of a petty offense, those actions prohibited by city or township ordinances (for example, spitting on the sidewalk, drunk and disorderly conduct), a short trial will often be held by the magistrate to determine the guilt or innocence of the party. A person accused of a misdemeanor can enter a plea at this time, and if the plea is guilty, a date will be set for sentencing. If the person pleads innocent a trial date will be set. In felony cases an individual will be scheduled for a preliminary hearing.

The Preliminary Hearing and Arraignment

In felony cases, the preliminary hearing serves a number of functions. First and foremost, it is a screening device, designed to ensure that only the most important cases get to the trial stage. Second, it acts as a check to ensure that the officials meet the appropriate standards of evidence in presenting a case. As the case proceeds from the time of arrest to the time of the trial, the standards for evidence become more exacting. What is considered probable cause for a police officer who has to make a decision in a brief period of time may not be considered probable cause when a case is reviewed at the various stages of the judicial process. Thus, the quality of evidence and probable cause have to be well established for the case to proceed from the preliminary hearing to the arraignment. Likewise, for the case to proceed from arraignment to trial also requires an exact standard of probable cause and evidence. In practice, this means that before a case reaches trial it has a great likelihood of being handled at a lower level of the judicial process. Only a small percentage of all the cases filed ever reach the trial stage. Thus, it is not surprising to find that most cases that come to trial result in a verdict of guilty. Weak cases are generally filtered out before they reach that stage, or the person pleads guilty to a lesser charge. If the case gets to trial, it generally means that the state has fairly strong evidence to convince either a judge or a jury that the person being tried is, in fact, guilty.

A third function of the preliminary hearing is to give the defense attorney a chance to ascertain the strength of the case presented by the state against the client. While in theory this particular function of disclosure is central to the concept of a preliminary hearing, in practice the preliminary hearing provides a very poor stage for reviewing the state's case. This is because, in general, the state will only present the minimum amount of evidence necessary to convince a lower court magistrate that the case should be allowed to proceed to the next step. Obviously, the prosecutor is not going to show the defense all his or her cards unless it is absolutely necessary.

Preliminary hearings, depending upon the volume of cases, will generally take place within a month of arrest. They are held in the magistrate or associate circuit court and are fairly brief, perhaps 15 minutes or so. The likely witnesses are the police officers involved in the arrest and perhaps the victim. The former is asked to relate the circumstances of the arrest, the latter the circumstances leading to the arrest. The prosecutor then moves to have the case bound over to the superior or trial court. If the magistrate agrees that there is sufficient evidence to do so, he or she will issue an information. This simply allows the prosecutor to file the charge in the felony court.

Arraignment is the first appearance in the state trial court. It will usually occur within four to six months after arrest, although the time can be longer or shorter depending upon case load. At the arraignment evidence is again reviewed to determine if there is sufficient evidence for a trial. A plea can also be entered at this time, and in 80–90% of the cases the defendant will in fact plead guilty at this point. Trial is the least likely outcome of criminal case processing. Most cases are settled prior to arraignment through a negotiated plea.

The Grand Jury

While what has been described thus far is typical case processing, variation is possible. The most likely variation is the use of a grand jury. The grand jury would replace the preliminary hearing.

Grand juries are made up of 12 ordinary citizens who get called to serve in that capacity for a year. The grand jury will meet mostly at night so as not to interfere with the workday of its members.

Prosecutors use grand juries primarily for sensitive cases. Thus, if a popular politician were accused of doing something untoward, the prosecutor would probably bring the facts of such a case before a grand jury. The grand jury would weigh the evidence. If it decides there is probable cause, the jury would issue a true bill, which is simply an indictment that comes from the grand jury rather than from a preliminary hearing. The case would then proceed to arraignment in the felony court.

Grand juries have been the source of much debate within criminal justice circles. The institution is clearly a tool of the prosecutor. Witnesses called before a grand jury may not have their own attorneys present in the room. Should they desire to consult counsel, they must leave the room to do so. Grand juries can shield prosecutors from making unpopular decisions. If a grand jury decides to indict someone who is a popular community figure, the prosecutor can always avoid negative publicity by saying he or she is simply carrying out the mandate of the jury. Similarly, in cases where the community demands vengeance, if the grand jury fails to indict, the prosecutor can shift the blame to them. An example of this latter use can be found in sexual assault cases. Sexual assault cases between people known to one another are extremely difficult to prove legally. Such cases are likely to be screened out. Yet, sufficient pressure can be brought to bear on prosecutors to treat such cases more harshly. In such a climate, the prosecutor might well bring the cases before the grand jury. If no true bill is issued, the blame shifts to the jury. If a true bill is issued and the case comes to trial and is lost, the prosecutor can again shift responsibility to the grand jury for issuing an indictment on a weak case.

Regardless of the route taken to arraignment, however, a plea bargain is still the most likely outcome. To understand the routine doing of justice, therefore, it is necessary to understand this key process.

Plea Bargaining

It is safe to assume that in most cases, all of the people representing officialdom (the prosecuting attorney, the defense attorney, and, later on, the judge and the probation officers) have all worked together before. Each probably has a fair idea of what the other actors will and will not accept as a definition of the situation in a particular set of circumstances. As noted above, these understandings result in what can be called a courthouse subculture. The subculture of the courthouse is simply the agreed-upon definitions, norms, and values that any work group arrives at from spending time, day in and day out, handling a work product. In the courthouse, the work product is literally the case. All of the main actors have an idea of how individual cases will be viewed by others on the courthouse stage. It is these understandings that allow attorneys to predict what various judges will do in particular instances and also allow attorneys to predict the reactions of each other to particular strategies and moves in the game. Thus the "worth" of any given case can be quickly and fairly accurately predicted. A prosecutor discusses the elements considered in establishing a case's worth:

> Who the judge is, is a very important factor. . . . You even know ahead of time whether it's worth arguing. There are certain judges you know that will never undercut a state's recommendation. Other judges, you know always will.

> My superior tries to evaluate a case in terms of what reasonably could be expected from a jury.[17]

The "going rate" for a particular type of case, that is, its worth in terms of the sentence likely to be imposed, establishes the guidelines upon which the plea bargaining process will be based. Put another way, all participants generally agree on what rules govern the construction of reality. This agreement significantly circumscribes the adversarial relationship existing between the prosecuting attorney and the defense attorney. If each were to act as out-and-out adversaries (that is, if each were to invoke different rules for the construction of reality), too much time and energy would be wasted and the efficient handling of cases impaired. Like the police, the attorneys, particularly those employed by public agencies, must be able to show their superiors that they are competent craftsmen. In order to do this, a case must be handled efficiently. Efficiency, the probability of winning measured against the cost both in time and money of pursuing a matter to the fullest, becomes the hallmark of the successful attorney-bureaucrat. Within this framework, the interests of the individual client, whether the accused or the state, is only one factor among many that need to be considered. Making it in the bureaucracy requires knowing when to cooperate. Therefore, much of the initial contact between prosecutors and defenders appears to be a matter of posturing. Each attempts to ascertain what the other will settle for and what the other will consider unreasonable. Actually the process is one of making sure that "typical" rules for social world construction will be involved in a particular case. As noted previously, in most instances this mutual understanding of how the world is to be put together allows for relatively quick agreement on an appropriate case disposition, limiting the need for trials.

Actual bargaining can take place over one of three case elements. The most common form of plea bargaining involves the dropping of charges. Prosecutors will typically charge an individual with a number of infractions related to a criminal incident. Thus, a person involved in a robbery might also be charged with carrying a concealed weapon and assault if the victim was threatened with physical harm. Depending on the specific circumstances of the case, either the major charge could be dropped in exchange for a plea of guilty on the lesser charges or the lesser charges could be dropped for a guilty plea on the major charge.

A prosecutor can also agree to reduce a charge in exchange for a guilty plea. A person initially charged with possession with intent to sell a dangerous drug might have the charge reduced to simple possession in exchange for a guilty plea.

Besides dropping charges and charge bargaining, a prosecutor can agree to a more lenient sentencing recommendation in exchange for a guilty plea. Since a prosecutor's sentencing recommendation can carry great weight with the court, the offer to recommend a more lenient sentence is a powerful lever to induce a guilty plea.

The person most likely to first suggest a guilty plea to an individual accused of a crime is the defense lawyer. As described above, defense lawyers act primarily as educators of rather than advocates for their clients. This is because the cases they receive are generally fairly strong against their clients. Weak cases have been previously screened out. And so the job is one of letting the individual know his or her options and describing from the attorney's standpoint which is best. The best option is almost never trial.

Deciding to Take a Plea

Research by Lynn M. Mather describes some of the methods public defenders use to both assess their client's chances and structure their own decisions on how to handle a case.[18] The public defenders in this study appeared in part to be guided by the following rules:

> You take a plea when there is a serious charge, but the prosecutor is willing to consider a lesser degree of criminal involvement than originally assessed.
>
> You take a plea when the charge will not result in a heavy sentence, and the prosecutor has a strong legal case.
>
> You go to trial when the charge will not result in a heavy sentence and there is reasonable doubt that the defendant committed any crime.
>
> You go to trial when the case is serious and the prosecutor has strong evidence, since the defendant has little to lose and much to gain.

The most difficult decision the public defender faced was in those cases where there was a serious charge but a reasonable doubt that the defendant was in any way involved in the act. Going to trial was a high risk–high gain venture due to the vagaries of juries. Bargaining for a lesser charge appeared to be the preferred strategy, but public defenders would go to trial on such cases if either the prosecutor or the client was unwilling to deal. Fortunately, from the public defender's standpoint, such cases were infrequent. Most cases were judged to be legally strong, but with comparatively light sentences, involving either probation or a short jail term. Thus rule two was the most frequently invoked in the structuring of case accounts by public defenders.

The discussion above, together with evidence cited previously by Sudnow and others noting defense attorney reliance on arrest reports and preexistent understandings of what a "typical" case is, suggests that from a defense attorney's standpoint, directly asking a client whether he is guilty or innocent is of little importance. Accounts presented on police reports and various other case documents provide the more "realistic" assessment of how a case will be perceived by those who will structure the final "legal" account of an event. Moreover, by avoiding a direct inquiry as to a client's guilt or innocence, the defense attorney can also avoid the ethical dilemma of the client who insists on testifying under oath to his innocence after having admitted the deed to his lawyer. By not asking the client, the attorney can put the individual on the stand without suborning perjury.

Why would an individual forego his or her right to a trial and instead plead guilty to a crime? First, in large urban court systems there is often a year or more delay between time of arrest and trial. If a person has not been able to make bail, the time awaiting trial is spent in jail. A plea settles the matter in a much shorter period of time. Since probation is the most likely case disposition, a person will be back on the street that much sooner. But even when the penalty will involve further incarceration, there is a powerful incentive for pleading guilty. A second reason for avoiding trial is to gain whatever leniency is possible. It is generally agreed that by going to trial a person forfeits any right to consideration at sentencing. The most severe penalty possible is likely to be imposed if a guilty verdict is rendered. This can be considered a trial tax for using resources without reaching a different outcome than the far more efficient bargaining process would have achieved. In cases of homicide, for example, prosecutors have been known to seek and obtain the death penalty after an individual has refused to plead guilty in exchange for prison time.

Function of Plea Bargaining

Plea bargaining performs a number of functions within the criminal justice system. First and foremost it gives courthouse workers control over their work product. Trials are unpredictable. Plea bargaining, on the other hand, has predictable outcomes and thus reduces worker ambiguity. This helps explain why plea bargaining goes on even in those courthouses with small case loads.

Obviously, plea bargaining does save time. This is a key consideration in large urban court systems that process thousands of cases a year. As noted, even though between 80 to 90% of all cases are settled with negotiated pleas, it is not unusual to have to wait a year to go to trial. Any decrease in negotiated pleas might result in even longer delays between arrest and trial.

Finally, plea bargaining can help those who work in our lower criminal courts negotiate a fundamental dilemma of their job. The principle of law dictates that all similar cases should be treated alike. At the same time, we as citizens expect our guardians of law to take into account individual circumstances. Plea bargaining offers a mechanism whereby these seemingly incompatible goals can be met. As discussed in Chapter 2, extralegal factors can be used to mitigate laws whose harshness would be inappropriate in a given set of circumstances. The use of the "typical case" to categorize individual circumstances allows for both mitigation and a kind of uniformity in case processing.

Although plea bargaining appears to be an integral part of our criminal justice system, it is often the target of criticism. While it gives attorneys and judges a sense of control over their work product, it takes control away from those initially involved in the incident. Victims and offenders both experience a system that has little to do with them and to which they have little input. This point can be illustrated by a brief description of the public conclusion to the bargaining process.

Public Rituals for Negotiated Pleas

The negotiated plea will be entered at the arraignment. Before the judge accepts the plea, however, he or she must ascertain if the plea was voluntary and if the defendant understands the consequences of the action. This is done through a series of pro forma questions, like the ones that follow:

Judge: "The Fifth Amendment to the Constitution provides you with the privilege against compulsory self-incrimination. You may remain silent at all times, and your silence may not be commented upon or used against you. Do you understand that?" The client had been previously coached to respond, "Yes."

"Do you understand that under the Sixth Amendment you are also entitled to confront your accusers, to require that they testify in open court at a public trial and to cross-examine the witnesses against you, and to call witnesses on your own behalf by the order of this court?" Again the appropriate response is, "Yes."

"Finally, do you understand that by your plea of guilty you are giving up all of these rights and subjecting yourself to sentence and punishment without a trial?" There is a final, "Yes."

"Were any threats, promises, or inducements made to cause you to offer this plea?" Here the correct response is, "No."

Everybody knows of course that certain promises were in fact made or implied, but this ritual has a number of functions other than to display the literal truth of the process.

The questions directed to the defendant and the mumbled responses meet the constitutional requirement that judges ascertain whether a plea is voluntary. Of course, voluntary is in the eye of the beholder. Some might argue that the threat of increased punishment for going to trial and being found guilty reduces the voluntariness of any plea bargaining arrangement. The courts, however, have held that increased penalties associated with going to trial do not really constitute coercion, in part because there is always a chance that a person could be set free.[19] If an individual chooses to roll the dice and go to trial, he or she must accept the consequences of the gamble, win or lose. Thus, a voluntary plea is defined as one in which the ritual of voluntariness, that is, pro forma judicial questions and equally pro forma answers by defendants, has been followed.

Besides meeting the legal requirement of determining voluntariness, the ritual also allows for a portrayal of justice, a making visible of that elusive quality the system is supposedly enhancing. At its best, this function of ritual is educative. The social system represents to itself its goals and its ideals and, in the process, recommits and reconfirms its image of itself as good, decent, and so forth. In short, the ritual of the court is a mini civics lesson, portraying to all who see it the type of society we think of ourselves as being. If you have ever seen a grammar school class on a field trip to a courtroom to observe the process of justice, you can gain a sense of the educative function of such a proceeding. After such encounters with the rituals of justice, the young students often express a very deep commitment to the process of government and a desire to avoid legal infractions which go against the ideals of our society. After such encounters, the commitment to law is at a peak. Unfortunately, the ritual of justice often only works in such a way for the occasional, naive spectator.

For those who are part of the process, either as legal functionaries or as defendants, the ritual emphasizes the value of either bureaucratic efficiency or displays another example of the system's discrimination against those it considers losers. Thus, many people found guilty of crimes deny their culpability, in part because the ritual has little to do with their actual circumstances. As indicated, the case and the individual are two separate entities. The ritual most often deals with the case and ignores the individual.

Finally, the ritual serves a function for the professionals involved in the process. In those cases where a private attorney is retained to defend an individual, the ritual arraignment allows counsel to plea publicly for mercy for the client (even if a deal has been previously worked out), thereby showing those who pay the bill that the lawyer is, in fact, worth the fee being charged. At the same time, prosecutors get a chance to show publicly that they are convicting those guilty of crimes. It appears, then, that many people are served by the ritual that takes place in accepting a plea. The defendant may not, however, be among them.

While liberals tend to criticize plea bargaining as being too harsh on the defendant, conservatives tend to see it as a loophole through which defendants escape the punishment they deserve. Assessments of programs to eliminate or restrict plea bargaining suggest, however, that this is not the case.[20] As the prosecutor quoted previously indicated, sentencing recommendations tend to be made on the basis of what a jury might do. In other words, serious cases are treated seriously with stiff sentence recommendations. Thus, reforms of plea bargaining tend to affect the less serious cases, for a "trickle-up" effect. Those involved in less serious criminal activity, cases on the bottom layer of the wedding cake, get harsher punishments when plea bargaining is eliminated or restricted.

It is important to note at this point that negotiated pleas are not arranged in a vacuum. The courthouse subculture establishes a going rate for offenses. This rate in turn is constructed on the basis of what a "typical" jury might do. While there is no such thing as a "typical" jury, the phrase emphasizes the importance of jury trials for the system. Although this is the least used method of disposition, its symbolic importance cannot be overestimated. The relatively few jury trials that take place form a kind of benchmark against which, day in and day out, pleas are measured.

The Trial: A Public Extravaganza

Ceremonies can be described as public extravaganzas that express in a special way the meanings and values of a particular group. While ceremonies express values and meaning, they also create and reinforce them. Thus, ceremonies are a necessary component of a group's social life. They strengthen the social bonds that tie the group together by reminding participants of a reality (or by creating a reality) that transcends individualistic needs and concerns. Trials represent such ceremonies in the context of society's concerns and beliefs about justice.

Jury trials represent the fullest expression of society's justice values. Yet they occur in only about 8% of criminal cases. While a jury trial must be available to defendants charged with a serious crime, that is, where the penalty carries a sentence of more than six months' incarceration, we have seen that most cases are settled through pleas. Defendants may also opt for a nonjury trial. These dispositions are preferable to courthouse workers because outcomes are more predictable. As noted, the "going rate" sets the parameters for the plea bargaining process, and thus attorneys and judges can be fairly accurate in their predictions of what others in the system will accept. With judicial trials there is perhaps a greater element of uncertainty as to the outcome, but judges too gain reputations and thus their behavior in a given case can be anticipated. Research suggests, however, that judicial decision making is influenced by far more than the letter of the law.

Judicial Decision Making

As early as 1914, a New York City group was beginning to suspect that logic and legalities were less important than were personality factors in influencing judges' decisions. Comparing how different judges handled similar cases in Magistrates Court, the Committee on Criminal Courts of the Charity Organization Society found wide variation. One judge heard 566 cases of alleged intoxication. He determined that 565 of the allegations were true and declared the individuals guilty of the offense. Only one person was discharged. His colleague, on the other hand, had 673 people come before him charged with the same offense but found only 142 of them guilty, discharging 531. Similarly wide variations were found among judges handling other kinds of cases within the magistrate court. Apparently, the committee was deeply disturbed by these findings, since they discontinued their study.[22]

A more rigorous study of judicial decision making, Frederick J. Gaudet's 1930s analysis of judicial sentencing behavior, also reveals marked inconsistencies. Gaudet examined 7,442 cases of certain select crimes assigned to six judges of New Jersey County Court over a 10-year period. His conclusion was that personality, in the broad sense of social background, education, religion, experience on the bench, temperament, and social attitudes, was of primary importance in determining a judge's decision of the appropriate sentence to give a person found guilty of a crime.[23]

In summarizing some of the studies done on judicial decision making, Anne Strick states, "Sentencing . . . depends less upon punishment fitted to crime, upon the contextual circumstances of the case, or even upon the particular criminal's history, than (in Judge Marvin Frankel's words) 'upon the wide spectrums of character, bias, neurosis, and daily vagary encountered among occupants of the trial bench.' "[24] The reader should exercise the normal caution of the social scientist when confronted with such a strong statement. Actually, the research problems confronting an investigator of judicial decision making are significant. Nevertheless, despite the admittedly serious methodological problems that have to be considered when examining such an issue,[25] the weight of the evidence to date is certainly suggestive of the need to analyze judicial decisions in light of unique judicial backgrounds. One of the most widely quoted studies in this regard is Stuart Nagel's study of the influence of certain background characteristics on judges' decisions. He found significant differences between Democratic and Republican judges, non-ABA members and ABA members, non–former prosecutors and former prosecutors, Catholic judges and Protestant judges, and relatively liberal judges and relatively conservative judges, as measured by their off-the-bench attitudes. Democratic judges were more likely to favor the defense than were their Republican counterparts. Not belonging to the ABA, not being a former prosecutor, being Catholic, and being scored as liberal in off-the-bench attitudes were also factors significantly associated with being more favorable to the defense position in criminal cases.[26]

Personality and background characteristics are not the only factors influencing judicial decision making. Whether somebody gets sent to prison may depend in part on how much room is left in the facility. Political pressure to "get tough with criminals" can also influence a member of the bench. Finally, it has been noted that the working relationships that judges develop with prosecutors, defense attorneys, and other courthouse personnel affect the decisions judges render in particular cases. Thus, a judge's pattern of decision making is somewhat stable and becomes known in the courthouse. Lawyers, police officers, and defendants familiar with how the criminal justice system actually works try to get the judge who would be most sympathetic to their particular plight. Such "judge shopping" is common practice and, as one judge has said, "Lawyers are always trying to psych the judge out, like people at the race track trying to figure out the horses. . . . That is what you pay a trial lawyer for—assessing the judge's discretion."[27]

Assessing a judge's discretion in anticipation of a bench trial is perhaps riskier than obtaining a negotiated plea, worked out primarily with the opposing council. However, it does permit some degree of control through the practice of "judge shopping." A jury trial eliminates even this control factor, and thus outcomes are least predictable with this form of case disposition. It is a wonder that there are any jury trials.

Jury Trials

One of the reasons for jury trials is the breakdown of negotiations. We have seen that negotiations are most likely to break down under two conditions. When the prosecutor has a serious case and strong evidence, there is no reason for him or her to negotiate. From the standpoint of the public defender, then, it makes sense to go to trial, since the defendant has nothing to lose. When the prosecutor has a weak case, but one with strong jury appeal, he or she may feel that a jury would assess a stiffer penalty than could be gotten through negotiation with a defense lawyer. From the prosecutor's standpoint, then, a jury trial makes sense.

Jury trials occur for more than pragmatic reasons, however. They serve to display and reinforce a number of values. Thus, defense lawyers are likely to seek jury trials when the charge does not carry a heavy sentence and there is a reasonable doubt concerning the client's guilt. In these instances, the ceremonies of justice can be as important as the outcome.

Jury trials symbolize the rule of law from an American perspective, namely that sanctions come ultimately from the community and not from the government. The doctrine of the jury's right of nullification illustrates this principle. In our system, juries have an absolute right to not enforce a law and to therefore find a defendant not guilty regardless of the weight of legal evidence. This right goes back to the founders' suspicion of government and the feeling that government power needed to be checked. Ironically, the right of nullification is often more symbolic than it is actualized since judges are reluctant to inform juries of this power. Defense lawyers do, however, attempt to impress upon juries their right to dismiss the legalities of a case by appealing to the sympathetic character of their clients.

Having a jury of peers sit in judgment is also a deeply ingrained value since it provides a potent symbol of democracy. Unfortunately, the term "peer" has varied in meaning over time. In small-town rural America, if an individual was a white male, he was indeed likely to have a jury of peers. If the accused was black or a woman, the jury would still likely be white and male. In this latter instance the notion of peer was broadly interpreted. In today's modern urban court system, the term "peer" is subject to similarly broad interpretation. It is likely to mean only that the individuals on the jury share a local geopolitical boundary with the defendant. They live in the same city, township, or county. As will be seen, other juror characteristics are sought based on case circumstances which may involve more than simply physical or biographical resemblance to the accused.

Trials by jury perform an educational function. As we have seen, they remind courthouse regulars of what "typical" juries do (whether or not in fact any individual jury does what is expected), and they instruct citizens as to their rights, duties, and responsibilities under our form of government. But the lessons are expensive in terms of time, resources, and inability to control and/ or predict an outcome. A plea negotiation can be arranged in a matter of minutes. A bench trial may take a day or less. The typical criminal jury trial is two days but can be much longer depending upon the nature of the case and in any event will involve the time of many more people.

Lawyers attempt to control the final outcome of a jury trial as much as possible, even though juries are unpredictable, an ironic state of affairs given the courthouse's reliance on the idea of a "typical" jury. This is done primarily through *voir dire*, the process of selecting jurors before the actual trial begins.

Voir Dire

Obviously, jurors, in their applications of the law, are affected by the same factors that affect judges and other legal functionaries. In fact, in the case of jurors, such background and personality characteristics are paramount in their selection for hearing certain cases. Lawyers do not attempt to pick impartial juries during the process of voir dire (literally, "to say the truth"). During the voir dire, lawyers question jurors in an attempt to discover which jurors are likely to be biased. Each lawyer is allowed to remove a certain number of jurors he or she feels would be biased against his or her side. Of course, each lawyer tries to get and to keep those jurors who would be biased for his or her side. The importance lawyers place on the biases of the jurors for winning or losing cases is illustrated by the following excerpt from *The Murder Trial of Wilbur Jackson*. The prosecutor and the defense lawyer are explaining what each looked for in putting together a jury. Jackson, a white, blue-collar worker, was on trial for killing his daughter and three hippie companions.

> *Prosecutor*: Jury selection in this case was completely different from the way it is in other cases. I wanted to get the most intelligent jury I could find, which is not the way I would normally approach it. Normally, I want followers. I want people who will follow the lead of one strong, middle-aged factory worker type who dislikes crime and whom the other jurors will follow. In this case, I wanted a really bright, intelligent jury who would disregard the clothes and beard and all that.

> *Defense*: Ordinarily, if you defend a homicide case in Pittsburgh, it would be fair to say that you are defending someone between seventeen and twenty-six who is charged with the commission of a felony murder, a murder which was committed in the course of the perpetration of a robbery, burglary, an arson, or a rape. About 90% of the time, but perhaps even more often than that, you're defending a black who is between eighteen and twenty-six and you want one particular kind of jury to try that kind of a case, but you want a very different kind of jury to try Wilbur Jackson. . . . What I was trying to do, to be quite frank with you, was to get as many people on that jury who came from the northeast part of Pittsburgh and who had Polish or Italian surnames.[28]

During the process of voir dire, attorneys are allowed two types of challenge to the sitting of a particular juror. Challenge for cause means the attorney is claiming a statutory exemption. If the juror knows the defendant or claims that he or she does not believe that people should judge others, the individual can be challenged for cause. These challenges are unlimited. A juror can also be dismissed through the use of a preemptory challenge. This simply means that the attorney does not want the individual on the jury. The attorney does not have to show cause as to why. Such preemptory challenges are, however, limited, with each side usually allowed only six or eight.

Given the fact that jurors are sometimes picked for their biases, that they are untrained in law, and that they have the right of nullification, how do the findings of juries compare with those of the professionals? Put another way, do juries work?

Do Juries Work?

The answers to the above queries are not straightforward. Studying juries is an extremely difficult undertaking beset with methodological difficulties. Yet the bulk of research suggests that juries and judges are in agreement on the majority of case outcomes.[29] At the same time, jurors have been shown to have low comprehension of judicial instructions and burden of proof requirements in criminal cases.[30] Also, there has been relatively little attention paid to questionable convictions. Recent research has suggested that there may be a greater problem than previously thought.[31] At this point, it appears that the answer to the question of jury competence is largely ideological in nature. Since facts concerning juries are unclear, ideology once again fills in the vacuum. Thus, how does one interpret the finding that judges agree with the bulk of jury decisions? Do judges themselves rely primarily on extralegal factors in deciding cases? Do juries fail to exercise their nullification function where it would be appropriate? Are juries biased toward the prosecution, thus having a problematic rate of questionable convictions? And, if you are following the thrust of this paragraph, what is a problematic rate of conviction anyway? Research conducted in England found a 6% rate of problematic convictions.[32] Is this too high? What about questionable acquittals? Is this a more serious issue? Obviously, these questions are ones of value, not science. Of course, if it were found that the overall rate of jury mistakes was low, or particular classes of defendants were far more likely to be victims of jury bias, this finding might call into question the values juries seem to express. At any rate, it is precisely because jury trials are symbols of values that their use, while low, will remain an integral part of our system of justice. In this sense, then, whether they work or not is irrelevant. It's the ceremony that seems important.

Juvenile Justice

A mixture of values, ideology, and legal processes fuels the operation of the adult criminal courts. The same kind of mixture fuels the operation of juvenile court, but here the ideological action is refined to a much higher level.

The juvenile court, first established in 1890, in the city of Chicago, is a clear outgrowth of ideological progressivism. Children were to be treated, not punished. Unfortunately, as Chapter 5 pointed out in its portrayal of the Elmira Reformatory, the difference between treatment and punishment was often one of terminology, not action. But since the ideology of the juvenile court stressed "child saving," the legal safeguards of adult justice processes were thought to be unnecessary. The juvenile court was interested in helping, not convicting and punishing. Today, these ideological roots are still apparent in the terminology used to describe the juvenile justice process.

Juveniles are taken into custody, they are not arrested. This first step in the juvenile justice process can result in a number of dispositions. Most encounters between the police and juveniles are for relatively minor incidents.[33] Thus, initial custody can result in a short lecture and release. This is the most likely occurrence. However, if the officer judges the situation to be more serious, the juvenile can be referred for formal system processing.

Referrals occur for a variety of reasons. These can include not only suspicion of involvement in serious crime, but also such things as protecting the child from harm (as in cases of child abuse), seeking appropriate supervision for the child (as in cases where adult supervision is lacking), or seeking to prevent a parent's removal of a child from a given vicinity. Thus, juvenile processes mix the purposes of crime control and social welfare. Should the police officer decide to refer a case, the next step is intake.

In juvenile case processing the intake interview replaces the first or preliminary court appearance of the adult system. A nonjudicial employee, after reviewing the case, can decide to release the juvenile with a warning; release on the condition that the child enroll in a community program or submit to informal probation; or decide to file a petition. A petition is the equivalent of an indictment. The intake officer can also decide to detain the child if further case processing is warranted. If the child is to be detained, the decision is reviewed by a court administrator or by a juvenile court judge at a detention hearing.

The juvenile court petition activates the court adjudication process. A juvenile court prosecutor will review the petition. He or she can dismiss the case, recommend the case be transferred to adult criminal court, or continue to process the case in the juvenile court system.

If the case continues in the juvenile court, the next step is adjudication. A juvenile being processed in juvenile court is not found guilty, rather he or she is adjudicated. A juvenile court judge reviews all the evidence presented in the petition at a formal hearing. At the hearing, the juvenile is represented by counsel, and interested parties, parents, social workers, police officers, etc. can make statements. The term hearing needs to be stressed. The process at this point is not a trial, but a procedure aimed at determining the best interests of the child and the community. Rules of evidence are only loosely applied. The judge may decide to release the child without further processing, thus rejecting the allegations made in the petition. He or she may withhold formal adjudication, on the condition that the child enrolls in a community program. If the judge accepts the allegations in a petition, the child can be adjudicated a delinquent, a dependent, or a child in need of supervision. The next step is then disposition.

If a child is found to be dependent or neglected, he or she can be placed in a foster family or in a juvenile institution. Such children can also be placed back with their families, with intensive social services provided to the entire family unit. If a child is adjudicated a delinquent who is found to be involved in activity that if committed by an adult would be a crime, the exact same case dispositions are available. Thus, because of the mixed purposes of the system, juveniles with entirely different problems are often treated the same way. This complicates a question that we have asked of the adult system. Is it too harsh or too lenient? We have seen that serious cases are treated seriously in adult criminal courts, and less serious cases are treated more leniently. The picture, unfortunately, is far murkier in the juvenile justice system.

As is clear, the juvenile may be detained at various points in the process. As is also clear, such detention is not simply based on legal evidence of criminal involvement. Detention can also be "in the best interest of the child," meaning that a child who is guilty of no crime can receive the same treatment as one who is. Thus, even prior to any formal adjudication, juveniles can be subject to fairly punitive treatment.[34]

Research on decision criteria used at the intake stage and at the stages of adjudication and disposition fails to present a clear picture.[35] It seems, however, that the theory of leniency is far greater than its actual practice. Thus, even in those cases that are handled informally, the presence of a program rather than strict need determines whether a juvenile will be subject to further intervention.[36] The juvenile court, therefore, seems to present a classic instance of the spreading criminal justice net. Serious offenders are treated seriously, and less serious offenders are treated seriously, in programs originally designed to lessen the control and punishment given the former.[37]

POLICY CONSIDERATIONS: THEORIES/ARGUMENTS/APPLICATIONS

What Should Be Reformed

A review of typical case processing suggests caution in the creation of reform policies. To date, most such reforms have failed to take into account the bureaucratic nature of case processing and the courthouse subculture that gives it meaning. As a result, policies aimed at increasing the punishment of serious offenders, whether adult or juvenile, have instead increased the punishment of less serious offenders. And, since the courthouse deals with cases and not crime, the end result has been inefficiency with no appreciable effect on the crime rate. This point will be even more clearly demonstrated in the next chapter, when the correctional system is described. The correctional system is at the end of the proverbial creek. Bad decisions flow down so that it is this system that suffers the most from ill-conceived policy decisions.

If the problem of the court system is not leniency, at least in the adult model, what is its problem? As with any bureaucracy, the problem appears to be one of impersonality. The system processes cases, but people, victims and offenders, are at the heart of the matter. Policies of reform need to take into account this basic fact. Without doing so, they risk increasing the alienation of these people from society, and thus inadvertently creating conditions for further crime. As Chapters 9 and 10 pointed out, there is a need for reintegrating both victims and offenders into the social fabric. Impersonal case processing does not further this goal. Before turning to alternative case processing methods, however, it will be enlightening to examine the consequences of policy innovations meant to reduce crime when these have been applied to a system that does not deal with crime, but with bureaucratic case production. The current state of corrections illustrates these consequences.

SUMMARY

What Was Said

- The courthouse deals with accounts, reconstructed views of past events.
- Prosecutors have been called the single most powerful figures in the criminal justice system.
- After an arrest, a prosecutor screens cases by deciding whether to issue a warrant.
- Warrants are issued in approximately 30–40% of arrests, although the number can vary widely by jurisdiction.
- Prosecutors, in making the decision to issue a warrant, use what can be called "a probable win test."
- The number of court appearances in a criminal case can include:
    —The first appearance
    —The preliminary hearing
    —The arraignment
    —The trial
- Most cases are settled by plea bargaining prior to trial.
- A grand jury can replace the preliminary hearing, and if it finds sufficient evidence it will issue a true bill, which then allows the case to proceed to the arraignment.
- Prosecutors, defense lawyers, judges, and juries use extralegal as well as legal criteria to decide the appropriate disposition of a case.
- These extralegal decision rules constitute what can be termed "the courthouse subculture."

- Reforms of this system need to take into account the values and work routines of the courthouse subculture.

What Was Not Said

- Plea bargaining should be abolished.
- Private attorneys are better than public defenders.
- Juvenile justice represents a "soft" approach to crime.

NOTES

1. Steven Marcus, "Introduction," in Dashiell Hammett, *The Continental Op* (New York: Random House, 1974).

2. The President's Commission on Law Enforcement and Administration of Justice, Task Force Report. Science and Technology (Washington DC: U.S. Government Printing Office, 1967), p. 61.

3. Charles Silberman, *Criminal Violence, Criminal Justice* (New York: Random House, 1978), pp. 257–61.

4. Ann Carter Stith, "Criminal Justice System," *St. Louis Currents* ed. Leadership St. Louis (St. Louis, MO: 1986), pp. 9–12..

5. James P. Levine, Michael C. Musheno, and Dennis J. Palumbo, *Criminal Justice, A Public Policy Approach* (New York: Harcourt, Brace Jovanovich, Inc., 1980), p. 202.

6. James F. Gilsinan, *Doing Justice* (New York: Prentice-Hall, 1982), p. 157.

7. Ibid., p. 156.

8. *Gideon* v. *Wainwright*, 372 U.S. 335 (1962).

9. *Argersinger* v. *Hamlin*, 407 U.S. 25 (1972).

10. Levine, Musheno, and Palumbo, *Criminal Justice*, p. 235.

11. Lynn M. Mather, "Some Determinants of the Method of Case Disposition: Decision-Making by Public Defenders in Los Angeles," in *Law and Society Review*, Vol. 8 (1975), 187–216.

12. See, for example, Abraham S. Blumberg, "Lawyers with Convictions," in *Scales of Justice*, Abraham S. Blumberg, ed. (New Brunswick, NJ: Transaction, July 1970), pp. 51–67 and Paul B. Wise, *Criminal Lawyer* (Beverly Hills, CA: Sage Publication, Inc., 1978), particularly Chapter 4.

13. Robert C. Welch, "Investigating and Marshalling the Facts Other than Formal Discovery," in *Missouri Criminal Practice* (Jefferson City, MO: The Missouri Bar, 1978), pp. I, 4.4.

14. Blumberg, "Lawyers with Convictions," p. 55.

15. Welch, "Investigating," p. 4.5.

16. Gilsinan, *Doing Justice*, p. 150.

17. Ibid., p. 156.

18. Mather, "Some Determinants," p. 216.

19. Arthur Rosett and Donald R. Cressey, *Justice by Consent* (Philadelphia, PA: J.B. Lippincott Company, 1976), pp. 29–31, 58–65.

20. Samuel Walker, *Sense and Nonsense About Crime* (Monterery, CA: Brooks/Cole Publishing Co., A Division of Wadsworth Inc., 1985), p. 135.

21. Ibid. pp. 127–130.

22. Anne Strick, *Injustice for All* (New York: G.P. Putnam's Sons, 1977), pp. 145–146.

23. Frederick J. Gaudet, "The Sentencing Behavior of the Judge," in *Encyclopedia of Criminology*, V. C. Branham and S. V. Kutach, eds. (New York: Philosophical Library, 1949), pp. 449–61.

24. Strick, *Injustice for All*, p. 147.

25. For a discussion of some of these problems see Edward Green, *Judicial Attitudes in Sentencing* (London: Macmillan and Co., 1961), pp. 8–20.

26. Stuart S. Nagel, "Judicial Background and Criminal Cases," *Journal of Criminal Law, Criminology and Police Science*, 53. No. 3 (1962), 333–39.

27. Judge Tim Murphy, "His Honor Has Problems Too," *The Center Magazine*, 3, No. 3 (May/June 1971), 51.

28. Philip B. Heymann and William H. Kenety. *The Murder Trial of Wilbur Jochman* (St. Paul, MN: West Publishing Co., 1975), pp. 296–97.

29. Levine, Musheno, and Palumbo, *Criminal Justice*.

30. Ibid.

31. Ibid.

32. Ibid.

33. Patricia M. Harris, "Is the Juvenile Justice System Lenient?" *Criminal Justice Abstracts*, Vol. 18, No. 1, (March 1986), 107–10.

34. Ibid. p. 110–15.

35. Ibid.

36. Ibid. p. 104.

37. Scott Decker, "Value Consensus Among Agencies in a Juvenile Diversion Program, a Process Evaluation," in Mary Morash, *Implementing Criminal Justice Policies* (Beverly Hills, CA: Sage, 1982).

XIII

Corrections

At the end of this chapter, the student will be able to:

A. Discuss the current crisis of correctional facility overcrowding including prison and jail overcrowding.
B. Discuss costs of an alternative to incarceration.
C. Note the various theories of prison subculture and their relevance for inmate reform.
D. Compare jail and prison experiences, noting their different dynamics.
E. Note and discuss the various alternatives to incarceration that are available.

ISSUE BACKGROUND

Prison Overcrowding in Eighteenth-Century England

The bouillon cube has an interesting place in the history of corrections. Moreover, as Robert Hughes notes, the bouillon cube was to the eighteenth century what the computer chip is to the twentieth. It helped extend the boundaries of the human frontier.

In his book *The Fatal Shore*, Hughes presents a fascinating account of the history of Australia's founding.[1] He demonstrates the connections among the seemingly disparate elements of bouillon cubes, microchips, prison overcrowding, correctional alternatives, and the founding of a new country. Because meat bouillon led to the defeat of scurvy, a disease caused by a dietary deficiency common on long sea voyages, ships from Europe could more easily make the arduous journey to the continent of Australia, an area originally colonized by prisoners from the overcrowded jails of England.

The industrial revolution helped create a crime problem in eighteenth-century England. Beset by unemployment, poverty, and social dislocation, many displaced workers turned to gin and crime in order to survive both psychologically and economically.[2] They came to be viewed as "the dangerous classes." It was the fear of this class that eventually led to the founding of the British police in 1829. But while the policy battle of whether Britain really needed a standing police force was being fought, the public relied on draconian laws to ease its fear of crime. Thus, during the 1700s, Britain experienced an enormous growth in the number of crimes carrying the death penalty. According to Hughes:

> One could be hanged for burning a house or a hut, a standing rack of corn or an insignificant pile of straw; for poaching a rabbit, for breaking down "the head or mound" of a fish pond, or even cutting down an ornamental shrub; or for appearing on a highroad with a sooty face.[3]

Had the government actually hanged all those guilty of capital offenses, bodies would have been everywhere. There was the innate understanding that such mass carnage would likely lead to rioting and a potential overthrow of the government. Therefore, the "royal prerogative of mercy" was used extensively. Death sentences would be commuted by the intervention of the king. This showed the mercy and benevolence of the Crown. At the same time, such a ritual still made clear that it was the king who held the power of life and death. Such criminal justice policy interventions in Georgian England had the same consequence as policy interventions today. By solving one problem, another was created.

The notion that people could be punished by taking away their liberty for a set period of time in an institution specifically designed for such a purpose is a modern invention. The first state prison was opened in 1796 in New York. Prison as a place of punishment was a largely American innovation. Traditionally, jails and prisons had been merely places of holding until the punishment decreed by the court could be carried out. Such punishments were usually physical in nature: flogging, branding, or death. By commuting large numbers of death sentences, then, the English king created the first modern situation of prison overcrowding. If people were not to be hanged, what could be done with them? While the answer to this question was being debated, the recipients of the king's benevolence simply began to pile up in English jails. Many of these were built in the Middle Ages and were privately owned. Conditions were abominable. All necessities had to be paid for by the inmate. Lack of funds meant lack of food, clothing, bedding, and any other necessities. Once confined, people simply waited until a decision was made about what could be done with them. Again, the concept that incarceration was itself punishment had not yet taken hold.

Eventually, it became clear that England was running out of space for housing its condemned prisoners. Further, the public began to become concerned that such a concentration of criminals in their midst merely increased the possibility of danger.

It was in response to these concerns that England developed the policy of transportation.[4] To relieve prison overcrowding, people were transported to other lands, first the American colonies and after the War of Independence to the far more distant land of Australia.

Long sea voyages had, however, always resulted in disease and death among crew and passengers. As noted, a major cause of illness was scurvy. Since fruits and vegetables would not keep on long sea voyages, travelers were deprived of necessary dietary supplements. The result was rotting gums, arthritic joints, and eventually death. By the mid-1700s, it was understood that scurvy was a dietary problem. Captain James Cook found that when he fed his crew sauerkraut, malt, and "portable soup," made by boiling down meat broth into gummy cake, he could defeat scurvy.[5] Thus, the bouillon cube and sauerkraut made possible long sea voyages, and eventually the exploration and colonization of Australia. The improved ability to survive the long sea voyage to Australia in turn provided an alternative to the prison overcrowding of eighteenth-century England. It was to this distant land that prisoners were now sent, thereby relieving the overcrowded jails and removing from the midst of respectable English society "the dangerous classes."

What lessons can be learned from this history? We now turn to that question.

The Lessons of History

The lessons of the eighteenth-century English experience are straightforward. First, as has been noted throughout this book, policy innovations often create more problems than they solve. Recall the discussion of the introduction of prisons in the United States in Chapter 5. Originally thought of as a humane alternative to flogging and other physical punishments, the prisons of Quaker charity became overcrowded dens of brutality and vice by 1850.

Second, getting tough with crime is not without cost. Overcrowded prisons and the expense of transportation resulted from the large number of capital offenses legislated in eighteenth-century England. In the United States, overcrowded prisons, riots, and extreme brutality arose from nineteenth-century long-term sentencing policies. And now in the 1990's history repeats itself, with prison populations far exceeding physical capacity. In the late 1970s, state

Table 13-1 A Record Prison Census

	Total Number of Inmates	Female Inmates	Percentage Increase From Previous Year	Male Inmates	Percentage Increase From Previous Year
1977	300,024	12,279		287,745	
1978	307,276	12,746	3.8%	284,630	2.4%
1979	314,457	12,995	2.0%	301,462	2.4%
1980	329,821	13,420	3.3%	316,401	5.0%
1981	369,930	15,537	15.8%	364,393	12.0%
1982	413,806	17,785	14.5%	396,021	11.7%
1983	436,855	19,020	6.9%	417,835	5.5%
1984	462,002	20,794	9.3%	441,208	5.6%
1985	503,271	23,124	11.2%	480,147	8.8%
1986	546,659	26,610	15.1%	520,049	8.3%

Source: Bureau of Justice Statistics.

legislatures decided to get tough on crime. Longer sentences and reduced opportunities for probation and parole caused a prison population explosion.

A third lesson to be learned concerns the impact innovative technology can have on social policy. The discovery of bouillon and the beneficial results of sauerkraut in the diet advanced the capacity to travel long distances by sea. At the same time, it made possible the transportation of thousands of Britons from a safe secure home to the uncharted wilds of Australia. In the process, brutal suffering was endured by these unfortunates. Today, the microchip has made possible travel to distant planets. At the same time, this technological innovation is beginning to make itself felt in the area of corrections. The microchip makes possible the confinement of people to their homes through electronic monitoring of their movements. The history of correctional policy has been and continues to be one filled with paradox and contradiction. In the 1990s, state legislators and correctional managers are being uncomfortably reminded of this fact.

Prison Overcrowding Today

By the mid-1980s, prison and jail overcrowding presented a serious challenge to the criminal justice policy community. At the end of 1986, the combined state and federal prison population was 546,659.[6] This represents a 66% increase in the population in six years.[7] The Bureau of Justice statistics estimated that state prisons were operating between 106% and 124% of their capacity.[8] Estimates of federal prisons suggest that they were operating at 127% to 159% of their capacities.[9] Table 13-1 shows the increase in prison population from 1977 through 1986. The strain this has put on the physical capacity of state and federal facilities can be underscored by noting current jail statistics.

While prisons are generally thought of as places of long-term punishment (anything beyond a year), jails are generally thought of as short-term facilities for those awaiting trial or for those who have been sentenced to less than a year's confinement. Prison overcrowding, has, however, caused a backup in the whole system. Those sentenced to terms in prisons literally have no place to go. Therefore, local jails are now housing state prison inmates who are awaiting an opening in the prison system. By the end of 1986, local jails housed 13,770 state prisoners.[10] This represents 2.7% of all state inmates. A combination of demographic and policy factors led to this booming population.

The perceived dramatic rise in the crime rate during the 1970s once again led to policy decisions aimed at doing something about "the dangerous classes." As we have seen, the question of whether or not the increase in crime was as dramatic as it appeared is open to question. Clearly, part of the rise was simply a demographic phenomenon as baby boomers entered the high crime–prone years. At any rate, by 1979 state legislators and the federal government were embarking on sentencing practices that would increase the minimum length of sentences to be served by those convicted of crime and would severely curtail the use of probation and parole. The results were both immediate and obvious. Prisons began to crowd up. More people went in and fewer came out. What was not obvious was the cost of such a policy.

Cost Factors in Overcrowding

A seemingly simple solution to the problem of prison overcrowding is the construction of new facilities. Upon examination, the solution is neither simple nor inexpensive. To illustrate, the state of Missouri at the time this is being written has approximately 4,000 inmates over its physical capacity to house prisoners. The prison system was initially built to house 6,000 inmates. It now holds over 10,000.[11] It would therefore take a minimum of eight 500-bed facilities to house the current population. Unfortunately, estimates are of continued increases in the prison population, so that the state of Missouri is anticipating 15,000 by 1990.[12] Even assuming eight new prisons could be built relatively quickly, the end result would be eight new but still overcrowded facilities. As it is, however, prison construction from the time of planning to when the doors open is usually three years. In the meantime, population growth has continued unabated. Its seems clear that construction alone cannot address the problem of overcrowding. Under current conditions, a new prison will not simply be overcrowded by the time it is open, but its design capacity will be seriously exceeded.

The issue of whether to build or not is made more complex by the cost of prison construction. The cost of a 500-bed medium-security prison can be conservatively estimated at $79,327 *per bed space*.[13] This does not include the cost of site acquisition. Thus, the total cost of a single prison would approach $40 million. The breakdown of this cost figure is indicated in Table 13-2. Notice that governments, much like individuals buying a house, finance the

Table 13-2 Base Capital Specifications and Costs 500-Bed Medium Security Missouri Prison

Type of Space	Gross Square Feet per Inmate Bed	Cost/SF	Total Costs
Management and Staff	47.9	$ 74	$ 3,545
Support	116.5	93	10,835
Program	136.9	76	10,404
Housing	302.6	100	30,260
Base Construction Cost/Bed			$55,044
Other Costs			
Architect's Fees (8% est., range = 7–9%)			4,881
Change Order Contingency Fee (5%)			3,050
Construction Supervision Fee (2.3%)			1,403
Equipment (13.5%)			8,237
Insurance and Bid (1%)			610
Subtotal			$73,225
Site Acquisition Costs			
Site Preparation Costs (10%)			6,102
Total Bed Cost			$79,327
			(+ site acquisition)
Total Prison Cost			$39,663,500
			(+ site acquisition)

Gross square feet include wall thicknesses, hallways, foyers, etc. 1982 dollars; New York = 100 (generally higher in West; lower in South). Moveable beds, bookcases, etc. Includes landscaping, utility lines, parking lots, driveways, etc.

Source: B. L. Wayson, G. P. Falkin and M. T. Cruz (consulting architect), *User's Manual for Estimating Standards Compliance Costs* (Washington, DC: 1981).

Year	Cost
1	$13,221,166
2	$14,937,166 ($13.2 million × 13%)
3	$16,887,166 ($14.9 million × 13%)
Total Cost with Interest	$45,045,498

cost of construction. This in fact raises the total cost of the project to over $45 million when interest on the loan is included. If a state were to embark upon the construction of eight such facilities, the cost would exceed $360,363,984. This figure does not include the cost of staffing such facilities. With the addition of operating costs, the total bill for this project would easily approach $2.5 billion. Keep in mind that this expenditure would not in fact solve the problem of overcrowding. In light of these physical and fiscal limitations, state legislators who in the 1980s supported stiff sentences are now beginning to rethink their position and introduce legislation that provides alternatives to minimum mandatory sentences. Nevertheless, as we have seen, the history of alternatives does not present a particularly optimistic answer to the question, "Can't we do better?" To understand why this is so, we need to explore both the practical and symbolic significance of punishment. In other words, "Why do we punish?"

CRIMINOLOGICAL/CRIMINAL JUSTICE CONSIDERATIONS

The Purposes of Punishment and Its Mitigation

Society punishes its miscreants for a number of reasons. Traditionally, punishment served the function of retribution. Literally, society demanded repayment in the form of punishment from those who violated its norms. The philosophy of retributive punishment was often supported by religious beliefs. Society would attempt to save the individual and atone for his or her transgression by making the individual suffer. As we have seen, this often meant some type of physical assault, literally beating the devil out of a person.

During the eighteenth century, the philosophy of retribution was slowly replaced by other justifications for punishment. The classical school of Beccaria and Bentham discussed in Chapter 10 argued that punishment could be used to deter people from committing crime. Such an approach involved both specific deterrence—the deterrence of a specific individual—and general deterrence—the deterrence of others through the example of what happens to those who violate the law. Isolation, the removal of the individual from respectable society, also provided a justification for punishment. This was the major justification for the policy of transportation. During the nineteenth century, a desire to reform the individual in a manner similar to the way physicians cured diseases came to the fore in correctional philosophy. Again, however, as we have noted, the rhetoric of medicine often merely camouflaged extremely brutal treatment. Finally, as the sociologist Durkheim showed, punishment served to clarify social norms. Rules for behavior are sometimes so general that the exact actions proscribed are not clear. Thus, while it is both morally and legally wrong to steal, it may not be clear when this prohibition is violated. If I take $.25 from my son's piggy bank, is this stealing? The answer is, "It depends." One of the things that it depends upon is whether or not such behavior is punished. Punishment helps define the limits of tolerable activity.

No matter what philosophy of punishment predominates at a particular historical moment, mitigation of the punishment has always been possible. Therefore, we need to ask why a state or government would want to mitigate the punishment it legally prescribes for a criminal act.

We have already seen one reason for such mitigation. Paradoxically, by mitigating a sentence, a sovereign reinforces the notion that he or she controls the power of life or death. By showing mercy, the king can also demonstrate control. Thus, punishment and mitigation in tandem perform an important symbolic function for governments. It reinforces important governmental prerogatives.

Punishment is also mitigated because it does not meet the goals envisioned for it. For example, its ability to deter can be challenged. While many studies have found some evidence for a deterrent effect, others seem to cast doubt on the efficacy of punishment in meeting this goal. As one authoritative panel has noted, the state of both available data and current research methods makes it difficult to show conclusively whether or not punishment deters.[14]

Mitigation may also come about as a response to the problems created by current forms of punishment. Transportation was an alternative to hanging, a punishment which if carried out in all cases might well have incited civil unrest. As Chapter 4 demonstrated, the rapid development of probation and parole was in part due to the prison overcrowding of the middle to late 1800s.

Finally, particular punishments may simply be too expensive for a society to engage in on a wholesale basis. Current prison overcrowding suggests the need for alternatives based on such monetary considerations.

Punishment and mitigation often seem to be different sides of the same coin. Both can symbolically reinforce the existing power arrangements within a society and strengthen the prevailing philosophy of punishment that justifies particular actions toward an offender. This dynamic can be illustrated by exploring the current place of prison in modern-day American correctional policy.

Prison as a Symbol

Prison is the least used correctional alternative. As Figure 13-1 shows, less than 20% of those under correctional supervision are in prison. Probation is by far the most used form of correctional supervision.

Given these figures, it is surprising that so much academic, policy, and popular attention is given to the institution of prison. The reason for this is simple. Prison forms the benchmark against which all other forms of punishment and correctional intervention are measured.

Prison as a Total Institution

How did prison gain such a symbolic stronghold on our ideas of punishment? The answer lies in the historical, sociological, and policy dynamics surrounding prison and its use.

Recall from Chapter 5 that prisons were largely a product of eighteenth-century rationalism and nineteenth-century progressive political thought. In a sense, prisons straddled three correctional eras. As noted, early prisons were somewhat like monasteries in concept and design. Their administration stressed a religious as well as a behavioral conversion. Prisons thus had connections to the earliest period of correctional history which stressed saving the soul of the miscreant. This period also supported, however, a philosophy of physical punishment. Indeed, it was because of a reaction to some of the excesses of this period that prison became viewed as a humane alternative. Prisons were therefore also anchored in the modern era which stressed humanitarian treatment and legal reform. Finally, as a physical expression of emerging social work sciences, prison became tied to the era of treatment, particularly through the reformatory movement in the United States.

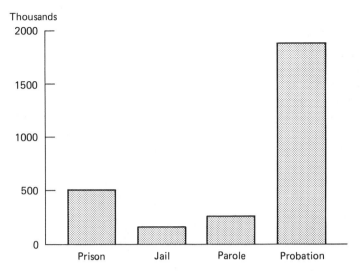

This chart is based on data from the Report to the Nation on Crime and Justice; 2ed., 1988. Jail data are for June 30, 1983. All other data are for December 31, 1985.

Figure 13-1 Persons under correctional supervision
Source: This chart is based on data from the *Report to the Nation on Crime and Justice*, 2nd ed., 1988. Jail data are for June 30, 1983. All other data are for December 31, 1988.

Given the prison's history as a bridge among the various historical periods of corrections, it is little wonder that prison occupies so much attention in correctional circles. Additionally, however, the dynamics of prison present a fascinating puzzle to those of us in the social sciences.

The Total Institution

The maximum security prison is an example par excellence of what social scientists would term a total institution. Other examples would be seminaries and convents, military academies, concentration camps, mental hospitals, and to a lesser extent, boot camps. All of these institutions have one thing in common. They attempt to resocialize individuals, literally to make someone over into a new or different kind of person.

To understand this process, it is first necessary to understand the socialization process itself. To socialize somebody means to make them fit for companionship with others and to take basic biological drives and needs and convert these to the needs of society. This process is often most intense during the period of infancy and early childhood. At this point, the aim is to take the newborn human animal and through the socialization process turn him or her into a human being. In a real sense, we learn how to be human.

The socialization process seeks to accomplish four basic goals. The first of these is the inculcation of discipline. The human infant must learn to control physiological impulses, restrict immediate gratification, and live up to the moral norms of society. Toilet training is an attempt to discipline the physiological impulse to eliminate. Weaning the child from the mother's breast or from the bottle and introducing solid foods involves disciplining the child's desire for food. Fortunately, most college students seem to be able to control these two impulses, at least most of the time. The important thing to remember is that the ability to do so resulted from the socialization process that provided the discipline to achieve these ends.

The second task of the socialization process is to instill aspiration, that is, the desire to achieve certain defined social objectives. Thus, American parents generally want their children to do well in school, to be polite, to be competitive, and to show initiative. The fact that some goals may be contradictory, for example, competitiveness and politeness, is of little concern. Societies develop myths to handle such contradictory expectations. Thus, everyone can be president, the United States provides unlimited opportunity, and people get what they deserve.

The third goal of the socialization process is to teach appropriate social roles. Social roles can either be ascribed or achieved. Thus, being male or female in this society is a biologically ascribed role that has considerable social learning attached to it. We learn the appropriate behaviors for males and females as defined by this culture. On the other hand, being a college professor is an achieved role. In this kind of role one learns specific job skills and appropriate social attitudes for successfully carrying out the role.

The final role of the socialization process is to teach specific sets of skills in order to accomplish socially desired ends. If the socialization process is successful, social ends will more often than not match individual desires. In our society, skills such as reading, writing, and computation are probably minimally necessary to get ahead. Were large numbers of people deficient in these areas, both the individual and the society would suffer.

Because of the intertwining of social needs and personal needs, society has a vested interest in seeing to it that individuals obtain at least a certain minimum degree of socialization. In fact, not everyone can be president, but everyone can work hard to achieve socially desirable ends. In the event the socialization process does not seem to take, society provides a number of alternatives. Removal from society has been the most historically popular. As we have seen, this can be accomplished through death, transportation, or isolation. However, society can also try to reform the individual. Since infants seem to be the most malleable of human beings, the more drastic the resocialization required, the more the process needs to reduce an individual to this state of infancy. This is the task of the total institution.

The total institution represents a basic social arrangement wherein the individual is confined to a relatively small space. Within this space sleeping, playing, working, and personal activities will all take place. Moreover, the activities will take place with a severely restricted group of people. Notice the parallels between this situation and that of the infant. By physically confining space, control is significantly increased. Thus, a person depends for privilege upon the largesse of those administering the institution. Things that we ordinarily take for granted as an adult cannot be taken for granted in such a situation. Thus, we do not generally ask for permission to take a shower. In a total institution such permission may be required and not routinely given. All other basic necessities and/or activities are similarly controlled. By making a person dependent upon the total institution for such basics, the individual theoretically becomes more malleable. To gain even the most insignificant privilege, it is necessary to adhere to the norms and values the total institution is attempting to inculcate. To regain adult status it is necessary to be made over into the image the total institution thinks best.

Within most total institutions, people resist this assault on their adult status. Thus, a much more complex social pattern is created than would be suggested by the theory of the total institution. Erving Goffman's *Asylums* is helpful in understanding this observation.[15] The book, a study of the social life of a mental hospital, points out that every institution has two faces. There is the public face, or the official goals and practices of the organization, and the private face, or the underlife of the institution. Both are real, and institutional life is a constant movement between the two faces. Thus, in the prison, there are the "make-do's" talked about by Goffman, those things that substitute for things not available on the inside. Prison hooch, exploitive homosexual relationships, a prison economy based on tobacco and/or cookies are examples. They also indicate that the total institution is far from successful in its attempt to control its inmate population totally. Thus, a complex social system develops. Within the prison, certain inmates learn how to work the system. These "con politicians" and "hustlers" get good jobs and, in doing so, are able to supply the goods and sometimes the services that help create a viable system of economic exchange. Because there are more inmates than guards, a certain consensual understanding develops which allows proscribed activities to go on. Within the prison, "free places" exist which guards ordinarily ignore on their rounds. These provide the locations where the underlife of institutions can flourish.

As within any social system, there are those who attempt to exploit rather than work for what the system has to offer. Therefore, prisons have inmates who are known as "low-riders," who steal and hijack from other inmates. This activity together with exploitive homosexual conduct can make prison a very tense place to be. Thus, prison creates a dynamic that in some ways defeats the official purpose of reform and resocialization. The deprivation of imprisonment leads to make-do's that are clearly deviant. Moreover, the institution, in creating a gulf between the watched and the watchers, makes the identification of the former with the latter (and therefore, presumably with the values of conventional society) difficult. If an inmate identifies with guards or administration he becomes in prison lingo a "square john" or a "snitch." The subculture of prisoners treats deviants the same way general society does. It seeks to get rid of those who violate its norms. In the New Mexico prison riot, the bloodiest in the history of the United States, the inmates who were brutally murdered were those who had reputations of cooperation with the administration.[16]

A comment from Claude Brown's book *Manchild in the Promised Land*, made by an inmate who had "graduated" from the state reformatory into a maximum security prison, underscores the paradox of imprisonment:

> Yeah. The time I did in Woodburn, the times I did on the Rock, that was college, man. Believe me, it was college. I did four years in Woodburn. And I guess I've done a total of about two years on the Rock in about the last six years. Every time I went there, I learned a little more. When I go to jail now, I live, man. I'm right at home. That's the odd part about it. If you look at it, a cat like me is just cut out to be in jail. It could never hurt me, 'cause I never had what the good folks call a home and all that kind of shit to begin with. So when I went to jail, the first time I went away, when I went to Warwick, I made my own home. It was all right. Shit, I learned how to live. Now when I go back to the joint, anywhere I go, I know some people. If I go to any of the jails in New York, or if I go to a slam in Jersey, I still run into a lot of cats I know. It's almost like a family.[17]

The dynamics of the total institution generally, and of the prison specifically, have fascinated social scientists. Despite the tremendous effort to control, inmates are able to create complex social dynamics that resist the onslaught of institutional intervention. Human ingenuity creates an oasis of freedom within a desert of deprivation. Gresham Sykes's book *Society of Captives*, written more than 20 years ago, underscores this point specifically as it relates to prison life:

> Indeed, the glaring conclusion is that despite the guns and the surveillance, the searches and precautions of the custodians, the actual behavior of the inmate population differs markedly from that which is called for by official commands and decrees. Violence, fraud, theft, aberrant sexual behavior—all are commonplace occurrences in the daily round of institutional existence in spite of the fact that the maximum security prison is conceived of by society as the ultimate weapon for the control of the criminal and his deviant actions. Far from being omnipotent rulers who have crushed all signs of rebellion against their regime, the custodians are engaged in a continuous struggle to maintain order—and it is a struggle in which the custodians frequently fail. Offenses committed by one inmate against another occur often, as do offenses committed by inmates against the officials and their rules. And the number of undetected offenses is, by universal agreement of both officials and inmates, far larger than the number of offenses which are discovered.[18]

The above discussion should make clear why prison has occupied much academic time and attention. The prison has also, however, captured the attention of the policy maker and the general public. Ironically, the attention that has been paid to it has often reinforced and condoned its most violent aspects.

POLICY CONSIDERATIONS:
THEORIES/ARGUMENTS/APPLICATIONS

Scared Straight

As reported by James Finkenaur, "Scared Straight" represents a program that simultaneously reinforces the most negative stereotypes of inmates while assuaging the public's conscience that something ought to be done to prevent people from engaging in a life of crime.[19] The program takes troublesome teenagers into a maximum security prison to be verbally abused by selected inmates. The abuse takes the form of horror stories about what it is like to be in prison. Accounts of homosexual rapes, assaults, and personal degradation, liberally sprinkled with four-letter words, are delivered to the youths. The purpose is to "scare the youths straight."

Although the program received a great deal of both popular and professional support when it was first introduced, its supposed efficacy was soon challenged by Finkenaur and others.[20] A public debate ensued, and eventually the program was modified. Nevertheless, Scared Straight–like programs still operate in some jurisdictions.

The horrors of prison life graphically portrayed were supposed to deter would-be offenders. Afterward, much of the debate centered around whether or not the program had obtained the success claimed for it. Interestingly, as Finkenaur points out, relatively few people asked the question of why conditions were so horrible in the prison in the first place. By having prisoners describe in graphic detail their prison experience, a number of diverse needs could be met. First, prisoners reinforced the stereotype the public had of them. This in turn justified the brutal conditions under which the prisoners lived. Second, the inmates who participated in the program themselves were rewarded by increased freedom and the ability to travel around and relate their experiences. Since these prisoners were for the most part lifers, this privilege was of some consequence. It gave them more freedom and provided a relatively tranquil stage wherein they could exhibit their toughness without the usual consequences. Finally, as noted above, everyone could feel that this display of aggression and horror was ultimately doing good. Wayward youth would be made better. With these obvious advantages, no one needed to concern themselves with prison reform.

Between the Attica uprising of 1971, where 39 people died, and the New Mexico state prison riots of 1979, there were 39 major prison riots in the United States.[21] A total of 300 inmates died in these uprisings.[22] As overcrowding increases the pressures on correctional institutions, prison unrest and brutality can be expected to continue. Why legislators do not act more vigorously to correct conditions that breed violence in these institutions is indicated by the symbolic place of prisons in our consciousness. They are a place to house violent, unsocialized predators. Thus, prison violence is to be expected. The fact that most inmates do not fit this stereotype has been irrelevant to state legislators. It has not, however, been irrelevant to federal judges.

Federal Judges as Correctional Policymakers

Beginning in 1972 with *Ruiz* v. *Estelle*, judges have taken a serious interest in the conditions that lead to prison violence. David Ruiz was an inmate of the Texas Department of Corrections. He filed suit against the prison director, Jim Estelle, claiming his constitutional rights had been violated and citing the cruel and unusual punishment clause of the Eight Amendment. Ruiz's suit was joined by seven other inmates and the Department of Justice. After seven years of investigation and a year-long trial, Judge William Wayne Justice declared virtually all aspects of the overcrowded Texas system to be unconstitutional.[23] To quote Judge Justice, "An unconstitutional atmosphere of fear and violence permeates prison life in the Texas Department of Corrections."[24] Overcrowding, inadequate health care, denial of due process, inaccessibility to the courts, inadequate safety, in short, the well-known secrets of prison life, were finally being dealt with officially. As of 1986, 38 states were under some kind of federal court mandate to improve local prison conditions. The violence of the prison subculture was no longer to be an accepted part of doing the business of corrections.

Changing prison life will involve more, however, than simply institutional reform. While the prison subculture develops in part because of deprivation, it seems clear that other factors also contribute to the violent aspects of some prisons. Most notable among these other factors is the presence of gang affiliations in prison. Thus, the prison subculture is also formed by cultural diffusion. Violent street values from outside the prison walls enter into the correctional facility with the inmates. Thus, certain prisons are hotbeds of gang violence and racial tension. White, black, and Chicano gangs war for turf just as they do on the streets of certain of our cities. Cultural diffusion plus deprivation plus the American tendency towards building large prison facilities all combine to create a tense violent atmosphere. Thus, by itself, reducing the size of the prison does not seem to lessen the atmosphere of violence. In fact, evidence from the Texas prison system shows that the amount of both inmate-on-inmate violence and inmate-on-guard violence increased after *Ruiz*.[25] Part of the explanation appears to be a shift in power relationships among inmates and staff which allowed for greater inmate gang activity.[26]

Unfortunately, despite its problems, the prison exercises symbolic control over the whole field of corrections. The consequence of using prison as a punishment benchmark for other kinds of correctional intervention is discussed below.

Alternatives

Since prison is a symbolic benchmark against which other forms of correctional intervention are measured, alternatives generally mean alternatives to imprisonment. Such alternatives can include the requirement of community service on the part of the person convicted of a crime, restitution to the victim, house arrest, probation and parole, and halfway house residency. Each of these represent a less restrictive mode of correctional control than the prison environment. Moreover, many of the alternatives are cheaper to administer. However, because these are measured against prison commitment, any alternative, no matter how punishing, is viewed as giving the offender a break. As a result, alternatives are often considered to be less punishment than a person deserves. In the strange calculus of criminal justice, therefore, alternatives to imprisonment end up being used as alternatives to the least punishing correctional strategy rather than to prison itself. An example will illustrate the point.

Mrs. Jones was picked up for shoplifting. The circumstances of her case were as follows. While shopping for groceries, Mrs. Jones put a large roll-on deodorant in her coat pocket. She was observed by a store security officer. At the checkout counter, she paid for her groceries in the cart. She then walked out of the store and was stopped by a security guard who claimed she took the roll-on deodorant without paying for it. She claimed to have forgotten the deodorant was in her pocket. Nevertheless, the store decided to prosecute. On advice of counsel, she pled guilty to stealing under $150. What would be the appropriate correctional disposition in this case?

Mrs. Jones paid approximately $200 in attorney's fees. She also lost three days of work attempting to get the matter settled. Thus, she already suffered a significant financial loss for her action, assuming that in fact she had intended to steal the deodorant. One could argue that given the circumstances of this case, Mrs. Jones had been punished enough. But the jurisdiction within which this occurred had recently established a community service alternative. Those sentenced to community service were required to work a specified number of hours a week in some community project. Since this alternative was now available, Mrs. Jones was sentenced to 300 hours of community service. For 25 Saturdays, eight hours a Saturday, she was required to help clean up and maintain a variety of public buildings. In light of her case, this punishment may seem quite severe. But at least it's not prison or jail.

This case illustrates a number of points about alternatives. First, they are often used to intervene with people who ordinarily would not be subject to formal correctional sanctions. Under ordinary circumstances, Mrs. Jones's travail through the court phase of the process would have been thought sufficient punishment. At her sentencing the judge may have admonished her, but that would be about the extent of correctional intervention. However, when a new correctional program is introduced, something more restrictive is now available to be used as a punishment.

A second characteristic of alternatives is that they seldom reduce prison populations. Instead, they end up correctionalizing a new population. Those ordinarily sentenced to prison still go there, and people like Mrs. Jones are given the "alternative."

Third, such an inversion of the process is possible because again prisons are the benchmark against which such alternatives are judged. Through a trick of language, the phrase, "At least it's not jail," seems to be giving the person a break. Obviously, most of us would prefer not to have these kinds of breaks.

The research literature on alternatives supports the rather gloomy caricature presented above. In an extensive review of research literature on alternatives, Austin and Krisberg note that criminal justice nets have become both stronger and more pervasive because of so-called alternative legislation.[27] As noted, rather than reducing reliance on prison, such legislation has often resulted in new forms of punishment that correctionalize new populations of offenders. These findings of course cast doubt on the cost-effectiveness of alternatives. New costs, not reduced costs, may result.

Unfortunately, this pessimistic assessment occurs at the time when many states face the dual crisis of extensive prison overcrowding and diminished economic resources. Thus, the search for alternatives continues. To be truly successful, however, an alternative must be viewed as a punishment in its own right and not as just a "break" being given to the offender. Without a change in this attitude, alternatives will continue to be simply adjuncts to the prison experience.

Probation

The long shadow that prison casts over the correctional enterprise can also be illustrated by examining the most used correctional intervention, probation. John Augustus is considered the founder of modern probation.[28] In the 1840s, this Boston bootmaker took it upon himself to have certain prisoners released to his care. John Augustus's work was clearly in the tradition of Beccaria and Bentham in that he firmly believed, "The object of the law is to reform criminals and to prevent crime, and not to punish maliciously or from a spirit of revenge."[29]

Then, as now, the custom of releasing prisoners to something other than the prison system was controversial. Thus, probation officers face a number of dilemmas in their task. From the point of view of the general public, as we have seen, anything less than imprisonment is viewed as being soft. Probation officers are often looked upon by both the public and others in the criminal justice system as "bleeding-heart" social workers. This view is not, however, shared by those subject to their control. For many on probation, the probation officer is simply an extension of that system of control that begins with law enforcement and ends ultimately in prison.

Added to these conflicting role definitions are the added burdens of large case loads, a court bureaucracy whose key decisions are made without the input of the probation officer, and a community that is reluctant to provide resources for the offenders in its midst. How a probation officer copes with these dilemmas shapes the use of probation in this society.

Although probation offices are organized differently depending upon state and local ordinances, two general models prevail. In some jurisdictions, probation is under the control of the local court. The probation officer literally works for judges. In other states, probation and parole are centralized in the executive branch of the state government. Regardless of how a local office is organized, the probation function will often consist of three distinct activities.

The first step in the probation process is an investigation to determine if an individual would make a good prospect for treatment in the community. This task is performed by a presentence investigator or a presentence writer. The presentence investigation is conducted during the time between a guilty plea or verdict and sentencing by a judge.

Presentence writers face a unique set of conflicts. While their main function is to assess treatment potential, and therefore their role seems to be anchored in the medical model, presentence writers must confront the fact that the court bureaucracy has already pretty much decided on an appropriate penalty through the plea bargaining process. Thus the medical model conflicts with the bureaucratic system of case processing. Large case loads, however, require a routine resolving of this dilemma. The large bulk of cases will receive probation. Therefore, the investigator will not spend a great deal of time looking at these. He or she will structure the recommendation based on what has typically happened in the past to these kinds of cases. At the other end of this seriousness scale, a relatively small proportion of cases will be given prison time. Here, too, the investigator is faced with a fairly clear-cut disposition and therefore need not spend a great deal of time on investigation. Finally, there are some cases that fall into a gray area. The person may be a repeat offender of property crimes, but still present some hope for reform. It is in this last type of case that the medical model may assert itself and an assessment of treatment potential actually take place. In most cases, however, bureaucratic values outweigh treatment values.

If the person is granted probation, he or she will be assigned to a probation officer. This is the most public function of probation and parole work and is the task usually associated with the term "probation." The case worker, however, faces a set of unique conflicts. At this level, the conflict is between the medical model and punishment and control. Organizational dynamics tilt the resolution of this conflict towards punishment and control. First, the only means of control a probation officer can exercise over clients is the threat of revocation, that is, imprisonment. Thus, he or she is viewed as an extension of the more intrusive correctional process. This of course tends to undermine any kind of therapeutic or helping relationship between client and officer. Large case loads require attention to bureaucratic processing. This is illustrated by the fact that in many jurisdictions probation is referred to as "making paper." Probation officers must keep a paper track on individual clients. Therefore, addresses must be updated, employment kept current, and a whole variety of details on a client's life that can be reduced to a written record must be kept track of and recorded. Unfortunately, most of the clients on probation are not particularly good at or concerned with bureaucratic record keeping. Therefore, a failure to report a change of address or a job change does not seem to be a particularly horrendous act. For the probation officer, however, such record keeping is crucial to his or her success within the bureaucracy. Therefore, the failure of a client to provide such information on a timely basis becomes viewed as indicative of more serious problems. The bureaucracy demands control of such details, and again the way to ensure control is to threaten prison for failure to comply with the bureaucratic rules.

The third reason for the tendency of probation to take on a control rather than a treatment orientation is the disposition of the clients themselves. By the time an individual arrives in front of the probation officer's desk, he or she has been through a system which has probably increased the bitterness and disorganization in his or her life. Many clients will have spent some time in jail. While jails share some of the characteristics of a total institution, they are different in a fundamental respect. Because jail sentences are relatively short, there is very little chance for the development of a stable subculture. Therefore, jail time often represents a cutting of familiar social bonds with nothing to replace them. Jail experience is truly one of disorientation. It is for this reason that suicide is often a problem for those confined in jail.[30]

The disorienting aspects of jail are often reinforced by the rest of the legal process. As noted in the last chapter, attorneys understand and control the court bureaucracy. Yet, from the point of view of the person accused of the crime, this system appears to be both secretive and arbitrary. The end result is a process which the client neither understands nor controls. Sentencing therefore appears to take place in a vacuum. The person will feel more a victim than a victimizer.

The probation office is often the first place where an individual has a chance to tell his or her story.[31] Of course, by this time it is too late. The person is already under a correctional jurisdiction. The bitterness and confusion this can engender does not add to the relationship of the probation officer and the client.

The final task of the probation or parole officer can be to garner community resources to reintegrate the individual back into the community. This role involves social advocacy. For most of us, medical treatment, job placement services, and adequate food and shelter are resources readily available in our community. This is often not the case with those subject to criminal justice processing. For example, the medical insurance I carry through my place of employment covers any treatment I may need for alcohol or substance abuse. Such treatment is generally quite expensive with costs running from $245 a day to over $1,000 a day.[32] Alcohol and drug treatment is therefore a growth industry as employers through employee health care benefits take on greater responsibility to provide care in this area. The key term is, however, "employees." Those without jobs cannot avail themselves easily of such services. This is precisely the circumstance in which most probationers find themselves. Given the tremendous number of people on probation, many probation offices are moving away from the idea of the probation officer being a counselor. Instead, probation officers are increasingly acting as brokers of community services. They put their clients in touch with existing resources rather than attempt to provide the resources themselves. Again, however, while such resources are available in most communities, they are not generally available to the clients of probation and parole. Therefore, the officer must sell his clients and the need for services to the general public.

This social advocacy task is often accomplished by a specific unit within probation and parole departments, often called community resource units. These workers, however, also face dilemmas. Here, the dilemma is between social advocacy and the prevailing political climate. In an era of get-tough crime philosophies, the notion of a community providing for its offenders is not popular, particularly when probation is viewed as being soft on crime. Again, such a view is reinforced because of the prison benchmark within correctional philosophy.

Finally, the importance of the prison benchmark for doing probation and parole can be illustrated by the legal mechanisms available to put somebody on probation. Two sentencing options are available to judges as a way of placing a person on probation.

The first of these is called a suspended imposition of sentence (SIS). Using this sentencing option, a judge can put a person on probation for up to five years. At the end of the probationary period, a person with no infractions will not be considered to have had a criminal conviction. The legal rule underlying this procedure is that a conviction on a criminal matter does not occur until a sentence has been imposed. Obviously, the SIS option has some distinct advantages for a defendant. Upon successful completion of the probationary period the individual can answer "no" on any employment application that asks, "Have you ever been convicted of a crime?" On the other hand, the individual does face some risk. Under the SIS option, if an individual violates the conditions of probation, he or she can be sentenced to a maximum prison term available for the original offense. Thus, a sword figuratively hangs over the head of the person put on an SIS probation. He or she can escape a permanent criminal stigma or face a longer period of incarceration than they would have, had an original sentence been imposed. Again, note that the sword is prison confinement.

The second method of imposing probation is through the suspended execution of sentence (SES). Using this option, a judge in fact imposes a specific prison sentence, say three years. He or she then suspends the execution of this sentence and puts the person on probation for the period of time indicated. Under this option, if a person violates the conditions of probation, he or she can only be sentenced for the amount of time originally imposed. On the other hand, the execution of the prison sentence can take place at any period during the probationary status. Thus, if a person were to violate the conditions of probation on the last day of his three-year sentence served in the community, he or she could then be sent to prison for three years. Also, under this option the individual does have a criminal record and could not answer "no" to the question of having ever been convicted of a crime. These two legal options permanently enshrine prison as the benchmark against which probation must be measured.

Other Alternatives

The doubling of the prison population during the last decade has led a strange collection of bedfellows to express interest in alternatives to incarceration. Warren E. Berger, the former Chief Justice of the United States, in calling for a major effort to change our prisons, stated, "We need not and must not suffer warehouses indefinitely." Humanitarian reformers, pragmatic correction officials, fiscally conservative state legislators and academics have joined together in chorusing a ringing "Amen!" As individuals have explored different kinds of alternatives to prison, a variety of new sentencing options have emerged.

Intensive probation provides an intermediate step between the relatively loose control of a normal probation and the extensive control of prison. Intensive probation usually involves much smaller case loads for the probation worker, frequent home visits and/or visits to the workplace by a probation officer, and special attention paid to any drug and alcohol problems. Obviously, for this kind of intensive community scrutiny, it is necessary to have an increased number of probation officers. Initially an expensive undertaking, increasing the number of probation officers can in the long run prove a much cheaper alternative than massive building programs required by current prison sentencing policies.

It is now possible to maintain an electronic surveillance of people in the community. Those on restricted probations in some jurisdictions are required to wear arm bracelets that send out an electronic impulse. If they go beyond so many feet from their telephone, a signal is sent to the appropriate probation office to indicate a violation. Thus, for instance, a person could be confined to his home in the evening. Electronic monitoring can help ensure compliance to this probationary condition.

Electronic monitoring and other alternatives to imprisonment raise a number of issues. Since the shadow of the prison pervades all of correctional philosophy, and since it is clear that prisons are places for cultural diffusion (that is, values of the outside world influence how prisons are run), one must ask whether or not there can be leakage of the prison mentality to the community. An ethic of control, applied to some members of our community while they are in their homes and neighborhoods, raises the specter of control becoming a dominant motif for the ordinary citizen. One only has to drive down the streets of our cities to observe homes barred and shuttered against the outside. At times, the homes themselves begin to resemble small prisons. Stores, parking lots, banks, and large shopping malls are monitored by cameras, mostly recording the ongoing activity of ordinary citizens. In such an environment, conformity can become a prized value and any deviance, criminal or not, quickly censured and curtailed. Under these circumstances the community itself becomes a kind of prison.

To fully explore the implications of this, it is necessary to turn to questions of how the state legislatures cope with the demands made of them, particularly in the area of crime, corrections, and community safety. We turn to these issues in Chapter 14.

SUMMARY

What Was Said

- Prison overcrowding is not a new phenomenon and a review of its history can teach a number of valuable lessons.
    - —Policy innovations often create more problems than they solve.
    - —Getting tough with crime is not without cost.
    - —Innovative technologies (such as bouillon cubes and microchips) can be used to enhance freedom or restrict it.
- State, federal, and local correctional facilities are all experiencing severe problems of overcrowding.
- A single 500-bed security prison built in the Midwest, where construction costs are relatively low, would cost approximately $45 million.
- States cannot afford to build their way out of the overcrowding problem, nor, because of the extent of overcrowding, can building solve the problem.
- We punish people for a variety of reasons, including:
    - —retribution
    - —deterrence
    - —reform
    - —isolation
- Throughout the history of punishment there have always been mechanisms for mitigation.
- Prison, while the least used correctional alternative, functions as the primary symbol of our correctional system.

- Prisons attempt to function as total institutions, whereby individuals are reduced to a state of childlike dependence so that they may be resocialized.
- Individuals attempt to resist such assaults on their adult self, and thus prisons often end up creating oppositional cultures which reinforce deviant behavior.
- Federal judicial policy making affecting the operations of prisons is now widespread as courts attempt to rectify constitutionally impermissible conditions.
- Alternatives to incarceration are often used to "correctionalize" new populations of defendants and thus can have little effect on prison overcrowding.
- Probation is the most widely used correctional alternative.

What Was Not Said

- Reform of the correctional system should not be attempted.
- A single reform, for example, the reduction of overcrowding, will solve complex prison problems.
- Alternatives are necessarily "soft" on criminal offenders.

NOTES

1. Robert Hughes, *The Fatal Shore: The Epic of Australia's Founding* (New York: Alfred A. Knopf, 1987).

2. Ibid., pp. 23–24.

3. Ibid., p. 29.

4. Ibid., p. 66.

5. Ibid., p. 49.

6. "A Record Prison Census," *The New York Times*, May 17, 1987, p. 4E.

7. Ibid.

8. Ibid.

9. Ibid.

10. "Statistic of the Week," *National Journal*, No. 29 (July 18, 1987), 1874.

11. Planning/Research/EDP Unit, Missouri Department of Corrections (unpublished report, October, 1985).

12. Gary N. Keveles, "Commentary: More Prisons Aren't the Answer," *St. Louis Post-Dispatch*, 6 March 1986, p. 3B.

13. B. L. Wayson, G. P. Falkin, and M. T. Cruz (consulting architect), *User's Manual for Estimating Standards Compliance* (Washington, DC: 1981).

14. Alfred Blumstein, Jacqueline Cohen, and Daniel Nagin, eds., *Deterrence and Incapacitation: Estimating the Effects of Criminal Sanctions on Crime Rates* (Washington, DC: National Academy of Sciences, 1978), pp. 6–7.

15. Erving Goffman, *Asylums* (Garden City, NY: Anchor Books, 1961), p. 207.

16. National Institute of Justice, Crime File Series, "Prison Crowding," No. 6, "Inside Prison," No. 2.

17. Claude Brown, *Manchild in the Promised Land* (New York: Macmillan, 1965), p. 412.

18. Gresham M. Sykes, *The Society of Captives* (Princeton, NJ: Princeton University Press, 1958), pp. 42–43.

19. James O. Finkenauer, *Scared Straight!* (Englewood Cliffs, NJ: Prentice-Hall, Inc., 1982).

20. Ibid.

21. National Institute of Justice, Crime File Series.

22. Ibid.

23. Helen Clarke Molanphy, "The U.S. Courts and Prison Reform: Ruiz v. Estelle," *Prison Journal*, LXN (Fall-Winter 1984), 68–75.

24. Ibid., p. 69.

25. Sheldon Ekland-Olson, "Crowding, Social Control and Prison Violence: Evidence from the Past Ruis Years in Texas," *Society Review*, 20, No. 3 (1986) 389–421.

26. Ibid., pp. 411–413.

27. J. Austin and B. Krisberg, "The Unmet Promise of Alternatives to Incarceration," *Crime and Delinquency* (July 1982) 374–409.

28. Paul F. Cromwell, George G. Killinger, Hazel B. Kerper, Charles Walker, *Probation and Parole in the Criminal Justice System* (St. Paul, MN: West Publishing Company, 1985), p. 10.

29. Ibid., p. 11.

30. *Sourcebook of Criminal Justice Statistics 1986*, p. 398, Table 6.21.

31. James F. Gilsinan, *Doing Justice* (Englewood Cliffs, NJ: Prentice-Hall, Inc., 1982), p. 240.

32. Based on a review of select facilities in the St. Louis area.

XIV

Legislating Criminal Justice Policy

At the end of this chapter, the student will be able to:

A. Discuss the various influences that shape the legislative process.
B. Note the types of rewards available for distribution through the political process.
C. Note the usefulness of crime as a political issue.
D. Be aware of the difficulty facing those who wish to evaluate the results of legislative policy making.

ISSUE BACKGROUND

Rationality and Lawmaking

It is tempting to view lawmaking as a way to rationally order community affairs. Norton Long suggests that our mythology encourages this view.[1] The ancient Greeks believed government, the representative of the whole, was morally superior to the individual, idiosyncratic, self-centeredness of the one. This tradition carried on through the institution of the divinely appointed sovereign, the representative of a whole people. As we have seen, a secularized version of the philosopher/divine king developed in the nineteenth and early twentieth century as a result of the planning movement. Divine inspiration was replaced by rational, scientific approaches to community problem solving.

While our mythology encourages a rational view of lawmaking, experience suggests otherwise. As this book has shown, lawmaking appears to be a rather haphazard affair. Legislators respond to a variety of demands, some of which are contradictory, with little in-depth knowledge of either problems or solutions.

This chapter will explore in some detail the legislative process. First, the various elements of legislative decision making will be examined. How do legislators decide which issues deserve their attention? How do they gain information to make decisions on such issues? And finally, how does this information get translated into a bill and ultimately become law?

Second, the chapter will explore the various outcomes of the legislative process. What kind of results can reasonably be expected from the lawmaking process? Who benefits, and in what ways?

These questions lead to a third consideration. How does one go about evaluating the impact of legislative initiatives? What is the role of social science in this type of policy-making process?

To illustrate some of the answers to these questions and to provide an overall context for understanding lawmaking, the chapter will conclude with a case study. The case study will also underscore the salience of criminal justice issues for those engaged in the game of politics. Crime is not simply a problem to be solved. It is an opportunity for those exercising political power to meet a variety of both personal and organizational ends.

CRIMINOLOGICAL/CRIMINAL JUSTICE CONSIDERATIONS

Myths Influencing the Legislative Process

Chapter 1 described what has been termed a garbage can model of decision making. Problems and their solutions float around in a random manner with one of the former occasionally bumping in and sticking to one of the latter. While the "garbage can" provides a cogent metaphor for understanding much of the decision-making process, it would be a mistake to think of this process as totally random. In the world of the legislative policy maker, actions and reactions are predictable. The "garbage can" has a shape which constrains the number of problems and solutions that can come together. What provides this constraining structure?

Robert B. Reich, in his *Tales of a New America*, suggests that the American world view, including problems and their solutions, is informed by four morality tales or myths.[2] Americans tend to think of themselves as a special group, historically isolated from the tyrannies and evil of European and Asian ancestors. Ours is the country that protects the fragile flame of liberty. From what are we protecting it? Reich's answer is the title of the first morality tale, "The Mob at the Gates."[3] As a nation, we tend to see evil "out there." People and movements are waiting to take advantage of our freedoms to destroy this noble experiment in liberty. Recall our discussion in Chapter 10 of the Red Scare. This historical event is but one example of our tendency toward believing that evil lurks at our gates and we must be ever vigilant in controlling and/or destroying it.

Reich terms the second morality tale "The Triumphant Individual."[4] This is the belief that despite all odds the little guy can make it big. Novels, movies, and autobiographies continually reinforce this tale. From Horatio Alger to the "Rocky" movies and the popularity of autobiographies by people like Lee Iacocca and Chuck Yaeger, we are continually reminded of the individual's ability to triumph over all odds.

The third story we tell ourselves about ourselves is "The Benevolent Community."[5] We are a nation of neighbors always available to help each other. Former President Reagan's appeal for volunteerism rather than government bureaucracy to solve social problems taps the belief in the essential willingness of the community to aid those in need.

The final tale is described by Reich as "The Rot at the Top."[6] This is our fundamental belief in the adage, "Power corrupts and absolute power corrupts absolutely." Too much centralization of power, whether political or economic, has always been distrusted. Thus, reform efforts for a smaller federal government, deregulation, and protections against monopolistic practices periodically arise on our policy landscape.

These tales help structure the political culture in which policy decisions are made. They give shape to the "garbage can." Thus, not all problems and all solutions will enter a legislator's reality. Problems and their solutions are preselected based upon these recurrent myths in our political and social culture. Each of these tales has, however, a liberal and conservative version. For the conservative, the key policy strategy involves the application of discipline to people and institutions. The liberal, on the other hand, tends toward a strategy of accommodation.

In the conservative view the mob at the gates, whether composed of foreign or domestic enemies, is to be controlled through the might of military or police power. The liberal version of how to deal with the mob at the gates would stress the need for accommodation and conflict resolution. Beneficial treaties and/or programs of integration into the larger society represent strategies flowing from this view of the folk tale. Some of the current controversies in criminal justice policy can illustrate these differing versions of the mob at the gate story.

How do we deal with criminals? We can have strict laws with strict sentences and support police efforts to catch those who would disturb our domestic tranquility. When prisons become overcrowded, we can build more of them. Law and order will ensure domestic tranquility.

What can we do about the crime problem? We can provide more jobs and other legitimate opportunities for those who would turn to crime. Sentencing policies should be geared toward rehabilitation. Prison overcrowding can be relieved by more emphasis on community correction and greater attempts to integrate law violators back into the community. Repressive police practices threaten all of us and turn those who have violated the law even more bitter and more likely to harm us.

What causes crime? In the conservative view of the triumphant individual, those who do not want to work, who would rather steal, and who fail to buy into the American dream are the culprits in the crime story. The answer to the question "What causes crime?" is straightforward. Bad people.

What causes crime? In the liberal view, the benevolent community has failed the individual. Crime is less an individual characteristic than the characteristic of a system and of a system's failure to integrate and support all of its members. The system has made it more difficult for the underdog to triumph.

Where should criminal justice resources be concentrated? For the conservative, the resources should be expended to control the crimes of the underclass. In this version of the rot at the top tale, the top lacks the political will to carry out the strategies that will truly result in crime control. Judges are too soft, prison administrators are too much concerned with rehabilitation, and the politicians too unwilling to take strong stands to defeat criminal interests.

Where should criminal justice resources be expended? For the liberal, rot truly is at the top. White-collar crime is viewed as far more costly and significant than the crimes of the underclass. Corruption and thievery are to be found in halls of government, the Pentagon, and the corporate board rooms. Too many criminal justice resources are wasted on crimes found in alleys and back streets. These represent an insignificant loss when compared to the crimes of those at the top.

It should be clear from this description that the variations of the four myths described by Reich limit the problem definitions and strategies available to legislators. The number of problems and strategies with which a legislator can deal are also constrained by limited time and resources. Each myth together with its liberal and conservative variations provide a wide range of potential problems to which a legislator might direct attention. What particular permutations of a myth will be used to shape a legislative agenda will in part depend upon the influence constituents, fellow legislators, lobbyists, and the executive branch exert on the process of lawmaking.

POLICY CONSIDERATIONS: THEORIES/ARGUMENTS/APPLICATIONS

Legislative Decision Making

Chapter 2 noted that categorizing and pattern making are highly developed human skills that allow us to make sense of our environment. Without the ability to classify, categorize, and in essence simplify our environment, we would be overwhelmed with stimuli.

Legislators, like the rest of us, simplify their environments. They have neither the time nor the resources to become highly involved and knowledgeable about every issue that comes before them. The research on legislative decision making suggests that legislators place issues into one of four broad categories.[7]

On certain issues, the individual legislator may be considered an expert. Either because of background, district concern, or previous legislative experience, an individual will become quite knowledgeable about specific policy areas. Issues arising in these areas of expertise will be decided largely based on fact situations. In such instances, the expert legislator will become a benchmark for others who are not as concerned or as knowledgeable about the specific issues being considered.[8]

A second category of issues involves those that are of particular concern to a representative's district. Regarding these legislative concerns, a representative might well follow the lead of his or her constituency in deciding the issue. This of course assumes that the issue is noncontroversial and that there is a unified body of opinion within the legislative district concerning it.[9]

Certain issues continually reappear on legislative agendas. Crime and what to do about it constitutes one set of these recurrent concerns. Regarding these kinds of issues, legislators develop a voting record. The member's personal disposition (that is, the myths to which he or she adheres), knowledge of constituent and interest group demands, and desire to remain consistent influence the vote on any particular one of these kinds of issues. Indeed, it is the consistency of the record in terms of continually reoccurring issues that a politician uses to get reelected.[10] A person with a history of conservative votes on the crime issue is not likely to run for reelection based on a conversion to liberal ideas.

Finally, there are issues that have low salience for a member of the legislature. Such issues do not raise a great deal of concern in the particular district the person represents, nor is the individual highly knowledgeable and involved in the particular policy area. These kinds of issues are likely to be decided on the basis of social cues.[11] How do members who are considered experts react to the bill? How do colleagues who share party affiliation view the matter? What are the desires of the executive and/or the interest groups for and against the legislation? These more social indicators will replace the more factual criteria when deciding issues within this category.

Legislative decision making involves a highly complex set of factors, some objective and some subjective. The process of making up one's mind on a particular legislative initiative, casting a vote, and fitting one's action into an ongoing pattern of a voting record is made even more difficult if the issue to be decided upon is a controversial one. What does a legislator do if there is conflict among the various groups to which he or she turns for advice? What if there are diverse opinions among constituents? What if constituents demand one thing and the party leadership another? It should be obvious why legislators prefer noncontroversial issues. Unfortunately, as we have seen, crime is not likely to be one of these. Therefore, legislators must establish priorities among the various groups competing for his or her support on issues that lack consensus. The basic myths and their liberal or conservative versions will often help a legislator accomplish such prioritizing. At the same time, the legislator must try to avoid alienating specific groups. Thus, many controversial issues result in legislation that is vague. This allows the legislator to convince diverse groups that their particular needs have been met. The opportunities for compromising, obfuscating, and watering down specific legislative initiatives are many. Figure 14-1 illustrates the route bills must traverse before they are made into law. At many points in the process, original intentions and goals may need to be modified in order to get the legislation passed.

How Bills Become Laws

A new bill can be introduced into the legislature from a variety of sources. Any person or group who has interest in a particular policy area may introduce a bill. This includes individuals, interest groups, legislators themselves, and formal organizations such as businesses, churches, and public agencies. Initial bills will often be drafted by particular interest groups sponsoring it.

Once introduced, a bill is usually assigned to the appropriate committee. This committee will hold hearings on the bill. The committee can decide to table the bill, amend it, substitute its own bill, or pass it on to the full body for deliberation unchanged. Legislative committees act as gatekeepers to the full legislative chamber. If the committee chair or the majority of the members of a committee do not support a bill, it can "die" before ever reaching the floor for debate.

Bills voted out of committee are reviewed by the whole of the legislative body. Bills can be amended at this point in the process also. Finally, a bill is "perfected." It is given a final reading and voted on for final passage.

In a bicameral legislature, that is, a legislature consisting of two chambers, a senate and a house, a bill passed in one chamber must then be approved by the second chamber. As the diagram shows, the bill essentially goes through the same process it went through in the first chamber. Committee hearings are held, floor debate takes place, the bill can undergo a variety of amendments, and then there is a final passage.

If the bill passed by the second chamber is exactly like the one passed by the first chamber, the bill then goes to the governor for his or her signature. If, however, there are differences between the versions of the bill, it must then go to a conference committee. The conference committee irons out differences between the two versions. Once these differences are resolved, the bill can then proceed to the governor's desk.

Governors of course can either sign the bill, in which case it becomes law, or they can veto the bill, in which case the process must begin again.

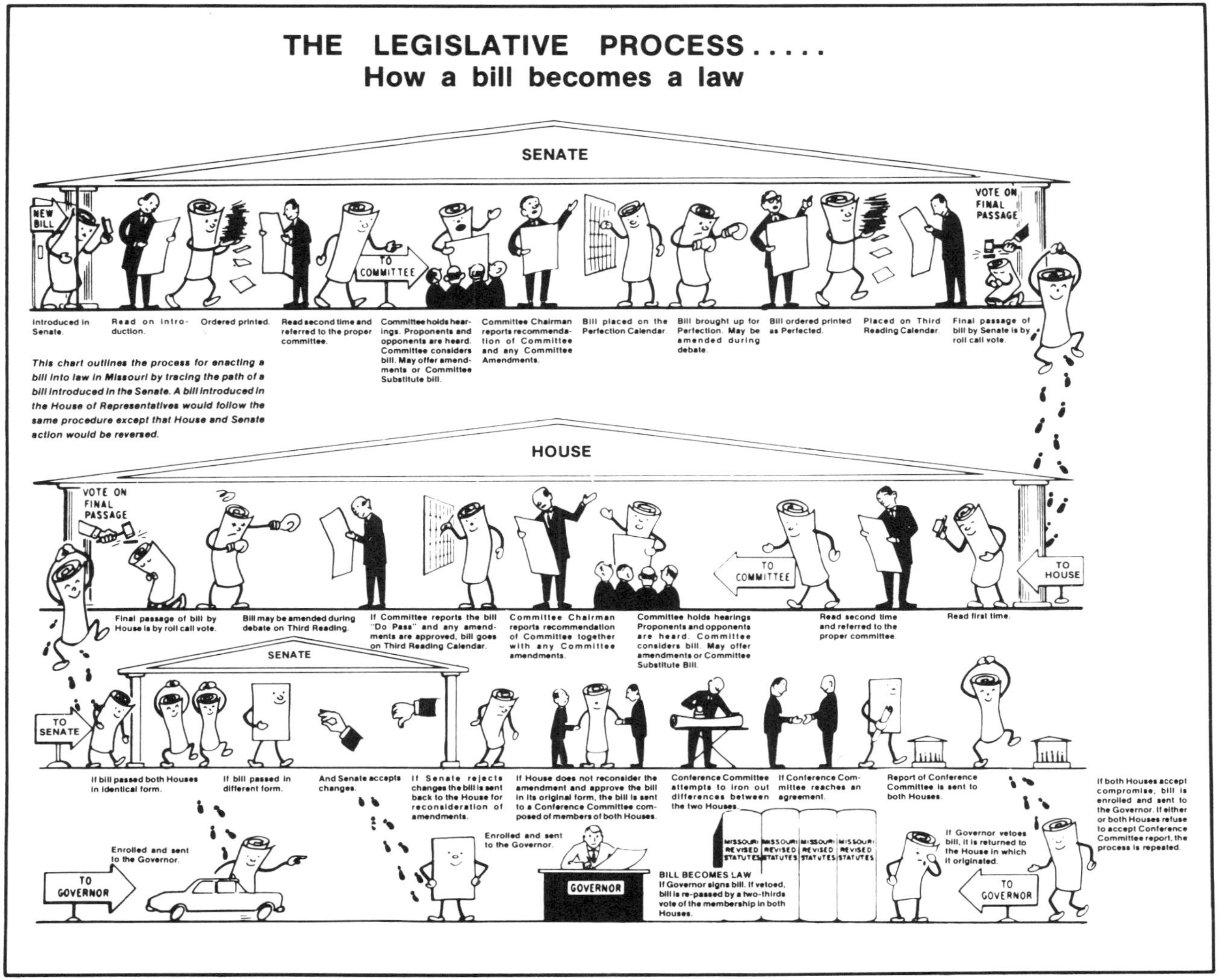

THE LEGISLATIVE PROCESS.....
How a bill becomes a law
SENATE
NEW BILL
TO COMMITTEE
VOTE ON FINAL PASSAGE
Introduced in Senate.
Read on introduction.
Ordered printed.
Read second time and referred to the proper committee.
Committee holds hearings. Proponents and opponents are heard. Committee considers bill. May offer amendments or Committee Substitute bill.
Committee Chairman reports recommendation of Committee and any Committee Amendments.
Bill placed on the Perfection Calendar.
Bill brought up for Perfection. May be amended during debate.
Bill ordered printed as Perfected.
Placed on Third Reading Calendar.
Final passage of bill by Senate is by roll call vote.
This chart outlines the process for enacting a bill into law in Missouri by tracing the path of a bill introduced in the Senate. A bill introduced in the House of Representatives would follow the same procedure except that House and Senate action would be reversed.
HOUSE
VOTE ON FINAL PASSAGE
TO COMMITTEE
TO HOUSE
Final passage of bill by House is by roll call vote.
Bill may be amended during debate on Third Reading.
If Committee reports the bill "Do Pass" and any amendments are approved, bill goes on Third Reading Calendar.
Committee Chairman reports recommendation of Committee together with any Committee amendments.
Committee holds hearings Proponents and opponents are heard. Committee considers bill. May offer amendments or Committee Substitute Bill.
Read second time and referred to the proper committee.
Read first time.
SENATE
TO SENATE
If bill passed both Houses in identical form.
If bill passed in different form.
And Senate accepts changes.
If Senate rejects changes the bill is sent back to the House for reconsideration of amendments.
If House does not reconsider the amendment and approve the bill in its original form, the bill is sent to a Conference Committee composed of members of both Houses.
Conference Committee attempts to iron out differences between the two Houses.
If Conference Committee reaches an agreement.
Report of Conference Committee is sent to both Houses.
If both Houses accept compromise, bill is enrolled and sent to the Governor. If either or both Houses refuse to accept Conference Committee report, the process is repeated.
Enrolled and sent to the Governor.
TO GOVERNOR
Enrolled and sent to the Governor.
GOVERNOR
MISSOURI REVISED STATUTES
BILL BECOMES LAW
If Governor signs bill. If vetoed, bill is re-passed by a two-thirds vote of the membership in both Houses.
If Governor vetoes bill, it is returned to the House in which it originated.
TO GOVERNOR

Figure 14-1

The Impact of Legislation

The outcome of the legislative process can affect many people, both directly and indirectly. Interest groups, constituents within legislative districts, as well as the legislators and their political parties stand to benefit from the passage of particular laws. Chapter 2 described how interest groups seek to advance their goals through legislation. Legislative districts also benefit from such processes. The placement of a new prison in a particular district, for example, can mean millions of dollars pumped into the local economy. Besides that, such a facility can provide both short- and long-term employment in construction and later on in correctional work. Finally, legislators need to pass laws in order to show their constituents that they are doing what they were elected to do. In turn, political parties point to legislative successes as examples of their concern and interest in the problems of the people.

Thus, the rewards available through the legislative process are both tangible and symbolic. Because of a favorable piece of legislation, a state agency can see its budget increased dramatically and therefore its power in relation to other state entities. Districts can experience a better financial climate, and its representative a secure political base for bringing it about. Besides these very tangible rewards, however, a number of intangible symbolic rewards are available. We have already seen that much of the impact of changes in criminal law is symbolic. When legislators raise sentences, people feel that something is being done about crime even if there is little relationship between the legislative action and the crime rate. On the other hand, we have also seen that symbolic legislation can have real, if unintended, consequences. Raising sentences, while having little or no effect on crime rates, has a very real effect on prison crowding. Therefore, legislators often find themselves passing laws to undo or limit the damage caused by previous legislative initiatives. Given the mixture of symbolic and tangible outcomes that result from the legislative process, assessment of impact can be quite difficult.

How to Evaluate the Impact of Legislation

Egon Guba's caution concerning what actually is evaluated when looking at the impact of legislation is germane:

> It is never the policy that is tested but only some treatment or program undertaken in the name of the policy, together with the experience of that treatment or program by the target group and other affected stakeholders.[12]

Guba argues that legislators primarily operate at the level of policy-in-intention. As noted in Chapter 2, this refers to general goals and general means for achieving them based on the commonly accepted values of a society. Since policy-in-intention constitutes an expression of values, it is not available for evaluation through the typical scientific method. To illustrate, a state legislature may pass a bill that mandates a minimum, mandatory sentence of three years for burglary. While this seems a concrete, straightforward expression of both an intent and a strategy, and thus easily evaluated, the reality is much more complex. The implementers, target groups, and other stakeholders actually determine what happens as a result of such legislation. Prosecutors (key criminal justice implementers) may use the new legislation to force more plea bargaining. Thus, fewer people get charged with burglary because they plead guilty to a lesser crime. Alternatively, more defendants (the intended target group) may opt for a trial rather than plead. This in turn may cause a backup in court dockets, thereby causing judges (another group of key implementers) to dismiss a greater number of cases because of evidenciary and procedural flaws. Juries (another set of implementers) may decide that three years is too harsh a sentence for the circumstances surrounding the crime and come in with more not guilty verdicts. Finally, correctional officials (a key group of stakeholders) may institute early release procedures in order to accommodate the increasing population caused by the original legislation. Failure to do so may result in court orders from the federal level to reduce overcrowding. In practice, therefore, the original legislation may have nothing to do with the actual program that is carried out. What is evaluated therefore is not the legislation, but an operational definition of what was intended. Again, as noted in Chapter 2, such operational definitions will be made by implementers according to what is best for their agency. The resulting program may be a considerably different animal than what was intended by those who passed the legislation.

As we have seen, social science can be somewhat useful at the level of program evaluation. At the level of policy-in-intention, however, the social scientist simply becomes one more interest group. In espousing goals and programs at this level, the scientist uses less of his or her expertise and more of his or her version of a particular American myth. Lloyd E. Ohlin, in commenting on the work of social scientists on the President's Commission on Law Enforcement and Administration of Justice captures this dynamic:

> . . . there emerged informal groupings of persons who shared similar, but non-specific, idealogic views about the causes of crime and delinquency and the effectiveness of existing criminal justice policies. For example, there were those who saw criminal offenders as essentially exploited underdogs of a repressive social system, especially offenders from minority groups in large urban areas and in the rural south. This faction in the staff and the commission advocate the plight of the poor and the discriminated-against urban classes who needed something more than greater repression by law enforcement agencies to deal with the problems that led to their acts of violence and crimes against persons or property. Another faction stressed a variation of a law-and-order approach. It was critical of permissive trends in the society and felt that restraints on the individual misconduct needed to be reinforced by strong laws and punitive measures by criminal justice agencies.[13]

Clearly, the differing versions of the "mob at the gates" formed the basic stuff out of which flowed the policy recommendations of Lyndon Johnson's Crime Commission. Thus, at the level of policy-in-intention, social scientists tend not only to be perceived as an interest group, but to act as one also.

To illustrate the legislative process, the effects of interest groups on it, and the difference between policy-in-intention and policy-in-implementation, a case study of a community corrections act is presented. This case study will also serve to introduce Chapter 15, which begins the discussion of a major new trend in criminal justice, that of privatization. Understanding how legislators generally approach criminal justice issues, and how the interaction of myths, facts, and interest-group pressure yields particular problem definitions will provide a framework for analyzing this important development.

The Odyssey of Community Sentencing in Missouri

A core group of six people, most of whom were church workers with extensive experience in corrections, sparked the community sentencing movement in the state.[14] After attending a conference on alternatives in Des Moines, Iowa, they resolved to push for nonincarcerative reforms in Missouri.

The first step in this direction was to organize a Missouri conference on alternatives. A statewide group formed as a result of this conference. Seed money and a consultant were provided by a large St. Louis–based corporation.

In their initial meetings, this now enlarged body struggled with defining what the fledgling organization should or could do. Immediate problems included setting a goal, getting sufficient monetary resources, and enlarging the membership base. A concerted effort was made to recruit people from both the business community and from the upper strata of the volunteer community, thereby hopefully solving the last two problems simultaneously. At the same time, the group began to focus on a specific goal, the passage of a community sentencing act.

With a specific goal, it became possible to attract foundation and grant support. This in turn permitted the hiring of an executive director. A board of directors with approximately 30 people was then formed, and the name Missouri Coalition for Alternatives to Imprisonment (MoCAI) was adopted.

MoCAI formulated a draft bill of 15 legal-sized pages. The bill contained innovations designed to limit the unintended, yet negative effects that had been observed in other states with such legislation. For a local jurisdiction to receive money under the bill, it had to reduce the number of individuals sent to state prison to a figure below that of the calendar year preceding the legislation. The draft called for local community penalty boards. These boards were to be responsible for the design and the submission of a comprehensive community corrections plan for the area and its eventual implementation. Thus, the term "community" in the draft legislation referred to both a place for corrections and the locus of administrative control. This latter point was underscored by mandating that community corrections would form a new division within the state's Department of Corrections. In the state of Missouri the Department of Corrections contains both the Division of Adult Institutions and the statewide Probation and Parole Division. The division of Community Corrections would operate as a third agency, independent from Probation and Parole. Finally, spending for construction was specifically prohibited.

The Missouri legislature passed a community sentencing bill in 1983. In its final version, the bill covered both sides of a single $8\frac{1}{2}$ by 11″ sheet of paper. It contained no specific formula for payback to a local jurisdiction for keeping otherwise prison-bound residents. No specific provision was made for local penalty boards, although "local involvement" was encouraged. Finally, the administration of the program was under the existing probation and parole bureaucracy.

A task force was appointed by the chairman of the Missouri Board of Probation and Parole to review the new legislation and to make recommendations regarding its implementation. One of the 14 members of this group belonged to MoCAI. The others were criminal justice professionals, legislators, and academics. The task force was chaired by the state's chief probation officer.

Nine recommendations were made for implementation of the Community Sentencing Act. Six of these stressed the importance of Probation and Parole to the success of the project and the need to increase their resources. The remaining three recommendations suggested a limited number of pilot projects, careful evaluation before statewide implementation, and judicial training to acquaint judges with community alternatives.

All of the recommendations were adopted. During the 1984 legislative session, $200,000 was appropriated for the implementation of the Act. Fifty thousand dollars was designated for administrative costs incurred by the central office of Probation and Parole, and $50,000 was awarded to each of the three pilot project sites: St. Louis, Kansas City, and Springfield, Missouri. Interestingly, during the same legislative session a 17% pay raise bill for Probation and Parole officers was passed, as was an appropriation to increase their number.

After the appropriation for community sentencing was approved, the Chief Probation Officer and his staff determined eligibility criteria and program design. A four-phase plan of maximum community supervision was developed and implemented for offenders under 25 years of age, with no prior felony convictions, a juvenile record of more than minor offenses, and with a history of substance abuse. Scanty employment history, noncompletion of high school, an adult arrest record, and a crime that would not present a current or future physical danger to the community were also typical characteristics of people who, in the judgment of Probation and Parole, were being incarcerated but could be safely treated in this new program.

The Odyssey of Community Sentencing in Missouri illustrates the effects of inter- and intraorganizational tensions on legislative activity. The interactions of four groups—reformers, legislators, probation and parole workers—and those connected with the Division of Adult Institutions helped structure both policy-in-intention and policy-in-implementation. In turn, each of these groups interacted with the others in particular ways to advance their own organizational ends. The end result was a piece of legislation and a program that more or less helped solve particular organizational problems. The legislation itself was not a rational plan to solve the problem of prison overcrowding, at least at the level of implementation. It was a value statement at the level of intention, however, that such a goal was certainly worthwhile! To borrow Norton Long's notion of the political process being a series of games, two distinct games had to be played. The goal of the first game was to get the legislature to endorse a proposal that legitimated the problem of prison overcrowding and the strategy of addressing it through something other than building more prisons. Winning this game had certain consequences for the organizations involved. A second game, only loosely related to the first, involved getting a program into operation. The outcome of this game too resulted in certain organizational consequences, and since the games were different, different stakeholders formed different teams from those that played in the first game.

MoCAI's first concern was to establish itself as a player in the correctional policy arena. To do this, it needed resources both in terms of people and money. Thus, to survive as an organization, it had to decide what to do, mobilize resources to do it, and define specific action strategies. To accomplish these organizing tasks, MoCAI continually changed the operational definition of what it was about. From a general concern with nonincarcerative reform, goal statements moved to support for community correction, then to support for a specific community sentencing act and finally to the supporting of an intensive probation program. These evolving goal statements attracted a wider constituency for MoCAI in terms of both membership and the support of relevant criminal justice decision makers throughout the state. MoCAI gained a secure financial base and a position within the network of criminal justice interest groups. Of course winning the organizational game meant backing away from some of its original goals, much to the dismay of its original founders.

MoCAI was not the only group grappling with organizational problems. Its appearance on the scene simultaneously added to and resolved tensions already extant in the multitude of organizations that constituted the correctional policy environment.

The Department of Probation and Parole had its unique set of problems. The division faced an increasingly militant group of probation and parole officers who were demanding significant pay raises. Moreover, turf battles were shaping up between the Chief Probation Officer and the director of the Department of Corrections over scarce budgetary resources and program priorities.

The director of the Department of Corrections, on the other hand, also faced a significant problem. The prison system was approximately 2,000 people over capacity. The director thus tended to define community corrections as small-scale prisons located in local communities. While this notion varied considerably from MoCAI's, he did support increased community control.

A conservative Republican senator, who eventually introduced the bill, was enmeshed in his own set of conflicts. Many of these involved the particular values he sought to represent. A group of constituents were complaining because of sewerage problems caused by a recently opened, but already significantly overcrowded correctional institution in their area. The legislator did not want to appear soft on crime, but neither did he want to appear insensitive to the needs of constituents directly and negatively affected by prison overcrowding. He was caught between liberal and conservative colleagues on the whole issue of correctional legislation.

MoCAI had recruited as its second board president a former member of the Missouri State Legislature. He was specifically sought because of his legislative experience. He, in turn, got his former staff, who now worked for the Republican state senator, to convince their new boss to introduce the bill. By stressing that the bill would allow longer incarceration for those who really needed to be locked away, the senator was able to maintain his law-and-order image while working with more senior and liberal legislators for community corrections.

The director of the Department of Corrections supported the original bill since it could provide some relief from overcrowding and political leverage vis à vis Probation and Parole. But because it took certain responsibilities away from Probation and Parole, this group wanted the bill killed or at least considerably modified. Thus, in the first game of getting the bill introduced, the teams were as follows. On the side of the legislation were the conservative Republican legislator, certain key liberal legislators, MoCAI, and the Division of Adult Institutions through the director of Department of Corrections. On the side opposed to the legislation were the Department of Probation and Parole and certain legislators with whom they had worked over a long period.

In the first game, those supporting the legislation won. The bill was introduced. This success, however, fundamentally altered the organizational context of the reform. Probation and Parole now attempted to gain control of the bill. They worked with the chairman of the House Committee on Corrections. He changed the bill to have community sentencing placed directly under Probation and Parole's jurisdiction. The Senate sponsor believed that this change was the only way the bill would have a chance of approval. Since this was his first session in the legislature, he was interested in getting a bill passed in order to show the folks back home that he was an active, concerned lawmaker.

The change in legislation put Probation and Parole in an awkward position. It did not really want the bill and thought it would be killed in the Budget Committee. But the bill came out of Budget Committee because of an agreement to eliminate the payback mechanism. Probation and Parole now found itself in a position of supporting a bill that it initially did not want,

The director of Corrections began lobbying for community prisons. This started his estrangement with MoCAI. At the same time, his support for a separate community sentencing agency increased the conflict between himself and the Division of Probation and Parole. When the director wrote a letter to House Corrections Committee recommending against the changes that would put community sentencing under the existing Probation and Parole Bureaucracy, Probation and Parole suggested that such a move would hamper rather than accelerate the use of nonincarcerative sentencing options. Thus, MoCAI and Probation and Parole formed a new team. The game was now to get the bill passed and implemented. MoCAI, or at least the pragmatic leaders in it, saw these goals as solidifying its organizational presence within the correctional arena. Similarly, the new state legislator saw the bill as solidifying his position within the legislature. Finally, Probation and Parole now saw the bill as a way to win greater resources in its battle with the Division of Adult Institutions.

The now considerably altered bill passed, despite the opposition of the director of the Department of Corrections. He, on the other hand, continued to lobby for increased construction. MoCAI, to appease those within their organization who thought that the legislation was a sellout, held a news conference denouncing further prison construction. This simultaneously ended the relationship of MoCAI with the director of the Department of Corrections while solidifying its relationship with Probation and Parole. Therefore, when the implementation game was played, MoCAI was an effective voice in getting at least some of its original goals met.

Conclusions

This chapter has attempted to illustrate the nonrational, gamelike features of the legislative process. In doing so, it provides lessons for both those interested in changing the criminal justice system and those interested in evaluating and assessing the results of such attempts. First, reform is obviously a process that does not cease when a specific piece of legislation is enacted. The continuous monitoring and assessment of the institutional environment is necessary if a reform group is to prevent the exclusive use of a reform by a single organization to solve its specific problems. It is such organizational hegemony that may be the main cause of expanding criminal justice nets. Reform groups seem most concerned with policy-in-intention and therefore do not involve themselves in implementation. But it is this next level that actually determines what goes on in a policy environment.

Second, if policy is a multilayered phenomenon, then assessment of reform efforts itself has to be multilayered. One should not only look at original goals and intentions, but at the various levels of implementation as well. Pressures toward the blunting of a reform may be most apparent at the level of goal statements and programmatic applications. But at the more general level of problem orientation, significant changes can occur that can have major, long-term effects. The introduction of new language categories for describing problems or solutions, as well as the rearrangement of institutional coalitions, represents a level of policy innovation that is often overlooked in the literature. Yet as noted, each of these may be more significant in the long run than the fate of any single reform effort.

Third, a given policy can be used to obtain multiple and sometimes contradictory goals. It would be very difficult to determine "the real" goal or intent of community correction legislation in Missouri. The question of successful goal attainment may therefore not even be relevant in most complex organizational environments. At the very least, however, evaluators should articulate success or failure in terms of whose goals are being used as benchmarks and why these goals should be considered most appropriate for purposes of evaluations.

SUMMARY

What Was Said

- While our mythology suggests that lawmaking is a rational process, experience suggests otherwise.
- According to Robert B. Reich, the American world view is informed by four morality tales or myths:
  —The Mob at the Gates
  —The Triumphant Individual
  —The Benevolent Community
  —The Rot at the Top
- Legislators use a variety of techniques to simplify their decision making regarding legislative issues including:
  —Their own expertise about an issue
  —Constituency demand
  —Past voting record on an issue
  —Other legislators and fellow party members
- Legislators generally prefer to deal with noncontroversial issues.
- While particular legislation can affect a variety of people, evaluating legislative impact can be quite difficult since they can be different at different policy levels.

What Was Not Said

- The legislative process makes no difference.
- Legislators act out of self-interest.
- Legislators do not work hard.
- The legislative process should depend more on experts.

NOTES

1. Norton E. Long, "The Local Community Is an Ecology of Games," *American Journal of Sociology*, LXIV (November, 1958), 251–61.

2. Robert B. Reich, *Tales of a New America* (New York: Random House, Inc., 1987).

3. Ibid., pp. 8–10.

4. Ibid.

5. Ibid.

6. Ibid.

7. Malcolm E. Jewell and Samuel C. Patterson, *The Legislative Process in the United States*, 3rd ed. (New York: Random House, 1977).

8. Ibid.

9. Ibid.

10. Ibid.

11. Ibid.

12. Egon G. Guba, "What Can Happen as a Result of a Policy?" *Policy Studies Review*, Vol. 5, No. 1 (August, 1985), p. 11.

13. Lloyd E. Ohlin, "The President's Commission on Law Enforcement and Administration of Justice," in *Sociology and Public Policy: The Case of Presidential Commissions*, Mirra Komarovsky, ed. (New York: Elsevier, 1975), p. 110.

14. James F. Gilsinan, "Creating a Reform Environment: A Case Study in Community Corrections and Coalition Building," *Criminal Justice Policy Review*, Vol. 1, No. 3 (September 1986), 328–43. This discussion is based on a summary of this article.

XV

The Privatization of Justice
Private Policing

At the end of this chapter, the student will be able to:

A. Discuss the various meanings of the term privatization.
B. Note the factors that have led to the growth of private policing.
C. Describe the scope of private security both in terms of numbers and amounts of money spent.
D. Discuss the social implications of the privatization of this part of the criminal justice system.

ISSUE BACKGROUND

Different Meanings of Privatization

The English language is not famous for its precision. In fact, it has been estimated that the average number of meanings per English word is 28.[1] The word "privatization" illustrates the point.

The decade of the 1980s saw a resurgence of faith in the free market. Spurred by the ideology and policies of the Reagan Administration, a business orientation that promoted government deregulation, fiscal conservatism, and success criteria based on profit dominated public policy discussions. The end result was a clarion call for less government interference in the world of business. Paradoxically, however, the world of business became the model for the delivery of public service. Government was not to interfere in the business world, but the business world was to show government how to do its job better. As a consequence, a wide range of activities formerly thought of as government responsibilities was transferred to private hands. This shift of public activity to the private sector is known as "privatization."

While the term seems a straightforward one, privatization actually encompasses a wide variety of arrangements. Thus, before its impact on criminal justice can be discussed and assessed, it is necessary to review the different uses of the term. Ted Kolderie of the University of Minnesota has begun the process of differentiating the ways the term "privatization" is applied.[2]

Kolderie notes that government performs two different activities when meeting a societal need. First, government makes a decision to provide the service. This is the policy decision. Second, government engages in an administrative action to produce the service. One or both of these functions can be privatized. Therefore, privatization can refer to different combinations of public/private enterprise. Kolderie provides examples of the different combinations based on a service called security.[3]

> *Case One:* Government does both—the legislature writes the law and provides the money; the Department of Corrections runs the prison. Neither function is private.
> *Case Two:* Production is private—the city of Bloomington decides to provide security when the high school hockey teams play at the city arena, and it contracts with Pinkertons for the guards.
> *Case Three:* Provision is private—government sells to a market of private buyers. The Northstars hockey team wants security at Metropolitan Sports Center, and it contracts with the Bloomington City Police.
> *Case Four:* Both activities are private—a department store decides that it wants uniformed security and employs (or contracts privately for) its own guards. Government performs neither activity.

While Kolderie's distinctions are useful, they still tend to oversimplify an extremely complex reality. The decision of government to provide a service is equivalent to Guba's description of policy-in-intention. The decision to produce the service is at the level of policy-in-implementation. While it is clear that government can withdraw from the provision of services, their production, or both, the resulting typology is considerably muddled with the addition of Guba's third level of policy, policy-in-experience. What are the public effects of any of the three types of privatization? In the area of criminal justice, is the term privatization even useful since most activity in this policy arena will have considerable public impact? The term "private" after all comes from a Latin word meaning "not belonging to the state" or "not in public life." Given the trend of Western history, can issues of order and justice ever again be considered purely private matters? The privatization of prisons, the most popular example of privatization in criminal justice, illustrates the difficulty. In this example, government provides the service but contracts with a private firm to produce incarceration facilities and/or to staff and manage these. But obviously at the level of policy-in-experience, corrections is still a public function, and no matter who produces it, it will have significant public impact.

The problem of what is or is not privatization is much more than just an academic exercise in semantics. As we will see, such distinctions have considerable legal implications, not the least of which is a citizen's right to protection from unwarranted government interference in his or her life. And so, another irony. In criminal justice, privatization may decrease the role of government while simultaneously increasing its power of control over citizen. The phenomenon of private policing illustrates this paradox.

CRIMINOLOGICAL/CRIMINAL JUSTICE CONSIDERATIONS

Who Maintains the Public Peace?

The demarcation between public space and private space at first glance appears to be a clear one.[4] When we are inside our homes, we are obviously in private space, while out on the street we are in public space. "A man's home is his castle" is a saying that captures the element of control a person may exercise in his or her private domain. On the other hand, public space is thought to be primarily under the control of the civil authorities, except "There is never a cop around when you need one."

Each of these sayings underscore some of the complexities of the public/private space dichotomy. The first one, while often heard, is in fact incomplete. The remainder of it states, "*and while he is quiet*, he is as well guarded as a prince in his castle."[5] Thus, civil authority recognizes a limit to the privacy and control a person may exercise even in his or her own home. Police officers may enter such private space if the individual creates a disturbance worthy of their attention. Moreover, government claims the right to control the use of private space through zoning ordinances, required building permits, and other administrative regulations governing land use. Of course, the police power of the state is limited by its ability to enforce laws. Limited personnel sometimes make enforcement a difficult proposition at best, as the second saying implies. Thus, even public space can be appropriated by less desirable people intent upon using such space for their own ends. A street robbery illustrates the point.

The history of law enforcement is in part a history of a common peace replacing separate private peaces.[6] The King's Peace, the responsibility and authority of government for the maintenance of order, now subordinates all other authorities to it. Thus, private policing, which as we saw in Chapter 11 predates the public police, is eventually replaced by a "new" police force responsible to the government. While it is tempting to think of these developments in a linear fashion, with private order maintenance eventually giving way to public authority, the recent growth of private policing clearly demonstrates that the conflict between public and private authorities is not finally resolved. Two reasons are offered for the resurgence of private police authority.

Theories of Growth in Private Security

The first theory relates to the saying, "There is never a cop around when you need one." This might be called the vacuum theory of private police growth.[7] Public forces are being overwhelmed because of the limited state resources they can draw upon. Into this vacuum steps the private police agent. Neighborhood associations, residents of apartment complexes, or owners of commercial property may contract with a private security agency to provide patrol personnel to protect the lives and property of those who are willing and able to pay for the extra security. Larger corporations and entities such as universities may have their own in-house police forces to perform the same functions. In either case, the emphasis is on prevention, particularly loss prevention.

A second explanation for the rise of private security forces can be found in the less familiar statement, ". . . and while he is quiet he is as well guarded as a prince in his castle." This statement hints at the blurring of lines between what is private and what is public. Under certain conditions, something private can become public. Similarly, what is public can be taken over by private interests. This last point can be illustrated by the increasing growth of what has been termed mass private property.[8]

A university, for example, has elements of both private and public space. Many public activities go on at a university campus, but if the campus is under the auspices of a private group and not a state university, is the university public or private property? Large, privately held housing developments, shopping centers, amusement parks such as Disneyland, and vast corporate complexes are other examples of mass private property. In these instances, police forces are both provided for and produced by a private entity. Thus, the growth of private policing can be associated with the growth of a particular form of property.[9] In this last instance, private policing does not augment the public force but in fact replaces it. And since the interests of private force are not parallel to that of the public force, conflict over which authority shall prevail can develop.

Loss prevention and crime prevention are not the same thing. Loss prevention emphasizes private interest. Within this framework, what is considered deviant is the creation of opportunities for loss rather than simply loss itself.[10] Thus, the potential pool of deviants is considerably expanded.[11] If you leave a door unlocked in your office that should be locked, security can cite you for a violation which may lead to a management reprimand. Continued violations may ultimately result in the termination of employment. In this kind of society, as Michel Foucault argues, conformity is not based on physical coercion but on surveillance. It is a "disciplinary society."[12] In the public arena, crime prevention emphasizes the detection and apprehension of offenders. It is largely reactive rather than proactive. The threat of physical coercion is what keeps people in line. However, the pool of potential deviants is considered much smaller.

It is clear that when private interests are at stake, there is less emphasis on enforcing the public law. Thus, as noted previously, embezzlement is often treated as a loss to be restored rather than as a crime to be prosecuted. This is but one example of where private interests may diverge from public interest. On the other hand, private security has the potential for being much more pervasive since the line between what is individual private space and the space that belongs to the corporate entity is considerably blurred.

In any event, it is obvious that the growth of privatization within the realm of policing raises a number of serious questions. Most of these questions center around the rights of citizens to privacy and control of space. Before these are discussed, however, it might be worthwhile to look at exactly how fast private policing has grown in the United States.

The Types and Numbers of Private Security Workers

Private security is another imprecise phrase that means different things depending upon who uses it and the circumstances to which it is applied. We have already seen that there are at least three meanings to the term private. In the context we are now using, it can refer to a private police force working for a private concern, a public police officer working for a private concern, and finally, a private agency working for a public concern. Sherlock Holmes helping Scotland Yard would be an example of the last case.

The *American Heritage Dictionary of the English Language* lists seven meanings for the term security.[13] The first three meanings are of interest to the current discussion. It can mean freedom from risk, a safe environment. It can also refer to having confidence in something, being free from anxiety and doubt. Finally, security can refer to anything that gives or assures safety. Ensuring a risk-free environment suggests the notion of a guard service, a group of individuals assigned the task of spotting and eliminating potential safety hazards. On the other hand, having confidence in something suggests having sufficient information about it. This points more to an investigative service. The last definition of security, anything that gives or assures safety, points to both human and technological risk reduction. Alarms, sensors, detectors, locks, and so on become part of the definition of security. Thus, when one attempts to assess the growth of private security, one is immediately faced with the question of growth in a particular aspect of this multifaceted phenomenon. A review of the data, however, seems to simplify the issue. Growth appears to be occurring in all sections of private security.

There are 470,678 sworn public police officers. This compares with 1.1

million private security guards.[14] The growth rate of the "rent-a-cop" business has been estimated at between 11–12% annually since about 1963.[15] Government work appears to be the industry's fastest growing sector. About 36,000 of the nation's private security guards work for a branch of government. Eleven thousand work for the federal government, 9,000 for state, and 16,000 for local governments.[16]

One of the problems that has accompanied the rapid growth in the number of private security guards has been the relative lack of standards and training. In a study by the Rand Corporation, the typical private security guard was described as "an aging white male, poorly educated, usually untrained, and very poorly paid." The typical guard averaged between 40 and 55 years of age, had not graduated from high school, and had only a few years of experience in private security. For many, the job seemed a last resort. Forty percent had not been employed immediately prior to their current guard job. Since the annual turnover rate rose as high as 200 percent, training was a low priority among most employers.[17]

There are many private-contract security firms that supply guards. However, the security field is dominated by three giants; Pinkerton, the William J. Burnes International Security Services, and the Wackenhut Corporation. A brief examination of the history of each of these corporations illustrates the problems and prospects of private security.

The history of the Pinkerton agency is intertwined with the history of industrialization and organized labor in the United States. The founder of the agency, Allan Pinkerton, was decidedly hostile toward the early efforts of unionization. The title of his 1878 book, *Strikers, Communists, Tramps and Detectives*, underscores the point. A passage from the preface further illustrates Pinkerton's hostility toward labor:

> . . . the working man is never the gainer—but always a loser, by resort to the reckless intimidation and brute force which never fail to result from the secret organization of the trades-union to force capital to compensate labor to a point where the use of that capital becomes unprofitable and disastrous.[18]

The building of railroads and the development of national corporations required a better organized form of protection for business than the system of local law enforcement could provide.[19] Pinkerton filled this gap. In 1850 he founded the North-Western Police Agency, the forerunner of the Pinkerton Agency, and very soon numerous railroads were utilizing these private agents in the pursuit of security and profits. The Pinkertons pursued such infamous railroad bandits as the James Gang and Butch Cassidy and the Sundance Kid. In pursuing these railroad nemeses, the Pinkertons developed some modern investigative tools, including the first use of photographs for criminal identification.

The pursuit of desperadoes was not, however, the only function performed by Pinkerton agents. Very soon they became involved in the brutal repression of various labor movements. The most notorious example of such repression became known as the Homestead Massacre, a strike-breaking attempt by Pinkerton agents at the Carnegie Steel Company near Pittsburgh in 1892. This action resulted in legislation passed in 1893 prohibiting the hiring of the Pinkerton Detective Agency or similar firms by the federal government. Pinkerton antilabor activity again became an issue in 1936. Management's use of private police, particularly the Pinkertons, was seen by Congress as inhibiting workers' free speech and their right to organize. A congressional resolution stated, "The so-called industrial spy system breeds fear, suspicion and animosity, tends to cause strikes and industrial warfare, and is contrary to sound public policy."[20] In response to this resolution, the Pinkerton Agency adopted a policy which stated that their operatives would no longer take sides in labor disputes.

The growth of mass private property, as illustrated by the spread of railroads, together with a lack of a national police force, clearly spurred the growth of a private police system. From the beginning, however, the line between private police and public law enforcement was blurred. Pinkerton and his agents, up until the time of the 1896 resolution, also provided services for the federal government, particularly during the Civil War period. Pinkertons acted as intelligence agents for the Union Army. These same dynamics, the growing security needs of private business and the blurring of public and private law enforcement functions, can also be seen in the history of the William J. Burnes detective agency.

William Burnes was a free-lance private detective for three years prior to joining the United States Secret Service in 1891. He soon gained fame for catching counterfeiters, uncovering corruption, and helping other federal agencies with their investigatory needs. At the request of some prominent residents of San Francisco, President Theodore Roosevelt granted Burnes and a few of his detectives a leave of absence from the federal government to fight corruption in the City by the Bay. After three years of fighting municipal corruption, Burnes decided not to return to federal service and instead went into business with his team of investigators. He was not entirely through with federal service, however. He came out of retirement during the early 1920s to head the Justice Department's Bureau of Investigation. He stayed three years as director, but was unable to clear up the corruption in the Bureau and was succeeded by his assistant, John Edgar Hoover.

Today, the Pinkerton Agency and the William J. Burnes International Security Services account for nearly one third of all the money spent on hired police yearly. Each agency employs approximately 40,000 people and does about $200 million of business annually.[21]

The Wackenhut Corporation was founded in 1954. Its first major contracts were with the federal government. By an ingenious legal device, the corporation was able to get around the 1893 Pinkerton Act. Although the Act prohibited the federal government's hiring of detective agencies, it did not specifically rule out the hiring of guards. Therefore, Wackenhut devised a wholly owned subsidiary made up exclusively of those providing guard services. The corporation has had contracts with the National Aeronautics and Space Administration, the Atomic Energy Commission, and other federal agencies.[22]

"Rent-a-cops" are not the only form of private policing. There are approximately 271,000 in-house private security personnel.[23] These are "company" police: hired for, trained by, and responsible to a single corporate entity such as a company, a shopping center, or a university. As might be expected, the history of in-house company police is itself intertwined with the history of organized labor. As also might be expected, they were not supportive.

The line between private and public was particularly blurry during the early days of the labor movement and industrialization. Factory or mine employees sometimes lived and worked in company towns. The corporation owned the land, housing, and stores and provided all of the services typically associated with government. Such company towns are clear examples of mass private property. But how does one classify those towns that, while not owned by a company, were so dependent upon a major corporation for jobs and tax dollars, they were for all practical purposes controlled by a private concern? In either situation, the use of police force becomes an issue of concern. Does public interest or private interest control its application? Historically, the latter interest seems to have predominated.

The Service Department of the Ford Motor Company did not fix cars. It was the name given to Ford's company police. Its early history illustrates the use to which such police were put and the difficulty that sometimes existed in distinguishing them from the public police.

In 1932, Ford Motor Company, once thought of as the most enlightened of employers, was experiencing serious labor troubles. On March 7, 3,000 men marched on the company's Dearborn plant to demand better working conditions.[24] The Detroit police simply escorted the marchers to the Detroit-Dearborn city limits. The Dearborn police were not as accommodating. Sixty-two percent of that city's tax base was supported by Ford. The chief of police was a former Ford Serviceman. Therefore, when the head of Ford security, Harry Bennett, wanted the marchers stopped, the chief did his best. Tear gas and fire hoses greeted the marchers. Despite their welcome, the demonstrators managed to reach the plant gates, where they were greeted by Ford's own police who had their guns and fire hoses ready. By the end of the day, four marchers had been killed and over 20 wounded.

In 1937, the Service Department was again used to repress labor organizing, this time relying on assistance from outside thugs hired for the occasion.[25] This "outside squad" together with the company police under the direction of Bennett severely beat four union representatives, including Walter Reuther, one of the founders of the CIO, when they attempted to pass out union literature.

The history of private patrol forces put to private use is scattered with instances of abuse. It would be inaccurate, however, to see private patrols as only a repressive force. Their presence can maintain and enhance security, prevent loss, and provide an extra margin of safety in areas such as fire prevention. Nevertheless, their use raises serious issues which have not yet been decided. Similarly, in other areas of the security industry, the limits of private power and the public interest have not been clearly established.

Although the private detective dominates our mystery fiction, such agents account for only a relatively small portion of private security workers. There are an estimated 32,000 licensed private investigators.[26] Of course, this figure does not include those who free-lance and do not bother with licensing requirements. Other security workers include those who are armored car personnel, and people who sell, monitor, and service a variety of security devices including alarms, cameras, and lie detectors. As this is being written, the last group of security workers is under Congressional scrutiny.[27] Lie detectors are being used increasingly in industrial settings to determine workers' job fitness. The polygraph records changes in pulse rate and skin moisture in response to questions. The theory is that a sudden change in pulse rate or skin moisture indicates a lie. Critics charge that "sweat" merchants pry unfairly into the private lives of potential or current employees and that the results of such tests are notoriously inaccurate. Polygraph results are not, in fact, admissible as evidence in federal courts. Legislators are trying to restrict the use of lie detectors by employers, particularly in the areas of preemployment screening and the random testing of current employees.

POLICY CONSIDERATIONS: THEORIES/ARGUMENTS/APPLICATIONS

Private Security and the Rights of Citizens

What are the rights of citizens when confronted with the demands of private agents? How can the potential conflicts between public and private enforcement needs be addressed? What constitutional guarantees are operative when dealing with private security? These questions in turn hinge on a central dilemma. How can we distinguish between what is private and what is public police action? As the history above demonstrates, policy-in-experience provides no easy answer. Pinkerton and Burnes were both intimately connected with the forces of public law. The Wackenhut Corporation's biggest contact is with the federal government. The Service Department of the Ford Motor Company and the Dearborn Police Department were at times indistinguishable. And at the federal level, Harry Bennett, the chief of Ford Security, worked closely with the FBI exchanging information with both local agents and J. Edgar Hoover himself. While policy scientists attempt to define the term "privatization" more precisely, courts and legislators must wrestle with the question of citizen rights in the context of private security. It is to these issues we now turn.

Private security agents, unless specifically deputized, have no greater authority than the average citizen to detain individuals. A citizen can effect a citizen's arrest if a felony has been committed in his or her presence. The person so detained must be turned over to a representative of public law enforcement without delay.

Generally, then, private security agents may not detain for misdemeanors nor for suspected felonies committed outside of their presence. Often, however, local and state shoplifting statutes will make an exception to the former rule by allowing the detention of shoplifters by store security personnel, even in a case of misdemeanor theft.

Although this restriction of arrest powers seems to provide clear protection to citizens, the statutes often assume knowledge on the part of both the citizen and the private security agent regarding the difference between felonies and misdemeanors. Based on the low level of training given most private security agents, such confidence seems misplaced. In fact, surveys of private security personnel have revealed that most think they have greater power to arrest than they actually have.[28] Further, most do not know the difference between misdemeanors and felonies.[29]

While their arrest powers are severely limited, private security agents appear to have more power than the public police when it comes to issues such as rights notification and search and seizure. It is in these areas that the distinction between what is private and what is public law enforcement is of crucial importance.

The majority of state courts have held that the Miranda rule does not apply to interrogations by private security personnel.[30] Regarding search and seizure, most courts have held to the precedent enunciated in *Burdeau* v. *McDowell*, a 1921 Supreme Court case that states, "The unlawful acts of private individuals in conducting illegal searches and seizures are not subject to constitutional proscription."[31] Given that the lines between public and private security are often blurred and that the growth of mass private property will cause more and more people to come into contact with the forces of private security, some commentators and courts are suggesting that these precedents are no longer adequate.

The foundation for a new legal approach to private security is based upon three principles.[32] The first involves the notion of public function. This principle was first enunciated in 1946. The Supreme Court, in *Marsh* v. *Alabama*,[33] held that a company town, even though privately owned, could not suspend First Amendment guarantees. The reasoning was based on the fact that the town provided all of the services and functions ordinarily performed by public government. Thus, when a private person or group carries out a traditionally governmental function, that entity is considered a government agent. This principle has not been widely applied to issues surrounding private security. Were it to be applied in cases of shoplifting, suspects detained by private security would be entitled to Miranda warnings. Further, when private agents produce a service at the request of government, all constitutional rights and protections would apply. Thus, when the Securities and Exchange Commission asked former Attorney General Griffin Bell to investigate irregularities at E. F. Hutton, Bell, a private agent, would have been bound by the procedural safeguards of constitutional law.

The second principle involves the Doctrine of Nexus.[34] This Doctrine holds that when there is sufficient government connection with the actions of private individuals, the actions can be considered those of the government. Thus, if a law enforcement officer asked a private security guard to obtain evidence without a search warrant, the evidence would be held to be illegally seized. A less clear-cut nexus is the revolving door between members of federal enforcement agencies and the managements of private security firms. Research has shown, for example, that former FBI agents now working in the security industry maintain contacts with their colleagues in the Bureau. Information exchanges among them are common. Some authors have, in fact, warned of a police-security complex that parallels the military industrial complex described first by Dwight Eisenhower.[35] Thus, information that law enforcement could generally get only through court order becomes available through the network of informal contacts maintained with former colleagues. Alternatively, private security agents have access to law enforcement files that ordinarily would be denied them. The need to consider constitutional protections in such circumstances is clear.

Finally, government may be unable to delegate certain responsibilities. This principle brings us full circle. How far can government go in relinquishing large sections of society to a private peace? A private peace is not necessarily congruent with the public peace, particularly in the application of procedural safeguards. Moreover, as the history of private security has shown, police power used exclusively in the service of economic ends is subject to abuse. Thus, new legal protections may be required as private security not only reinforces but sometimes supplants public law enforcement.

As appellate judges and legal scholars try to decide whether and how constitutional guarantees should be extended to cover areas of private security, another legal remedy remains available. This is tort law. Private wrongs between private individuals can be addressed through civil suit. This is the approach that courts have generally endorsed regarding private security. Again, however, there is serious question as to the sufficiency of this kind of legal redress.

Legislative remedies to the problem of private security have involved such things as the setting of qualifications for entrance into the field, mandated training, and licensing procedures. While the training of private security agents has traditionally been minimal, training opportunities have increased in response to public concern and industry growth. There has been a rapid growth of academic degree programs in private security.[36] Increasingly, local police departments are requiring some police academy training before security guards can be licensed to carry a firearm. Such efforts may be the harbinger to the increasing professionalization of the security industry. Nevertheless, at the present time, the delivery of security services is often in the hands of a poorly paid, poorly trained individual who believes he or she has the authority of the public police. Moreover, such remedies do not begin to address another variation of the private police theme. This is the growth of community patrols or what might be termed the private, not-for-profit sector of security.

Community Patrols

If two youths wearing red berets and white T-shirts approached you on a dark, deserted city street, would you be worried? If two tall, silent black men approached you a little later on, what would you do? If a jeep with three white men in it kept circling the block you were on, might you call the police? In each of these instances, you were probably not faced with a threat to your safety. Instead, you were probably confronted with individuals dedicated to making the neighborhood safer. By one estimate, there are more than 800 resident patrols active in U.S. urban areas. These extragovernmental patrols, organized by citizens themselves, began to blossom during the 1970s to augment the work of the public police.

The best known citizen patrol is the Guardian Angels, founded in New York in 1979. Originally a subway safety patrol, the Guardian Angels now have chapters in over 40 cities and claim 3,000 members.[37] While on patrol, the Angels dress in red berets and white T-shirts. They are unarmed. Before they can go out on patrol, prospective members must complete training in martial arts, "physical and mental conditioning," citizen's arrest procedures, cardio-pulmonary resuscitation, and first aid.[38] According to a study funded by the National Institute of Justice and carried out by the San Diego Association of Governments, a typical Angel patrol consists of four to eight members and lasts four hours. The Guardian Angels only infrequently encounter or intervene in a crime incident. The majority of activities involve giving directions, escorting the elderly, and assisting drunks.[39]

Evidence of the Angels' crime control effectiveness was inconclusive. Their activity did, however, reduce residents' fear of crime.[40] While residents generally supported the activity of the Guardian Angels, police were less supportive. In the majority of the 35 cities studied, police officers expressed a cautious neutrality toward the patrols, although many thought the Guardian Angels provided some benefit.[41] More enthusiastic police support and cooperation was found in a community patrol sponsored by Muslims in the Bedford-Stuyvesant section of Brooklyn.[42] This community patrol seems successful in being able to move the drug trade and associated crime out of their area.

A study by the Rand Corporation suggests that community patrols can be usefully divided into four types.[43] Building patrols seemed effective in preventing property crime and increasing residents' sense of security. Neighborhood patrols seemed less clearly successful and were the subject of more complaints by residents. Social service patrols which sought to provide service to those in need and community protection groups which dealt with a wide range of safety issues such as fire prevention and traffic congestion rounded out the categories of community patrols. These last two were not common enough to evaluate at the time of the study, however.

The issues raised by citizen patrols are the same ones that have plagued security policy since the Middle Ages. Who should have primary responsibility for peace keeping, and what are the social consequences of reliance either on a public peace or a series of privately maintained peaces? The movement toward a King's Peace was in part an effort to regularize punishment and protect the rights of citizens. If peace keeping is increasingly done by citizens or private security forces, is punishment itself likely to be decentralized and beyond the view of the state to regulate? Lynchings in the old South and West, often carried out by citizens organized into vigilance committees, illustrate an extreme example of private peace keeping. But loss of a job or a ruined career because of a faulty lie detector test are certainly modern-day possibilities in the context of a private peace with its own punishment. Runaway vigilantes are always a possibility whether on the western plains or in the corporate boardrooms. It is certainly this possibility that police officials worry about when confronted with groups like the Guardian Angels. At least regarding the latter group, however, such fears appear unfounded. In the study alluded to earlier, very few instances of inappropriate intervention by Guardian Angels were found. Nevertheless, this does not rule out such activity among those groups that are less well trained and less subject to public scrutiny because they are not as well known.

Conclusion

This chapter has also dealt with the problem of a citizen's rights when faced with private peacekeeping activity. As it now stands, a citizen is not entitled to the normal procedural safeguards available in the context of public law enforcement. The growth of private security and the negative impact private sanctions can have on an individual may require a broadening of such safeguards. Finally, a public peace assumes everyone is equally entitled to the protection of the sovereign. A private peace makes no such assumption. Security in person and possessions is a function of the ability to pay for it or to organize fellow citizens to seek it. Parallel production in the delivery of security, whereby citizens or companies act on their own to secure a public good or service, may discriminate against those who can least afford a decrease in their safety or their ability to obtain justice. This quality of justice issue is central in the next realm of privatized justice, dispute adjudication. We turn to it in the next chapter.

SUMMARY

What Was Said

- The term privatization has different meanings and can refer to the privatization of provision, production, or both.
- While the history of law enforcement is in part a history of a common peace replacing separate private peaces, the recent growth of private security demonstrates that this development is not complete.
- The vacuum theory of the growth of private security suggests that public forces are being overwhelmed and need to be supplemented.
- The growth of mass private property has also been offered as an explanation for the growth of private security.
- Private security workers fall into a number of categories including for-hire guards, company police, private investigators, public police hired by private concerns, and armed-car personnel, and people involved in the manufacture and sale of security devices.
- Private security agents, unless specifically deputized, have no greater authority than the average citizen to detain individuals.
- Generally, constitutional protections have been held *not* to apply to actions of private security personnel.
- Potential for increased protection from the actions of private security agents exists in the following legal principles:
  - When a private concern offers the services typically provided by government, that concern is restricted by constitutional guarantees.
  - The doctrine of nexus holds that when a sufficient connection exists between a government agency and the actions of a private individual, those actions are considered to be performed by government.
  - Government may be unable to delegate certain powers.

What Was Not Said

- Private security is sufficiently regulated.
- Private security cannot perform a valuable function.
- Private security assumes everyone is equally entitled to protection.

NOTES

1. James F. Gilsinan, "Information and Knowledge Development Potential: The Public vs. Private Sector Jobs Demonstration Project," *Evaluation Review*, 8, No. 3 (June 1984), 371–88.

2. Ted Kolderie, "The Two Different Concepts of Privatization," *Public Administration Review*, 46, No. 4 (July/August 1986), 285–91.

3. Ibid., pp. 285–86.

4. For a further discussion of this issue see Albert J. Reiss, Jr., "The Legitimacy of Intrusion into Private Space," in *Private Policing*, Vol. 23, Clifford D. Shearing and Philip C. Stenning, eds. Sage Criminal Justice System Annuals (Newbury Park, CA: Sage, 1987), pp. 19–43.

5. Shearing and Stenning, *Private Policing*, p. 12.

6. Ibid.

7. Clifford D. Shearing and Philip C. Stenning, "Modern Private Security: Its Growth and Implications," in *Crime and Justice: An Annual Review of Research*, Vol. 3, Michael Tonry and Norval Morris, eds. (Chicago, IL: The University of Chicago Press, 1981), pp. 226–27.

8. Ibid., p. 228.

9. Ibid., pp. 227–28.

10. Ibid., p. 212.

11. Ibid., p. 213.

12. Michel Foucault, *Discipline and Punish: The Birth of the Prison* (New York: Pantheon, 1977).

13. *American Heritage Dictionary* (New York: American Heritage Publishing Co., Inc., 1969), p. 1173.

14. Martin Tolchin, "Private Security Guards Doing Government Work," *St. Louis Post-Dispatch*, Nov. 30, 1985, Sec. B., p. 1.

15. George O'Toole, *The Private Sector: Private Spies, Rent-a-Cops, and the Police Industrial Complex* (New York: W. W. Norton and Co., Inc., 1978), p. 5.

16. Tolchin, "Private Security Guards."

17. James S. Kakalik and Sorel Wildhorn, *Private Police in the United States*, 5 vols. (Santa Monica, CA: The Rand Corporation, 1972).

18. Allan Pinkerton, *Strikers, Communists, Tramps and Detectives* (New York: G. W. Carleton & Co., Publishers, 1978), p. XL.

19. For an extended discussion of the "big three" in security, see O'Toole, *The Private Sector*, pp. 20–31. Facts in the following discussion are drawn from this work.

20. Ibid., p. 27.

21. Ibid., p. 30.

22. Ibid., p. 31.

23. Shearing and Stenning, "Modern Private Security," p. 201.

24. Robert Lacey, *Ford: The Men and the Machine* (Boston, MA: Little, Brown and Company, 1986).

25. Ibid.

26. O'Toole, *Private Sector*, p. 202.

27. William Safire, "The Sweat Merchants," *The New York Times*, February 29, 1988, p. 21.

28. O'Toole, *The Private Sector*, p. 5.

29. Ibid.

30. Steven Euller, "Private Security and the Exclusionary Rule," *Harvard Civil Rights–Civil Liberties Law Review*, 15, No. 3 (Winter, 1980), 649–84. Nigel South,

"Private Security, The Division of Policing Labor and the Commercial Compromise of the State" in Steven Spitzer and Andrew T. Scull, *Research in Law, Deviance and Social Control*, Vol. 6 (Greenwich, CT.: JA1 Press, Inc., 1984), pp. 171–98. Joan C. Szuberla, "Reality and Illusion: Defining Private Security Law in Ohio," *University of Toledo Law Review*, 13, No. 2 (Winter, 1982), 377–419.

31. 256 U.S. 465 (1921).

32. Euller, "Private Security and the Exclusionary Rule."

33. *Marsh* v. *Alabama*, 326 U.S. 501; 90L Ed. 265, 66 S.Ct. 276 (1946).

34. Euller, "Private Security," p. 665.

35. O'Toole, *The Private Sector*, p. 227.

36. William C. Cunningham and Todd H. Taylor, "The Growing Role of Private Security," *National Institute of Justice Research in Brief*, October, 1984.

37. "Demystifying the Street Punk," *Criminal Justice Newsletter* 14, No. 12 (June 6, 1983), 7.

38. " 'Guardian Angels' Given Good Marks for Avoiding Vigilantism," *Criminal Justice Newsletter*, 17, No. 23 (Dec. 1, 1986), 5.

39. Ibid.

40. Ibid.

41. Ibid.

42. Thomas Morgan, "Muslim Patrol Reduces Crime in Brooklyn Area," *New York Times*, Feb. 25, 1988, p. 204.

43. "Citizen Involvement: Resident Patrols Get Positive Evaluation," *Criminal Justice Newsletter*, 8, No. 5 (Feb. 28, 1977), 6.

XVI

The Privatization of Justice

Dispute Resolution

At the end of this chapter, the student will be able to:

A. Distinguish among the terms conciliation, arbitration, mediation, and reconciliation.
B. Discuss the strengths and weaknesses of the neighborhood justice center movement.
C. Describe the private court movement.
D. Discuss the social consequences of privatization in this sector of the justice system.

ISSUE BACKGROUND

The Nonjudicial Settlement of Disputes

The typical criminal courtroom drama depicts a good guy and a bad guy. Increasingly, the good guy is seen as the state and the crime victim, the bad guy is the defendant and sometimes his or her attorney. As Chapter 9 noted, however, the good guys and the bad guys have not always been divided this way. Indeed, many of our procedural safeguards have assumed that the government is as likely to be a bad guy, using its power to unduly interfere in the lives of citizens. And of course, the criminal trial may well show that the accused is indeed an innocent party, not a bad guy at all.

Terms like "victim," "defendant," "offender," and so on suggest a degree of certainty and clearly delineated roles that may not in fact exist. Again, as data cited previously show, the designation "criminal," and by extension the designation "victim," are contingent terms. Their application depends upon the context of their use. Who is applying them, in what circumstances, and at what times are factors needed to be understood in order not to oversimplify the complexities of a case. By oversimplifying the characters involved in traditional court proceedings, the processes of the system also tend to oversimplify the disputes that brought the parties into court in the first place. Lon Fuller has argued that, often, disputes categorized as criminal, and thus disputes perceived of as having clearly delineated good guys and bad guys, are really polycentric.[1] That is, they contain complex webs of cause and effect and complex rules for creating, indexing, and manipulating social patterns. This suggests that a different vehicle for understanding and processing such disputes may be helpful, one that takes into account the complex nature of disputes and puts less emphasis on determining a "guilty" party.

In 1969, the Philadelphia Municipal Court Arbitration Tribunal was established to provide disputants with the option of binding arbitration for minor criminal matters.[2] This small step in alternative dispute resolution has grown into a national and, indeed, international movement. In the United States, the search for alternatives to typical case processing can be placed within another context, that of privatization. The rapid growth of alternative dispute resolution mechanisms has resulted in an innovation with multiple goals, critics and supporters, and numerous organizational structures. Two things seem clear, however. First, alternative dispute resolution procedures seem to more readily admit of the complexities underlying seemingly straightforward criminal encounters. Second, the climate of privatization created by various federal and state policy initiatives will provide a hospitable environment for further experimentation in this area. The complex issues raised by the nonjudicial settlement of dispute, particularly in crime-related situations, must therefore be addressed. As always, the first problem is with terminology. What exactly is meant by "Alternative dispute resolution"?

CRIMINOLOGICAL/CRIMINAL JUSTICE CONSIDERATIONS

Alternative Dispute Resolution: What Is It?

There are many forms of alternative dispute resolution (ADR). Landlords and tenants, divorcing couples, large corporations, government agencies, and crime victims all have nonjudicial dispute resolution mechanisms available to them. Groups providing these services will vary by type of dispute. Some organizations are primarily community based, have few paid staff, rely mostly on volunteers, and handle neighborhood disputes involving property (landlord/

tenant) or minor criminal matters. On the other hand, some agencies are primarily based within the criminal justice system. They rely on professional staffs, have a high case load, and carry out their function in a more formal manner than found within the community agencies.[3] ADR procedures can also be anchored within a professional practice. Increasingly, lawyers offer divorce mediation as an alternative to the advocacy proceedings of divorce court. Couples negotiate the splitting of property, child custody, and so on. The aim is to avoid the sometimes long and embittering process of divorce litigation.[4] Large companies can hire what amounts to private courts to settle their grievances. Judicate of Philadelphia and EnDispute of Boston are private concerns that specialize in dispute resolution.[5] Judicate provides a courtroom where private civil disputes are heard by retired judges. These judges don robes and decide cases according to Pennsylvania law. EnDispute provides both this kind of service and mediation and arbitration services. Government agencies are increasingly turning to mediators to help negotiate the distribution of government funds among special interest groups.

Dispute resolution will vary not only according to the type of disputes dealt with and the type of sponsoring agency, but it will also vary according to the process used. There are four kinds of dispute resolution processes. The first and least intrusive is conciliation. This process involves a neutral third party assisting in the resolution of a dispute without bringing the parties together for a face-to-face discussion of the matter. Often the third party will engage in a kind of "shuttle diplomacy" bringing information back and forth between the parties.[6]

A second approach to dispute resolution involves the process of mediation. Mediation refers to a situation where a third party helps individual disputants work out their own solution to the problem in a face-to-face encounter.[7]

A third form of dispute resolution involves arbitration. Arbitration refers to the process in which the party hearing the dispute makes a decision regarding its resolution. Such decisions are usually binding on the disputants.[8]

Finally, reconciliation can use any of the methods described above. Its goal is not, however, just the resolution of a specific problem. Reconciliation seeks to heal the damaged relationship between the parties. The emphasis is on bringing the two parties back together in a harmonious relationship.[9]

As the discussion of reconciliation suggests, dispute resolution centers vary according to the goals they seek to achieve. Those founded initially in the late 1960s and early 1970s often had an official base within the criminal justice system. Their goals were, therefore, straightforward. They acted as a kind of case-screening mechanism, to remove minor cases from the criminal justice system thereby decreasing case loads, costs, and case processing time. However, as the idea of alternative case processing caught on, other groups emphasized different goals for the procedure. Neighborhood justice centers, for example, were often started by individuals from religious communities. Actually, as noted

Table 16-1 Typical Features of the Major Types of Community Dispute Resolution Programs

	Justice System–Based	Community-Based	Composite
Sponsorship	Justice System	Nonprofit Agency	Governmental or Nonprofit
Area Served	Entire City or County	Either Entire or of a City or County	Mixed Approach
Major Referral Source	Justice System Agency	Sources Outside Justice System	Both Justice System and Other Sources
Intake Coercion	Typically High	Typically Low	Intermediate
Hearing Length	Typically Brief	Typically Long	Intermediate
Hearing Settings	Typically Formal	Typically Informal	Intermediate
Caseload Size	Typically Large	Typically Small	Intermediate
Budget Size	Typically Large	Typically Small	Intermediate

Source: Daniel McGillis, *Community Dispute Resolution Programs and Public Policy*, U.S., Department of Justice, National Institute of Justice, Office of Communication and Research Utilization, 1986, p. 21.

in Chapter 9, the idea of mediating or arbitrating disputes outside of the formal legal system has a long history. Various religious and ethnic communities have often avoided the civil or criminal system for dispute settlement, choosing to rely instead on their own community mechanisms. Indeed, whole cultures have opted for dispute mediation over judicial intervention. China, for example, has traditionally used dispute resolution mechanisms more often than formal court settings.[10] Interestingly, China is now experiencing the increasing legalization of its system, while the United States and other Western countries are experimenting with less legal forms of dispute resolution.

Neighborhood justice centers founded by those with a religious commitment stress community values over and above efficiency and cost-effectiveness. Groups like the Mennonites have been very active in the neighborhood justice center movement. They see it as a way to emphasize values of peace and community harmony. Reducing community tensions, developing indigenous leaders, and decentralizing decision making so that communities can control their own destinies are some of the specific goals these programs might incorporate.

Still other programs seek primarily to improve the lot of the victim and the offender. In short, they want to humanize the process of justice. This is done primarily by treating a criminal matter as a civil dispute. Each side gets to tell his or her story and then negotiate over what the appropriate remedies should be.

Table 16-1, taken from a National Institute of Justice study on community dispute resolution, illustrates the different types of community dispute resolution programs. The composite type program, the last column on the chart, will often encompass the multiple goals of efficiency, community betterment, and criminal justice system humanization. In order to better illustrate the use of dispute resolution in criminal justice, a community program of composite type will be described.

POLICY CONSIDERATIONS: THEORIES/ARGUMENTS/APPLICATIONS

A Neighborhood Justice Center

Neighborhood justice centers are defined as "facilities . . . designed to make available a variety of methods of processing disputes including arbitration, mediation, referral to small claims court, as well as referral to courts of general jurisdiction."[11] Cases are referred to the center in a number of ways. After a case has been adjudicated through the formal system, a judge can order an individual found guilty to make restitution to the victim and to report to the neighborhood justice center to arrange it. These programs are termed Victim/Offender/Reconciliation Programs (VORP). The emphasis here is to arrange restitution and to bring about a reconciliation, a healing of the relationship between the victim and the offender. A case can also be referred to the center prior to actual determination of guilt or innocence. In such instances, the system does not forego control. It will retain the right to prosecute if an agreement cannot be reached. These referrals from the criminal courts are not the only source of cases for the program. In some instances, cases come to the center entirely through community referrals, sometimes involving suggestions by police officers, but for all practical purposes avoiding any kind of formal system referral.

Once a case has been accepted by a paid staff member, the staff member will contact a volunteer mediator. The mediator will then attempt to contact the two parties involved. In a criminal case referred by the court, the mediator will first contact the victim to ascertain his or her willingness to participate in the process. Many times victims are reluctant to do so. However, the prospect of restitution and the opportunity to gain information about the crime will often overcome victim reluctance.

Once the victim and offender have agreed to participate in the process, a time and place for the meeting is arranged. In this particular program, most meetings take place at the program site, a church hall. Other programs, however, arrange meetings in the home of the victim if the victim is amenable.

The meeting has a set format and a predictable flow.[12] First the mediator will introduce the parties to each other. After everyone is settled, the mediator then explains the goals of the session. Each party will have a chance to describe his or her perception of the event. How the person felt during the event and questions that they now have are important elements of this stage. Victims are often concerned about why they were targeted for victimization. In a burglary situation, they will want to know, for example, if their house had been under some kind of surveillance. Perpetrators are asked to repeat the details of crimes. They are often surprised that the victim had the feelings that were expressed. Many crimes are crimes of impulse and do not involve a great deal of planning and/or surveillance. The perpetrators will often express remorse for the fear that they created in the victim and will express surprise at the value of the items taken. Perpetrators often do not consider sentimental value of items.

Once perceptions and feelings about the event have been aired, the mediator will attempt to establish the specific value of the items taken. Then, a discussion of how to pay the victim back will take place. After agreement on payback, either monetary or service, the mediator will draw up a contract. Each party signs the contract and agrees to abide by its conditions. The session ends with the victim and offender having established at least some common ground on which to proceed.

Such face-to-face meetings often involve surprises for both the victim and the offender. The process of justice tends to dehumanize each of these two key actors. Coming face to face requires the offender to take responsibility for his or her actions. It also requires the victim to drop stereotypes that he or she may hold regarding offenders. Often in the process of mediation, the victim will begin to express some sympathy for the plight of the offender.

In cases referred by the court, the contract is returned to the judge. Failure to live up to the contract can result in the judge imposing more severe punishment on the offender. Cases not referred by the court require follow-up by the mediator.

Obviously, the processes described above allow for the greater control over outcomes by those most intimately associated with the event, the victim and the offender. Nevertheless, there are cultural roadblocks to the use of such procedures.[13] Our criminal justice system has reinforced the notion that in judicial processing there should be a clear winner and a clear loser. Criminal events designate the offender as the loser and the victim as the winner. Yet this is seldom the case. Research evidence suggests that both victim and offender often lose.[14] The victim loses time from work, is frustrated by the slowness of the system, and usually does not get restitution. The offender feels railroaded and, therefore, does not take personal responsibility for his or her actions. But, the desire to punish often outweighs the more pragmatic aspects of case processing. Offenders think they can beat the system, and victims think they can righteously see the offender "get his or her just desserts."

An obvious question that arises from experience with neighborhood justice centers is whether or not they achieve the goals intended. Since there are myriad goals ascribed to these centers, the question is not an easy one to answer. Nevertheless, recent research has attempted to untangle the complex expectations surrounding such community dispute resolution processes.

Evaluation of Community Dispute Resolution Programs

Whether or not alternative dispute resolution "works" depends upon the goals focused on in the evaluation. Based upon the history of the movement, three broadly defined categories of goals can be articulated. These are system goals, punishment goals, and community goals. Each of these broad goal categories can be further subdivided. System goals include such things as greater efficiency and reduced cost, as well as a more humane process. Punishment goals can include reform of the offender, deterrence, and incapacitation. Finally, community goals can include such things as power sharing, decentralization of decision making, and reconciliation of the offender and the victim. A community goal can also be improved access to justice.

A review of the evaluation literature suggests that alternative dispute resolution is neither the panacea claimed by its supporters nor the dark conspiracy described by some detractors. The evaluation literature instead cautiously argues that alternative dispute resolution "works, *but.* . . ."[15]

The qualified support found in the literature can be illustrated when one looks at program goals from a system perspective. Using the efficiency criteria of lowered case-processing time, reduced dockets, and cost containment provides mixed results. Case-processing time appears to be much less in ADR programs than in the courts. In a study of three neighborhood justice centers, the Justice Department found the average processing time was less than two weeks from referral. Similar cases taken to court would take two to three months from the time of filing until a trial.[16] While these data clearly point to the efficiency of alternative dispute resolution programs, it must be remembered that these programs contain a built-in advantage. Their case loads are far less than the case loads of the court. Therefore, when one looks at the ability of alternative programs to reduce case loads in the criminal courts, the evidence is far less favorable for the alternative. The American Bar Association's *Dispute Resolution Program Directory* lists 182 alternative programs.[17] One hundred and thirty-six (136) of these mediation centers provided information regarding the number of case referrals. Only 4% indicated that they received over 5,000 referrals annually. Sixty percent of the programs received fewer than 500 referrals per year.[18] The case load size of alternative dispute resolution centers, then, implies that impact on court dockets is minimal. This, in turn, suggests that dispute resolution programs have not had significant effect on court costs. While it is no doubt cheaper to process a case using an alternative center, the small number of people who choose to do so keeps court costs relatively high. At the same time, money is being spent on the alternative. Thus, while a case-by-case cost comparison favors ADR, overall system costs may be unaffected or indeed rise if funding is provided the ADR by criminal justice agencies.

System goals can also include humanitarian concerns. These can specifically address such issues as client satisfaction and compliance with agreements. In a 1980 evaluation of three centers (Atlanta, Georgia; Kansas City, Missouri; and Los Angeles, California), it was found that nearly 90% of the disputants said they were satisfied with their experience in the centers. Moreover, in a six-month follow-up, 80% of the agreements arrived at were working well.[19] An increasing body of data supports these findings. Disputants are generally well satisfied with their treatment in the neighborhood justice centers. In the few comparative studies that have been done, those going through regular court channels have been found to be far less satisfied with both the way they were treated and the personnel handling their cases.[20]

One of the common outcomes of the ADR process is the offenders' agreement to pay restitution to the victim. Restitution can be either monetary or in the form of service. If the goals of alternative dispute resolution are viewed from a punishment perspective, the question arises as to whether this outcome is to be considered sufficient punishment for violating the law. Unfortunately, this question cannot easily be answered because it involves a more complex issue, namely, what should the goals of punishment be? VORP-like programs tend to stress rehabilitation as a goal. However, there has been very little systematic research on this point. The little that has been done suggests that restitution may have some positive benefits for juvenile offenders. Less promising results have occurred when adult restitution programs are examined.[21] Two other factors complicate the picture even further. In some programs, restitution has been ordered in conjunction with a short jail sentence. Moreover, the studies of the effects of restitution have not been in the context of ADR. In some instances, the cases represented court-ordered restitution or service. Thus, from a punishment perspective using the goal of reform, there is no clear data for the purposes of evaluation.

Clearly, from a perspective of incapacitation, ADR outcomes are likely to be less restrictive. If a person is given a short jail sentence, even this will usually be less than if restitution has not been agreed to. Thus, a person is likely to be back in the community much more quickly using an alternative dispute resolution mechanism.[22] Again, however, there are no systematic data to address the issue of whether the lessening of incapacitation causes more or less crime. It does appear, however, that judges are more likely to support the nonincarcerative aspects of ADR if the offender clearly knows restitution or unpaid labor is a form of punishment.[23] Further, the fact that most contracts are fulfilled suggests that behavior is being monitored, or that the offender anticipates such monitoring, while he or she remains in the community.

A similar lack of research does not permit an answer to the question of whether VORP-like processes deter offenders. Theoretically at least, bringing the offender face to face with a victim forces the former to take responsibility for his or her deeds. This, in turn, may encourage a greater sense of community responsibility. Some theorists have also argued that giving the offender the chance to make things right with the victim restores self-esteem, further lessening the likelihood of repeat offenses.[24] While these theories relate to specific deterrence, there is very little conceptual development regarding VORP's influence on general deterrence. And, of course, data supporting either a specific deterrent or a general deterrent hypothesis are minimal. However, data cited previously about the beneficial effects of the process on juveniles are promising.

Regarding community goals, the multiple demands made on neighborhood justice centers continue to provide a less than focused picture. Critics, for example, worry that alternative dispute resolution represents second-class justice.[25] Thus, rather than contributing to power sharing and decentralized decision making, such community-based procedures are seen as reinforcing the position of the powerless vis-à-vis the powerful. Those opposed to this privatizing of justice note that most clients of neighborhood justice centers are poor. Moreover, they contend that a major function of courts is to set public standards. Neighborhood justice centers keep records confidential and, therefore, the standard setting function of justice is lost. This, in turn, trivializes certain offenses, particularly in the area of family life, such as spouse abuse.

Three things must be kept in mind when assessing this criticism. The possibility of second-class justice clearly exists. If an individual does not have his or her grievance fairly addressed and no attempt is made to restore to the victim that which has been lost, second-class justice has triumphed. Unfortunately, this state of affairs seems to describe more closely the circumstances of typical case processing in the formal system of justice. In the context of a neighborhood justice center, the emphasis is on discovering what the victim needs, what the offender can do to meet those needs, and what the community can do to restore both to full participation.

If second-class justice is defined from the point of view of the offender, the use of neighborhood justice processes and jail raise the specter of the spreading net. Here, the charge of second-class justice seems more cogent. In a review of VORPs, Robert Coates and John Gehm found that 80% of both a VORP and a non-VORP matched sample did not go to jail. Yet, in the non-VORP sample the 80% did not have to participate in *any* program. VORP was an extra for those referred to the process. On the other hand, of those in both samples that served postconviction time, the VORP participants served a significantly shorter amount of time and were more likely to be incarcerated in a local jail than in a state prison.[26] Generally, then, it appears that neighborhood justice centers provide participants with a greater say in the outcome of their cases, but from the point of view of the defendants, they may receive more punishment if their offense would not have resulted in incarceration no matter which system they participated in. VORP participation seems to ameliorate punishment if the individual is likely to be given a confinement sentence.

Neighborhood justice centers do seem to decentralize justice by involving far more people in the process. As noted, most mediators are volunteers and come from all walks of life. Some people have argued that justice is too important to be left exclusively to judges and lawyers.

One of the goals of neighborhood justice centers has been to strengthen the sense of community in a local area. This was to be accomplished through reconciling the victim and the offender and by improving access to justice. Unfortunately, movement toward these goals is difficult to measure. The terms "justice," "reconciliation," and "access" are not easily defined. It appears the neighborhood justice centers make every effort to advertise their services, but as noted, relatively few people take advantage of them. Thus, while justice access has been theoretically improved, practically there has not been a marked change in people's access. Reconciliation is also not well defined. If it is taken to mean a healing of a relationship between two parties, this is probably not the typical outcome of most mediations. However, it does occur in some instances where there has been a prior relationship. And, in those cases involving stranger-to-stranger confrontations, the VORP process can make it more difficult to maintain the stereotypes victims and offenders may hold about one another. Perhaps this, too, is a type of healing.

At this stage in the ADR movement, it appears that the process is indeed promising. Participants are generally more satisfied with what they experience when compared to those who go through regular court channels. At the same time, some of the lofty goals that have been proposed for the alternative have not been met. Concerning systemic goals, there is no reason, at least in principle, why the ADR movement cannot contribute to greater court efficiency. If a larger volume of cases were to be shifted to alternative dispute mechanisms for resolving conflicts, the courts could alleviate log jams in their dockets. In some jurisdictions, such as Atlanta, Georgia, neighborhood justice centers do relieve the courts of a significant number of cases.[27] Nationally, however, use is still relatively small. Finally, the caution of critics must be taken seriously. Privatization of formerly governmental functions can have a downside. We turn next to the privatization of dispute resolution within the broader framework of privatization generally.

What Disputes Should Be Settled Publicly?

Privatization of justice services raises two key issues: equity and responsibility.

The equity issue was first addressed in the history of Anglo-Saxon jurisprudence in the year 1215 with the signing of the Magna Carta. King John accepted the principle that no one should be denied justice because of monetary considerations.[28] The poor, as well as the rich, deserved their day in court. In

Table 16-2 Missouri Court Surcharges

Amount	Purpose
$3 per case (criminal, civil and probate)	Sheriff's Retirement Fund
$36 or $26 per criminal case depending on date of offense	Victim's Compensation Fund
$2 per criminal case	Sheriff's Training
$3.50 per criminal case	Prosecuting Attorney's Reimbursement Fund
$1 per criminal case	Prosecuting Attorney's Training Fund
$10 per dissolution case	Domestic Violence Shelters (optional county surcharge)
$2 per municipal case	Law Enforcement Training (optional municipal surcharge)
Up to $10 ($15 in county required to hold circuit court in two cities)	Law Library

Source: Richard Dohm, "Are We Selling Justice?" *Governmental Affairs Newsletter*, 22, No. 7. (March, 1988).

the last chapter, we saw that the provision of a secure environment is often based on the ability to pay. Privatization of police service may well mean, then, that those without sufficient resources will have to sacrifice the level of security enjoyed by the better off in society. Considerations of equity have a somewhat different outcome when applied to dispute resolution.

Courts are required to levy charges on those who use them. These need not be necessarily related to the actual costs of judicial administration. Table 16-2 shows Missouri Court surcharges from a study by Richard Dohm on the cost of justice in Missouri. These are exclusive of the approximately $50 in fees related to courtroom administration. If found guilty, therefore, a defendant can be held responsible for approximately $90 in court-related costs.[29]

As noted, the costs of a neighborhood justice center are much less than the costs associated with formal case processing. Moreover, fees are not assessed from offenders, only restitution for victims. Thus, from an equity standpoint, the privatization of this part of the justice system may increase rather than decrease access to dispute resolution.

The responsibility issue is much more difficult. As noted, dispute resolution has more than a personal dimension to it. Some disputes may be so important that society as a whole must take responsibility for both settlement and the articulation of a standard. Indeed, the history of criminal justice has been one of the state claiming increasing responsibility for the settlement of disputes because of the need to establish a socially acceptable norm. Thus, critics of neighborhood justice centers accuse the state of shirking its responsibility for norm setting, particularly in the area of family violence.

Perhaps if the use of alternatives were to become both more widespread and better known, with some form of a public admission of guilt being required, both the goal of norm setting and the goal of personal dispute resolution could be met. Unfortunately, when the state takes over the function of dispute resolution, the very real and specific needs of both victim and offender seem to get lost. With imaginative linkages between private dispute resolution and the public courts, it might be possible to better achieve the needs of society and the specific individuals. For now, courts act primarily as overseers of contracts, providing a potential threat to future liberty if the contract is not fulfilled. Perhaps courts can also become public forums, where offenders state their commitment to the contract and their sorrow for having harmed the offender. Such a public ritual could supplement the private arrangement worked out between the parties.

The issue of responsibility becomes even more pronounced when punishment is considered. We turn to this issue in the next chapter.

SUMMARY

What Was Said

- Traditional criminal court practices can oversimplify the nature of disputes.
- Alternative dispute resolution (ADR) can involve conciliation, mediation, arbitration, and reconciliation.
- Evaluation literature of ADR suggests that it works, but that it is not a panacea for the problems of the criminal courts nor is it without some problems.
- The costs of alternative dispute resolution are less than formal case processing.
- Critics of neighborhood justice centers accuse the state of shirking its responsibility for norm setting, particularly in the area of family violence.

What Was Not Said

- ADR is appropriate for all disputes.
- ADR is a modern concept.
- ADR has proven to be an unqualified success.

NOTES

1. James F. Gilsinan, *Doing Justice* (Englewood Cliffs, NJ: Prentice-Hall, Inc.), p. 241.

2. Daniel McGillis, "Community Dispute Resolution Programs and Public Policy," in National Institute of Justice, *Issues and Practices in Criminal Justice*, December 1986, p. 5.

3. *Ibid.*, p. 40.

4. Richard H. Weiss, "Divorce Mediators Make Peace Out of Domestic War," *St. Louis Post-Dispatch*, Nov. 4, 1985, p. 1B.

5. Martin Tolchin, "When the Justice System Is Put Under Contract," *New York Times*, Aug. 4, 1985, p. E5.

6. McGillis, "Community Dispute Resolution," p. 31.

7. Gilsinan, *Doing Justice*, p. 240.

8. Ibid.

9. Robert B. Coates and John Gehm, "VORP Research Project Preliminary Findings" (unpublished paper, March 15, 1985).

10. McGillis, "Community Dispute Resolution," p. 15.

11. Daniel McGillis and Joan Mullen, *Neighborhood Justice Centers, An Analysis of Potential Models* (Washington, D.C.: U.S. Government Printing Office, 1977), p. i.

12. Coates and Gehm, *VORP Research*, pp. 5–6.

13. McGillis, "Community Dispute Resolution," p. 14.

14. For a review of this evidence see Gilsinan, *Doing Justice*, p. 224.

15. McGillis, "Community Dispute Resolution," p. 13.

16. R. Cook, J. Roehl, and D. Sheppard, *Neighborhood Justice Centers Field Test: Final Evaluation Report* (Washington, D.C.: U.S. Government Printing Office, 1980).

17. McGillis, "Community Dispute Resolution," p. 4.

18. Ibid., p. 77.

19. Cook, Roehl, and Sheppard, *Neighborhood Justice Centers Field Test*.

20. McGillis, "Community Dispute Resolution," p. 71.

21. Douglas C. McDonald, "Restitution and Community Service," in *National Institute of Justice Crime File* (Washington, D.C.: U.S. Government Printing Office, 1988), p. 3.

22. Coates and Gehm, "VORP Research Project," pp. 18,19.

23. McDonald, "Restitution and Community Service," p. 3.

24. Ibid., p. 2.

25. Tolchin, "When the Justice System Is Put Under Contract." Also, Martin Tolchin, "Mediated Justice Being Put to Test," *New York Times*, July 21, 1985, p. Y13.

26. Coates and Gehm, "VORP Research Project," pp. 18–19.

27. Tolchen, "Mediated Justice Being Put to Test."

28. Richard Dohm, "Are We Selling Justice?" *Governmental Affairs Newsletter*, 22, No. 7 (March, 1988).

29. Ibid.

XVII

The Privatization
of Justice

Punishment

At the end of this chapter, the student will be able to:

A. Discuss the political importance of the power of punishment.
B. Describe the trend toward privatization in the area.
C. Note the pros and cons of this privatization effort.
D. Discuss the difference between for-profit and not-for-profit privatization in correction.

ISSUE BACKGROUND

American Mythology and the Privatization of Corrections

Clayton Hartjen, in his book *Crime and Criminalization*, notes that the principle of double jeopardy resulted from a conflict between the church and the state about who should have the power to punish.[1] By enunciating the principle that a person could only be tried once for an offense, the state was claiming the prerogative of punishment. The prerogative allows the person who exercises it considerable power. The move toward privatization in the punishment sphere of criminal law suggests that the state is now willing to share some of that power. To understand why this is occurring, it is necessary to review some points discussed earlier.

During the 1970s, there was intense concern about the crime problem and the seemingly dramatic rise in crime rates. A law-and-order philosophy prevailed. The following captures the sentiments of the time:

> In California, the population has made it clear that it wants people locked up for a long time. Alternatives to incarceration are no longer the focus of debate. The issue is how to build more prisons as cheaply as possible. California voters don't want a Cadillac prison system. They simply want criminals out of their lives.[2]

The feelings expressed during this period were often conveyed through variations of "the mob at the gates myth." Our society was being inundated by criminals who needed to be isolated from the rest of society. The notion of rehabilitation, a liberal approach to "the mob at the gates," was replaced by a conservative version of the myth which stressed punishment and control.

Legislators responded to the demands for more law-and-order legislation. Mandatory sentences and the loss of good time through restrictions on the activities of parole boards became the legislative norm.

The policy consequences of these actions soon became clear. Prisons are now, by the beginning of the 1990s, seriously overcrowded. Each week the prison population in the United States grows by 750 people.[3] The incarceration rate per 100,000 people is at 228, a dramatic jump from the rate of 110 per 100,000 that held steady for a number of decades.[4]

The 1980s saw another myth gain ascendency. The triumphant individual, the symbolic bulwark of free enterprise and capitalism, was hailed through myth and story by many spokespersons of the Reagan Administration. Thus, the private sector, controlled by the forces of the free market, was superior to the public sector where government regulation was the engine that drove decision making. As we have seen, therefore, government was encouraged to privatize at all levels of service.

Garbage collection, fire safety, port and waterway authorities, dams, and public parks were some of the service domains opened to the for-profit sector of the economy. The myth and the practice were particularly appealing in the area of corrections.

Legislators do their best to avoid controversial issues. A vote one way or another on a contentious matter is bound to alienate some part of the electorate. Being as noncontroversial as possible helps ensure a continuing political career. Issues surrounding the whole field of corrections place legislators in exactly the kinds of situations they seek to avoid. People want tough laws for dealing with criminals, but they do not want to increase their tax liability in order to pay for the extra prison space such laws require. People do not want criminals on the street, and so expanding probation and parole options in order to better manage institutional populations and resources is viewed with suspicion. And, of course, prisoners themselves do not have a strong lobby. Finally, as we have seen, while state courts have responded to a "get-tough" policy by imposing longer sentences, federal courts have sought to remedy overcrowding by demanding that states either reduce their prison population or provide more space. Thus, legislators see themselves as better off if they can avoid correctional issues altogether. Privatization represents a seemingly painless way to deal with such problems. The controversies they raise can be externalized to the private sector.

Three distinct streams feed the privatization movement in corrections. The conservative version of the mob at the gates led to legislative decisions dramatically increasing our prison population. The myth of the triumphant individual makes privatization of certain public services seem very desirable. Finally, the private sector offers legislators a convenient way of externalizing the controversies raised by correctional policies.

CRIMINOLOGICAL/CRIMINAL JUSTICE CONSIDERATIONS

History and Meanings of Privatization in Corrections

As with many so-called new reforms in criminal justice, the privatization of correctional services has a long, if not to say notorious, history. Unfortunately, both policy analysts and policy makers tend to overlook some of the early experiments in correctional privatization, particularly as these relate to prisons.

Although private prisons and probation services predate public corrections, by the early 1800s the preeminent role of government, at least in the running of prisons, was firmly established. Unfortunately, the policy decisions of early state legislatures resulted in overcrowded, extremely costly, and brutal prisons by as early as 1850.[5] Thus was born state experimentation with "prisons for profit."

Early court decisions regarding the legal standing of inmates held that prisoners were "slaves of the state."[6] Since most state legislatures were interested in defraying the cost of incarceration, inmate labor provided an obvious commodity for sale. In numerous states, particularly in the South, inmate labor replaced the labor of plantation slaves. The "inmate slaves of the state" replaced the slave class freed by the Civil War.[7] By selling inmate labor to private contractors, both public monies and private profits could be generated. The selling of inmate labor did not, however, solve the economic woes of the prison system. In Texas, for example, the main prison was growing at a faster rate than the state could accommodate. This meant that the prison still constituted a drain on state resources. Further privatization was suggested to remedy this problem. In 1871, the entire penitentiary operation was leased to private interests.[8] By 1875, however, it was clear that expanded privatization was not the answer to the problems of the prison. A legislative commission noted that conditions had considerably deteriorated.[9] Brutality, overcrowded conditions, and inefficiency had increased dramatically. By 1883, the state had once again assumed responsibility for the prison system, but continued to contract with private interests for inmate labor.[10]

While state legislatures were struggling to make prisons economically viable enterprises, others, both inside and outside of government, were questioning the benefits of incarceration for the majority of offenders. In 1841, John Augustus began to accept responsibility for convicted persons released to his custody.[11] This early effort at probation grew and with the help of private donations, Augustus was able to make this alternative a permanent option at the Boston Criminal Court. In 1878, the city of Boston, authorized by state statute, took over the probation function when the mayor appointed a paid probation officer.[12]

The early history of privatization and the field of corrections illustrates both the varying definitions of the concepts and issues that such efforts raise. There are at least seven distinct meanings for the term "correctional privatization." Four of these relate to prison facilities. Privatization in the residential prison market can refer to *private management, private financing for construction, inmate labor for profit*, or *any combination of these*. Regarding privatization of probation or parole services, the term can refer to *private control responsibility, private treatment planning*, or *private contracting for services in the community*. Each type of privatization raises particular issues. It is to these that we now turn.

POLICY CONSIDERATIONS:
THEORIES/ARGUMENTS/APPLICATIONS

Issues in the Privatizing of Punishment

The Corrections Corporation of America, Behavioral Systems Southwest, Buckingham Security, Ltd., the RCA Service Company, a Division of the Radio Corporation of America, and American Corrections Corporation are all for-profit corporations whose business is the financing and/or management of correctional institutions. To date, the largest user of these services has been the federal Immigration and Naturalization Service (INS).[13]

The Corrections Corporation of America (CCA), formed in 1982 and based in Nashville, Tennessee, currently controls 1,600 correctional bedspaces.[14] Among the facilities they run are two INS detention centers, a work farm, and a high-security jail. As this is being written, CCA has completed contract negotiations with the State of Texas to provide two 500-bed state prison facilities.[15]

Behavioral Systems Southwest operates one short-term facility for the INS in Colorado, five reentry centers for prison inmates in California, and four community treatment centers for the Federal Bureau of Prisons in Arizona and California. The remaining firms operate primarily low-security, short-term facilities.[16]

The movement of these companies into the operation of adult state prisons has been considerably slowed by the controversy the management and building of prisons by private concerns raises. The State of Tennessee, for example, rejected CCA's offer to buy the state's entire prison system for $250 million.[17] Even in those jurisdictions where the effort to privatize corrections has succeeded, controversy remains.

The private management of prisons raises certain fundamental questions. Among these are the legal rights of persons confined to such facilities, the criteria by which management is to be judged, and the cost savings such management can realize.

Opponents of privatized prison management argue that government cannot contract away certain fundamental functions. Civil libertarians argue that the right to deprive a person of his or her freedom and to impose punishment should belong exclusively to the state. By introducing a profit motive, some fear that the power to punish will be used for the good of the corporation rather than for the good of society or the individual involved.[18] For example, if the private contractor is paid on a per-prisoner basis, it may be in the interest of management to maximize the length of incarceration. Decisions about release for good time or increased sentences for institutional infractions get caught up in the profit needs of the corporation. The need for maintaining a profitable operation, in the view of critics, will negatively affect physical conditions and treatment programs as well as fundamental due process rights. Supporters of privatization, on the other hand, counter that the private sector is able to maintain a higher overall quality in the physical, legal, and treatment aspects of confinement than is found in the public sector.[19] CCA, the largest private correctional company, offers potential government clients a kind of guarantee in this regard. They claim that every facility under their management will meet the vigorous certification standards of the American Correctional Association. These standards cover all aspects of confinement. To date, however, no CCA facility has been ACA certified.[20]

How does one appropriately gauge the effectiveness of private prison management? Students of privatized mental health facilities, schools, nursing homes, and so on, suggest that privatization has resulted in greater efficiency, that is, in the providing of better service for fewer dollars. Unfortunately, such studies also indicate that this result has been achieved through "creaming."[21] Typically, private concerns reduce or eliminate services provided to the most difficult or unprofitable cases. Thus, the burden on public facilities is increased, as they attempt to serve increasingly large concentrations of the most troubled clients. Specifically regarding prisons, would privately run corporations only want the "best" offenders? If they were prevented from this kind of creaming, would they then reduce expensive therapy and work training programs to concentrate instead on the cheaper alternative of simple warehousing?

Cost savings can also be realized by staff reductions and the limiting of staff development. CCA reports that its facilities are designed to operate with fewer employees.[22] Further, employees are given considerably less training than their public sector counterparts.[23] These facts raise both labor relations and treatment issues. Public employees will fight to maintain their jobs and benefits. Moreover, treatment supposedly is enhanced by contact between the treated and the treater. Fewer employees, with less training, may subvert this aspect of institutional corrections.

Some critics argue that CCA's failure to achieve American Correctional Association accreditation is directly related to labor–management conflicts.[24] While CCA reports a turnover rate in employees of 28%, other figures suggest the employee turnover rate is 70% annually. The average in corrections has been estimated at 35% a year.[25]

Labor–management problems can raise rather than lower operating expenses. To this cost can be added the social cost of those public sector guards displaced by privatization. Thus, at this point in the privatization saga, it is unclear whether the approach has really saved any taxpayer dollars. Jurisdictions that have privatized some of their confinement facilities have been unable to verify any significant cost savings.

The privatization of correctional construction financing raises its own set of dilemmas. Currently, most states and local jurisdictions finance the construction of new prison or jail facilities by attempting to get a bond issue passed by voters. There are two major types of bonds.

Revenue bonds are paid for by the revenue produced from whatever is built. Thus, if the local government decides to build a sports arena, the money it must borrow to do so plus interest will presumably be paid back to the lender through the revenues the arena produces. CCA convinced both Tennessee and Florida to issue these types of bonds to finance its construction of facilities in these two states. The company has assumed as part of its long-term debt the obligation to pay off the Tennessee bonds. It will pay back the Florida bonds by reducing the rate it charges for prisoners. So far, the company has not paid back any of its bond indebtedness.[26]

Prisons obviously have a difficult time producing revenue. How, then, do state and/or local governments pay for, or more accurately, get citizens to pay for, their construction? Typically, they would ask voters to approve a general obligation bond. By approving such a bond, voters allow the state to borrow money with the understanding that the state puts its credit behind the bond. In the event that there are insufficient tax revenues in the general fund to pay back the loan and interest, citizens agree to let the state raise taxes in order to pay off the debt. The recent past has made clear the voters' reluctance to approve such bonds.

The private financing of prisons or jails avoids the necessity of gaining voter approval for such projects. The prison or jail is built with private money and then leased back to the state. Under this arrangement, the cost still becomes part of the general governmental operating budget. Tax levies would still be required if the state could not meet its obligation under leasing arrangements. But this form of financing avoids the political consequences of prison construction.[27] By bypassing the voters, prisons and jails can be built more rapidly. At the same time, however, the question of whether or not they should be built is removed from the public agenda. Red tape is avoided, but so too is the vital give and take necessary for an informed body politic. Decision making is left entirely to those whose vested interests lie in the direction of expanded incarcerative facilities. It is hard to judge whether this serves the public good if, in fact, the public has no voice in deciding the issue. Moreover, the public remains financially obligated, at least potentially, despite its lack of voice in how tax dollars are allocated.

Private sector participation in the prison system is also found in prison industry and work programs. "Factories with fences" can take a number of forms. As a brief history of privatized corrections shows, the use of inmate labor was often tied to the agricultural industry or to public works, the building of roads, bridges, etc. The early use of inmate labor was, however, curtailed by a number of factors. Among these were the brutality, corruption, and exploitation that often seemed to accompany the use of inmate labor for private profit or institutional gain. Despite these problems, significant legislative curtailment of the practice did not occur until the Depression as policy makers sought to ease civilian unemployment.[28] The legacy of this era has been a type of prison work with few transferable skills. Being able to make a good license plate does not ensure employment outside the walls. Hence, the renewed interest in factories with fences.

In its modern reincarnation, prison industry is being oriented toward the manufacturing and the service sectors of the economy. Many states, however, still limit the participation of prisons in the private economy. Prison goods are seen by labor interests to have an unfair advantage in the market place, since the manufacturing of such goods are in a sense being subsidized by the state. The extensive use of inmate labor may also threaten the jobs available to those on the outside. California, for example, wants to employ inmates in meat, fish, and poultry processing for state-run institutions. The United Food and Commercial Workers Union argues that such a program would cost civilian workers at least 100 jobs. Union opposition continues to slow such privatizing.[29] Nevertheless, there have been a number of states wherein the "factories with fences" movement has gained momentum. In Arizona, a hotel chain installed reservation computers in a women's facility. The inmates are used to make reservations for the chain. In Minnesota, inmates manufactured disc drives for Control Data Corporation.[30] Other states are actively pursuing an expansion of prison-based industries. While some of these innovations are promising, past history suggests that inmate labor is easily exploited. Real-world work experience seems to reduce idleness and provide useful skills, but careful monitoring to ensure adequate and safe working conditions will be required. Policy makers will also have to make sure that prison labor does not compete with free labor for jobs and resources, particularly in the troubled manufacturing districts of the Northeast and Midwest.

The need for careful monitoring in all aspects of institutional privatization suggests a hidden cost which may further affect the fiscal attractiveness of their venture. As Bowditch and Everett note, the state would have to create a regulatory bureaucracy to ensure compliance with contract provisions, state and local laws, and constitutional guarantees.[31] Thus, government officials appear quite limited in their ability to externalize the problems of institutional corrections. There is no legal doctrine that supports the idea that governments can escape legal liability by privatizing the production of a service.[32] Yet the attractiveness of being insulated from lawsuits appears to be a major selling point for elected officials.[33] The need for a regulatory structure further entangles lawmakers with prison systems run by private companies. Finally, since the for-profit sector will control a wide variety of secondary employment opportunities, from contracts for pest control to landscaping and food services, opportunities for conflicts of interest and corruption abound. Part-time legislators or council members who own businesses that could profit from contracts with a private prison company might base privatization decisions on mutually beneficial business considerations rather than on considerations of sound public policy.[34]

The privatization of jails and prisons has a common theme, namely privatization for profit. As noted, the privatization of probation and parole services has traditionally been a not-for-profit enterprise. Indeed, in this latter segment of corrections, the impetus for change has been reform rather than profit. Thus, correctional privatization has a kind of schizophrenic character to it.[35] For-profit privatization seems to encourage an increased reliance upon facilities for incarceration. Buildings can be erected more cheaply and more quickly so that a larger number of inmates can be housed at less cost to the government. The not-for-profit privatization movement has, on the other hand, largely been involved with alternatives to imprisonment. From John Augustus in Boston to modern-day private advocacy for client-specific planning, the impetus has been on getting people out of jail and prisons. A brief review of the types of not-for-profit privatization highlights this emphasis.

Halfway Houses and Private Service Vendors

John Augustus exercised a kind of privatized control function. Today, such privatized control is largely exercised through the institution of the halfway house. Halfway houses form an intermediate step between total freedom in the community and incarceration away from the community. Often run by not-for-profit organizations with religious or philanthropic ties, their purpose is to ease the transition from confinement back to the community or to provide the offender headed for prison one more chance at a community alternative. The origins and history of halfway houses is instructive.

Although no one is certain exactly when halfway houses began, they can be traced at least as far back as the first century. The monk, St. Leonard, established a monastery for offenders whose early release he had obtained.[36] The religious affiliation of most halfway houses remained strong through the 1960s. In 1845, the Quakers established a halfway house in New York City that still operates today.[37] The work of the Salvation Army in housing homeless men included work with men recently released from prison. But halfway houses have always generated opposition, and their development remained slow. The movement gained new vitality in the 1950s when Dismas Clark, a Jesuit priest, established Dismas House in St. Louis. By 1960, Attorney General Robert Kennedy gave his endorsement to the movement. Growth was further spurred by the availability of Law Enforcement Assistance Administration money during the 1960s and 1970s. Today the community corrections movement has provided a new role for halfway houses, encouraging their use for offenders who would ordinarily be sentenced to prison, but who appear to still have rehabilitative potential in the community.

Community corrections' reliance on local treatment centers has spurred the growth of private service vendors. Vendors provide a wide variety of services including drug/alcohol counseling, employment training and referral, remedial education, budgeting and family services, and so on. State or local agencies will contract with these various groups to provide a certain number of program slots for those under state or local correctional jurisdiction. As noted, probation and parole officers increasingly become brokers of service rather than providers of service.

Reforms can sometimes go awry. Probation and parole services have often been criticized as too supportive of jail- or prison-based programs. The seemingly too easy use of revocation by these workers has dismayed those committed to less incarcerative reforms. Thus, continued privatization in the area of community-based corrections has directly challenged the hegemony of probation and parole in this area. Privately prepared presentence reports and privately formulated client specific plans have been innovations which directly challenge the judgment of probation and parole workers. In some instances, judges now have two presentence reports to choose from, one arguing for continued community corrections, the other for incarceration. It is the latter that is usually produced by probation and parole, while the former is a private product.

Conclusion

Clearly, privatization has different impacts in different segments of the justice system generally, and corrections, specifically. Private for-profit groups seem mainly concerned with institutional corrections. As noted, the privatization of this segment of correction may actually encourage the use of prisons and jails. Sophisticated lobbying, promises of quick fixes, and reduced roadblocks to financing and construction encourage the current prison population problem to be defined as lack of space.

Private not-for-profit activity is mainly centered in community alternatives to imprisonment. Here, the problem definition that is encouraged is the overuse of prison because of mandatory sentencing and other law-and-order policy decisions. Therefore, it is not lack of space but lack of sound policy that has created the overcrowding crisis.

Policy makers need to avoid a panacea phenomenon, seeking a simple answer to a very complex problem. Getting the right answers and solutions depends upon asking the right questions and defining the right problems. This chapter has articulated some of the questions and problems that arise when looking at an issue like the privatization of corrections. The next chapter will explore the ways policy makers and public managers can expand in a systematic way their visions of problems and solutions by generating imaginative questions.

SUMMARY

What Was Said

- Three distinct streams feed the privatization movement in corrections: a conservative version of mob at the gate; the myth of the triumphant individual; a way for legislators seemingly to avoid a controversial issue.
- The history of privatized corrections suggests that such efforts have not been particularly successful.
- The key issues that the private management of prison raises include the rights of prisoners, the criteria used to judge such management, and the cost savings that can be realized.
- Privatization in the residential sphere can refer to private management, private financing for construction, inmate labor for profit, or any combination of these.
- Privatization of probation and parole services can refer to private control responsibility, private treatment planning, or private contracting for services in the community.
- Privatization of jails and prisons has generally been a for-profit endeavor, while privatization of probation and parole services has been a not-for-profit enterprise.
- For-profit privatization seems to encourage an increased reliance upon facilities for incarceration.
- Not-for-profit privatization has largely been involved with alternatives for imprisonment.

What Was Not Said

- Legislators and government can avoid issues of liability by privatizing prisons.
- Privatized prisons are cheaper than publicly run facilities.
- State probation and parole services always favor community rather than residential programs.

NOTES

1. Clayton Hartjen, *Crime and Criminalization* (New York: Praeger Publishers, 1974).

2. J. P. Levine, M. Musheno, and D. Palumbo, *Criminal Justice in America: The Law in Action* (New York: John Wiley, 1985).

3. Peter Applebome, "With Inmates at Record High, Sentence Policy Is Reassessed," *New York Times*, 25 April, 1988, p. 11.

4. Ibid.

5. David J. Rothman, "Sentencing Reform in Historical Perspective," *Crime and Delinquency* (October, 1983), pp. 631–49.

6. Steve J. Martin and Sheldon Ekland-Olson, *Texas Prisons* (Austin: Texas Monthly Press, Inc., 1987), p. 5.

7. Ibid.

8. Ibid., p. 6.

9. Ibid.

10. Ibid., p. 7.

11. Paul F. Cromwell, Jr., et al., *Probation and Parole in the Criminal Justice System*, 2nd. ed. (St. Paul, MN: West Publishing Co., 1985), p. 10.

12. Ibid., p. 11.

13. Christine Bowditch and Ronald S. Everett, "Private Prisons: Problems Within the Solution," *Justice Quarterly*, 4(3) (September 1987), 443.

14. Deborah Davis, "2 'Model' Prisons Cast Doubt on CCA Claims," *The Nashville Tennessean*, 15 May, 1988, p. ID.

15. Deborah Davis, "5-Year-Old CCA Has Yet to Make a Profit," *The Nashville Tennessean*, 15 May, 1988, p. 5D.

16. Bowditch and Everett, "Private Prisons," p. 443.

17. Bill Finger, "The Great Break Out," *Southern Magazine*, June 1988, p. 51.

18. Jan Elvin, "A Civil Liberties View of Private Prisons," *Prison Journal* 65(2) (Autumn–Winter 1985), 48–52.

19. Joan Mullen, "Corrections and the Private Sector," *Prison Journal* 65(2) (Autumn–Winter 1985), 8–11.

20. Deborah Davis, "CCA Falls Short on Accreditation, Insurance Vows," *The Nashville Tennessean*, 16 May 1988, p. 4E.

21. Bowditch and Everett, "Private Prisons," p. 446.

22. Davis, "5-Year-Old CCA Has Yet to Make a Profit," p. 5D.

23. Davis, "CCA Falls Short on Accreditation, Insurance Vows," p. 4E.

24. Ibid.

25. Ibid.

26. Davis, "5-Year-Old CCA Has Yet to Make a Profit," p. 5D.

27. Elvin, "Civil Liberties," pp. 48–52.

28. "Convict Labor Has the Unions Worried," *Business Week*, April 16, 1984, p. 51.

29. Ibid.

30. Ibid.

31. Bowditch and Everett, "Private Prisons," pp. 449–50.

32. Mullen, "Corrections," p. 9.

33. Davis, "2 'Model' Prisons Cast Doubt on CCA Claims," p. 1D, 4D.

34. For a discussion of this entanglement, see Davis, "2 'Model' Prisons Cast Doubt on CCA Claims," pp. 1D, 4D.

35. Dennis J. Palumbo, "Privatization and Corrections Policy," *Policy Studies Review*, 5 (February 1986), 598–605.

36. Belinda Rodgers McCarthy and Bernard J. McCarthy, Jr., *Community-Based Corrections* (Monterey, CA: Brooks/Cole Publishing Company, 1984).

37. Ibid.

XVIII

Does It Work? Can It Work? How Do We Know?

At the end of this chapter, the student will be able to:

A. Discuss the current revolutions in both the physical and social sciences.
B. Describe how these paradigm shifts affect the study of crime and crime control policies.
C. Note ways of stimulating creativity in the management of public policy problems.
D. Describe strategies that are realistically possible in light of current knowledge and political and economical realities.

ISSUE BACKGROUND

Revolutions

Science, both physical and social, is in a state of crisis. This state has been brought about in part by a questioning of one of the fundamental assumptions of scientific endeavor, namely, the assumption that the world is a logical, coherent construct, knowable through a rigorous application of the deductive method. This assumption is now, however, no longer taken for granted.[1]

In the physical sciences, one illustration of the revolt against commonly accepted scientific assumptions is found in the problem of parallel universes.

Some physicists argue that how we observe the physical world determines the reality of that world.[2] In other words, we cannot take the physical world as a given. How we interact with it determines what it is. Now, this notion applied to physical reality seems startling enough. But a school of physicists have taken this notion even further. If I observe a physical reality in a particular way, what happens to the other potentials contained in the object? One answer is that they too exist, but in a parallel universe. Despite the evidence of our senses, therefore, there are many physical worlds that exist simultaneously with the one we happen to be in at the moment.[3]

If this theory were true, it would be difficult to construct universal laws to explain the functioning of the physical world. After all, such a quest rests on the assumption that the world is objectively knowable. The scientist attempts to construct universal laws through the application of the "scientific method," that is, testing a general proposition by constructing a statement of what should happen in a specific set of circumstances. This statement, or hypothesis, is then tested. A positive outcome adds to the validity of a particular general theory, while a negative outcome suggests the need for altering the theory or general statement. But if the scientist's observations constitute only one of many multiple realities, how can objective truth be arrived at using the traditional methods of science?

Obviously, the rumblings of certain physicists attack the foundations upon which science has rested. The inability of traditional science to answer new problems raised by different understandings of the physical environment is precipitating what Kuhn has called a scientific revolution.[4] Such revolutions involve, according to Kuhn, paradigm shifts. Paradigms are "universally recognized scientific achievements that for a time provide model problems and solutions to a community of practitioners."[5] When such assumptions and models no longer appear to be able to answer new questions, a paradigm shift or revolution occurs within the scientific community.

The paradigm of traditional science has provided the model for social scientists and their inquiries into the nature of social life. We have seen throughout this book, however, that new understandings and models are emerging in the field of social scientific inquiry. These new models and understandings are in part a response to the inability of traditional social science to answer a variety of questions. The effects of a policy depend, it seems, upon who observes them and under what conditions. Moreover, policy interventions seldom result in what was intended by the policy maker. In fact, they often seem to make a problem worse rather than better. Traditional social science has been unable to provide solutions to the dilemmas faced by policy makers and has been slow to understand the multiple realities of the organizational and policy environment. And so, a significant question remains. How do we make sense out of our political environment, and what guidance can be offered to those who want to affect it in a positive way?

At first glance, the revolutions of science seem to offer a rather pessimistic prognosis. Not only is the political world seemingly beyond comprehension, but the model upon which such comprehension has been based is itself under serious challenge. On the other hand, revolutions always offer hope for a better situation. Certainly, in the history of science, periods of confusion often turn out to be the most creative moments within a discipline. Unshackled from the frameworks of the past, investigators are free to put together ideas and concepts in new and exciting ways that stimulate new and exciting insights. Thus, confusion within organizational, criminological, and policy sciences may herald imaginative new insights that will break down old understandings and in their place provide new problems and solutions. For this to occur, however, it is not sufficient to understand only the shifting paradigms of science. An understanding of the changing ideological infrastructure of public institutions is also required. It is to this shift that we now turn.

Ideological Shifts

A political shift away from the government interventionism of the 1960s and the 1970s, combined with certain fiscal realities and the pessimistic conclusions of evaluation research, have created a climate negatively disposed to supporting government action in many policy areas. The generalizability of the "nothing works" argument can be seen in recent attitudes toward the presidency. Lyndon Johnson, Richard Nixon, Gerald Ford, and Jimmy Carter shared a common fate. These recent presidents all had shorter tenures in office than they legally could have had. Ronald Reagan was the first president since Dwight Eisenhower to serve two full terms. But even with the high expectations and "Teflon coating" that surrounded him, foreign policy scandals, indictments and convictions of key aides, rising deficits, and a recurring sense that the president was not in control plagued even this popular political figure.

At the beginning of the 1990s there is a pessimism that goes beyond the feeling that government cannot solve our problems. Our traditional myths seem unable to provide answers to the problems faced by the body politic today. Thus, in the social and political realms as in the realms of physical and social science, basic assumptions are being challenged.

The consequences of this social/political paradigmatic shifting have been uneven. On the one hand, we still look at potential presidents in terms of the quick fixes they can provide. Political campaigns become media events wherein complex problems and their solutions are reduced to one-minute commercials. Slogans replace analysis. The candidate who presents the image of the best mechanic, the Mr. Fix-It, has the best opportunity to win an election. On the other hand, honeymoon periods for new presidents tend to be short. The complexities of the problems encountered do not allow for quick fixes, and the gap between promises and possibilities soon becomes apparent. Skepticism may well be a healthy byproduct of a shifting social/political paradigm. While people search out new assumptions around which to build a consensus, gurus are paradoxically sought after and criticized. Thus, simple answers to complex problems, although initially appealing, soon lose credibility. Changes in the criminal justice policy arena illustrate these points.

CRIMINOLOGICAL/CRIMINAL JUSTICE CONSIDERATIONS

Nothing Works, Again

The criminal justice enterprise, as we have seen, is replete with examples of failed policies and of policies that had unintended consequences. While it may seem obvious that there are no simple solutions to the complex problems associated with the phenomenon called crime, criminal justice, as other policy areas, first tends to embrace the simple solution. It is a field in which gurus, at least initially, are easily accepted. Pass a law, increase a penalty, substitute a treatment, spend more money, get tough, be lenient, do less, do more, do something. Underlying all of these reforms is the notion that the crime problem is solvable. During the last 20 years, the system has seen a dramatic rise in both the amount of money spent and the personnel employed to deal with the crime issue. Despite this there has been no dramatic change in crime patterns. Further, people are increasingly questioning such expenditures. The old assumptions about the liberal and conservative approaches to crime therefore no longer seem to hold. Conservative legislators argue the need for increased prison sentences until the bill comes due. Then they, together with their constituents, balk at paying the tremendous price entailed by massive prison construction. Liberal legislators support sentencing guidelines which decrease the discretion of judges but might potentially increase the time to be served for an offense. National organizations of police personnel publicly split with the National Rifle Association, ending a decades-long alliance. Bullets that penetrate body armor, automatic weapons, and plastic guns that can evade metal detectors seem, in the eyes of the police, to stretch beyond acceptable limits the meaning of the right to keep and bear arms. Police agencies and their national associations therefore increasingly sound the liberal concerns about unlimited weapons availability. Shifting alliances seem to be the norm rather than the exception within the criminal justice area. These shifts may in fact be heralds to new policy paradigms for dealing with crime.

One emerging trend seems to be the renewed interest in the policy potential of the local community. Rather than simply being seen as the receiver of policy initiatives, the neighborhood and local community is being viewed as a key source of successful criminal justice policy innovation.

The Local Community and Criminal Justice Policy

To be successful, new criminal justice policy paradigms will have to build on the fundamental myths of the past. Thus, creative policy approaches involve less the invention of new myths and more the recombination and reformulation of old ones. One such emerging framework within criminal justice involves policy elements of neighborhood, family, and employment.[6]

It is immediately clear that the elements of this emerging policy framework build on traditional American myths. Elements of the triumphant individual and the benevolent community are apparent. As being applied in certain areas of criminal justice, the negatives associated with "mob at the gates" and "rot at the top" are lessened. The following discussion illustrates these points.

The decade of the 1970s fostered a policy of neighborhood crime prevention. Programs that encouraged block watching, security surveys, property identification, and so on shifted some of the burden of crime prevention from the police to the local neighborhood. Unfortunately, the results of such efforts were marginal. Evaluations were unable to document significant decreases in crime rates, and the success of program implementation depended on middle-class involvement in the projects. It became increasingly clear that programs devoted to the single issue of crime prevention could show only marginal results and these only in neighborhoods not known as high-crime areas. Neighborhoods that suffered from a complex of pathologies, high crime, high unemployment, a large number of school dropouts and general disorderliness, were not amenable to such neighborhood crime prevention strategies. Moreover, in urban areas undergoing gentrification, such crime prevention programs took on characteristics in keeping with the "mob at the gates" orientation. Closing off streets to restrict public access and the building of cul de sacs illustrate the point. Crime prevention strategies became a way of solidifying the middle class against the poorer residents of an area.

High-crime areas clearly needed more than simple crime prevention. The youth of these areas needed stable families, the opportunity to finish high school, and potential for employment that would provide more than a marginal income. Yet such areas often lacked the institutional supports necessary to address the multiple problems of residents. By definition, family life was in disarray. Churches and schools had little influence particularly with resident youth. What could be done?

An emerging answer seems to lie in the success of certain community-based organizations (CBOs).[7] These organizations have used crime prevention strategies as a means to more fundamental goals including community regeneration, economic development, and youth employment and education. Such an approach has been endorsed by at least four presidential commissions, going back to the Eisenhower Violence Commission in the 1950s.[8]

One of the keys to a successful CBO seems to be an ability to perform certain functions ordinarily carried out by the family.[9] In this sense, it acts as a kind of extended family. For youth, it provides discipline, a sense of purpose, and a crucial network for employment possibilities. This last factor turns out to be particularly important for placing a youth on a road to productive citizenship. Inner city black youth, particularly, seem to lack the contacts most other youth have that enable them to get jobs. The community-based organization, with a board of directors usually made up of people with contacts in the wider community, overcomes this significant hurdle to successful employment. For the older resident, the CBO can provide a mechanism for community improvement and political strategizing. Thus, crime prevention becomes simply a means to an end rather than an end in itself. The ultimate goal is improvement of the neighborhood and the life chances of the people within it. In this sense, the CBO model parallels the police community service approach discussed in Chapter 11. Crime becomes viewed as part of a larger more complex picture.

Successful programs include the Argus Community, Inc., a South Bronx community-based organization; the House of Umoja in Philadelphia; and the Ponce Playa Project in Puerto Rico.[10] Each of these projects report significant success rates in dealing with delinquent youth. They provide a disciplined family environment in both residential and nonresidential settings so that youth can obtain the skills necessary to complete their high school education. Moreover, these CBOs act as advocates for the youth and the general community. Their functions include job development, skill training, drug education and rehabilitation, and concern about general community development.

A recent evaluation of 10 similar projects in a wide variety of urban areas shows similarly promising results. Although not as well established as the three programs described above, these demonstration projects in their early evaluation were quite promising.[11]

The utilization of community-based organizations as a vehicle for crime fighting fits in well with certain prevailing policy directions within the federal government. As noted, there is a movement away from large-scale federal interventions. Thus, a neighborhood orientation is in keeping with the current mood prevalent on the national policy scene. Moreover, the three-legged stool of neighborhood, family, and employment builds on prevailing myths of the benevolent community and the triumphant individual. Finally, such an approach seems cost-effective. Youth involved in community-based organizations have lower recidivism rates than those processed through the normal juvenile justice correctional system.[12] CBOs operate at a far lower cost with seemingly more significant effects than official agencies.[13]

POLICY CONSIDERATIONS: THEORIES/ARGUMENTS/APPLICATIONS

New Research and Policy Agendas

The growth of CBOs suggests both a different policy and a different research agenda for local and national governmental units. In the more traditional policy model, policy effects are seen as trickling down from a centralized government bureaucracy. The CBO approach emphasizes instead a bubbling up. Using indigenous community leaders and resources, these organizations are able to put together programs that more effectively meet the needs of the local community. To get started, however, funding from a centralized government source is necessary. Thus, government becomes an enabler rather than a controller of such organizations. Research suggests that successful CBOs eventually become self-sustaining.[14] By addressing a multitude of problems, rather than simply the problem of crime control, they are able to garner widespread community support. Thus, government money used as seed grants for such organizations appears well spent. The emphasis on local community does, however, require a new research agenda.

At this point evaluations should be formative rather than summative in nature. By acting in the local community and observing the consequences, programs can become stronger while simultaneously teaching about the dynamics of the successful community. Research on how communities can better respond to crime victims, on how to overcome neighborhood resistance to treatment facilities, and how to prevent neighborhood and family disputes from escalating into serious crime are all topics suggested by the local community emphasis.

Local community involvement in the process of justice is not a panacea. Nevertheless, the three-legged stool of neighborhood, family, and employment provides a creative policy framework for addressing the issues of crime and crime control. It is clear, however, that to deal successfully with the problems of crime in this society, imagination is needed.

The decade of the 1980s witnessed dramatic changes in work life, family life, and the nature of the community. By 1983, over 35 million lived below the poverty line in the United States.[15] This represents an increase of 10.8 million people since 1978 or an increase of 44% in a five-year period. Most of this poverty increase could be accounted for by the changing occupational structure.[16] Over half of the increase was in the 18 to 44 age group. Fourteen percent of the poor lived in inner city ghettos, but 25% lived in suburbs.[17] The sons and daughters of middle-class, blue-collar families were finding it increasingly difficult to maintain a middle-class life style. Many were slipping below the poverty line. By the middle of the decade, family values were becoming an issue of public discussion and concern. But the traditional family, defined as a working father, a stay-at-home mother, and children accounted for only 6% of all households.[18] The "typical American family" wasn't! Central cities continued to lose population as did ring suburbs. The fastest growth was experienced in formally rural communities.[19] New suburbs sprang up with an interesting mixture of rural, urban, and traditional suburban people, each group with its own set of values. Demographic trends indicated a deconcentration of populations. The norm was no longer a large central city surrounded by the core suburbs but instead a series of smaller population concentrations in formally rural areas. Chicago, St. Louis, and Denver were losing population to places like Wheaton, Illinois, St. Charles, Missouri, and

Fort Collins, Colorado.[20] These new types of suburban communities will continue to challenge policy makers on a variety of issues including crime. What is learned about local community efforts in inner cities may provide guidelines for how to empower these new communities for dealing with their problems. Again, imagination is a key to dealing with rapidly changing situations. Policy maker and manager of tomorrow must have a systematic way of stimulating such imagination. It is to this issue that we now turn.

Stimulating the Imagination

This book has stressed the function of simplification. Scientists simplify in order to research a problem; policy makers simplify in order to act; all of us simplify in order to understand just a piece of our complex environment. While such simplification is necessary, it can at times be overdone. Simplifications are, after all, essentially false. They present only a piece of the puzzle. For example, most explanations of crime, whether theoretical or based on folk wisdom, can be compared to still photography. A snapshot captures the moment. But, in a way, a snapshot is always false. It holds still an instant of time and freezes it. Life, however, goes on in a continuous stream. A still photograph is unable to capture process, and is therefore unable to illuminate change. Similarly, many theories and policy pronouncements tend to use language in a way that suggests rigid, nonfluid, absolute categories. The sense of law as a process, the sense of criminal behavior as being a moment in time rather than an immutable definition of self, the sense of judgments about such behavior being flexible and responsive to a variety of circumstances is lost. Many theories and policy pronouncements tend to take a snapshot and freeze one moment or instance, which then serves as the foundation for a particular explanatory structure and plan of action. In freezing the instant and ignoring the process of which the instant is just a fraction, such theories and pronouncements oversimplify. To avoid the pitfalls of simplification, managers and policy makers of the future will need systematic ways to stimulate imagination, that is, to bring needed complexity to discussions of problems and their solutions.

Many authors have argued that one of the goals of policy analysis and program evaluation is to raise the level of discourse about a particular topic.[21] Raising the level of discourse can have a number of meanings. At the most basic level, it refers to avoiding sterile debates. Again, discussions of crime control seem particularly vulnerable to emotional rhetoric, with slogans substituting for understanding. People take and defend positions rather than define and solve problems.

Improving discourse about a problem can also help people see more facets to its nature and consequently more avenues for amelioration. This "complexifying" will mean that at first situations will increase in ambiguity rather than in clarity. But as Karl Weick eloquently argues, ambiguity is often an aid to imagination.[22] It forces the breakdown of old stereotypes and the search for new understanding. Weick goes on to show that in ambiguous situations "chaotic action is preferable to orderly inaction."[23] By doing something, observing the results, and then reflecting on these, new lines of action are generated. Simply waiting for something to happen provides neither insight nor solution. This is simply another way of stressing the importance of a formative evaluation approach in the field of policy. Action seeks to both deal with an immediate issue and provide understanding for the future and perhaps more effective programming.

"Complexifying" can also mean an avoidance of a traditional scientific procedure, that is, the elimination of competing explanations for a phenomenon. As noted previously, this approach is encouraged by the normal process of hypothesis testing. Within social policy, however, there is not a single truth. Social policy is basically a political endeavor and thus competing explanations of phenomena do not disappear. Within this kind of framework, the social scientists's obligation may be to describe competing explanations and the likely consequences flowing from alternative problem views and solutions.

The advantage of stimulating multiple rhetoric about a phenomenon, and thus multiple problem definitions and solutions, can be illustrated by James Thurber's story *Many Moons*. After the king's daughter was taken ill, he went to her and offered to get anything her heart desired. The little girl said that she wanted the moon and that if she got it, she would be well again. The king gathered his consultants and quizzed them on how the moon might be obtained. Each gave a different description of the distance and size of the object, but all agreed that the moon could not be brought to the kingdom. In despair, the king called on his court jester who described both the "experts" and the solution to the problem:

> "They are all wise men," he said, "and so they must all be right. If they are all right, then the moon must be just as large and as far away as each person thinks it is. The thing to do is find out how big the Princess Lenore thinks it is, and how far away."[24]

Princess Lenore thought the moon was as small as her thumbnail and made of gold. The jester took these data and provided the princess with a small gold locket that she could wear around her neck. Her health instantly improved.

Discourse about a problem can be aided by the use of social theory, as well as by a good story or parable. Programs and individuals immersed in the day-to-day doing of justice are likely to miss crucial elements in the process, unless some mechanism is available that allows them to maintain a broad view of the overall system. Prison reformers, for example, often talk only to prisoners and administrators. Thus, there is little understanding of the world of the prison guard, an oversight that causes this group to block the effects of suggested correctional innovations. Theories from organizational analysis, criminology, sociology, anthropology, and psychology can be used to generate alternative understandings and to keep both managers and program evaluators aware of the broad view. Chen and Rossi suggest a systematic way for using theory in a policy and evaluation context. They suggest that theory can be used in an a priori fashion to generate lists of possible outcomes for a program. This "multi-goal, theory driven" strategy has advantages for both utilitarian and theoretical concerns:

> Certainly both social science and policy are better served by the ability of the completed evaluation to decide among competing understandings of the social problems or treatments involved. Hence, all the outcomes deemed possible by social science theory and knowledge should constitute the pool out of which outcomes are to be selected for evaluation testing.[25]

Glaser has also shown the advantage of theoretically anchoring program evaluations. As discussed in Chapter 7, the use of theory improves discussions for what works and what doesn't work by causing the articulation of circumstances under which a given intervention might prove beneficial.

Theory used in the ways described can provide the policy maker with alternative viewpoints, a method for systematically exploring unintended program consequences, and even better theoretical categories for the development of more sophisticated theories. The improvement of discourse about a problem has definite practical consequences.

The above discussion contains a moral for those concerned with change in society generally and with change in criminal justice specifically. The moral is, "Do not become a true believer, either in your own plans for change or in the plans of others." Nobody had *the* answer, *the* public policy that will solve all or even most, of society's ills, even you (or, in this case, I). The sentiment was captured in the title of a book, *If You Meet the Buddha on the Road, Kill Him.*[26] Despite the title, the book is not about violence, but rather about the need to be cautious in accepting uncritically the sayings, strategies, and directions of gurus. People actively participate in and create their social worlds, often at variance with what scientists and policy makers say they will or should do.

Improving conversation about these worlds can help individuals by helping people appreciate the rich complexities of their lives.

SUMMARY

What Was Said

- Science, both physical and social, is undergoing shifts in how the nature of reality is to be understood.
- Political and ideological shifts are blurring the lines of traditional issue coalitions, particularly in criminal justice.

- An emerging trend seems to be a renewed interest in the policy potential of the local community.
- A three-legged policy stool of neighborhood, family, and employment has shown significant promise in alleviating problems of high-crime neighborhoods.
- The community-based organization (CBO) model parallels the police community service approach in that crime is viewed as part of a larger more complex picture.
- The decade of the 1980s has witnessed dramatic changes in work life, family life, and the nature of community, requiring imagination on the part of policy makers in solving problems.
- Social science theory can be used to improve discourse about a problem, which in turn can suggest new problem definitions and solutions.

What Was Not Said

- The traditional methods and theories of science are no longer relevant to policy analysis and evaluation.
- CBOs, a police community service orientation, neighborhood justice centers, and criminal justice reform legislation will dramatically alter crime patterns in the short run.
- Gurus are useful for policy problem solving.

NOTES

1. For a discussion of their revolution specifically within sociology, see James F. Gilsinan, "Symbolic Interactionism and Ethnomethodology: A Comparison," *The Rocky Mountain Social Science Journal*, Vol. 10, No. 1 (January 1973), 73–83.
2. Tom Siegfried, "Schroedinger's Cat: A Problem of Parallel Universes," *St. Louis Post-Dispatch*, December 22, 1987, p. 10.
3. Ibid.
4. Thomas S. Kuhn, *The Structure of Scientific Revolutions* (Chicago: University of Chicago Press, 1970).
5. Ibid.
6. Lynn A. Curtis, "Preface," *The Annals of the American Academy of Political and Social Science*, Vol. 494, (November 1987), 9–18.
7. Elizabeth Lyttleton Sturz and Mary Taylor, "Inventing and Reinventing Argus: What Makes One Community Organization Work," *The Annals of the American Academy of Political and Social Science*, Vol. 494, (November 1987), 19–26.
8. Lynn A. Curtis, "Preface," p. 10.
9. Elizabeth Sturz and Mary Taylor, "Inventing and Reinventing Argus."
10. David Fattah, "The House of Umoja as a Case Study for Social Change," *The Annals of the American Academy of Political and Social Science*, Vol. 494 (No-

vember 1987) 37–41. M. Isolina Ferre, "Prevention and Control of Violence Through Community Revitalization, Individual Dignity, and Personal Self-Confidence," *The Annals*, (November 1987) p. 27–36. Elizabeth Sturz and Mary Taylor, "Inventing and Reinventing Argus."

11. Lynn A. Curtis, "The Retreat of Folly: Some Modest Replications of Inner-City Success," *The Annals*, (November 1987) p. 71–89.

12. Ibid.

13. Ibid.

14. Ibid.

15. William P. O'Hare, "Poverty in America: Trends and New Patterns," *Population Bulletin*, Vol. 40, No. 3 (June, 1985).

16. Ibid.

17. Ibid.

18. Ibid.

19. John Herbers, *The New Heartland* (New York: Times Books, 1986).

20. Ibid.

21. Leo J. Cronbach and Associates, *Toward Reform of Program Evaluation* (San Francisco: Jossey-Bass, 1980).

22. Karl E. Weick, *The Social Psychology of Organizing*, 2nd ed., Topics in Social Psychology Series (Reading, MA: Addison-Wesley Publishing Company, 1979).

23. Ibid., p. 245.

24. James Thurber, with illustrations by Louis Slobodkin, *Many Moons* (Orlando, FL: Harcourt Brace, 1971), p. 18.

25. Huey-Tsyh Chen and Peter H. Rossi, "The Multi-Goal, Theory Driven Approach to Evaluation: A Model Linking Basic and Applied Social Science," in *Evaluation Studies Review Annual*, Vol. 6, H. E. Freeman and M. A. Solomon, eds. (Beverly Hills, CA: Sage, 1981).

26. Sheldon B. Kopp, *If You Meet the Buddha on the Road, Kill Him* (Ben Lomand, CA: Science and Behavior Books, 1972).

Name Index

Subject Index